FDR's Mentors

FDR's Mentors

NAVIGATING THE PATH TO GREATNESS

MICHAEL J. GERHARDT

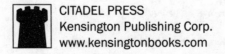

CITADEL PRESS
Kensington Publishing Corp.
www.kensingtonbooks.com

CITADEL PRESS BOOKS are published by

Kensington Publishing Corp.
900 Third Avenue
New York, NY 10022

All Kensington titles, imprints, and distributed lines are available at special quantity discounts for bulk purchases for sales promotions, premiums, fund-raising, educational, or institutional use. Special book excerpts or customized printings can also be created to fit specific needs. For details, write or phone the office of the Kensington sales manager: Kensington Publishing Corp., 900 Third Avenue, New York, NY 10022, attn Sales Department; phone 1-800-221-2647.

CITADEL PRESS and the Citadel logo are Reg. U.S. Pat. & TM Off.

10 9 8 7 6 5 4 3 2 1

First Citadel hardcover printing: May 2024

Printed in the United States of America

ISBN: 978-0-8065-4253-9

ISBN: 978-0-8065-4254-6 (e-book)

Library of Congress Control Number: 2023951994

To my wife Deborah,
who makes everything joyful and meaningful

Democracy cannot succeed unless those who express their choice are prepared to choose wisely. The real safeguard of democracy, therefore, is education.
—Franklin D. Roosevelt, Message for American Education Week, September 27, 1938

A leader may chart the way, may point out the road to lasting peace, but... many leaders and many peoples must do the building. It cannot be the work of one man, nor can the responsibility be laid upon his shoulders and so, when the time comes for peoples to assume the burden more fully, he is given rest. God grant that we may have the wisdom and courage to build a peaceful world with justice and opportunity for all peoples.
—Eleanor Roosevelt, "My Day," April 17, 1945

All the world's a stage, and all the men and women merely players...
—William Shakespeare, As You Like It (1599–1600)

Contents

Preface

O N DECEMBER 10, 1887, A five-year-old boy visited the White House for the first time. He came with his father, who introduced him to his friend, Grover Cleveland, the twenty-second President of the United States. Three years earlier, Cleveland, a Democrat and New Yorker, like the boy's father, had won the presidency in an upset, succeeding the incumbent Chester Arthur, another New Yorker, who had been a year ahead of the boy's father at Union College.

After showing the father and son the White House, Cleveland stopped, put his hand on the boy's head, and said, "My little man, I am making a strange wish for you. It is that you may never be President of the United States."

It was not the first or last time Cleveland missed the mark. At the end of his first term, he bet the public would support his plan to reduce tariffs as an economic fix for an ailing economy, but he lost the bet and the White House in 1888. Four years later, he won a second, nonconsecutive term, and the boy and his father visited him again in the White House. But Cleveland floundered during the Panic of 1893, a devasting depression that hurt every sector of the economy and cost him the presidency a second time. A few years later, the boy and his father returned to the White House a third time, this time to visit their cousin, also a New Yorker, who was president.

Cleveland did not live long enough to see what became of the boy: that each visit to the White House fueled his ambitions to become a great leader. A leader whose meteoric rise in Democratic politics culminated in his twice being elected governor of New York and the thirty-second President of the United States, Franklin Delano Roosevelt was no ordinary Democrat or New Yorker. Nor was he any ordinary president: George Washington launched the presidency and the republic, Abraham Lincoln preserved the Union and helped to end slavery, and Franklin D. Roosevelt led the nation through two major crises, served longer than any other president, and launched the era of big government, which endures to this day. Unlike Cleveland, Franklin relished nearly every moment of being president.

Many Americans know what Franklin D. Roosevelt did, but do not know how he learned to do it. He had many gifts—he was charming, optimistic, theatrical, emotionally intelligent, and quick-witted. He benefitted from family connections, deeply held religious convictions, ruthlessness, stoic resolve, and surprising eloquence. He was rarely still. He always seemed to be constantly moving forward, though sometimes he looked to the past for guidance from the successes and failures of the men who had preceded him as president. From those he knew personally—Cleveland, Teddy Roosevelt, Woodrow Wilson, Warren Harding, Calvin Coolidge, Herbert Hoover—and earlier leaders such as George Washington, Thomas Jefferson, Andrew Jackson, and Abraham Lincoln, Roosevelt learned valuable lessons on campaigning, assembling cabinets, mastering foreign affairs, and cultivating the image, messaging, vision, and congressional, public, and party support needed for political success. Even when he was improvising, as he often did, Roosevelt was mindful of his audience and the impact of his actions and rhetoric on his stature, both in how he compared with earlier presidents and the model he was crafting for his successors to consider following.

This book tracks these lessons in telling the story of how Franklin Roosevelt learned to lead and examines Roosevelt's interactions with the mentors who influenced his ambition, vision, and actions. Presidents, even great ones such as Roosevelt, are not to the manor born but shaped by the people they know, as inspirations, cautionary tales, and teachers.

From some presidents, Roosevelt learned what not to do. This is true for the three New Yorkers who preceded him as president—Martin Van Buren, Chester Arthur, and Grover Cleveland (in both his terms)—who each lacked boldness and popular support in addressing economic crises. Determined to be their opposite, Franklin mastered audacious solutions backed by congressional and popular support.

By the time Franklin visited his distant cousin Teddy in the White House at the turn of the twentieth century, he was old enough for the power and pageantry to make lasting impressions on him. Franklin modeled himself on Teddy, right down to the clothes and glasses he wore, the college and law school he attended, his first government job in Washington, and his becoming governor of New York, a vice-presidential candidate, and president in his own right. From Theodore, Franklin learned the values of mastering the bully pulpit, challenging the status quo, and working directly with the people who could help him achieve his goals, wherever they were, in his administration or not.

For seven years, Franklin served as assistant naval secretary to President Woodrow Wilson, spanning the entirety of the First World War. From Wilson, Franklin learned the risks of being sanctimonious and elitist in governing, dragging his feet when making important decisions, and stubbornly adhering to the hierarchy of power. Yet he also became familiar with the intricacies of military command, foreign affairs, and the men who became important leaders in the Second World War. From Theodore, Wilson, and Lincoln, Franklin understood presidents are responsible for providing the moral leadership the nation needs to advance and address problems and to become a model for other nations.

Roosevelt's project extended the nation-building legacy of Washington, Jefferson, Lincoln, and Wilson. He shared their constitutional vision in promoting a democracy capable of addressing economic and other crises. He overcame a number of obstacles to do so, not the least of which was overcoming the devastating effects of polio. The physical courage Roosevelt mustered to achieve that shared political and personal vision was nurtured and inspired by a cohort of earlier leaders such as Andrew Jackson and Teddy Roosevelt (each of whom survived a bullet wound near his heart) and intimate advisors, especially his wife Eleanor and political mentor Louis Howe.

As governor of New York, Franklin won two terms as a model of leadership through his unique combination of the attributes he adapted from leaders whom he admired, including charm (he became a less annoying version of his cousin Teddy), ruthlessness (from Jackson and Lincoln), bravado (from Teddy), and optimism (from Teddy and his first significant mentor, Endicott Peabody).

Once the national economy crashed in 1929, Roosevelt prepared to realize his dream of becoming president. He promised to do for the nation what he had done for New York. Challenging the incumbent Herbert Hoover for doing too little in addressing a great depression, Roosevelt promised bold action and innovation. He grew frustrated with Hoover's obstinance and refusal to acknowledge the merits of any views other than his own, even forcing himself to leave their last meeting together to avoid punching the President. Once in the White House, Roosevelt put into practice the lessons he had learned, burnishing his image as relentlessly optimistic, educable, and unafraid to tackle America's toughest problems.

Like Jefferson, Jackson, and Lincoln before him, Roosevelt was consumed with building a legacy, beginning with the image he cultivated and cast as president. He was everything he learned presidents had to be—motivator, visionary, communicator, entertainer, and pragmatist. Above all, he learned, presidents are moral leaders: They are instrumental in linking the past to the present, connecting current projects and challenges to those faced by the men who founded the country and the Constitution, and securing not only congressional, public, and judicial support for their programs but also formulating visions and projects in which subsequent presidents and Americans will be eager to invest. Yet, he learned, like Lincoln, to lead from behind. Often, in the darkest hours of his presidency, he put into words not just the fears Americans faced but also their highest aspirations. Roosevelt pushed policies and initiatives only once he was certain of their political appeal and effectiveness.

In 1962, President John F. Kennedy, who entered Congress two years after Roosevelt's death, told Lincoln scholar David Herbert Donald, "No one has the right to grade a President—not even poor James Buchanan—who has not sat in his chair, examined the mail and the information that came across his desk, and learned why he made decisions." We cannot begin to assess the performance of any president, including Franklin Roosevelt, without knowing how they led and how their learning informed their leadership.

Franklin Roosevelt knew from history—his own and that of the presidents who preceded him—that he could not succeed without the right people around him. "I'm not the smartest fellow in the world," he said, "but I can sure pick smart colleagues." In every phase of his political life, he surrounded himself with the best advisors he could find. In doing so, he learned to prize above all else loyalty, experience, and judgment.

Mentors vary in their impact and guises. Aside from presidents like his cousin Theodore and Woodrow Wilson, among the most impactful of his mentors were Louis Howe, a streetwise New York journalist who taught both Franklin and Eleanor how to campaign, win elections, and cultivate the image and support Franklin needed to succeed in office; Felix Frankfurter, who urged Roosevelt to hire many of his former students and to be bolder in pushing Congress and challenging the Supreme Court, which had blocked key elements of Roosevelt's New Deal; Franklin's wife Eleanor and his friend Henry Morgenthau, who both urged Franklin, largely in vain, to champion civil rights legislation and to save Jews fleeing from Nazi oppression and extermination in the 1930s and 1940s; the veteran New York Democratic leader Al Smith, who mentored Franklin and modeled both successful and unsuccessful forms of leadership; and Frances Perkins, a longtime advisor who taught Franklin nearly everything he knew about the burgeoning labor movement. Prime Minister Winston Churchill tried, with but limited success, to mentor Roosevelt in his approach to the war in Europe and interacting with other leaders, especially Soviet leader Joseph Stalin, whose cunning eclipsed Roosevelt's. But, once outfoxed by Stalin, Roosevelt learned his lesson and adapted to ensure it would not happen again.

Mentors teach, but mentees do not always heed the lessons they are taught. Such was often the case with Franklin, who, by his own admission, was never a great student and whose stubbornness sometimes made him his own worst enemy. Yet what he lacked in learning he made up for with his extraordinary self-confidence. No one knew for sure where it came from, but it gave him the courage of his convictions.

Roosevelt eschewed the label "mentor" to describe the people who had advised or taught him, because he wished never to appear weak or to be reliant on others but rather to be the man in charge, the man who was on top of things, and the man who knew best. Yet he borrowed from previous presidents when it was useful, and he made the exception of acknowledging as the most powerful influence on his life a mentor—the headmaster of the Groton School, which Franklin had attended, at his cousin Teddy's behest. Endicott Peabody was the charismatic proponent of "muscular Christianity," which demanded the performance of patriotic duty, good deeds, self-sacrifice, and toughness in the form of Spartan-like devotion to duty and refusal to acknowledge weakness or failure. Peabody's faith, which both informed and inspired Franklin's, demanded much but promised great reward. Most importantly, it resonated with Franklin's upbringing to follow the doctrine of noblesse oblige: the obligation of the privileged to give charity to those less fortunate. The two men stayed in nearly constant touch for forty years, until Peabody died shortly after Roosevelt's fourth election as president. Franklin internalized the lessons of his parents and of Peabody and made them the driving force of his crusade to secure the American dream and America's moral leadership in the fight against tyranny and for democracy in the world.

CHAPTER ONE

Model Citizens (1882–1910)

Franklin Delano Roosevelt was born into a world fraught with conflict. There was conflict over race: Just seventeen years before his birth in 1882, the Civil War had ended, but throughout his life, America was riven with Jim Crow—state-mandated segregation of the races—designed to keep African Americans unequal and powerless. There was conflict over the rights of women: Defined more as property than people, they had no power to vote. America was a man's world. There was conflict over religion: America was hardly a harmonious melting pot as the influx of Jews and Catholics was met with violence and discrimination in many quarters of America. There was class conflict: Franklin Roosevelt's youth coincided with the end of the Gilded Age, the period from 1870 until 1900 marked by sharp disparities in wealth and ostentatious displays of fortune. In one world lived the wealthy, while in another lived the people who worked for and yearned to be like them. Franklin Roosevelt was born into the first, but he made his mark by uplifting the second. The first called Franklin a traitor for challenging the legitimacy of their wealth and urging its redistribution to the underprivileged. The second regarded him as a savior.

Conflicts signaled the world was changing, but Franklin D. Roosevelt refused to let the times define him. Through force of will,

relentless optimism, grit, and conviction in the capability and com-
passion of government, he defined the times in leading the nation
into a new age marked by the rise of progressive government, the
defeat of great evil forces unleashed on the world, and the indom-
inable spirit of America.

I

Franklin D. Roosevelt came of age as New York City was rising to
prominence and centrality in the life of the nation. New York had
been the nation's first capital, after the Constitution was ratified in
1788; George Washington took the oath of office as the first president on the balcony of City Hall; and many New Yorkers had
distinguished themselves during the founding era, including the nation's first chief justice of the United States, John Jay, and its first
treasury secretary, Alexander Hamilton. Less than a year after the
founding, the United States moved its capital to Philadelphia for the
next decade, and over the next century, several states—Virginia,
Massachusetts, Ohio, and Tennessee—each had more men become
president than did New York.

In the nation's first hundred years, only one New Yorker—Martin
Van Buren in 1837—had been elected president, though he failed to
stem the devastating effects of the first great depression in the United
States and lost reelection, in 1840, to a political journeyman of no
great talent, William Henry Harrison. Harrison became famous not
as the first Ohioan to become president or as the man who fixed the
first great depression, but for having the shortest term of any American president—dying thirty-one days after his inauguration.

Yet, as New York was establishing itself as the financial center of
the nation, it began taking center stage politically: New Yorker Mil-
lard Fillmore ascended to the presidency in 1850 after the death of
President Zachary Taylor, and four different New Yorkers, from 1882
through 1945, took the presidential oath of office, for a total of nine
times—Chester Arthur (once), Grover Cleveland (twice), Theodore
Roosevelt (twice), and Franklin Roosevelt (four times). Franklin was

hardly responsible for the rise of New York's political and financial significance, but he became its fiercest advocate and visionary.

One year before Franklin's birth, Chester Arthur had become president as a result of the death of the incumbent James Garfield. Arthur, a lieutenant in a corrupt political machine in New York, had become Garfield's running mate to appease a staunchly conservative wing of the Republican Party known as the Stalwarts. Two years after Franklin's birth, Arthur was on his way out while Grover Cleveland, a Democrat, was elected as the fourth New Yorker to occupy the White House. Cleveland's first term, 1885–1889, was a disaster as he resisted aggressive federal meddling while the nation fell deeper into a great depression. But, in his second term, beginning in 1893, he became a different kind of president with a different outlook, having learned from his mistakes. He became the first progressive in the White House. He was determined to use all the levers and influence he had to ease the second great depression. Though his efforts to stem the depression failed, then–political scientist Woodrow Wilson considered Cleveland in his second term the most significant president in the latter half of the nineteenth century, because he had dared to use the powers of the presidency to steer the national government. When, in 1901, Franklin's cousin, Teddy Roosevelt, became the fifth president from New York, national leaders battled over the impact of big business on American life. Teddy vowed to contain its impact, which he and other progressives believed had crushed the American dream.

Teddy walked away from the presidency and the Republican Party in 1908, but he did not linger long on the sidelines. In 1912, he ran unsuccessfully as an independent candidate for the presidency, losing to New Jersey's Democratic governor, Woodrow Wilson. After leading the nation through the First World War with Franklin at his side as his deputy navy secretary, Wilson left office a defeated man, having failed to broker a meaningful and lasting peace.

Nonetheless, like both Theodore Roosevelt and Woodrow Wilson, Franklin was a proud progressive who lived by the doctrine of noblesse oblige. Franklin was the sixth New York governor to be sworn into office as president. (In 2016, Donald Trump became the seventh New Yorker to become president.)

Franklin took the mold of the presidency shaped by those who had come before, shattered it, and reassembled it in his own image—charming, relentlessly optimistic, shrewd, inspiring, a problem-solver, a patrician with a heart, boyishly curious, eager to please and to appear as a family man, and far-seeing. Franklin relished making everything look easy. He loved performing.

Roosevelt's critics complained that the image he presented to the public was false and that he was just a "trimmer," someone who tailored his opinions to the prevailing political mood for his own personal advancement. There was more than a little truth to the charge. Franklin's father had introduced him to sailing, which became one of Franklin's favorite pastimes and a metaphor for his life. On March 8, 1938, he told a hurting nation that "to reach a port, we must sail—Sail, not tie at anchor/Sail, not drift."[1] To reach safe harbor, Franklin learned to trim his sails to catch the winds that carried him from one office to another and to help the nation find solutions to a great depression and the Second World War. His rise is the story of how he learned to navigate the path to presidential greatness.

II

In the nineteenth century, men who wished to learn trades or certain skills sought mentors who taught them what they needed to know. But Franklin D. Roosevelt was not one of those men. From the moment of his birth, on January 30, 1882, he had teachers aplenty. Home for Roosevelt was the modest country estate of his parents, Sara and James Roosevelt, in Hyde Park, New York. Franklin was the center of everyone's attention. The estate's servants—and his parents—served his every need. His governesses taught him German and French. He wanted for nothing. He loved every moment.

Franklin's mother and his father were patricians, who shared with their only child stories of their ancestors. His father's family came to the United States from the Netherlands in the seventeenth century. Franklin liked to call himself "a stubborn old Dutchman,"[2] implying he had the traits of entrepreneurship, good citizenship, and stubbornness as many successful Dutch men did.

At the time of Franklin's birth, James was a railroad executive, whose investments were failing. He relished spending his afternoons with his son sledding, fishing, boating, and touring his estate, often in the family's private railcar. Franklin's mother, Sara, was twenty-six years younger than James, whose first wife had died several years before. Though James and his first wife had a son whom they called Rosey, Sara hoped to bear James a son, too, and more. But her pregnancy with Franklin was so difficult that she was unable to have any more children. Initially, she hoped to name him Warren Delano in honor of her late father, but her grandfather objected that neither he nor his wife could endure having another child in the family named Warren so close to when he died. Instead, she named him Franklin to honor a favorite uncle of hers.

Sara was protective to a fault. She watched young Franklin like a hawk, refused to allow him to bathe alone until he was eight, and maintained a written record of his daily activities until he was in his twenties. (She never slacked off, insisting later that Franklin and his new bride live next door to her in the same building.)

Franklin loved what his parents loved, particularly what he learned from his father. He crewed for James until he was tall enough to see over the tiller. When he was nine, his father bought him a fifty-foot sailing yacht. He spent summers sailing until he left for boarding school in 1896. Franklin loved books about adventures at sea and loved traveling like his parents did. They took Franklin to Europe nine times before he turned fourteen. Indeed, as a young boy, he spent as much time abroad as he did at home, perhaps accounting for his distinctive, British-sounding accent. (Such travels distinguished Franklin from earlier presidents, several of whom—notably Abraham Lincoln—never ventured abroad in their lifetimes.) Franklin met European royalty and visited English manors, the French Riviera, and German spas, where his father frequently stopped in the hope the waters would help his weak heart.

Sara declared Franklin was pure Delano, "not a Roosevelt at all,"[3] a proud lot of merchants and businessmen. Together, she and James taught Franklin that family and hard work were what mattered most. She took pride in the fact that her family came to America long before the Roosevelts did, and she shared extensive details about her family tree with her son. Only one ancestor on his father's side, Isaac, had been a politician, and an avid supporter of the Revolutionary War and the new Constitution, and he helped draft New York's first constitution after the start of the war. Isaac had been a Federalist who, like fellow New Yorker Alexander Hamilton, supported the Constitution's ratification on September 17, 1787, over the objection of many powerful landowners along the Hudson River.

Boasting and ostentatiousness were not tolerated in the Roosevelt or Delano households. Nor was any vulgar display of religion. James and Sara took their faith seriously but regarded it as a private matter rather than for public show. They taught Franklin that he, by virtue of his birth into a wealthy family, had inherited the duty to help the poor and destitute. They saw greater virtue in businessmen than politicians. James liked to say that businessmen, who spoke little but earned their way through life, were more important to the livelihood, vitality, and future of the United States than politicians in Albany or Washington. He liked to say that, while businesspeople built things, employed people, and contributed to a strong economy, politicians did little but talk.

Despite their travels and worldliness, Franklin's parents shielded him from the harsh realities of the times. They never spoke, at least in his presence, about the hardships of the depression that had hit the country in the mid-1880s. Nor did they discuss when the nation's railroads ground to a halt in 1894 because of a nationwide strike of railway workers protesting their wages and living conditions, prompting President Cleveland to direct thousands of U.S. Marshals and more than twelve thousand army troops to forcibly get the trains moving again. Franklin might have been vaguely aware of Cleveland's proclamation of the first Labor Day in 1894 to conciliate organized labor after the strike.

Instead, Franklin busied himself with activities on the estate, and he went on a bicycle tour through Germany during the presidential election in 1896. He knew of his father's failed investments, but their estate was an oasis for Franklin, regardless of what else was happening in the world. Sara's sister Dora once described Franklin as having been "brought up in a beautiful frame."[4]

While Franklin showed no early interest in politics, James did. When he was on his honeymoon with his first wife in England in 1853, James met the United States minister who convinced him to work for him as his secretary. James was later elected town supervisor in Hyde Park, New York, but he turned down other opportunities to serve or run for political office. Instead, he preferred to give money to Democratic candidates, particularly his friend Grover Cleveland in his successful runs for governor of New York in 1882 and for the presidency two years later and again in 1892. James took pride in visiting the White House with Franklin at his side.

Besides meeting President Cleveland and several foreign leaders, Franklin attended nearly every extended family event, where he met his cousins. He was a little boy when his parents first traveled south more than one hundred miles to Sagamore Hill, where he was introduced to his father's fourth cousin, Teddy. Franklin adored the boisterous man who never stopped moving.

Teddy loved giving advice and making introductions. He fancied himself a matchmaker. Indeed, matchmaking was a favorite Roosevelt pastime: Teddy's mother and older sister introduced Franklin's father James to his sixth cousin, Sara, at a dinner party in 1880. Before the end of the year, the two were married. By the time Franklin was fourteen, Teddy had introduced him to two other people, one a friend, Endicott Peabody, who became Franklin's lifelong mentor, and the other, Teddy's niece Eleanor.

III

James Roosevelt made one exception to his support for Democratic candidates: He gave money to his cousin Teddy, a progressive Republican. The family rallied around Teddy, an early but important reflection of their credo that family came first. As Franklin learned to walk, Teddy was blazing a path in New York politics.

Born in 1858, Teddy was a sickly child during the Civil War. He had a high voice and was nearly blind in one eye and severely asthmatic. When he was twelve, his father, Theodore Sr., encouraged him to develop his physical strength. He did so with gusto, lifting weights, doing pull-ups, boxing, wrestling, hunting, and riding horses, a pastime he loved above all others. He had three sisters, who doted on him as he did them.

Teddy adored his father. He called him "the best man I ever knew. He combined strength and courage with gentleness, tenderness, and great unselfishness. He would not tolerate in us children selfishness or cruelty, idleness, cowardice, or untruthfulness."[5] Besides inheriting his father's predilection for using racial and antisemitic epithets (a common mindset in the era), Teddy inherited his father's devotion to public service. The elder Roosevelt supported the Union in the Civil War (though, possibly to appease his Southern wife, he hired a replacement to fulfill his obligations when he was drafted by the Union); was one of the founders of the Union League, a society established to support the Union and President Lincoln's war policies; led numerous campaigns and causes to help destitute children; was one of the founders of the American Museum of Natural History in New York City; and had been among the first prominent people to join Lincoln's new Republican Party.

The winner of the controversial presidential election of 1876, Republican Rutherford B. Hayes prioritized cleaning up the corruption infesting the Customs House of New York City, the source of more than 75 percent of the federal government's revenue in that era. He fired the acting head, Chester Arthur, who had been the faithful deputy of Roscoe Conkling, a colorful but corrupt senator from New York. Hayes nominated Theodore Roosevelt Sr. to lead the Customs House, but Conkling, in retaliation against the Senate's failure to confirm Arthur for the post, persuaded a majority to reject Roosevelt.

The battle for confirmation left the elder Roosevelt severely depressed. Two months after the Senate defeated his nomination , on February 9, 1878, he died of a gastrointestinal tumor. When Teddy, then a student in his second year at Harvard, learned his father was seriously ill, he got on the first train to New York he found but did not arrive until two hours after his father had died. Teddy stood stiffly by his father's coffin when President Chester Arthur came to pay his respects.

Teddy spent months grieving and the rest of his life determined to do whatever he thought would have made his father proud. His sister Corinne recalled "when [Teddy] was entering upon his duties as President of the United States, he told me he never took any serious step or made any vital decision for his country without thinking first what position his father would have taken on the question."[6]

Teddy was determined to make the most of everything, though some college classmates disliked his exuberance. "A fish in a strange pond," as one biographer described his time at Harvard, Teddy irked many classmates, who considered his boundless energy "a vulgar thing" and thought his loud, boisterous greetings offensive. One classmate said, "When it was considered not good form to move at more than a walk, Roosevelt was always running."[7] Teddy studied biology, boxed, rowed crew, and graduated Phi Beta Kappa, ranking 21st in his class of 161. Later, he said, "I thoroughly enjoyed Harvard, and I am sure it did me good, but only in the general effect, for there was very little in my actual studies which helped me in afterlife."[8]

Perhaps the most important thing Teddy did while attending Harvard had nothing to do with the school: He got engaged his senior year to Alice Hathaway Lee, whom he married on October 27, 1880. In little more than a month, he entered Columbia Law School and joined, as his father had done, the Republican Party. In 1881, the year before Franklin's birth, Teddy became the youngest person to be elected to the New York State Assembly, and he was appointed a member of the New York Civil Service Association. He later explained, "I intended to be one of the governing class" and vowed "to hold my own in the rough and tumble."[9] Over the next year, he published his first book, *The Naval War of 1812* (based on his senior thesis at Harvard), later assigned as required reading at the Naval Academy. In August 1882, he joined the National Guard. In January of 1883, Teddy was elected the minority leader for the Republicans in the State Assembly. Later that year, he traveled to the Dakota Territory, where he enjoyed hunting and established Elkhorn Ranch, his western home away from home.

In 1884, Teddy's world collapsed again. On February 12, Alice gave birth to their daughter, Alice, but Teddy was so busy in Albany that he did not receive the telegram until the next day. As he planned to rush home that afternoon, he received another telegram informing him that Alice and his mother Martha, who lived in the same house, were both ill. Teddy arrived home around midnight. Early the next morning, on February 14, Martha died of typhoid fever. With Teddy by her side, Alice languished throughout the morning in a semicomatose state. That afternoon, she died of Bright's disease, an inflammation of the kidneys that her doctors had overlooked because of her pregnancy. "The light has gone out of my life forever,"[10] he later admitted having written in his diary at the time.

Teddy was so distraught that he barely could mention Alice's name thereafter. He burned the letters they had written to each other and destroyed the pages in his diary in which he had written about her. He never spoke to their only child, Alice, about her mother, to young Alice's everlasting frustration and resentment.

Teddy went west to find himself. He developed a close bond with the people he met and tried his hand at being a rancher. In 1885, he published his second book, filled with stories of western experiences, and completed building his family home, Sagamore Hill, near Oyster Bay, New York. The next year, Roosevelt ran unsuccessfully for mayor of New York City; married his childhood sweetheart Edith Carow; and, as a deputy sheriff, tracked down and captured the thieves who had tried to steal his boat. In 1887, Teddy published a third book, this one on the life of Senator Thomas Hart Benton, who had been a Democrat and friend of Andrew Jackson, one of the founders of the modern Democratic Party. Teddy continued his writing in 1888, completing a book on the life of Gouverneur Morris, an influential founder of the Constitution, and another one on what he called "practical politics." That same year, Teddy campaigned against Grover Cleveland in the presidential election, but Cleveland won.

Over the next few years, Teddy wrote several more books, welcomed into the world his and Edith's daughter, and, in 1888, campaigned for Benjamin Harrison, who defeated Cleveland for the presidency. Harrison rewarded Roosevelt with an appointment to the United States Civil Service Commission, but Roosevelt irritated Harrison to no end with proposals for reform. In 1895, he resigned from the commission to become police commissioner for the City of New York. That same year, he was elected president of the Board of Police Commissioners. He was thirty-seven years old. As Teddy once described himself, "I rose like a rocket."[11]

Never shy about giving advice to others, Teddy encouraged James and Sara to send Franklin to a new boarding school run by his friend, Endicott Peabody. Peabody had established a private school for boys in Groton, Massachusetts, and appropriately named it the Groton School for Boys. Unable to part from their boy, James and Sara delayed his entry for a year. But, in 1896, they dropped an anxious Franklin off. A year later, Teddy left New York to work for President William McKinley as assistant secretary of the navy. He arrived just in time for the Spanish-American War.

IV

Theodore Roosevelt, Jr., and Endicott Peabody appeared unlikely friends. Teddy was a gregarious, robust, barrel-chested man who was two inches shy of six feet. Peabody was tall, athletic, and serious. Teddy spoke in a high register but without artifice, while Peabody's voice was powerful, theatrical, and resonated with the word of God. Teddy had little patience for religion, while Peabody was an Episcopal priest. Peabody was educated at Cambridge in England, Roosevelt at Harvard in America's Cambridge. Peabody evinced a stern, no-nonsense demeanor, in contrast to Teddy's childlike exuberance at life. Teddy made his name in political exploits in New York City and hunting out West and in Africa, while Peabody's exploits were more rustic and humbler: His first post was in Tombstone, Arizona, where he built an Episcopal church. He arrived just after the famous gunfight at the O.K. Corral. He became known as "a parson who doesn't flirt with the girls, who doesn't drink beer behind the door, and when it comes to baseball, he's a daisy."[12] Peabody left six months later because he was homesick.

Yet both Teddy and Endicott made their way through the world
on their own terms. Teddy's second wife was Peabody's cousin, several of Teddy's friends were benefactors of the new Groton School,
and both men agreed a good education was mandatory for men who
ran the world. They agreed on what a good education entailed—
reading the classics of literature, understanding the rigors of science,
studying foreign languages, and engaging in lots of physical activity.
They agreed that young people should be taught certain values, especially hard work and devotion to public service. Teddy never had the
patience to teach, while Peabody devoted his life to teaching the word
of God as he understood it. Teddy disliked the elitism and class-con-
sciousness bred at British boarding schools, but Peabody modeled
Groton on them. Teddy urged Franklin to attend Groton, where he
would acquire "personal influences to strengthen his character."[13]
Teddy and Peabody each commanded any room they entered, but in
different ways—Teddy through his exuberance and curiosity and Peabody through his erect bearing, rectitude, and booming voice.
Neither feared anyone or anything.

Peabody's prospectus explained that the school's objective was
to ensure "every endeavor [would] be made to cultivate manly,
Christian character, having regard to [the] moral and physical as
well as intellectual development" of the students.[14] He dressed im-
peccably and repeatedly emphasized that the essential element of
his teaching was that "obedience comes above all else," meaning
obedience to authority, religion, parents, and teachers. Averell Harriman, a year behind Franklin at Groton and later a close advisor
to Franklin on foreign affairs, said Peabody "would be an awful
bully if he weren't such a terrible Christian."[15] Peabody's students
were almost entirely the children of the rich and famous, and most
went on to become financiers, captains of industry, lawyers at the
fanciest law firms, and the landed gentry like Franklin's family. Peabody devoted sermons to urging his students to be unafraid of the
world, to be truthful and rugged and not allow any weaknesses to
interfere with their success and commitment to public service,
never compromising with evil and helping those less fortunate. In
1894, Peabody worried aloud, "How distressing the political out-

look seems to be! One looks in vain for men who will serve their country. Those who are not for themselves seem to be hopelessly bound to their party interests, and country comes in a certain last."[16] Many graduates contributed to the less fortunate, and, for those who did not, Peabody kept score and singled them out for reckonings in his sermons.

Yet many of Peabody's boys believed that the activity that mattered most to him was not scholarship or good works but athletics. Peabody said, "I am not sure I like boys who think too much."[17] Franklin endeared himself to Peabody by serving as a counselor at a summer camp that Peabody ran for poor children and where the campers were in motion nearly all the time. Said another student attending Groton at the same time as Franklin, "Instinctively [Peabody] trusted a football-player more than a non-football-player, as the boys did."[18] Such trust, however, could have been based in part on Peabody's belief that competitive sports tested people's mettle and brought out the best—and worst—in competitors. Most of all, athletics allowed students to learn how to be good teammates.

When Franklin first entered Groton, his biggest worry was that he did not belong. Peabody preferred that his students attend all six years of the school, but Franklin was fourteen and had entered as a third-former (sophomore in today's parlance). He knew only one or two other students, and he was a mediocre C student in his early years there. Since D was a failing grade at Groton, Franklin had every reason to worry about his ability to compete academically with the other boys. It took some time for the boy who had complete freedom in Hyde Park to adjust to the regiment of getting up by 6:45, followed by cold showers, breakfast, chapel, classes, dinner, mandatory sports activity, supper, evening prayers, and the ritual of the students standing in line each night to say good night to Peabody and his wife.

Groton was Franklin's first experience being around other children. The only children he had been around before entering Groton were his cousins. Having largely been isolated from other children until he was fourteen, Franklin often got sick. By the time he graduated from Groton, he had survived scarlet fever, whooping cough, mumps, the flu, broken bones, and numerous colds.

Not surprisingly, after being razzed by upper class students and finding many other students irritatingly immature (though they thought the same of him), Franklin was unhappy much of the time he attended Groton. Years later, he told a friend, "I always felt entirely out of things," and he told Eleanor that something had gone "sadly wrong" at Groton, adding that "the other boys had formed their friendships" by the time he had become a student there. Thus, he confessed, he was "always a little the outsider."[19] Eleanor speculated that his sense of isolation helped him to sympathize with outcasts, though, instinctively, he made his way by pleasing the majority rather than defending the students who were mistreated. Nor did it help that one of the other students was Tadd Roosevelt, a year ahead of Franklin and James's son with his first wife. Tadd was perpetually in trouble and set an example to avoid at all costs.

Yet rather than share his anxieties with his parents or his teachers, Franklin became adept at masking his emotions. When his parents dropped him off at Groton, he did not cry or show any outward signs he was loath to go. He badly wanted to be popular, but he did not yet know how to navigate a world where he was not the smartest, the best athlete, or the most handsome or talented. When he was once cornered by a group of older students who demanded that he dance for them, he immediately did with exuberance. "He did what he was told," a classmate recalled, "with such good grace that the class soon let him go."[20] Eventually, he joined the more popular boys in razzing the newer students. In his second year at Groton, he won the Punctuality Prize. Franklin dutifully attended the lectures given by prominent figures visiting campus. He got along by getting along.

By senior year, Franklin had managed the baseball team, played second squad in football, was a dormitory prefect, sung in the choir, debated (he had the annoying practice of taking contrary positions on issues just to rankle other students), joined the Groton Missionary Society, and distinguished himself as an actor in a play that the seniors put on, *The Wedding March—An Eccentricity in Three Acts*. His major disappointment was not to be selected as one of the senior prefects, but he had raised his grades to a B average in time for graduation and received the senior award for best Latin essay.

Franklin's parents never knew the toll his time there had taken, though his letters contained numerous clues, including his injuries and illnesses. Nevertheless, Franklin graduated from Groton with undying adulation of its rector, Endicott Peabody. The impression Peabody had on Franklin loomed larger as the years went by. In 1939, Roosevelt, then in his second term as president, wrote, "As long as I live, the influence of Dr. and Mrs. Peabody means and will mean more to me than that of any other people next to my father and mother."[21] After a meeting with Peabody in the White House, Roosevelt confessed to an aide, "You know, I'm still scared of him."[22] Throughout his life, Franklin and Peabody maintained copious correspondence, and Peabody regularly visited the White House and officiated on special occasions. Through the decades after Franklin attended Groton, Peabody addressed him as "Dear Franklin," while Franklin, throughout his adult life, addressed his old headmaster, "Dear Mr. Peabody."

Whether the sentiments Roosevelt expressed about Peabody reflected his genuine feelings or were elaborate efforts to project the image of a loyal and grateful alum, no one knows for sure. There were many aspects of Groton that fed baser attitudes. Among the worst were the racial stereotypes it fostered. Being a dutiful son of Groton, Franklin wrote his parents to share the exciting news that Peabody had appointed him as one of two head "mail n------," whose job was to sort student mail and "take breakfast with the rector twice a year during the term."[23] The racial epithet was common in both Franklin's family and social class at the time.

After Groton, Franklin lied about his experiences there, for instance once telling a reporter in 1911 that he had been "quite the boxer" at Groton.[24] In fact, he had never boxed there. In 1939, he confided to his friend (then–Treasury Secretary) Henry Morgenthau that, while his doctors thought he had sinus problems while he was at Groton, he had broken his nose twice playing football. There is no record to confirm the injuries.

Franklin took to heart other sentiments from Peabody, especially the comfort provided by faith. Peabody once preached, "It used to bother me when I made mistakes, and I wasted a lot of time fretting. Now I have learned that if one does the best he can in the light of all his available knowledge and judgment, then . . . there is no use grieving over it. I do the best I can under the circumstances and go on to something else. One thing at a time, that is the great thing."[25] Time and again throughout his life, Franklin repeated the lesson word for word.

The isolation of Groton made it easier for Franklin and Peabody to spend time together. Franklin attended Peabody's confirmation class and accompanied Peabody on his visits to neighboring towns where he preached and paid charitable visits. Franklin joined the Boston Missionary Society, where Peabody helped underprivileged boys and elders, who were unable to help themselves, to get food and fuel.

There was only one college that Peabody, Teddy, and James allowed Franklin to consider, Harvard, where James had attended law school. (When Franklin told his father he was considering Annapolis, James quickly dismissed the idea.) With Teddy and James as alumni, Franklin was sure he would be admitted, and he was. Indeed, eighteen out of the twenty-three members of his Groton class were in his class at Harvard. Just thirty-five miles south of the school, Harvard, with its great name and resources, was a natural choice for Groton students, but the road ahead, for both Franklin and the nation, was not as easy as he might have hoped.

V

The new century bristled with possibilities. As far as America was concerned, the world was at peace: Two years before, Cuba had secured its independence after the Spanish-American War had been fought and won by the United States (which had retaliated as well to the sinking of the USS *Maine* in Havana Harbor). In January, Franklin looked forward to his eighteenth birthday, graduating from Groton in the spring, and becoming a Harvard man in the fall. Cousin Teddy was skyrocketing to fame: He had left his post as McKinley's assistant naval secretary to fight for the liberation of Cuba, returned home a war hero to run successfully for the governorship of New York, and was drafted, later in the year by popular demand, as President McKinley's running mate in his bid for a second term (his first vice president had died in 1899).

Come fall, Franklin moved into in a four-bedroom suite with his Groton classmate and friend, Lathrop Brown. They lived in an area near campus called the "Gold Coast," a name based on the profits of bootleggers who operated between Cambridge and Somerville.[26] It was lined with large apartments, eating houses, and clubs for the children of especially well-to-do and socially and politically well-connected parents. Franklin no longer wore braces for his teeth, for which he had been teased at Groton. He had grown into a tall, lanky young man, with hair parted down the middle, and he wore a pair of pince-nez, just like his cousin Teddy did. He left Groton with a concern that Peabody's "favoritism" accounted for why he had not been chosen as senior prefect. But from his first days at Harvard through his last, he spent most of his energy, not in class or studying or athletic activities, but on "the social life," which he mentioned repeatedly in his letters home. His primary objective was social acceptance.

Franklin joined the Harvard Republican Club, and he marched eight miles in a torchlight procession of Harvard and MIT students in support of the Republican ticket of McKinley and his cousin Teddy in 1900. Franklin's family had put aside their traditional Democratic allegiances to support Teddy in his successful races for New York governor in the fall of 1898 and as McKinley's vice president two years later. The favorites of the monied classes, McKinley and Teddy won, and a jubilant Franklin and his family came to celebrate with Teddy in Washington.

Though he had benefitted from having the popular New York governor on his ticket, President McKinley ignored Teddy once they were in office, finding his excitable curiosity to be more of an annoyance than anything helpful.

A month later, on December 8, 1900, Franklin's dreamy world collapsed. His father James's heart condition, which the family had closely monitored throughout Franklin's childhood, had sharply declined after James's yacht exploded in the fall of 1900. Franklin rushed home but arrived too late to see his father before he passed on December 8, 1900. Franklin consoled his mother. He needed consoling, too, and Teddy came to the rescue, reminding him that his own father had died while he'd been a student at Harvard and that he, too, had arrived too late to see his father before he died.

After James's death, Franklin grew closer to his mother and to both Teddy and Endicott Peabody. When Franklin was at Groton, Teddy had often invited him to his home, where Teddy recounted stories of his western adventures and political exploits and plotted the boy's next steps. Peabody arranged for Teddy to deliver the commencement address at Franklin's graduation, providing yet another opportunity for the three of them to bond. Teddy made it a point to invite Franklin whenever he could to the White House.

The time Franklin had spent with Peabody at Groton had sensitized Franklin to religion, an attachment made stronger after the death of his father. Peabody pointedly invited Franklin back for public events, including lectures by Booker T. Washington, the renowned African American educator, and by Teddy, who was by then the vice president. Having once been in the situation that Franklin now found himself in, Teddy redoubled his efforts to give suggestions to his younger cousin on the activities, courses, and clubs he should pursue at Harvard. He made a point of hosting Franklin when he came to Washington to revel in his cousin's ascension to power.

Franklin stayed with Sara through the Christmas holidays but returned to campus in January 1901. Sara could not stay away. Before the end of Franklin's first year in college, she moved to Boston, where she leased an apartment near campus. With Teddy, Sara, and the expanded family rallying around him, Franklin returned to school more determined to make a success of himself. At the same time, he continued to skipper the sailboat that his father had given him, often en route to the family's new summer home at Campobello Island in Maine, which he and his father had discovered years before. Campobello became one of his favorite homes away from home.

Teddy was a tough act to follow at Harvard, where he had done well academically, earned a reputation as a good boxer, and joined several clubs, including the prestigious Porcellian Club, a "final" club (meaning its membership was for life). Franklin yearned to be an even bigger man on campus than Teddy had been. Frustrated that he was unable to make the Harvard football and rowing teams, Franklin joined lots of clubs—the Glee Club, the Newell Boating Club, and the Hasty Pudding Club (the only social club on campus that had members for all four years). He competed hard to be asked to join Porcellian, but he never got the invite. He was chosen instead to join Fly, a club that Teddy had been invited to join as well. Years later, when he was serving as the deputy assistant secretary of the navy during the First World War, Franklin said his rejection from the Porcellian Club "was the biggest disappointment of my life."[27] Eleanor believed his rejection made him more attentive to democratic values.

Though Teddy had been an editor of Harvard's literary magazine the *Harvard Advocate*, Franklin set his sights on becoming an editor on the elite campus daily, the *Harvard Crimson*. His fellow editors praised him for getting stories others did not, including getting the college president, who generally refused to be interviewed, to say he would vote for McKinley in the 1900 presidential election, and getting the scoop that his cousin Teddy, then the vice president of the United States, was coming to lecture on campus. In his junior year, he was selected editor in chief of the paper. Though he had amassed enough credits to graduate early, he stayed on for an extra year doing graduate work so he could continue working on the *Crimson*. He thought editing the paper was his greatest achievement at Harvard.

Classes and studying were never priorities for Franklin. He graduated with a gentleman's C, usually the mark of a clever student who did not dirty his hands with hard work because his path was already set in the world. He took classes in government, but he found them dull and filled with constitutional formalities and legal abstractions rather than real politics. He described his studies "like an electric lamp that hasn't any wire."[28] He hoped to gain a "practical idea of the workings of a political system—of the machinery of primary, caucus, election, and legislature."[29] He once recalled, "I took economics courses in college for four years, and everything I was taught was wrong."[30] He quit his only philosophy class after three weeks.

Roosevelt biographer James MacGregor Burns describes Franklin's views at that time as "a mixture of political conservatism, economic orthodoxy, and anti-imperialism, steeped in a fuzzy altruism and wide ignorance." These views came from his elders, particularly his father James and cousin Teddy. While his articles and editorials focused almost entirely on student life at Harvard, the influences of his elders and those around him were reflected in the obstinance of his views on race. "Yes," he wrote in an article during his junior year, "Harvard has sought to uplift the Negro, if you like, has sought to make a man out of semi-beast."[31]

Franklin bragged that he had fought for reform at Harvard through his editorials, but in fact he rarely wrote about politics and usually only to report public events at Harvard. His editorials were about such non-weighty matters as insisting boards be placed between Harvard buildings during the rain, so that the students did not get their shoes muddy. The few papers he wrote in his classes showed a peculiar contrariness and stubbornness that he never fully grew out of. The fact that his cousin had become president in 1901, after President McKinley was assassinated, did not keep him from (accurately) criticizing Teddy's "tendency to make the executive power stronger than the Houses of Congress."[32] (It became practically impossible for Franklin not to think of the presidency, given that his favorite cousin was president and that he had lived all four years at Harvard in Adams House, which had been named for two presidents who attended Harvard, John Adams and his son John Quincy.) Though Franklin had taken a class from the eminent historian Edward Channing, who taught his students to verify their facts, no matter where they led, Franklin wrote an effusive paper praising Alexander Hamilton that was filled with inaccuracies. The C average may have been well deserved after all.

While at Harvard, Franklin dated several young women, but marriage, more than dating, was on his mind. In 1902, he proposed marriage to a seventeen-year-old Jewish debutante, Alice Sohier from Boston. Too effusive for his own good, Franklin scared her off when he told her that he wanted six children. Her father was opposed to their marrying in any event, and sent her abroad as quickly as he could to sever the relationship. Within a year, Franklin's attention was elsewhere, more than a couple hundred miles from campus, thanks to his cousin, the matchmaking President of the United States.

VI

Eleanor Roosevelt's childhood was as bleak as Franklin's was idyllic: Her mother Anna Hall, whom Eleanor described as "one of the most beautiful women I have ever seen,"[33] died of diphtheria when Eleanor was eight. Anna had "belonged," according to Eleanor, "to that New York City society which thought itself all-important." Eleanor found that world, where "you conformed to the conventional pattern," to be repulsive.[34] Whereas Franklin's mother doted on him, Anna tortured Eleanor. She was emotionally aloof, berated Eleanor for her "plainness"[35] and needled her as "Granny."[36]

Yet, Anna's death did not bring relief to Eleanor. She went to live with her father Elliott, who had been separated from Anna earlier that year. He was distraught over both Anna's death and his failure to match his older brother Teddy's successes; he drank too much, and he was addicted to opiates, which he took to relieve the pain from a riding accident that had shattered his leg. Though he adored Eleanor, who loved him dearly, Elliott was often absent—recovering in sanatoriums and hospitals. "Though he was so little with us," Eleanor recalled, "my father dominated all this period of my life. [His] visits were irregular, and he rarely sent word before he arrived,"[37] but when she heard his voice, she "slid down the bannisters and usually catapulted into his arms before his hat was hung up." His wife's death intensified his self-destruction. He died of a fatal heart attack six months after Anna did. Elliott was, Eleanor said, "the love of my life for many years after he died."[38]

Not yet ten, Eleanor was now an orphan. She was sent to live with her grandparents. They were cold and callous. Believing it would do more harm than good, they forbade her to attend her father's funeral. She was lonely, stubborn, duplicitous, and physically fearful (because of the deaths of her parents and her own narrow escape at the age of four when a ship she was traveling in collided with another ship and began to sink before she was rescued).

Like Anna, Eleanor's grandparents enjoyed berating her, and they restricted her visits to other Roosevelts to once or twice a year. To make matters worse, living with her grandparents meant living with her uncles (on her mother's side), who were not only alcoholics but physically abusive. In a rare move to protect Eleanor, her grandmother installed three heavy locks on the door to her bedroom. When a girlfriend, whom Eleanor's grandmother had allowed to sleep over one night, asked Eleanor why she had the locks, Eleanor replied, "To keep my uncles out."[39] Eleanor learned to lie to keep up appearances and, especially, to keep her grandparents from taking any enjoyment from her discomfort.

Freedom arrived when Eleanor became old enough to attend boarding school. Her grandfather arranged for her, then fifteen, to attend Allenswood, a school for girls on the south side of London. She grew close with the headmistress, Mademoiselle Marie Souvestre. The two spoke French together, Mlle Souvestre had Eleanor sit with her during meals, and she took Eleanor with her on trips abroad. Eleanor was devasted to return to the United States after she completed boarding school at seventeen.

Eleanor's years abroad changed her. She was far from the plain woman her late mother had tortured: She was now nearly six feet, wore her brown hair long, was fit and trim, and had a pleasant, smooth face. Her cousin Alice pointedly remarked that Eleanor "was always making herself out to be an ugly duckling, but she was really rather attractive. Tall, rather coltish-looking, with masses of pale, gold hair rippling to below her waist, and really lovely blue eyes."[40] Perhaps Eleanor saw herself as the ugly girl her mother berated, perhaps she put herself down as a way of lowering expectations or putting other people at ease, or perhaps she just never could shake her insecurities.

Eleanor was serious, indeed, sometimes too serious. While her family presented her as a debutante in December 1902, she was shy, thought the event "utter agony," and was "miserable through all that."[41] Only one boy paid her any attention, her distant cousin Franklin.

Eleanor and Franklin had first met when he was four and she was two. While she had been in England, Franklin had begun meeting regularly with Teddy. In 1902, he met Eleanor by accident on a train heading back to her grandmother's house. Afterward, they saw each other by both accident and design. On November 17, 1902, Franklin and Eleanor were two of the attendees at a dinner hosted by his half brother Rosy. Soon thereafter, they slipped away to have tea together. In January 1903, Eleanor attended Franklin's twenty-first birthday party. The more time they spent together, the more comfortable they were, and the more they found they had in common. By July of that year, Franklin recorded in his diary that "E is an angel."[42]

On a weekend trip to Groton in the fall of 1903, Franklin proposed marriage to Eleanor. She was surprised but pleased. She insisted that they not move forward without the blessing of Franklin's mother. Knowing that would be difficult to arrange, Franklin had the three of them visit together during Thanksgiving. Sara said she would not reject the engagement outright, but she persuaded the two to wait at least a year before marrying. Afterward, Franklin and Eleanor both wrote letters lobbying Sara. Eleanor said, "I do so want you to learn to love me a little. You must know that I will always try to do what you wish."[43] This was the right message to send, which might have made it easier for Sara to read Franklin's missive declaring that "I know my mind, have known it for a long time.... Result: I am the happiest man just now in the world; likewise the luckiest." Eleanor knew of Sara's efforts behind the scenes to scuttle the marriage, but they ultimately failed.

Eleanor worried that she loved Franklin more than he loved her. Shortly after Franklin told her, when he proposed, that he hoped to achieve something significant in life, her insecurities had gotten the better of her. She replied, "Why me? I am plain. I have little to bring you."[44] A few days later, she told Franklin she felt more confident in his love for her, though Eleanor often downplayed her own needs.

No one was more excited about their engagement than the President of the United States. In 1904, Theodore had won the presidency in his own right, and he eagerly took charge of the wedding plans. He liked that he had nurtured the bond between Franklin and

Eleanor by bringing them together at various social and political events, including his re-inauguration on March 4, 1905. He arranged for the two to marry nearly two weeks after his inauguration, on St. Patrick's Day, March 17. With the Secret Service everywhere and every guest questioned before they could take their seat, Endicott Peabody presided over the ceremony, which was held at the brownstone of Eleanor's cousin Susie Parish on East 76th Street in New York City. When Peabody asked who gave the bride away, the President roared, "I do." Once the ceremony was done, Teddy joked, "Well, Franklin, there's nothing like keeping the name in the family." To no one's surprise, the President dominated the reception with his stories and jokes, leaving the "young married couple ... standing alone." As a relative said of Teddy, "When he goes to a wedding, he wants to be the bride, and when he goes to a funeral, he wants to be the corpse."[45]

After honeymooning in Europe, the couple returned to New York City, where they lived in an apartment that Sara had rented and furnished. Two years later, they moved to a town house Sara had built that was directly adjacent to another that she owned. Sara came and went as she pleased through a door, which was always open, connecting the two homes.

It took no time for Eleanor to feel as if she were a prisoner, as she increasingly bristled over Sara's interruptions. Eleanor hated Sara's constant efforts "to bend the marriage to the way she wanted it to be." Sara's bedroom was closer to Franklin's than Eleanor's was, and the young bride often cried alone. She never stopped resenting that she was forced to live in a home, "which was not in any way mine, one that I had done nothing about and which did not represent the way I wanted to live."[46]

Franklin was oblivious to her anguish. He expected her to be a wife and mother (as did both Teddy and Sara), and she accepted that circumstance, at least for a while. At Teddy's urging, Franklin had begun Columbia Law School in the fall after his graduation from Harvard, and he completed his first year there before his marriage to Eleanor. He entered his second year after returning from his honeymoon.

Franklin hated law school as much as Teddy had. Like Teddy, he thought the courses dreary and useless. Both thought there were too many lectures on theoretical subjects and not nearly enough on how law functioned in the real world. Uninspired and bored, Franklin did no better than a C average. When he passed the bar examination in his third year, he immediately dropped out, just as Teddy had done, to begin his life in politics.

Years later, when Franklin was governor of New York, Columbia's president Nicolas Murray Butler chided him, "You will never be able to call yourself an intellectual until you come back to Columbia and pass your law exams." Laughing, Roosevelt said, "That just shows how unimportant the law really is."[47] Years before, when he dropped out of Columbia, Teddy had said, "Some of the teaching of the law-books and of the classroom seemed to be against justice."[48] Teddy cared about practicalities and results, and so, too, did Franklin. Teddy followed his passions, as did Franklin, and one of Franklin's passions was emulating Teddy, not just in how he dressed and where he attended college and law school but in finding the quickest route into politics.

It was difficult to best Teddy, but Franklin never stopped trying. If Teddy could be assistant naval secretary in Washington, governor, vice president, and eventually president, Franklin figured he could, too. He would follow that path as a Democrat, though he first had to enter the game. Franklin understood that if you don't play, you can't win, and he always played to win.

CHAPTER TWO

Taming the Nation and
the World (1910–1921)

I N 1908, THEODORE ROOSEVELT BACKED his war secretary William Howard Taft for president. After Taft defeated his Democratic rival, William Jennings Bryan, in Bryan's third and final run for the presidency, Roosevelt left for a safari in Africa. It did not take long before he wanted his old job back.

Roosevelt and Taft had once been political allies and friends, so close that Teddy had chosen him as his secretary of war and heir. But, once Taft became president, tensions developed between them that ripped the Republican Party apart. Whatever had been their bond, the years sharpened their differences: Teddy was an unapologetic progressive, loved mingling with people and regaling them with stories, and welcomed the women's suffrage movement and the rise of social activism and political reform. Taft was rigidly conservative, hated shaking hands and small talk, and loathed the presidency as much as Teddy loved it. At the heart of the Progressive Era was the belief, shared by Teddy Roosevelt, that the world could be changed for the better and that government's job was to manage the conflicts between business owners and their employees and between those who were wealthy and those who were out of work and needed government assistance to survive. Taft was uncomfortable with change and wanted more than anything to be chief justice of the United States, a position occupied by Taft's own appointee, Edward Douglas White. As one of the foremost conservative jurists and scholars of the era, Taft believed big business was an unalloyed good, championed smaller government and less regulation, and expansively read the protections accorded to private property owners in the Constitution. Teddy wrote books about his adventures in the wild, while Taft wrote books about the Supreme Court, the presidency, and the Constitution. Taft was consumed with the operations of government, while Teddy had little patience for them. Teddy believed the Constitution empowered presidents to do whatever they wanted for the public good unless the public objected. Taft believed presidents were constrained to do nothing unless specifically authorized by the Constitution.

Their differences drove Teddy to run for the presidency again in 1912 but as an independent, while Taft ran for reelection largely to defend himself against Roosevelt's attacks that he was a traitor to reform. Taft's speeches were stiff and uninspiring. Teddy crisscrossed the country, while Taft rarely left the White House.

Teddy's zeal was nowhere more apparent than on October 14, 1912, in a speech in Milwaukee, Wisconsin. He began in a somber voice, "Friends, I shall ask you to be quiet." He paused, and then added, "I don't know whether you fully understand that I have just been shot." With the crowd gasping in disbelief, Teddy unbuttoned his vest to reveal his bloodstained shirt. "It takes more than that," he said, "to kill a bull moose." He pulled out of his jacket pocket his fifty-page speech with two bullet holes through each page. Holding pages above his head, he told the audience, "Fortunately I had my manuscript, so you see I was going to make a long speech, and there is a bullet—there is where a bullet went through—and it probably saved me from it getting to my heart. The bullet is in me, so I cannot make a very long speech, but I will try my best." Teddy then spoke for ninety minutes. "I give you my word, I do not care a rap about being shot, not a rap."[1] With his staff nearby to catch him if he fell, Teddy persisted, even as his speech slowed, and his breath shortened. Once he was done, he was rushed to the hospital. Doctors determined that the bullet could not be removed without risking serious damage to his heart; it remained in his body for the rest of his life. It did not take Teddy long to recover.

Most everyone thought Franklin was no Teddy. Teddy made no secret of his views and was notable for his directness, candor, and tactlessness. Artifice was not a part of his skill set. In contrast, artifice and posturing seemed among the things Franklin did best. It was hard to pin him down. Franklin desperately wanted to be liked. Critics viewed his self-confidence as arrogance, which most law-makers, particularly in New York, regarded as unwarranted. He talked a good game. As Grenville Clark, a Harvard classmate and law-yer who later worked with Franklin, recalled, "I remember him saying with engaging frankness that he wasn't going to practice law forever, that he intended to run for office at the first opportunity, and that he wanted to be and thought he had a real chance to be Pres-ident. I remember that he described very accurately the steps which he thought could lead to that goal. They were: first, a seat in the State Assembly, then an appointment as Assistant Secretary of the Navy . . . and finally the governorship of New York. 'Anyone who is governor of New York has a good chance to be president,' he said."[2] Franklin was adapting Teddy's path for his own.

Yet, in the 1912 presidential election, Franklin left no doubt which of the three candidates he favored. It was not the Republican Taft or the now-Independent Roosevelt. For Franklin, blood was not thicker than his own ambitions, which led him to support the third candidate in the race, the Democratic nominee, New Jersey governor Woodrow Wilson.

More than a few scholars have suggested that Franklin's choosing the Democratic Party was opportunistic. It might have been (given that much of what Franklin did was), but, as early as college, Frank-lin had declared he was a Democrat. Before his first run for office, he asked Teddy for his blessing to run as a Democrat, and Teddy gave it. Teddy wrote his sister, "Franklin ought to go into politics without the least regard as to where I speak or don't speak."[3] In fact, the Dem-ocratic Party was a natural fit for Franklin. He adored his father, James, who had been a Democrat, and by 1912, there was no question which of the major political parties better suited Franklin, for whom, because of his upbringing and the influence of Endicott Peabody, noblesse oblige was a guiding principle. In contrast, most Republicans, with the obvious exception of Teddy, viewed government as bad, charity as the responsibility of the private sector not the government, and people whom the government supported as weak and shiftless. That Franklin hitched his political wagon to the most progressive candidate in the race, Woodrow Wilson, the first Democrat elected president in the twentieth century, underscored that he was not a Democrat in name only but instead a genuine party member committed to paying the price for his beliefs.

By the beginning of the Wilson administration, in March 1913, the constellation of Franklin's mentors was largely coming together. Frances Perkins, a young labor activist, befriended him in 1910, believing (correctly) that he was destined for the presidency. Teddy was a role model, not just in how Franklin dressed but in how he rose and fell from grace in the rough-and-tumble of presidential electoral politics. And Wilson, as New Jersey governor and in two terms as president, became the model of progressive leadership that Franklin followed. In 1912, New York journalist Louis Howe thought the moment he first saw Franklin that he was looking at a future president; he was attracted not just to Franklin's charisma but to his bona fides as a progressive committed to making government work for the people. Howe would be instrumental in tutoring Franklin and Eleanor on how to stage and win political campaigns.

By 1920, Franklin had become so popular among Democrats that they nominated him as their candidate for vice president. Though he—and Ohio governor James Cox, who led the ticket—lost the general election, Franklin was not yet forty. He had more than enough time to begin preparing runs for governor of New York and President of the United States.

I

In 1910, Franklin Roosevelt was done with the law. He turned to other priorities. The first was starting a family with Eleanor. Over the next six years, they had six children, though Franklin Jr. died in infancy. Franklin left the task of child-rearing to Eleanor (subject to constant harassment by Sara) and their nannies. He immersed himself in his greatest passion, the world of politics.

Franklin believed in learning by doing, so he wasted no time in making his first run for office in 1910. Franklin leapt at the opportunity to run for a safe Democratic seat for the Second Assembly District in the New York State Assembly. The only problem was that the opening Franklin thought that he had to run for the State Assembly quickly evaporated when the Democratic incumbent changed his mind and declared his intention to run for reelection. Initially distraught, Franklin learned he could run for an open seat in the state senate, which held greater prestige than the one he had previously considered in the assembly's other chamber.

In opening his state senate campaign, Franklin told the Democratic caucus in Poughkeepsie, New York, on October 6, 1910, "I am pledged to no man; and I am influenced by no special interests."[4] The Democratic machinery in that part of the state quickly fell behind him. Though initially skeptical that Franklin's plan to hit the campaign trial in his car might backfire with the farmers whose support he needed, the electorate loved that Franklin frequently stopped to chat with folks all along his way. He helped himself further by inviting Richard Connell, the editor of the *Poughkeepsie-Press*, to travel with him. Connell taught Franklin the tricks of the campaign trail, including advising him to stop wearing the pince-nez he had worn at Groton because it fed into the narrative that he was arrogant and an elitist.[5]

Franklin ran his first campaign for office. Besides ordering thousands of campaign buttons, designing campaign posters, and spending his own money to fuel his campaign, Franklin crafted his campaign narrative to avoid mentioning any substantive issues that could be controversial. Fortunately, as well, for Franklin, 1910 turned out to be a banner year for Democrats, who won ten seats in the United States Senate and more than half the governorships and a majority in the House for the first time since 1892. The opposition to his election came too little too late, largely consisting of charges that he was an elitist and a trimmer. At twenty-eight, Franklin had won his first election.

Once in the state senate, he was chosen as the leader of a small but tenacious group, called the "insurgents," that opposed the domination of the Democratic Party by Tammany Hall, the renowned headquarters for the party in New York City. Believing Tammany Hall was corrupt, Franklin's insurgents opposed their candidate for the U.S. Senate, William Sheehan. They did not want Tammany Hall telling them what to do. "Sheehan," Franklin said, "looks like [Tammany's] choice.... There is no question in my mind that the Democratic Party is on trial and having gotten control of the government chiefly through up-state votes, cannot afford to surrender its control to the organization in New York City."[6]

The insurgency sparked the first in a series of clashes between Franklin and Al Smith, a favorite of Tammany Hall, which helped to elect him as the Democratic leader in the state senate in 1911. Smith had grown up in a tenement in one of the poorest districts of Manhattan. He took pride in his growing up there and his Irish roots. Unlike Roosevelt, Smith pulled himself up by his bootstraps, learning how to read people while he worked at the Fulton Fish Market and how to entertain them by acting in several vaudeville shows. He had a sly, often biting sense of humor. From the beginning of their relationship, Smith distrusted and disliked Franklin Roosevelt, whom he thought effete and largely if not wholly out for himself. Identifying with the working people, Smith became one of Tammany Hall's most beloved leaders, and Franklin dubbed him "the Happy Warrior." Untutored in lawmaking, Smith taught himself the mechanics by spending nights in the New York Public Library reading the details of the laws he was asked to support and introduce in the legislature. The head of the Citizens Union, an early organization devoted to good government, praised Smith for having "displayed a practical knowledge of the workings of the state government not rivaled by anyone else."[7]

Tammany Hall responded just like everyone expected to Roosevelt's insurgency, exerting maximum pressure on the insurgents to relent: Pet projects were shelved, patronage dried up, hometown constituents were mobilized, local newspapers counseled against delay, country chairmen, bankers, and prominent businesses threatened to withdraw support.

In the first of many confrontations between Franklin and Smith, Smith broke the insurgents apart by dropping Sheehan as their candidate and instead proposing State Supreme Court Justice James Aloysius Gorman, whom even Franklin conceded the insurgents "would have taken... at the very beginning and been perfectly satisfied." Though Franklin got considerable publicity for leading the insurgents, not all of it was good. Worst of all, he was tagged as anti-Catholic and anti-Irish, a label that took years for him to overcome.[8]

Once Gorman was seated, the state legislature went back to work. In 1911, Franklin introduced the Seventeenth Amendment, which provided for the direct election of U.S. senators by the voters in each state. The Democrats in both chambers voted for the amendment, while most Republicans opposed it. Luckily for the Democrats, President Taft had no formal role to play in the ratification process, though he voiced no opposition since he reflexively deferred to legislatures on policy matters. On May 13, 1912, Congress adopted the measure by the two-thirds vote required in the Constitution, and once it was formally ratified in three-fourths of the states, the amendment became official on May 31, 1913. (On January 15, 1913, New York became the fourth state to ratify the amendment.)

As the amendment was heading toward ratification, Franklin persisted in challenging Tammany Hall. He opposed such measures as a Tammany-sponsored charter for New York City even though it provided equal pay for women who were schoolteachers; a bill to reorganize the State Highway Commission; and other bills to legalize prizefighting, Sunday baseball, and racetrack betting. The persistence of his opposition played well with Republicans and his constituents, who were mostly farmers and small business owners. But he could not have expected Tammany Hall, the seat of Democratic power in the state, to ignore the new boy begging for notoriety.

Al Smith, now the Democratic leader in the state assembly, regarded Franklin as "a damn fool," while Robert Wagner, who led Democrats in the state senate, derided Franklin as a publicity-hound, declaring once, "Senator Roosevelt has made his point. What he wants is a headline in the newspapers." Tom Grady, who had served with Teddy years before in the state legislature, said that he found Franklin to be the more obnoxious of the two men; and Tim Sullivan, a legislator who rarely had a bad word to say about anyone, declared Franklin "an awful arrogant fellow."[9]

Even politically friendly people found Franklin insufferable. One was Frances Perkins, one of Franklin's earliest and most enduring supporters. After graduating from Mount Holyoke in 1902, she had been among the first women selected to attend the prestigious Wharton School of Business at the University of Pennsylvania. After earning her master's degree there, she earned another from Columbia in social work. She made the most of her connections with wealthy New York families, such as the Vanderbilts and the Astors, provided editorial support for the writer Upton Sinclair, whose works illuminated the plight of working-class Americans and immigrants during the Progressive Era, and became an assistant to Florence Kelly, the head of the National Consumer League. Perkins took to heart Kelly's insistence "on rigorous research before proposing reforms."[10] On March 25, 1909, while attending a ladies' tea in Manhattan, she and the other guests heard an explosion nearby. When she determined that the explosion had come from the Triangle Shirtwaist Factory, she rushed to help, but 146 people, mostly immigrant women, perished in the fire that followed because of the unsafe working conditions. Perkins used the incident to rally the New York Assembly to enact a new law requiring improvements in worker safety.

One of the assemblymen she lobbied in 1910 was Franklin Roosevelt. "There was nothing particularly interesting about the tall, thin young man with the high-collar and pince-nez," she wrote in 1946, except for the fact that he "made a spirited defense of Theodore Roosevelt, being careful to proclaim that he was not his kin except by marriage." She did not pick up his first name then, but she soon observed him in the state legislature: "I have a vivid picture of him operating on the floor of the Senate: tall and slender, very active and alert, moving around the floor, going in and out of committee rooms, rarely talking with the members, who more or less avoided him, not particularly charming (that came later), artificially serious of face, rarely smiling, with the unfortunate habit—so natural that he was unaware of it—of throwing his head up." She found that "This, combined with his pince-nez and great height, gave him the appearance of looking down his nose at people." She believed that "he started that way... because he really didn't like people very much and because he had a youthful lack of humility, a streak of self-righteousness, and a deafness to the hopes, fears, and aspirations which are the common lot." She was not alone in thinking that his Harvard education was "a political handicap," since it reinforced his image as an elitist who was not a man of the people at all. Yet, she said, "the marvel is that these handicaps were washed out of him by life, experience, punishment, and his capacity to grow."[11] That Perkins was a loyal political ally who eventually became Franklin's secretary of labor makes her observations more insightful.

II

The origins of the term "muckrake" date back to one of the first English novels, John Bunyan's *Pilgrim's Progress*, published in 1678. It is the tale of a young man who must overcome various challenges to achieve salvation. One character was "the Man with the Muck Rake," who succumbed to the world's earthly temptations and corruption.

The term became popular in the United States during the Progressive Era. Muckrakers were journalists (such as Upton Sinclair) and politicians bent on reform and exposing corruption, and it was associated with the growing number of newspapers and magazines, such as *McClure*, that spread stories of scandal and corruption in the nation's businesses and government. In 1906, President Theodore Roosevelt helped to further seal the term in the nation's firmament, declaring that "muckrakers should rake less muck." In his address, President Roosevelt explained that the character the Man with the Muck Rake "is set forth as the example of him whose vision is fixed on carnal rather than spiritual things. Yet he also typifies the man who in this life consistently refuses to see aught that is lofty [and] fixes his eyes with solemn intentness on that which is vile and debasing."[12]

Franklin had no problem with muck so long as it raked the results he wanted. When he entered politics, he looked for allies among newspaper editors and reporters. He knew that newspapers could make, or break, a political career. Franklin understood positive coverage could reach more people than he could on his own. Thus, he used the press to promote the image he thought could attract the support he needed to win. In leading insurgents (unsuccessfully) to thwart Tammany Hall's domination of the race to fill the open Senate seat in 1911, Franklin relished the coverage, telling the *New York Times* that "there is nothing I love as much as a good fight." Indeed, he added, "I never had as much fun as I am having now."[13]

Reporters flocked to cover Franklin because he made news as much as Teddy did. The *New York Post* commented that Franklin had "the strong insurgent tendencies of the family." (He turned the insurgency to his advantage.) The *American* reported, "His face is boyish, but those who remember Theodore Roosevelt when he was an assemblyman say the Senator bears a striking resemblance to the Colonel."[14] The New York papers depicted Franklin as a heartthrob, and Franklin enjoyed playing that part to the utmost.

The Sheehan battle brought Franklin exactly what he wanted—national attention. It did not take long before Roosevelt turned his defeat into a victory by focusing exclusively on the fact that Sheehan was defeated. The *Cleveland Plain Dealer* declared Franklin as Teddy's successor, "May it not be possible that this rising star may continue the Roosevelt dynasty? Franklin D. Roosevelt is, to be sure, a Democrat, but this is a difference of small import. In other respects, he seems to be thoroughly Rooseveltian."[15] In North Carolina, Josephus Daniels, editor of the *Raleigh News & Observer*, praised Franklin as "A Coming Democratic Leader."[16] New Jersey governor Woodrow Wilson acknowledged Franklin's rise as well, while Teddy wrote Franklin, "Just a line to say that we are really proud of the way you have handled yourself."[17]

Yet, it was another man, a reporter for the *New York Herald* in Albany, who saw something more in Franklin than others were seeing.

Franklin first met Louis Howe when Howe interviewed him for the
Empire State Democracy, and the connection between the two men
was immediate. Howe told Eleanor and Franklin that he believed
that Roosevelt had the potential to become president. That was all
Franklin needed to hear. Tammany Hall had stymied his short-lived
effort to secure the Democratic nomination for the Senate in 1911.
When a bout with typhoid fever stalled his efforts to win reelection
to his state senate seat, Franklin asked Eleanor to arrange a meeting
with Howe to discuss his political future.

Near the end of 1911, Franklin traveled to New Jersey to meet Governor Wilson to express his support for Wilson's presidential
campaign. Franklin begged Howe, "If you can connect me with a job
during the campaign, for heaven's sake help me out."[18]

Asking Howe for help was risky, because most people found him
repulsive. He was short, barely five feet tall, and gaunt, and had
"gnome-like features," which other reporters never ceased to call out.
Whereas Franklin had been educated at the nation's most elite institutions, Howe was a college dropout. Whereas Franklin was treated
like a matinee idol by favorably disposed reporters, Howe's face was
scarred from a childhood bicycle accident. While Franklin was always well groomed, Howe dressed sloppily, often in attire with
various stains that prompted most other people to keep their distance. He smoked incessantly, and never cared for his personal
appearance, indeed, claimed with perverse pride that he was "one
of the four ugliest men" in New York. "Children take one look at me
and run," he once said. Though detractors belittled Howe's appearance, he took pride in his (small) stature. Franklin was an optimist,
while Howe was a cynic.[19]

Yet Howe never doubted Franklin's potential. "I was so impressed
with Franklin Roosevelt," he explained, "his seriousness, his earnestness, his firm dedication to his cause, that from that moment [when
first we met] we became friends—and almost at that very first meeting I made up my mind that he was Presidential timber and that
nothing but an accident could keep him from becoming President
of the United States."[20]

Howe's wife Grace recalled that, in 1911, "The first time that I saw [Franklin Roosevelt] was when we were coming out of St. Peter's Episcopal Church in Albany. Louis said, 'There's young Roosevelt—the man I was telling you about. A man of great promise.'"[21]

Howe shared Franklin's dislike for Tammany Hall, counseled the insurgents, and gave Franklin his first extensive interview in the national media. Howe's position as a journalist covering state politics in Albany allowed him to keep a watchful eye on Franklin's progress: "Keeping close tabs for my newspaper on every move of the insurgents brought me into daily contact with Franklin Roosevelt. I had ample opportunity to study his potentialities as a leader."[22] He also shared Franklin's allegiance to the Democratic Party but not to a particular political philosophy. What mattered most for Howe was the same thing that counted for Franklin—the bottom line.

In 1912, Franklin turned his state senate campaign over to Howe. Muckrakers like Howe were common in that era for aligning themselves with a political party or partisan; and, for the next six weeks, Howe was Franklin's surrogate. He moved to Poughkeepsie, decorated the same car Franklin had used in his first campaign with Roosevelt banners, and personally lobbied legislators to vote for Franklin. A brilliant tactician, Howe devised strategies to appeal to different constituencies, such as devising a scheme to protect farmers from New York City commission merchants, mailing more than eleven thousand letters to inform farmers of Franklin's priorities, promising apple growers that Franklin planned to introduce a bill standardizing the size of barrels, assuring fishermen that Franklin would help lower licensing fees, and telling the farming community that Franklin aimed to become a chair of the Senate Agriculture Committee. He took out full-page ads in upstate New York promising Franklin's support for women's suffrage and determination to reform working conditions.

Howe overspent Franklin's money, forcing him to get loans from friends, but he was so energetic and creative in directing the campaign that very few voters were aware that Franklin was ill throughout the campaign. Yet Howe's enthusiasm never waned, even addressing one letter to Franklin, "Beloved and Revered Future President."

Franklin won the district with a larger margin than he had two years before—but without ever having appeared there. "I for one was convinced that day," Howe said, "that Franklin Roosevelt was on the threshold of a brilliant public career."[23]

Eleanor, however, took an immediate dislike to Howe. His appearance initially disgusted her, and she found his boasting annoying. But, in time, she changed her opinion and grew to love the "gnome-like looking little man." In 1936, she said, "My husband was reelected thanks to Louis Howe."[24] As Franklin and Eleanor's son Elliott noted years later, "Louis Howe was probably the greatest influence in both my father and my mother's lives."[25]

III

Teddy Roosevelt had the highest vote of any non-major-party candidate in history, but the 1912 presidential election marked the end of Teddy's colorful electoral career. He had had an extraordinary ride as president, including becoming the first world leader to win the Nobel Peace Prize[26] and for fashioning a new foreign policy that expanded the Monroe Doctrine to oppose the colonization of any Western nations and to underscore the United States' unique role in protecting order, life, and property in those countries. His foreign policy had become popularly associated with the words "walk softly and carry a big stick."[27] The 1912 presidential election is the most recent election in which the candidate finishing second was not from one of the two major political parties, as well as the last one in which four candidates each had more than 5 percent of the popular vote. Eugene Debs, the Socialist candidate, finished with 6 percent of the vote.

Taft finished with the lowest number of electoral votes (eight) and percentage of the public vote of any incumbent in American history. If the election had been based solely on résumés, Taft likely would have won: Before becoming president, he had been a federal appellate judge, solicitor general, governor of the Philippines, law school dean, and secretary of war. He was the first person elected president directly from the cabinet since James Monroe in 1816.

Unlike Taft, Wilson was not a career politician. Among the first scholars in the country to specialize in Congress, Wilson had taught political science at Princeton before becoming its president. He relished the job until he lost a fierce battle involving modernizing the university, which would have involved relocating the graduate school on the main campus. Fed up with academic politics, he entered the political arena and ran for the governorship of New Jersey in 1910.

In the first political campaign of his life, Wilson cast himself as a progressive, a label that loosely encompassed beliefs in the government's capacity for acting on behalf of the common good. He pledged to do away with machine politics, including ridding New Jersey of political bosses (who happened to support his candidacy). He proved surprisingly effective in debates in which his opponents underestimated him and his command of the facts was incomparable. His landslide victory convinced him of the necessity of party rule for political success and marked him as a new political star on the national stage. In his first year in office, he rallied his fellow Democrats to champion workers' compensation and electoral reforms such as secret ballots and direct primaries for all elective offices and party officials. Former rival George Record conceded it was "the most remarkable record of progressive legislation ever known in the political history of this or any State."[28] Wilson could not help but gloat, "After dealing with college politicians, I find that the men with whom I am doing with now seem like amateurs."[29]

Wilson's successes in his first year as governor attracted national attention and interest among some Democratic Party leaders that he run for the presidency. It had been nearly two decades since a Democratic had won the White House (ironically, Grover Cleveland had clashed with Wilson when the latter was president of Princeton and Cleveland headed the university's Board of Trustees). While Wilson had little interest in quixotic ventures, he listened to the power brokers and agreed to run.

The year before the Democratic convention in 1912, Franklin traveled to New Jersey to meet Wilson. Franklin hoped to ingratiate

himself by being one of the first people to express support for a presidential bid by Wilson, while Wilson, then fifty-five, was primarily
interested in knowing how Franklin could help him win over the
New York delegation for the upcoming Democratic convention.
New York had ninety votes at the convention, only a third of which
might support Wilson. But even that level of support seemed unlikely because the delegation operated under the unit rule, which
meant that the person who won the state primary would win all of
the delegation's votes. Tammany Hall boss Charles Murphy controlled the delegation, and Wilson was not Murphy's choice.

Nor was Wilson the front-runner by any means; at best, he was
a dark horse candidate, far behind Champ Clark, a Missouri progressive who was house speaker and widely viewed as the favorite.
Franklin did what he could do—he arranged a dinner the night before the convention, for Wilson to meet his supporters from upstate
New York. Only a few came, and Murphy dominated the New York
convention from start to finish. A slate of ninety uninstructed delegates was chosen, with Tammany Hall holding the decisive majority.
Franklin failed to be chosen as either a delegate or alternate.

He was undaunted. With Louis Howe's help, he secured the chair-
manship of the New York State Wilson conference, which convened
mostly disaffected Democrats who were willing to rally to Wilson's
side. Roosevelt was able to get 150 Wilson supporters to attend the
national convention in Baltimore. Fortunately for both Franklin and
Wilson, Senator O'Gorman favored Wilson, too, and arranged for
the Democratic National Committee to obtain seats for the Wilson
conference in the gallery, where they chanted incessantly for Wilson.
Franklin got credentials to access the convention floor.

Franklin loved working the convention. He lobbied folks in the
hotel lobby and dining rooms, touting Wilson's virtues all the while.
Reporters craved time with Franklin, Josephus Daniels among them.
"Franklin and I became friends at that convention," Daniels later wrote.
"It was a case of love at first sight."[30] The convention operated under
two rules—the unit rule and the rule that the nominee had to receive
at least two-thirds vote of the convention. The latter gave the Southern
states veto power over the nominee—something Clark expected to

work to his advantage—but ensured voting would last for days. On the first ballot, Wilson finished second to Champ Clark. Though Murphy announced New York's support for Clark during the second round of balloting, the move alienated William Jennings Bryan, known as the "Great Commoner" for his faith in the common people. Bryan switched his support from Clark to Wilson in response. For the next dozen ballots, Clark's support held, but it began to fall part on the thirtieth ballot when Indiana governor Thomas Marshall withdrew from the contest and threw his support behind Wilson, who now pulled ahead 460–455. On the forty-third ballot, four days after the voting started, Illinois switched its fifty-eight votes from Clark to Wilson, and the landslide began. Three ballots later, Wilson secured the nomination. Marshall's switch won him the vice-presidential nomination.

The day after Wilson's nomination, Franklin visited him at his summer estate. Wilson agreed to have Franklin assemble pro-Wilson Democrats in New York to fight in the general election. Two weeks later, Franklin announced the formation of the Empire State Democracy, a grassroots progressive movement with a national agenda. As the leader of the new faction in New York, Franklin waged war yet again against Tammany Hall. Though Wilson did not want the New York delegation to splinter, his concern turned out to be unwarranted when Tammany Hall's Murphy announced their support for Wilson. Murphy's move was not just an expression of his commitment to the party but signaled to Wilson that reciprocity would be welcome. Wilson asked his principal advisor, Colonel Edward House, to negotiate behind the scenes to arrange a Tammany victory in the New York governor's race in 1912.

During the general election, Franklin found himself sidelined while Wilson's team worked with Murphy and Tammany Hall to secure the outcome in New York. He learned the hard way that he was expendable.

In the general election, Republicans had the advantage of an incumbent, William Howard Taft, but Teddy's third-party insurgency split the Republican vote, ensuring the victory for Wilson. For the first time since Grover Cleveland's election in 1892, Democrats had one of their own in the White House. The election marked the end of Teddy's electoral career. While Wilson's share of the popular vote was the lowest percentage of any winning candidate since Abraham Lincoln in 1860, his share, albeit a plurality, coupled with Theodore Roosevelt's 27.4 percent, meant that nearly 70 percent of the American people had voted progressive. Thus, the popular vote, along with winning the electoral votes of all but eight states, gave Wilson a solid mandate. His 435 electors were the largest number yet for a single candidate in a presidential election.

As Democrats around the country flooded Wilson with requests for appointments, Wilson filled his cabinet with prominent progressives, including two men whose help had won him the Democratic nomination—William Jennings Bryan as secretary of state and William McAdoo as treasury secretary. Franklin pleaded with Howe to help him land an appointment. Howe in turn urged Roosevelt to make peace with Murphy and Tammany Hall to help both his reelection to the state senate and chances of serving in the upcoming Wilson administration. Determined not to be left on the sidelines again, Franklin, with Howe's support, moved his family to Washington before he had been appointed to anything.

IV

If there was anyone in Franklin's past that Wilson resembled, it was Endicott Peabody. Both were serious men who embodied moral rectitude. Neither suffered fools gladly.

But Wilson was unlike the one president whom Franklin knew best, his cousin Theodore. To be sure, Wilson and Teddy shared some progressive values, but, as Franklin recalled many years later when he was president, "Theodore . . . lacked Wilson's appeal to the fundamental and failed to stir, as Wilson did, the truly profound and social convictions. Wilson, on the other hand, failed where Theodore Roosevelt succeeded in stirring people to enthusiasm over specific individual events."[31] In 1913, however, Franklin's primary concern was less with how to meld the two presidents' leadership styles without their limitations than with his own immediate future.

When Franklin arrived in Trenton at the president-elect's invitation to discuss possible appointments within his administration, Franklin made clear he wanted only one thing—the position of assistant secretary of the navy. Besides trying to fill Teddy's old shoes, Franklin understood the job was a big one: At the time, the United States had the third largest navy in the world, and it was the responsibility of the assistant secretary to hone the navy into a formidable fighting force in the Western Hemisphere and the Pacific. Returning to the state senate held nothing nearly as interesting and important as filling Teddy's old shoes. There was no question the job would give Franklin the national visibility and credibility he craved.

Franklin left the meeting without any commitment from Wilson. As Franklin waited for further news, Wilson's incoming treasury secretary, William McAdoo, offered Franklin the chance to serve as an assistant secretary within his department or as the collector of the port of New York, seemingly an unimportant post except that it entailed the distribution of considerable patronage and overseeing the collection of most of the funds required for the federal government to operate. While Franklin waited impatiently, Wilson tapped Josephus Daniels as navy secretary. A North Carolina newspaper editor, Daniels had no qualification for the post other than the facts that he was an old friend and early supporter of Wilson and his father had built ships for the Confederate Navy during the Civil War. A leader of the white supremacist movement in North Carolina, Daniels convinced Wilson's choice for secretary of state, William Jennings Bryan, who knew Teddy well, to agree to Franklin's appointment as Daniels's deputy. Though Wilson, Daniels, and Bryan knew next to nothing about naval affairs, Bryan and Daniels believed that Franklin's interest in naval history and connection to Teddy made him an ideal choice to serve under Daniels.

As luck would have it that, on the morning of the inauguration, Franklin ran into Daniels at the Willard, where both were staying. As Daniels recalled, Franklin was bubbling with enthusiasm, "as keen as a boy to take in the inauguration ceremonies." Franklin congratulated Daniels on his appointment as secretary of the navy, and Daniels responded, "How would you like to come to Washington as

assistant secretary of the navy?" Bursting with excitement, Franklin
told Daniels, "It would please me better than anything in the world.
All my life I have loved ships and have been a student of the Navy,
and the assistant secretaryship is the one place, above all others, that
I would like to hold."[32] Franklin told Daniels of his offer from the
treasury secretary but added, "nothing would please me so much as
to be with you in the Navy." Later, Daniels noted in his diary that
Teddy "went from that place to the Presidency. May history repeat
itself." Daniels's paper reported, "He's following in Teddy's footsteps."
Teddy saw the connection, too. He wrote Franklin, "It is interesting
that you are in another place which I myself once held. I am sure you
will enjoy yourself to the full as Ass't Secty of the Navy and that you
will do capital work."[33]

Daniels cleared the appointment with New York's two senators.
New York's Democratic senator, O'Gorman, was thrilled to assent,
especially because he understood the debt that he had owed Franklin
for his own seat in the Senate. New York's other senator, Elihu Root,
who had served as secretary of state under Theodore Roosevelt,
greeted the news with less enthusiasm, asking Daniels, "You know
the Roosevelts, don't you? Whenever a Roosevelt rides, he wishes to
ride in front."[34] Root gave his consent, acknowledging that as "a Republican, I have no right to make any suggestion." Daniels told Root
he was not concerned that Franklin had great ambitions, since he
wanted a strong man as his deputy. He told Root, "A chief who fears
an assistant will outrank him is not fit to be the chief."[35] With the
backing of New York's senators and the good will Teddy enjoyed
with most Republican senators, Franklin was swiftly confirmed in
the Senate.

V

On March 17, 1913, Franklin Roosevelt took his oath as assistant secretary of the navy. At thirty-one, he was the youngest person yet to
have held the post, and his eagerness to prove himself was widely
perceived as a virtue. As the only assistant in the Navy Department,

Franklin got attention even if he did not want it. When Daniels was not in town, Franklin had the run of the department and easy access to the President. Later, when he was in the White House, Franklin recalled several of the lessons Wilson had taught him during their eight years together, involving such diverse matters as working with Congress, the importance of shaping public opinion, and expecting that Democratic candidates' best chance to win the White House would be during economic downturns.

Franklin relished the opportunity not just to wield power but to learn about leadership. Newton Baker, who served as secretary of war from 1916 to 1921, told Frances Perkins, "Young Roosevelt is very promising, but I should think he'd wear himself out in the promiscuous and extended contacts he maintains with people." He added, "But as I have observed him, he seems to clarify his ideas and teach himself as he goes along by that very conventional method."[36]

A harder lesson for Franklin to learn was respecting the chain of command. (Indeed, Daniels was the only administrative superior Franklin ever had in his career.) In public, Franklin deferred to Daniels, but he ridiculed him behind his back. Calling him "the funniest looking hillbilly I have ever seen," Franklin entertained his friends with imitations of Daniels and expressed disdain for Daniels's outspoken advocacy of white supremacy, segregation, and Prohibition. His disdain for Daniels became so apparent that at one point Interior Secretary Franklin Lane told Franklin either to be more respectful or to resign his office. Franklin learned how to be more discreet.

Franklin loved touring naval ships. He especially enjoyed the seventeen-gun salutes he received when boarding vessels, but he hated the paperwork. He hired Howe as "clerk in the Secretary's Office, Navy Department (detailed for duty in the Office of the Assistant Secretary)."[37] Louis acknowledged, sometimes with pride and sometimes with bitterness, that "I am hated by everybody. I always have been hated by everybody, and I want to be hated by everybody."[38] This was true, except for the Roosevelt family. Franklin's son Elliott recalled Franklin's "striding down Connecticut Avenue with Louis at his side. The two of them looked uncannily like Don Quixote and Sancho setting out to battle giants."[39]

Howe did more than handle the paperwork; he was constantly attentive to how Franklin could advance his career. Eleanor observed that "Louis had enormous interest in having power, and if he could not have it for himself, he wanted it through someone he was influencing." Franklin was happy to be that person. As the veteran journalist John Gunther wrote, "If FDR had come out for the Devil, it wouldn't have mattered much to Louis Howe."[40]

Howe was at least as quick a study as Franklin. He mastered the navy's intricacies to such an extent that Admiral Emory Land once said, "Louis Howe was a damned smart able man and the best advisor Roosevelt ever had, because he had the guts to say 'no.'"[41] "Howe, the older man, always called Roosevelt by his first name and spoke out whenever he thought FDR was mistaken."[42] Howe was once overheard shouting on the phone at Franklin, "You damned fool! You can't do that! You simply can't do it... If you do it, you're a fool—just a damn idiotic fool." Howe jokingly said that his principal function in Washington was to provide "toe weights to keep Franklin's feet on the ground."

Howe was one of the very few people whose advice Franklin accepted without question. Over their years together in the Navy Department, Howe taught Franklin how to deal with organized labor, while both Daniels and Howe taught Franklin about "the diversity of the Democratic Party, the need to accommodate regional politicians, and the importance of small favors and gestures." Franklin endeared himself to many members of Congress by fulfilling nearly every request made by a representative or senator to grant early discharges, promotions, and other favors. As Franklin told Frances Perkins many years later, congressmen wanted more for the administration or president to have "a nice jolly understanding of their problems than lots of patronage. A little patronage, a lot of pleasure, and public signs of friendship and prestige—that's what makes a political leader secure with his people and that is what he wants anyhow."[43]

Daniels agreed Howe "knew all the tides and eddies in the Navy Department, in the administration, and in the political life of the country. He advised [Franklin] about everything. His one and only ambition was to help steer Franklin's course so that he could take the tide the full. He was totally devoted. He would have sidetracked both President Wilson and me to get Franklin Roosevelt to the White House."[44] Daniels recognized as well Louis's talents in serving Franklin: "Always fertile in resources and suggestions and with a keen sense of public opinion. Howe had boldness in as large measure as his chief. And he could write, having a style that was luminous and convincing. Franklin leaned upon Howe whose devotion made him sensitive to every wind that might affect Franklin in his public career."[45]

"The laboring men all liked" Franklin, Daniels remembered. "If there was any Groton complex, he did not show it."[46] Eleanor acknowledged that, thanks to Howe, Franklin's experience visiting the nation's navy yards and the men working there was largely responsible for having made Franklin "more than a very nice young man who went out in society and did a fair job but was perfectly conventional about it." Eleanor credited Howe with helping Franklin overcome the elitist mannerisms and attitudes of his background.[47]

Wilson, Daniels, and Bryan were pacificists, but Franklin was not. Bryan and Daniels were linked together by the fact they were old friends, Daniels having been Bryan's publicity director in each of his presidential campaigns. They resented men of wealth and special privilege. Together, they promoted the values of an old-fashioned, rural, small-town America: pacifist, prohibitionist, and religiously fundamental. They railed against sin wherever they found it. The only thing Franklin had in common with them was that he represented farmers in rural New York, but he hated the trio's myopic provincialism.

Daniels's small-town values and rectitude were unpopular not just with Franklin but throughout the Navy Department. Daniels dreamed of disarmament, saw the navy in terms of Wilsonian neutrality, and was more concerned with the welfare of the enlisted men than building warships or expanding the office corps. And yet, in 1913, the Navy Department was its own little world. Taft's departing secretary of war, Henry Stimson, described it as devoid of logic and as "a dim religious world in which Neptune was God and [Alfred] Mahan[, a widely revered naval historian,] his prophet."[48] Annapolis graduates regarded Mahan's work as their bible.

Wilson's concern was civilian control of the military. He had given Daniels his marching orders to modernize the navy, disbanding the board of four admiral aides that had stood between him and the department; limiting the terms of bureau chiefs to four years; and requiring every officer to put to sea. Daniels visited naval facilities throughout the United States, often breaking ranks to shake the hands of enlisted men; routinely overrode admirals' orders; and ordered the fleet to cross the Atlantic in winter.

He even criticized naval nomenclature. On May 18, 1914, Daniels issued General Order No. 98, which required that directional instructions henceforth be given as "right" and "left" and not as "port" and "starboard."[49] Daniels got rid of choker-collar uniforms, took engineering officers out of dress whites, implemented a promotion system based on merit, and dismantled many of the artificial barriers between officers and enlisted men. He banned wine on ships and issuing condoms to sailors on shore leave.

Though he agreed on the need for greater professionalism in the navy, Franklin cared more for improving naval strategy and performance. Yet two incidents changed Franklin's attitude about Daniels. The first dealt with the chain of command. California had enacted a law forbidding Japanese citizens from owning land in the state. On May 9, 1913, Japanese authorities lodged a formal complaint with Washington, declaring that the law violated both treaties Japan had with the United States and international law. Wilson rejected the complaint.

The secretary of war and the Joint Board of the Army and Navy were convinced Japan would likely attack the Philippines if the United States did nothing. Franklin, in private, "did all in my power" to ready American forces for an attack.[50]

But Daniels vehemently disagreed, and Wilson agreed with Daniels that every effort should be made to avoid military conflict. When the admirals appealed the decision, Wilson was outraged and ordered the Army and Navy Board not to meet without his express authorization. That Wilson backed Daniels over his military leaders left a deep impression on Franklin.

The second incident involved the navy's contracting authority. Daniels hated monopolies, and he ordered three of the nation's largest steel manufacturers to resubmit their bids the next day after they had each come up with the exact same bid for the armor plate to be used in constructing the battleship *Arizona*. "I loved his words," Franklin recalled, and both he and Daniels enjoyed seeing the disappointment on the faces of the steel magnates as they left the room. The next day, the companies presented the same bids again. Daniels told Franklin to meet with the leader of a British consortium, which submitted a substantially lower bid. Once the American companies learned the news, they quickly matched the British offer. Daniels gleefully reported to Congress that he had saved the navy more than $100,000. (Franklin wrote Eleanor in July 1913 that "the Secretary and I worked like n——-s all day.")[51]

Roosevelt could not, however, resist testing boundaries. During an inspection tour of American bases out West, Franklin told reporters of his support for President Wilson's hard line in threatening to use military force to free three American sailors whom the Mexican government had arrested when they had come ashore for supplies. Daniels was not amused. He ordered Franklin back to Washington, but, on the train trip back, Franklin told reporters that he expected that "sooner or later, it seems, the United States must go down there and clean up the Mexican political mess."[52] By the time Franklin arrived in Washington, Wilson had backed down, following the advice of Daniels and Bryan to withdraw American forces from Mexico and to accept a mediation effort led by Argentina, Brazil, and Chile. Daniels told Franklin to tone down his rhetoric or resign. Franklin did not resign.

But Franklin considered a third option—running for a statewide office in New York that would enable him both to get out from under Daniels's watchful eye and to reassert his independence. He tried in vain to get Wilson's endorsement for a gubernatorial run, but Wilson stubbornly remained neutral in the hopes of not alienating Tammany Hall, whose support he needed for his reelection campaign in 1916. Teddy refused, too, saying that he was too busy mending fences

with liberal Republicans, whose support he needed if he ran again
for president.

When Elihu Root, New York's Republican senator, declared he
would not run again, Franklin saw his chance to run for the open seat.
Howe was more than eager to lead Franklin's campaign, and Treasury
Secretary McAdoo encouraged Franklin to enter his name as a candidate. On August 13, 1914, Franklin became the first Democrat to enter
the race. Tammany Hall put up James Gerard for the seat, creating
the problem of Franklin's having to compete with a State Department
colleague who was ambassador to Germany. Wilson stayed out of the
contest, leaving Franklin to battle Tammany Hall on his own. Without any compelling message driving his campaign (despite Howe's
efforts to drum up support in upstate New York), Franklin lost the
primary. Gerard's pledge that, if elected, he would represent everyone
and not Tammany Hall won Franklin's support in the general election.

Franklin's loss was a reminder that it was long overdue to make
peace with Tammany Hall; he had no future in the state without its
help. Tammany, too, learned that it needed Franklin and his supporters, as their candidate lost the general election without the
support of a unified party.

As Franklin looked for ways to make peace with Tammany Hall,
he kept his distance from Teddy. He maintained contact with many
of Teddy's friends, such as Supreme Court Justice Oliver Wendell
Holmes, but he understood that, as one of the most visible members
of the Wilson administration, he had to be careful about interacting
with Teddy, who made no secret of his animosity toward Wilson. In
turning down an invitation to stay at Hyde Park during a visit to the
Hudson Valley, Teddy wrote Franklin's mother, "Now, Sara, I am very
doubtful, from Franklin's standpoint, whether it is wise that we do
so. . . . I shall be in the middle of a tour in which I am attacking the
Administration, and I think it might well be an error, from Franklin's
standpoint, if we stayed with you. . . . I hope you understand, dear
Sally, that it is the exact truth that I am thinking of Franklin's interest."
Whether Sally understood or not, Franklin did, especially as Teddy's
bellicose rhetoric intensified as armed conflicts broke out across Eastern Europe with more violence seeming likely every day.

VI

On June 28, 1914, a Serbian national assassinated Archduke Franz Ferdinand and his wife during a state visit to Serbia's capital, Sarajevo. As the presumptive heir to the throne of the Austro-Hungarian Empire, his death set in motion a chain of events that threatened the security of the entire Western world: On July 28, Austria declared war against Serbia, which refused to disavow the assassination; Russia mobilized to support Serbia two days later; France mobilized its forces to support Russia on July 31; on August 1, Germany declared war against Russia, and on August 3 they declared war against France and moved into Belgium to outflank the French Army. The violation of Belgian neutrality brought Great Britain into the conflict.

As assistant secretary of the navy, Franklin was convinced that it was just a matter of time before the United States was drawn into the war ripping Europe apart. Summoned back from Reading, Pennsylvania, to the Capitol after Germany declared war, Franklin wrote Eleanor, "A complete smashup is inevitable, and there are many great problems for us to consider. These are history-making days. It will be the greatest war in the world's history. [Daniels] totally fails to grasp the situation and I am to see the President Monday a.m. to go over the situation."[53]

Once he arrived, Franklin was stunned that "nobody seemed the least bit excited about the European" crisis. Daniels worried aloud about his loss of confidence in the nature of men, while Franklin "started in alone to get things ready and prepare for what ought to be done by the Navy end of things." Franklin never wavered in his belief that preparedness was the only reasonable alternative; "it is," he wrote Eleanor, "my duty to keep the Navy in a position where no chances, even the most remote, are taken."[54]

Over the next two and a half years, Franklin often felt as if he were the only one in the Navy Department who understood the ramifications of the conflict abroad. He was the principal civilian advocate for preparedness in the country, a role he took seriously. Occasionally, he had to temper his public rhetoric given that Wilson, Bryan, and Daniels all hewed closely to the administration's policy of neutrality. Privately, Franklin pushed whenever and wherever he could for the administration to prepare for war. He wrote Eleanor that "I am running the real work; although Josephus Daniels is here! He is bewildered by it all, very sweet, but sad!"[55]

Yet Franklin again underestimated Daniels, who was moving rapidly to solidify the nation's neutral stance. On August 4, 1914, Wilson, agreeing with Daniels, issued the first of ten neutrality proclamations that he would promulgate during the first three months of the war. These committed the United States to remain neutral and made it a crime for anyone to be partial beyond the "free expression of opinion." Two days later, on August 6, Wilson ordered Daniels to direct all officers "to refrain" from any political or social commentary on the conflict. With help from Daniels and Franklin, Wilson placed the navy on alert to watch the coasts, protect the neutrality of American ports, and prevent the shipment of any munitions to combatants.

At the same time, Franklin was feeding information to hawks in Congress led by Senator Lodge of Massachusetts, even while President Wilson was reassuring the nation that it "was at peace." With news of the war having reached Congress, the House Naval Affairs Committee invited Franklin to testify on December 16, 1914. During his five hours as a witness, Franklin studiously avoided discussing administration policy. Instead, he stressed the facts about the navy's preparedness, including the need for naval expansion in the event of war. Franklin was elated that the newspapers gave his testimony high marks.

Wilson's hopes for American neutrality took a sharp blow on May 7, 1915, when the British ocean liner *Lusitania*, the largest and fastest in the Atlantic, was torpedoed and sank into the Irish Sea. With Teddy and Lodge proclaiming the necessity for American involvement, Wilson put the nation at ease by asking Germany to respect the rights of Americans to sail the high seas and demanding reparations for the loss of American lives. Germany blamed the owner of the ship for its demise, which led Wilson to take his rhetoric up a notch, demanding Germany issue an apology and declaring the sinking as "a crime against humanity."

Wilson's militaristic tone backfired: Williams Jennings Bryan, a lifelong pacificist, submitted his resignation on June 9 because he believed Wilson's rhetoric meant war. The cabinet, as well as Daniels and Franklin, rallied to the President's side. Daniels was uneasy, but Franklin was thrilled. He hoped Daniels would also resign, but Daniels proved he was in no hurry to return to North Carolina.

With Bryan gone, Franklin tried appeasing both Wilson and Daniels and upgrading the navy. He had learned the importance of party unity from both Wilson, who as governor and now president saw himself as the leader of his party whose support was indispensable to Franklin's success, and political boss Charles Murphy, who famously remarked, "They may be sons of bitches, but they're our sons of bitches." When Daniels summoned him to Washington to draft plans for naval expansion, Franklin arrived with drafts he had already prepared. A month after Bryan's departure, Wilson instructed Daniels and Secretary of War Lindley Garrison to prepare a program for "an adequate national defense." Taking over as acting secretary while Daniels vacationed, Franklin worked with the navy's General Board to propose what was at the time the largest peacetime construction plan in American history. Despite his pacifist leanings, Daniels shepherded the program through Congress, which authorized completion of the program in three years.

When President Wilson agreed in the fall of 1915 to develop a preparedness program, Franklin was enthusiastic. During Wilson's reelection campaign the next year, Franklin publicly expressed strong support for Wilson's domestic policies, but Franklin continued to have difficulty toeing the administration's foreign policy line of complete neutrality. He hoped Wilson's reelection in 1916 might make Wilson more open to modifying his position, especially after Germany on February 1, 1917, resumed waging unrestricted submarine warfare, which Franklin worried would soon claim American lives and vessels. When the Senate filibustered a law authorizing arming merchant vessels, Franklin urged President Wilson to use his authority under an older law allowing him to arm the vessels. Wilson said he would but did not do more. Though Wilson rarely explained the reasons for his decisions, this time he did, telling

Franklin, "I want history to show not only that we have tried every diplomatic means to keep out of the war; to show that war has been forced upon us deliberately by Germany; but also that we have come into the court of history with clean hands."[56] Franklin never forgot. He repeated the words virtually verbatim when he was president.

VII

In the four presidential elections held from 1900 until 1916, Theodore Roosevelt had been a candidate in all but one. In 1916, he begrudgingly came back into the Republican fold, though now too nativistic for most voters. Franklin blunted Teddy's appeal beyond his party. For Franklin was not just a Roosevelt but he became a symbol of Democrats committed to preparedness and an asset to Wilson in taking on much of the leadership in readying the navy for war. Wilson was enjoying his recent marriage to a much younger woman not long after the death of his first wife, but his neutrality turned off hawks as well as pacificists concerned with his occasional martial rhetoric, and conservatives found his progressivism offensive. When the Republican Party nominated as its candidate for president Charles Evans Hughes, a former New York governor who was then an associate justice on the Supreme Court, few expected Wilson to prevail. No Democratic president had been reelected to consecutive terms since Andrew Jackson in 1832.

Hughes was an unusual nominee. After he had won reelection as governor of New York, President Taft nominated him to the Supreme Court in 1910. Hughes's credentials were stellar; he had graduated at the top of his class at Brown University at the age of nineteen and first in his class at Columbia Law School, followed by practicing with two prestigious law firms on Wall Street for a few years, teaching for two years as a professor of law at Cornell, overseeing the state's investigations into public utilities and insurance companies, and being handpicked by then-President Theodore Roosevelt to run against—and defeat—William Randolph Hearst for the governorship of New York in 1906. On the Supreme Court, he became well known for his photographic memory, well-reasoned opinions, and erudition.

To nearly everyone's surprise, Hughes ran a poor presidential campaign. His speeches were dull and offered nothing inspirational and little insight on the prospects of war. Though not in the race, Teddy turned his ire on both Wilson and Hughes, whom he derided as "Wilson with whiskers," "the bearded lady," and "the bearded iceberg."[57] Yet Hughes was leading in the vote counts late into the evening of Election Day and early into the next, having swept the South and the Northeast. By morning, Hughes was nineteen electoral votes shy of winning the presidency. In its edition the day after the election, the New York Times reported Hughes's victory as a landslide. But by morning the returns had broken heavily in favor of Wilson. Wilson wound up defeating Hughes in the Electoral College 277–254. He won the popular vote by more than 5 million.

Despite having campaigned on the slogan "he kept us out of war," Wilson did not take long to abandon neutrality. Previously, he had rejected Franklin's proposal to form a Council of National Defense to take over war production, but when Franklin approached him again, Wilson agreed. Germany's unrestricted submarine war had recommenced, while public support for American military intervention grew after the discovery of a secret telegram from the German foreign minister to his ambassador in Mexico vowing "to keep the United States neutral."[58] On February 3, Wilson informed Congress he had severed diplomatic ties with Germany. Daniels called Franklin back to Washington from Santo Domingo, where he had been inspecting Marine Corps operations, and once Daniels left for vacation, Franklin tried in vain to get the President to approve bringing the Atlantic fleet north from Guantánamo Bay to ready itself for war.

Germany's aggression pushed the United States closer to war. When its submarines sank three more American steamships, Wilson met with his cabinet to discuss the prospects for war. In tears, Daniels agreed that the "German government left us no other choice."[59]

On April 2, 1917, Wilson convened both chambers of Congress to request a declaration of war. "The world must be made safe for democracy," he told Congress, and he pointedly reminded everyone in the chamber that war "has been thrust upon us." The joint session erupted in applause. Four days later, on April 6, Congress easily approved the declaration the President had requested.[60]

When Congress declared war, the United States was at best a second-rate military power. Within six months, the navy's strength increased fourfold. By the war's end in 1919, nearly half a million men had joined the navy and the navy had more than two thousand ships. While the army was expanding in numbers and strength, Franklin busied himself contracting for vast amounts of matériel and equipment, pressed for expanding enlistment, ordered training camps expanded and ship construction increased.

Franklin became the naval liaison with both France and England. He met with French officials for hours before they met with any other Americans, and, without the knowledge or approval of Wilson and Daniels, he pledged to deliver thirty American destroyers to the British. He tried without success to schedule a meeting with his counterpart in the British government, Winston Churchill, a veteran of two military campaigns in the late nineteenth century. Franklin had more success in implementing several winning strategies, including laying a North Sea anti-submarine mine barrage (a chain of underwater explosives stretching twenty miles from the Orkney Islands to Norway).

Franklin was persuaded, as Teddy had been, by the insights and historiography of Admiral Alfred Thayer Mahan, a lecturer at the Naval War College in the latter half of the nineteenth century. Though Mahan had died in December 1914, before the United States got involved in the First World War, his book, *The Influence of Sea Power upon History, 1660–1783* (1890), had become a classic on naval warfare. His second book, *The Influence of Sea Power upon the French Revolution and Europe, 1793–1812* (1892) was more popular and made him world famous and among the most influential American writers in the nineteenth century. The thesis of both books was that a strong navy was crucial for economic and political welfare and preserving international leadership. Teddy's positive review of Mahan's first book helped to popularize it. Mahan's arguments provided crucial support for both Theodore's and Franklin's visions of the navy.

From 1916 to 1920, Franklin and Howe oversaw the rapid construction of training centers, the laying of a North Sea mine barrage to contain German submarines, the expediting of military contracts, adopting a plan for a naval reserve, and going abroad to coordinate strategy with world leaders. In 1918, Franklin crossed the Atlantic to visit, much as Lincoln did at home, military bases and battlefields. He returned home sick with double pneumonia and the Spanish flu. Yet his trip abroad brought him nearly universal positive coverage in newspapers, which, by the end of the war, gave him credit as an effective administrator and as a progressive leader to watch for in the years ahead.

Franklin became a good team player to a fault. He was silent when Wilson and others in the administration referred to African Americans in derogatory terms, which he was prone to use as well. When the Wilson administration extended the Jim Crow system to the federal workforce, Franklin was again mute. Wilson was a huge proponent of the newly proposed eighteenth amendment, which prohibited the production, distribution, and sale of alcoholic beverages. Franklin skirted the law later whenever it suited his purposes. The espionage and sedition laws, enacted in the early days of the war effort with Franklin's support, remained in effect after the armistice, and the attorney general A. Mitchell Palmer led a series of raids on leftist organizations in 1919–20. When marines committed atrocities in Haiti, Franklin said nothing. Wilson's administration deported hundreds of immigrants and did nothing to stop private violence against both labor organizers and minorities. When Palmer's Washington home was blown up (not long after Franklin and Eleanor had passed on their walk home from a dinner engagement), dozens of people were killed, and hundreds wounded in the center of Wall Street.

Even with a world war on his hands, Franklin made time to mend fences with Tammany Hall through the placement of navy yards and personal favors for influential members of Congress. Thawing, Tammany Hall invited Franklin to give the keynote address at Tammany's upcoming Fourth of July celebration, where Franklin relentlessly tried to charm his former enemies. Tammany did nothing to stop rumors of a possible run by Franklin for the governorship in 1918.

Wilson himself encouraged Franklin, but Franklin followed the advice of both Howe and Daniels to stay put. In 1918, Franklin endorsed Tammany's gubernatorial candidate, Al Smith, and at the 1920 Democratic convention, he made a point of chatting Charles Murphy up and gave a speech seconding Al Smith's nomination for president.

VIII

As the year 1919 opened, Teddy was planning another third-party run for the presidency and was working late into the night of January 5 correcting copy for a forthcoming magazine article assailing Wilson again for his domestic and foreign affairs blunders. He suddenly began having trouble breathing and summoned his family doctor, who put him to bed after treating his symptoms. During the early morning hours, Teddy died in his sleep from a coronary embolism.

Franklin and Eleanor got the news while they were traveling across the Atlantic to attend the Paris Peace Accords, which Wilson hoped would lead to the signing of the Treaty of Versailles. Wilson issued a presidential proclamation on January 7 paying homage to the old lion and ordering the nation's flags half-mast. On February 9, Congress held an elaborate memorial ceremony as well, attended by numerous luminaries, to honor the former president. While there was a private ceremony held on January 8 in Oyster Bay, Franklin and Eleanor were notably absent from both the private and public ceremonies. Neither of them made any public comments, perhaps too crushed for words. Yet Franklin told the family that Teddy was "the greatest man I ever knew," and Eleanor acknowledged, "Another great figure off the stage,"[61] and wrote letters of condolences to her aunts, Teddy's sisters.

Franklin and Eleanor put Teddy's death behind them as they thrilled to the adoring crowds of millions of Parisians who flocked to the streets to honor Wilson for his leadership during the war. The Roosevelts visited battlefields and naval bases.

They eagerly accepted the President's invitation to voyage back to the United States, a voyage they recalled as being consumed by

Wilson's enthusiastic defense of the League of Nations, which had been established in the Treaty of Versailles "to promote international cooperation and to achieve peace and security."[62] Wilson was determined to use the occasion of the end of the war to secure a lasting peace in Europe and the world.

Once the ship landed in Boston, the battle over the League of Nations intensified. Franklin was largely a bystander, though he had a front-row seat. The League was Wilson's fanciful idea, and he devoted his remaining energies and time in office to secure the treaty's approval in the Senate and place the United States as an important signatory to it. Though Wilson had hoped his stop in Boston might give him the opportunity to get Senator Lodge on his side in the upcoming storm, Lodge never budged in his opposition. He delivered several major speeches in 1919 demonstrating the flaws and dangers of such a league (declaring at one point that "I cannot share the devotion [to this country with] a mongrel banner created for a League"[63]) and led months of hearings in the Senate Foreign Relations Committee to pummel the treaty into smithereens. With little comment, Franklin, along with other administration officials, watched helplessly as Wilson drove himself sick.

Few people inside the administration knew that Wilson had suffered a major stroke in October 1919. For weeks, he was hidden away in a sickroom, which only his wife, doctor, and secretary visited. Neither Franklin nor the cabinet knew how ill he was, as Wilson's wife purported to speak for him on all matters. In November 1919, the Versailles treaty came before the Senate for a vote. Ratification required at least two-thirds of the Senate to approve, but it garnered less than a majority. Rather than let the matter die there, Lodge kept the debate going so that Republicans could bash Wilson and the Democrats for its deficiencies in the congressional and presidential elections of 1920. In March, another vote was taken in the Senate, this time failing by a vote of 49–35. The treaty's rejection provided another reason to expect Democrats to lose big in the fall election.

Franklin saw little reason to stay in the administration to the bitter end. In mid-March 1920, he agreed to set up a law practice with two friends. Yet Franklin's passion was politics, and he believed that, even if Democrats were crushed in November 1920, progressivism would make a comeback. He had good reason to believe this, since, by the middle of the summer, political developments had placed him at the center of the debates shaping the 1920 presidential election.

The Democratic convention nominated Ohio governor James Cox as its candidate for president and Franklin as its vice-presidential candidate. His place on the ticket promised the possibility of the Democrats taking both Ohio and New York. He had gained enormous popularity within the party as an advocate for preparedness, and Democratic Party leaders became convinced that, with Teddy's death and the Republican Party's selection of Warren Harding as its presidential candidate, the Democrats could benefit from having the one remaining Roosevelt as a progressive leader. Cox agreed and saw nothing but an advantage in having a running mate with his "magic name."[64]

Though thrilled to be the vice-presidential candidate, Franklin was realistic about the outcome that fall. When an aide "asked him if he had any illusions that he might be elected," Franklin responded, "Nary an illusion." Nonetheless, he threw himself into the campaign because he believed the experience would help him in future elections. While many die-hard Democrats responded well, the press gave him mixed reviews, some dismissing him as merely a playboy and a few making note of the enthusiastic crowds as he barnstormed the country. Wilson himself thought very little of the ticket, dismissing it as comprised of "a nonentity and a mediocrity." He described then-thirty-eight-year-old Franklin as "affable and deferential but also bumptious." Though Cox arranged a meeting with the President, Franklin, and himself, Wilson had difficulty speaking and said nothing of note.

Franklin asked Louis Howe to manage his 1920 campaign. Howe arranged for local papers to cover the vice-presidential candidate's speeches,[65] and encouraged Eleanor to be a part of the day-to-day work of speechwriting and developing campaign strategies to get Democratic voters to the polls. It was during these meetings that Eleanor's contempt for Howe began to melt. She appreciated that he saw her value even if Franklin did not. Howe helped her to overcome her concerns about being overshadowed by Franklin and to understand that, as Franklin's partner, both she and he could benefit. "Being a sensitive person Louis knew that I was interested in the new sights and the new scenery, but that being the only woman was embarrassing. The newspaper fraternity was not so familiar to me as it was to become in later years, and I was a little afraid of it. Largely because of Louis's early interpretation of the standards and ethics of the newspaper business, I am to look with interest and confidence on the writing fraternity." She noted further, "Louis Howe began to break down my antagonism by knocking at my stateroom door and asking if he might discuss a speech with me. I found myself discussing a wide range of subjects." She found, too, that she liked the involvement in a campaign that mattered. "I did receive an intensive education on this trip, and Louis Howe played a great part in this education from that time on."[66] From Louis, she learned how to make allies among the press corps, to draft speeches, and to answer questions.

IX

The Democrats had expected disaster and got it. The outcome in the 1920 presidential election was worse than both Cox and Franklin had imagined. Harding won 61 percent of the popular vote. In commenting on the rout, Franklin said, "People tire quickly of ideals[,] and we are now repeating history." He told Cox that he did not expect a Democratic candidate for president to win the general election until the country faced a serious economic downturn.[67]

Throughout the war and the years immediately following, America was changing. The influx of immigrants altered the country's demographics, and some outside groups, such as Catholics and Jews, were beginning to prosper financially and to become influential financiers, lawyers, and statesmen. Franklin and Eleanor were the products of their upbringing and class and never rid themselves entirely of their prejudices against people who looked different than they did.

Eleanor had grown up among antisemites, whose attitudes she
often shared. In January 1918, she unhappily attended a gala honoring Bernard Baruch, then the head of the War Industries Board. She
wrote Sara that it would be "mostly Jews. [I'd] rather be hung than
seen there." After the gala, she told her mother-in-law, "The Jew
Party was appalling. I never wish to hear money, jewels, and sables
mentioned again." When Franklin invited Felix Frankfurter, a Harvard law professor, to join him and Eleanor for lunch, she did not
mince words, describing Frankfurter, later one of the influential
members of Roosevelt's Brain Trust, as "an interesting little man but
very Jew."[68] These attitudes were hard to square with Franklin's progressivism, though in time they would dissipate as both Franklin
and Eleanor worked closely with Jewish lawyers, scholars, advisors,
and business leaders.

X

Throughout 1910–20, Howe and Franklin projected to the nation and
the world an image of Franklin as energetic, charming, and devoted
to progressive ideals and family. His bigotry, and that of Eleanor, were
relatively well hidden from their adoring public. Their image masked
Franklin's various illnesses and infidelity. Franklin had cultivated many
relationships successfully throughout the decade, but the one that suffered most was the one he most neglected—his marriage to Eleanor.

Lucy Mercer had come to Franklin's attention in 1913 through an
accidental meeting on the staircase of his own home. Through family
connections, the twenty-two-year-old Lucy had been recommended
to work with Eleanor as a social secretary, but once she and Franklin
met, flirting quickly ensued and an affair soon thereafter. Eleanor
found her helpful, but her presence made Eleanor uncomfortable
from the beginning, as she never could shake her self-image as unat-
tractive and matronly, while nearly everyone agreed with Sara,
Franklin's mother, that Lucy was "so sweet and attractive." Franklin
obviously thought so, too, and his absences from home grew longer,
intensifying Eleanor's suspicions and insecurities further.[69]

Franklin managed to keep the affair hidden from Eleanor until after he returned from Europe in 1918. As he recovered from influenza, Eleanor arranged his correspondence and discovered a packet of love letters from Lucy. Confronting Franklin with evidence, she gave Franklin two choices—either grant her a divorce or stop seeing Lucy.

The news did not surprise the Roosevelt family. Franklin's aunt Alice's husband, Nick Longworth, was notorious for his frequent marital infidelities, and Alice herself recognized the signs early: "Lucy was beautiful, charming, and an absolute delightful creature.... I would see her out driving with Franklin, and I would say things like, 'I saw you out driving with someone very attractive indeed, Franklin. Your hands were on the wheel, but your eyes were on that perfectly lovely lady.'" Without skipping a beat, Franklin responded, "Yes, she is lovely, isn't she?" Alice approved of the relationship, saying, "Franklin deserved a good time. He was married to Eleanor." Alice even offered her house as a place where Franklin and Lucy could liaison. She enjoyed taunting Eleanor as much as she despised her own husband's dalliances.

While Franklin and Eleanor had often argued and she made no secret that she regarded sex as "an ordeal to be borne" (she had told this to her daughter Anna on Anna's wedding day),[70] Franklin needed to maintain the image of a happy family as a political asset.

As the oldest of Franklin and Eleanor's children, Elliott was keenly aware of the constant bickering between his parents, later describing their relationship as "a cold war." He recalled being shown a letter that his mother had written to Franklin while he was working in the Wilson administration that demanded Franklin join the family on vacation. Elliott understood the ultimatum at the end of the letter, "I count on seeing you on the 26th. My threat was no idle one." "There was no mystery," Elliott wrote. "She threatened to leave him."[71]

Franklin's broken marriage disturbed his superiors—and his mother. Daniels told Franklin to do what he needed to do to save the marriage, while it was made clear to Franklin that Wilson would have hated for muckrakers to feast at length on Franklin's moral failings—and Daniels's by association with the philanderer.

Sara told Franklin she would disown him unless he fixed the marriage. She was convinced Franklin's future political success depended on his image and his image relied on his being perceived as a good family man. Howe, too, warned Franklin that a divorce would end his political career.

Louis Howe "intuitively grasped that Franklin would remain catnip to female voters only by having a publicly working marriage."[72] He helped Eleanor because he did not want her to suffer from Franklin's taking her for granted, because he had gotten to know her well enough to know she was an asset to Franklin's future, and because he knew it was just a matter of time before she discovered Franklin's sometimes humiliating behavior.

The more Howe took her under his wing, the more their friendship thawed. An embarrassing *New York Times* story praising her "thrift" during the war had caused her to distrust the press and keep her distance from reporters. But the more closely the two worked and the more time they spent together, the more her respect for Louis's calmness under fire and her affection for him grew. In later years, her son Elliott suggested "that he was the first suitor treating her as the dissatisfied, incomplete woman he knew her to be. Louis and Mother made an extraordinarily well-matched pair."[73]

Eleanor had made Franklin promise that he would end the affair or grant her a divorce. Franklin hated ultimatums. He could not fix the marriage in any conventional way, but, with the help of several enablers, including his aunt and his daughter Anna, he mastered the illusion of having a happy family life while (mostly) hiding his sins from his family and the nation.

Franklin's marriage troubles bothered him more than the loss in the 1920 election. He looked forward to being progressives' best hope when the economy tanked under Republican leadership, whenever that day came, but Eleanor expected the worst. They were both right.

CHAPTER THREE

Learning to Run Again (1921–1932)

EVEN BEFORE REPUBLICANS ROUTED DEMOCRATS in the 1920 presidential election, Woodrow Wilson had warned Franklin that the American people rarely devoted themselves to some grander cause—and, even then, for a short while. With the war over and the economy stabilizing, Americans yearned for what Republican candidate Warren Harding promised—a return to "normalcy," by which he meant a rejection of "nostrums" or the elitist attitudes, ideals, and rhetoric of Wilson and his cronies, like Roosevelt, in favor of restoring small-town American virtues.[1]

Harding was the third Republican elected president in the twentieth century. Republicans occupied the White House for twenty-four of the first thirty-two years of the century, controlled both chambers of Congress for all but six of those years, and transformed the Supreme Court into a conservative bastion devoted to protecting private property and curbing congressional power. Republican presidents appointed fourteen Supreme Court justices during those years, while Wilson, the lone Democratic president, appointed two.

While progressivism was most manifest in the four constitutional amendments approved to grant women the right to vote, to prohibit and then allow the sale of liquor, and to allow the popular election of

65

United States senators, the roaring twenties were a decade of deca-
dence, rapid economic growth, and widespread prosperity. Whereas
progressives, such as Woodrow Wilson and Franklin Roosevelt, had
supported extensive federal intervention to serve the public welfare,
conservative Republicans championed individualism. Republican
Presidents Taft, Harding, Calvin Coolidge, and Herbert Hoover regarded governmental regulation as more of an evil to contain than
an engine of reform. Except for the brief period of Prohibition, Republicans oversaw the scaling back of the national government, and
Americans reveled in their return to normalcy.

Franklin Roosevelt hardly wished disaster on America. He bided
his time until the good times ended. But as the Scottish poet Robert
Burns wrote in 1785, "the best laid schemes of mice and men oft go
awry." In Franklin's case, they cratered when polio struck. It was, as
Eleanor said, "a blessing in disguise."[2]

I

After the 1920 presidential election, Franklin felt unsettled. He accepted the vice presidency of a surety bonding firm; tried but failed
to become re-engaged with the practice of law, which he still found
boring; tried smaller ventures, such as advertising, which also bored
him; served as president of the American Construction Council; and
joined forces with Calvin Coolidge's commerce secretary, Herbert
Hoover, to develop trade associations to promote economic stabilization and efficiency. Nothing came from their collaboration since
Hoover was unable to obtain governmental support.

Without much enthusiasm, Franklin agreed in August 1921 to vacation with Eleanor and their family at Campobello Island, a favorite
family retreat near Lubec, Maine, in the Canadian province of New
Brunswick. He invited Louis Howe and his family to join them, but
it was not the vacation everyone expected.

At Campobello, Franklin quickly busied himself, deep-sea fishing,
sailing, swimming, playing tennis and baseball, and doing whatever
else the children wanted. On August 10, while the family was sailing,

they spotted a small forest fire on a nearby island. Franklin moved the boat in as close as he could and led Eleanor and the children ashore. They fought the blaze with pine boughs for hours, until it was extinguished. Upon returning home, Franklin took the kids on a two-mile jog to Lake Glen Severn, where they played in the tepid water, and he then took a dip into the icy waters of the nearby Bay of Fundy.

Once back in the family cottage, Franklin felt a sudden chill and an unusual sensitivity in his legs, which he first ignored. "I didn't feel the usual reaction, the glow I'd expected," he later recalled. "I sat reading for a while, too tired even to dress. I'd never felt that way before. . . . The next morning when I swung out of bed my left leg lagged but I managed to move about and shave. I tried to persuade myself that the trouble with my leg was muscular, that it would disappear as I used it. But presently it refused to work, and then the other."[3] On August 12, he awoke with a fever, and he felt paralyzed from the waist down.

Louis Howe and Eleanor scrambled for medical help. The first doctor they found in Lubec said Franklin had a bad cold. Howe then placed calls to the resort towns in southern Maine, where, he knew, wealthy families spent most of their summers, and located Dr. William Keen, a revered surgeon who once operated secretly on then-President Grover Cleveland to remove mouth cancer. Keen thought Franklin had a blood clot and prescribed heavy massages, which worsened his condition.

Howe suspected that neither of the first two doctors were right, and he reached out to Franklin's Uncle Fred in Boston for his assistance in finding the right physician. They found Dr. Robert Lovett, a professor of orthopedic surgery and infantile paralysis at Harvard. Lovett traveled to Campobello, where, on August 25, he diagnosed Franklin with polio.

The news stunned Eleanor, who recalled that, on receiving the news, Franklin "was completely calm. His reaction to any great event was always to be completely calm. If it was something that was bad, he just became almost like an iceberg, and there was never the slightest emotion that was allowed to show."[4]

Franklin told Frances Perkins that he had briefly fallen into despair, but after a week his temperature dropped, and his buoyancy slowly rebounded. Eleanor slept on a nearby sofa, and, with the help of Louis Howe, she moved him, bathed him, massaged his legs, brushed his teeth, and gave him enemas. At the time, she wrote, "I think he's getting back his grip and a better mental attitude though he had of course times of great disappointment."[5] Two weeks later, a Boston specialist confirmed the diagnosis of polio but assured Franklin and Eleanor (mistakenly) that it was a "mild" case that would soon pass. It never did.

Franklin entered a New York City hospital, where he suffered acute pain for several weeks. Sara pleaded with him to retire to Hyde Park and live a life of leisure as his father had done. Eleanor and Howe disagreed. They insisted he remain active in politics. Howe, Eleanor, and Franklin "hid their inner anguish behind a façade of optimism and jollity."[6] Franklin broadcast to the world that he had every intention to continue his career. Eleanor said that he had come to this decision at a time when he was flat on his back, struggling to move a single toe.

Franklin quickly manifested the stoicism he had learned from Teddy, who had famously sworn to live a "strenuous life,"[7] and Endicott Peabody, who preached never showing weakness. After the *New York Times* reported the diagnosis, Franklin reached out to the publisher, Adolph Ochs, to say that his case "was very mild" and he agreed with the doctor interviewed for the article that "no one need have any fear of any permanent injury from this attack." As the journalist Ernest Lindley reported on looking back at Franklin's condition a decade later, "Roosevelt gaily brushed aside every hint of condolence and sent them away more cheerful than when they arrived. None of them has ever heard him utter a complaint or a regret or even acknowledge that he had had so much as a bit of bad luck." Franklin told Daniels, "I am sure you will be glad to learn that the doctors are most encouraging."[8]

Howe's role expanded, not only continuing to be a cheerleader and campaign manager and advisor but now also managing Franklin's recovery. Like Eleanor, Howe appreciated having more of Franklin's attention than before, but Franklin hated their constant poking and pushing him to recover. Howe tracked down doctors, drove them to and from Franklin's home, and communicated regularly with reporters and Democratic leaders. Looking back, Eleanor said, "Thank heavens. [Howe] has been the greatest help."[9] Eleanor and Louis both appreciated that it was their job to keep Franklin's hopes up. Louis maintained a steady drumbeat of encouragement about Franklin's prospects, prompting Eleanor one day to ask him, "Do you really believe that Franklin has a political future?" He replied, "I believe someday Franklin will be president."[10]

Yet Howe recognized Franklin had no future as a candidate bound to a wheelchair, so he constructed a different image of Franklin as slowly recovering. Over the next seven years, Franklin tried vainly to get his legs working again (he routinely took hot baths and immersed himself in mineral waters). He strengthened his upper body through constant exercise, so he could carry an extra fourteen pounds of painful steel braces and swing his hips. He succeeded in creating a semblance of walking, in which he leaned heavily on the arm of someone strong, and he stood unassisted by leaning against the podiums from which he spoke. Not yet forty, Franklin reinvented himself.

II

Through trial and error, Franklin Roosevelt worked on himself and his image. In 1922 and 1923, he increased his exercise routine and hid, as best he could, his exhaustion and despair from those around him. He assailed his therapists and doctors with innovative plans to regain the use of his legs, but none panned out. By February 1923, he was sailing again, which lifted his spirits, as did the purchase of a houseboat, on which he spent the winters of 1924, 1925, and 1926.

At Eleanor's invitation, Howe moved into Franklin's home, and his constant presence and steadfast loyalty to the Roosevelts warmed her heart (though she and the children were disgusted by his lack of hygiene). Frances Perkins recalled, Eleanor "had called for help and Louis came. I know that Mrs. Roosevelt loved Louis Howe. She loved him the way you love a person who has stood by you in the midst of the valley of the shadow and not been afraid of anything."[11]

Maintaining that Franklin's political future was bright, Howe planted stories with the press and wrote cheery letters to Franklin's wide array of correspondents. Confined to a wheelchair himself, Wilson got the message, responding to Franklin on April 30, "I am indeed delighted to hear you are getting well so fast and so confidently. I shall try and be generous enough to envy you."[12]

Eleanor was a whirlwind of activity. She invited a steady stream of visitors to see Franklin, and she joined Howe in insisting Franklin stick with his regimen of arduous exercise. Howe balanced Eleanor's sternness and lack of humor with gossipy anecdotes that made Franklin laugh.

When Franklin moved back to Hyde Park, his mother Sara took over from Eleanor, allowing her to focus on her own self-improvement. She learned to type, write shorthand, and cook. Howe went further to convince her that she had an entirely new role in life—she could be a leader on behalf of women's causes. Franklin would no longer be the only one in the family with a political future.

Only once did Eleanor's veneer crack. She recalled this period as "the most trying of my life," as she and Howe devoted most of their time to Franklin's recovery and eventual return to politics, while Sara was trying just as hard to persuade Franklin to give up politics and follow in his father's footsteps. "My mother-in-law thought we were tiring my husband and that he should be kept completely quiet. This made the discussions about his care somewhat acrimonious on occasion." The stress became too much for Eleanor, and one night after dinner she began to sob uncontrollably. It became so bad that, when Howe tried to comfort her, he ended up sobbing, too. After some time, Eleanor pulled herself together. She splashed some water on her face and helped Howe pull himself together, and then she went back to work. Later, she recalled, "That was the one and only time I ever remember in my entire life having gone to pieces."[13]

Howe encouraged Eleanor to make appearances on behalf of her husband, much to Sara's annoyance. He helped her to write speeches, and he gave her tips on speaking before public audiences. Sometimes, he would sit in the far back of the room where she expected to speak so that he could measure how loud she had to speak to be heard.

He suggested she take deep breaths when she felt panicky, grip the lectern when her hands trembled, maintain eye contact with her audience, stand up straight rather than slouching, and stop giggling when she was nervous. She later wrote about how Louis helped her to become a better speaker at public events: "His cardinal principle was: have something to say, say it, and sit down." She added, "I have tried to remember that ever since. He used to say that beginners often went on talking, repeating themselves over and over again because they did not know where to stop."[14]

Eleanor cultivated many new friends, who would be instrumental in guiding her public life. Nancy Cook, a New York Democratic Committee member, gave her political advice and became a frequent visitor and dinner guest at Hyde Park. Eleanor looked to her as a role model and dressed like her. She grew close to Nancy's domestic partner, Marion Dickerman. Marion and Nancy introduced Eleanor to liberal women activists. Howe said, "She had to become actively involved in Democratic politics in order to keep alive Franklin's interest in the party and the party's interest in him."[15] But now the once shy, retiring, insecure Eleanor was being introduced to an entirely different society, which energized her and captured her imagination. She raised funds for causes and candidates other than Franklin and became an active member of the League of Women Voters, the Women's Trade Union League, the Women's Division of the New York State Democratic Committee (led by Nancy Cook), and the Women's City Club of New York.

Franklin enjoyed thinking of Eleanor, Nancy, Marion, and himself as "our gang." He liked discussing politics and plotting campaigns with them. They supported his career, which they viewed as instrumental for achieving their own progressive ideals. Franklin decided to build a home for them to socialize at; he donated land from his estate at Hyde Park and oversaw the construction. He called it, "The Honeymoon Cottage,"[16] or Val-Kill, after the fact it had once housed a business called Val-Kill Industries. Though Franklin occasionally visited, Val-Kill was primarily a refuge for the women and their friends to relax and be themselves. "At Val-Kill," Eleanor said, "I became an individual."

III

The political world had not stopped while Franklin was struggling to overcome polio. A year before Franklin was diagnosed, Al Smith, then in his first term as governor of New York, had asked Franklin to serve as his floor manager at the Democratic National Convention. The New York Democratic Party had also asked Roosevelt to second Smith's nomination for president. Smith wanted Roosevelt's endorsement because he hoped to capitalize on Roosevelt's popularity from his leadership during the First World War and to demonstrate unity among Democrats. Franklin had support within the party as a Protestant upstate New Yorker, name recognition, and bona fides as a progressive leader. Roosevelt had established a friendly relationship with Tammany Hall boss Charles Murphy, which was beginning to produce dividends. It was imperative to Franklin's political future, especially since the Democratic convention had chosen Franklin, not Al Smith, as Ohio governor James Cox's running mate in the 1920 presidential election.

Though the 1920 presidential election was the worst political defeat of Franklin's career, he did not view it as a setback. The votes had barely been counted when Howe and Eleanor began plotting Franklin's comeback. Howe appointed himself chief strategist and assumed primary responsibility for figuring ways for Franklin to get publicity and manage his correspondence to rally support from state and federal Democratic allies.

Eleanor was becoming increasingly comfortable with being Franklin's eyes, ears, and voice. Both Howe and Franklin recognized her value in rallying women, now empowered with the right to vote after ratification of the nineteenth amendment in 1920, to support Franklin or those he endorsed. Franklin advised her on how to organize the best crowds for rallies. He was already scouring newspapers daily for news on political developments. She began a practice of leaving at his bedside the books he needed to read to be fully prepared for political meetings and campaigning. She introduced him to women, in the state and across the country, including those who educated him about the plight of the under-privileged and women in general.

By 1922, the dynamics between Smith and Franklin were shifting yet again. Smith urged Franklin to run for governor, but Franklin demurred. When Smith learned that William Randolph Hearst was considering a run for the governorship as a Republican, Smith could not stay out of the race. Franklin helped by playing to Smith's ego: "Many candidates for office are strong by virtue of promises of what they will someday do," he wrote. "You are strong by virtue of what you have done." Smith's entry convinced Hearst to drop out before officially entering. Smith "punctured the Hearst boom," Franklin said.[17] Six weeks later, Al Smith won reelection, as the fluctuating prices of agricultural products worried New Yorkers and Prohibition was wearing thin.

In 1924, Smith turned to Franklin for help in securing his party's nomination for president. Though Smith had lost reelection as governor to Republican Nathan Miller in 1922, his advisors Robert Moses and Charles Murphy rallied supporters within the party to boost his chances for the nomination. When Murphy died suddenly on April 25, others—notably including Judge Joseph Proskauer and Belle Moskowitz, both Smith allies—took charge of the campaign. Though he had initially hesitated in enlisting Franklin's help again, Proskauer settled matters, telling Smith, "You're a Bowery mick, and he's a Protestant patrician and he'd take some of the curse off you."[18]

Two days after Murphy's death, Franklin accepted Smith's invitation to be the campaign's national chairman and to give the chief nominating speech on behalf of Smith's candidacy for president. On June 26, 1924, Franklin's son Elliott helped him maneuver to the stage. He had practiced the walk, but initially there had been some confusion (and even later uncertainty) about whether he would deliver his or Judge Proskauer's draft of the nominating speech. Though, in the end he gave Judge Proskauer's version, he got the credit for the phrase "Happy Warrior" Proskauer had used to describe Smith. Franklin predicted the phrase would "be a flop" because it was too poetic, but he was wrong, as the line became the most memorable one in the speech. Attempting to bridge the divide

between the two major parties, Franklin invoked Abraham Lincoln
near the end of his speech: "I ask you in all sincerity . . . to keep first
in your hearts and minds the words of Abraham Lincoln: 'With ma-
lice toward none, with charity for all.'"[19] Roosevelt found common
ground with Lincoln in trying to heal the divisions that had riven
the nation. For Roosevelt, those divisions were primarily economic.
It was Franklin's first major appearance since he had contracted
polio. When he concluded the thirty-four-minute speech, the convention howled with applause.

Neither Howe nor Franklin expected Smith to win the nomination, and they were right: Ending the longest convention in
Democratic Party history on the 103d ballot, the party nominated
John Davis, a one-term representative from West Virginia who was
a prominent Wall Street lawyer, had served as solicitor general in Wilson's Justice Department (he had argued more than 140 cases in the
Supreme Court), and been Wilson's ambassador to Great Britain.

Yet, Franklin, not Davis, may have been the real beneficiary of
the convention. The *New York Times* reported, "The most popular
man in the convention was Franklin D. Roosevelt. Whenever word
passed around the floor that Mr. Roosevelt was about to take his seat
in the New York delegation, a hush fell over [Madison Square] Garden. On his appearance each time there was a spontaneous burst of
applause." Other political leaders agreed. Tom Pendergast, who had
run the Democratic Party for years in Missouri, said, Franklin "has
the most magnetic personality of any individual I have ever met, and
I predict that he will be the candidate on the Democratic ticket in
1928." Howe and Franklin accurately predicted a landslide for Coolidge, as the Democrats failed to unite over such issues as Prohibition,
the Ku Klux Klan, immigration, and teaching evolution in public
schools.[20] Afterward, Franklin, echoing Wilson, mused to a friend
that "in 1920 after the poke we got that year, I remarked . . . that I did
not think the nation would elect a Democrat again until the Republicans had led us into a serious period of depression and
unemployment. I still [believe] that forecast holds true. . . . The
people will not turn out the Republicans while wages are good and
the markets are booming. Every war brings after it a period of ma-

terialism and conservatism; people tire quickly of ideals and we are now but repeating history."[21]

Smith was not, however, content to lose. Two years later, in 1926, he was overwhelmingly reelected governor and became the front-runner for the Democratic Party's candidate for president in the next election. He asked Franklin to lead his campaign and to deliver his nominating speech. This time around, Smith expected no serious competition for the nomination. He was right—he was nominated on the first ballot, thus becoming the first Roman Catholic to win a major party's nomination for president.

Whereas the Democratic convention had been held in New York in 1924, it was held in Houston in 1928—the first time since the Civil War that either of the two major parties held their national convention in the South. The star was as much Franklin as it was the nominee himself. The delegates erupted with applause and glee at the end of a rousing tribute to Franklin. When the time came, he made his way to the platform without crutches, helping to reinforce the impression that he was no longer an invalid. Franklin added to that image a new side of himself, as he took great pains to tailor his speech for the more than 15 million people likely to be listening on the new medium of radio. By nearly all accounts, his nominating speech on this occasion was even better than his last. The *New York Times* described the speech as "the address of a fair minded and cultivated man."[22]

Franklin said that, to be a great president, the candidate had to have "the quality of soul which makes a man loved by little children, by dumb animals, that quality of soul which makes him a strong help to those in sorrow or trouble, that quality which makes him not merely admired but loved by all the people—the quality of sympathetic understanding of the human heart, of real interest in one's fellow man." Franklin was speaking of a quality that he and Smith shared, though few at the time, and fewer later, overlooked how much the description fit himself. Smith was nominated on the first ballot, and then Senate minority leader Joseph Robinson of Arkansas was chosen as his running mate.[23]

Nearly everyone expected Smith to lose, and he did—in another rout by the Republicans. He was a lackluster candidate at best. It was

obvious the party needed someone else as its standard-bearer, someone with charisma, someone who could energize voters and could
bring energy and new ideas to the fight for America's soul. It was no
secret who that might be.

IV

It was not just polio that kept Franklin from fully re-engaging with
politics. Twice, in 1922 and 1926, he had declined Democratic movements to nominate him for a Senate seat. Nor did he think 1928
would be a good year for Democrats, since the economy still appeared strong. The position he now coveted was governor of New
York. While he expected (rightly) that there would be a sharp downturn in the economy at some point in the 1930s, Franklin understood
his route to the governorship would be easier with Smith's support
than without it.

    Franklin and Smith maintained a friendly front during the years
1925–1928, but a break seemed inevitable. The tensions between
them began surfacing during the 1928 presidential campaign as they
differed over how best to win back the White House. As FDR biographer Robert Dallek noted, "Although Smith admired Franklin and
his courageous fight to overcome his disability, he also didn't trust
him, remarking to a friend, he 'isn't the kind of man you can take
into a pissroom and talk intimately with.' Roosevelt reciprocated the
wariness. For all his progressive actions as governor in support of
women, children, the least advantaged, and public power, Smith also
showed an affinity for self-made millionaires."[24] Franklin thought
Smith too stubborn in opposition to the side of the party dominated
by Wilson's former treasury secretary William McAdoo (who, unlike
Smith, had not denounced the Ku Klux Klan) and too insensitive to
the concerns of voters outside the Northeast. He thought Smith well
intentioned but ultimately nothing more than a "crude politico."[25]

    Nevertheless, Franklin encouraged Eleanor to campaign for
Smith's bid for a third term as governor in 1924. Smith's opponent was
her distant cousin, Teddy's son Theodore, whom she charged with

being supported by "stupid or dishonest public servants."[26] Eleanor enjoyed driving around the state in an automobile with "a steam-pouting teapot," which reminded voters of the Teapot Dome scandal, a bribery scheme that had involved the fraudulent sale of oil leases on government property.[27] She did not mind insinuating that Teddy Jr. was involved in the scandal. Teddy Jr. lost big, but Smith's landslide victory set up his next run for the presidency in 1928.

Franklin was maneuvering carefully, building his political reputation and devoting himself again to the candidacy of Al Smith. He tried, but failed, to persuade Smith to go on a speaking tour throughout the country. Smith felt that the nomination must come to him. It did, but, in 1928, the still-booming economy, anti-Catholic bigotry, and the absence of war heavily favored the Republican candidate, Herbert Hoover, for president. Even Southern Democrats did nothing to stop Smith from running, expecting he would get trounced. He did.

Both Franklin and Howe had expected that 1928 would not be a good year for Democrats. On Howe's advice, Franklin declined the party's nomination for governor and ventured to Warm Springs to ride out the disaster to come. Warm Springs was a second home he'd built in Georgia. He first went there in 1924 because of its warm waters, and by 1927, he had established the Warm Springs Foundation to assume ownership over the property, which he transformed into a renowned national center for the treatment of polio. It later became the site for his "Little White House" in Georgia.

However, Democratic leaders believed Smith had no chance to win the presidency unless he carried New York in the general election, and he had no chance to carry New York without Franklin as the Democratic candidate for governor. Smith pleaded with Franklin, who responded in a telegram on the eve of the gubernatorial nomination, "As I am only forty-six I owe it to my family and myself to give the present improvement a chance to continue." But party elders did not back off, and neither did Smith. He telephoned Warm Springs and pleaded with Eleanor to put Franklin on the phone. She told Smith she expected it would make no difference as she rushed out the door to catch a train to New York so that she could teach a class the next day.[28]

Once he had Franklin on the phone, Smith knew he had him. Smith first had Franklin talk to John Jakob Raskob, the party chairman, who pleaded with Franklin to run for the sake of the national party. Then Smith took the phone, saying, "Take the nomination, Frank. You can make a couple of radio speeches and you'll be elected. Then you can go back to Warm Springs. After you have made your inaugural speech and sent your message to the legislature you can go back there again for a couple months."[29]

With Franklin still not convinced, Smith gave the phone to Herbert Lehman, a senior partner in his family's investment business and an experienced labor negotiator. He told Franklin that if he agreed to run for governor, Herbert would agree to run for lieutenant governor, and as lieutenant governor he would fill in for Franklin whenever Franklin desired. Franklin still said no, but, when Smith asked him whether he would run if the party nominated him, Franklin was silent. "Thanks, Frank. I won't ask you any more questions." The deal was struck. When the following day the party nominated Franklin by acclamation, Howe sent a characteristically blunt telegram, "Mess is no name for it. For once I have no advice to give."[30]

The smart money expected Franklin to lose. But Howe, Franklin, and Frances Perkins loved a challenge, and they each rose to the occasion. Howe recognized he needed a team to help, and he systematically assembled one. He began with Edward Flynn, who had left his position as the Democratic boss of the Bronx to focus full-time on winning the governorship for the Democrats. Flynn ran the machine, while Howe oversaw the campaign. Frances Perkins, then serving as labor secretary for Smith, joined Franklin on the campaign trail along with a young New York legislator, Sam Rosenman. Rosenman was immediately impressed. "I had never seen anybody who could grasp the facts of a complicated problem as quickly and as thoroughly as Roosevelt."

Though she had been underwhelmed with Franklin when he was in the state senate, Perkins still believed Franklin could rise to the occasion, and he did, as he listened to her counsel on issues and wowed crowds across the state with his humor and stamina. To assist him on the campaign trail, Franklin also enlisted Raymond Moley, a Columbia political science professor, to write campaign speeches, and James Foley, an influential Tammany Hall surrogate, to mobilize voters upstate and fellow Catholics around the state to support Franklin. They joined a team of regulars, which included Henry Morgenthau, Jr., who, besides being a fellow farmer, was the publisher of the *American Agriculturist*, and a helpful strategist in mobilizing farmers to vote for Franklin. They all helped Franklin hone a message of hope for the disabled and underprivileged who lacked his resources to help themselves. Like Smith, he made the case for public control of waterpower and electric utilities, which would remove them from the control of private businesses only interested in making profits and leave them instead able to serve the public welfare. "I am horribly afraid you are going to be elected," Howe told Franklin a week before the election.[31]

By early evening of Election Day, it appeared that the Democrats, including Franklin, were heading toward the disastrous outcome Franklin had expected. But Howe, Perkins, and Sara vowed to stay with Franklin until the last vote was counted. Through much of the evening, each refused to give up. Franklin had gone home in the early evening when he was still behind.

Frances insisted on staying to keep Sara company through the long night ahead. She had once observed that, because men loved their mothers, women in politics would succeed if they acted maternally toward the men in power. She had previously earned Smith's attention after growing close to his mother. She did the same that night with Sara. They knew the votes from upstate had not yet been counted, and, in the early morning hours, Franklin began to pull ahead. The lead held, as Franklin ended up winning by just over twenty-five thousand votes, though the Republican candidate, Albert Ottinger, did not concede until November 19. By the time the vote counting was over, Franklin had won the election, and Frances had won Sara over.

Al Smith, on the other hand, in his campaign for the presidency did little to ignite any serious interest outside his home state. Smith got more votes than Davis had gotten in 1924, but he lost the presidency by a wide margin. Hoover won the popular vote with more than 15 million votes, besting Smith by more than 6 million. Hoover won the Electoral College 444–87. Hoover was the first president to be elected directly from the cabinet since Taft had won in 1908. Like Taft, Hoover's first run for political office was for the presidency.

With Smith's fate sealed as a two-time loser as a presidential nominee, the party needed a new standard-bearer, someone who shared Smith's progressive politics but who had less baggage and could project optimism, strength, and hope. Franklin's own transformation to fit the bill was unfolding as Smith's star began to fade. By 1928, Franklin had parlayed his years as assistant secretary of the navy into becoming the Democratic Party's spokesman on foreign policy. He mastered the "tripod system," which was a scheme for walking that his doctors had taught him: With his legs locked in braces, he would hold a cane in one hand and take a tight grip on his escort with the other, so that he could move slowly forward. Throughout the campaign, Howe closely monitored photographs and images of Franklin to ensure none showed him as disabled.

With Franklin's victory in the 1928 gubernatorial election, Democrats believed they were seeing the future of the party, and it was not Al Smith. When, during the 1928 campaigns Franklin spoke of Smith's qualifications, many heard instead how qualified Franklin himself was. He grew most passionate, not when hailing the virtues of Smith, but talking about how government could help the farmers, underprivileged, and destitute in the state. Though Smith's manager wired Rosenman that Franklin "is not running for president but for Governor" and that he had better "stick to state issues," he did not. He championed a national vision for the future of the country throughout the campaign, and though Franklin appeared to be four years ahead of schedule, there was no turning back. He set his sights on Washington and never lost another election. He declined Smith's invitation to become the chair of the Democratic National Committee, preferring the freedom of being available as a candidate at a moment's notice.[32]

The momentous journey Franklin had taken in the 1920s from contracting polio to overcoming its debilitating effects, with the help of Eleanor and Louis, to win the governorship of New York in 1928 did not, however, stop Franklin's wandering eye. He had grown fond of Missy LeHand, who had become his personal secretary in 1921. She was a vivacious young woman, known for her discretion and devotion to Franklin. She became more than his secretary, subsequently acting as his confidante, companion, and hostess for the rest of her life. Eleanor did not distrust Missy as she had Lucy Mercer, perhaps, as one biographer speculated, "because Missy was of a different social class, and certainly her attendance upon Franklin freed Eleanor to serve her husband as his political surrogate and adviser, a role she preferred."[33]

Nor did Eleanor mind Franklin's fondness for extended visits, without her, at his second home of Warm Springs. Visiting Warm Springs allowed him to indulge his other new respite—driving a car, which enabled him to be in control without walking. Both Warm Springs and his driving brought him the joy and relaxation he needed to forget his limitations, at least for a while. Howe indulged Franklin's pastimes because they rejuvenated him, while Eleanor herself announced, "I am not excited about my husband's election. I don't care. What difference can it make to me?" She seemed content to work on a "range of social initiatives aimed at strengthening government protection for women and children."[34]

V

On January 1, 1929, Franklin Roosevelt was sworn in as New York's forty-fourth governor. He was forty-six, five years older than Teddy had been when he became governor, but Franklin was four years ahead of when he initially planned to run for the office. Teddy had been governor only a year before William McKinley tapped him as his running mate, but Franklin's sites were on the presidency not the number two job.

It was no secret that Al Smith wanted Franklin's election to be conducted as his own fifth term as governor. Within a month after the election, Smith visited Franklin at his East 65th Street home in New York City, and he urged Franklin to keep both Robert Moses and Belle Moskowitz on staff. He suggested Franklin could have

Belle draft his inaugural address and his legislative agenda (taking orders, of course, from Smith). Smith had already reserved a suite of rooms in Albany, where he expected to reside and manage the state when Franklin went home or to Warm Springs. He told Franklin, "Well, Frank, you won't have to worry about being governor. You can come to Albany for the inauguration and stay around for a while and get the hang of things, and when you get a chance you can hop back to Warm Springs. And we'll be here to see that things go right."[35]

Eleanor and Frances Perkins had warned Franklin that Smith wanted him as a figurehead who would be guided by his closest confidants to do what Smith wanted. Eleanor distrusted both Moses and Moskowitz and told Franklin to dismiss them immediately. One week after the election, Eleanor wrote Franklin, "By all signs I think Belle and Bob Moses mean to cling to you and you will wake up to find R.M. Secretary of State and B.M. running Democratic Publicity at her old stand unless you take a firm stand." Louis Howe agreed and was especially opposed to Moskowitz, whom he saw as a competitor for Franklin's attention.

Initially, Franklin responded politely to Smith. He thanked him for his offer but told him that he had already drafted his inaugural address and that he would show the drafts to Belle and Smith when he was done (he never did). Though Moses had told Smith that Franklin "rubs me the wrong way," Franklin said he would keep Moses in his present position, but then he asked Smith, "Did you ever leave Albany for any extended stay during a legislative session?" Smith said, "No." "Then I won't either," Franklin declared.[36]

Franklin then dropped both advisors, based not only on the advice he got from Eleanor and Howe but also his own experiences with each—Robert Moses, Smith's brilliant, strong-willed, power-hungry secretary of state who had blocked several of Franklin's projects when Moses led the State Council of Parks but was widely regarded as a master legislative draftsman in Albany; and Moskowitz, who had blocked Franklin's access to Smith during the last campaign. Smith was displeased with both decisions and with Franklin's decision to write his own inaugural address. (Indeed, both as governor and president, Franklin generally wrote the initial drafts of important speeches.)

Franklin kept other advisors in place, notably Frances Perkins. She had been instrumental in delivering women voters to the Smith and Roosevelt campaigns. Franklin appointed her as the state's inaugural industrial commissioner, who oversaw more than eighteen hundred employees and was the highest paid woman in New York state government, the first woman, in fact, appointed to a cabinet-level position in the state. Roosevelt's motivation had not just been to please her or to make history but also to upstage Al Smith. As Perkins noted later, "One of the reasons Franklin Roosevelt thought of it, and he often said so, was 'Al would never have thought of that. Al would never have thought of making a woman head of the Department.' [Franklin] was quite vain about how much better he was than Smith."[37]

Often dismissed as "Eleanor's friend," even though the two never grew nearly as close as Frances did with Franklin, Perkins had closely studied Franklin before joining his ranks. He had impressed her in many ways, noting years later her impressions of Franklin as not a "simple man" to understand but as having a penchant for "shrewd planning" on every little detail of his path to the presidency, "a capacity for living and growing that remained to his dying day," the capacity of being "essentially adaptable to new circumstances, always quick to understand the changing needs and hopes of the people . . . and to vary his action to meet challenging situations," and as a consummate actor, as vain, and as becoming an expert on geography through stamp-collecting and "being an avid atlas reader."

She was impressed that "in the years of his illness," Franklin studied labor history, learned about unions, read "political history, political memoirs, books of travel" as well as continuing his study of "naval history and naval technical works[,] farm and agricultural journals and . . . developments in modern agriculture and [he] was particularly interested in their application to the small farm which is so characteristic of the East," "acquired a taste" for "detective stories," and continued "his study of the history and political and economic development of his home region."

Though Perkins acknowledged Franklin was never a great student nor seemed interested in learning about economics, she believed he "grew to greatness by a full utilization of all of his talent and personality; he began where he was and used what he had. He ignored his handicaps, both physical and intellectual, and let nothing hinder him from doing the work he had to do in the world." "He was not born great but he became great,"[38] she concluded.

The Republican legislature could not stop Franklin from reorganizing the governor's office. In doing so, he introduced a new style of governing. "It looks like I have a man-sized job on my hands for the next two years," Franklin wrote to Teddy's son Archie, soon after his victory.[39] Understanding that Republicans who controlled the state legislature would give him no victory as governor, he spoke to them directly in his inaugural address on January 1, 1929. The rupture with Smith was already apparent. Looking back at that inauguration day several years later, Franklin reminisced, "It had become pretty evident I was going to be my own Governor.... You know, too, the politics in any Capitol.... The crowd began to flock around their new Governor. Thus, without any premeditation or action on my part, Al, I think, got the impression that to hang around would be a grave mistake." It is hard to imagine Franklin improvising on that occasion or being uninterested or indifferent to the symbolism and substance of his actions. If Smith felt a lack of love coming from the direction of the new governor and his people, it was likely not happenstance.[40]

Once in office, Franklin was a flurry of activity and ideas. He used radio to apply pressure on Republicans to support certain legislation. He developed to perfection a simple, conversational way of talking, in sharp contrast to the political oratory common to Smith and other politicians.

While Franklin showed nearly every day as governor that he did not need Smith's help to succeed, he and Howe understood that the gubernatorial term was only two years and there was no Democratic president to help his reelection. Republicans understood that, too, and they controlled the legislature. Accordingly, they shot down nearly every initiative Franklin proposed, and after his first year in office, he had nothing significant to show for his efforts.

Though the prospect of getting the Republican legislature to work with him was nil, his appointments reflected his agenda: He reappointed sixteen of Smith's department heads, but his inner circle did not include Smith, Moskowitz, or Moses. He had told Rosenman, "I do not expect to call on these people whom Al has been using." Franklin replaced Moskowitz with Howe and replaced Moses with Ed Flynn. He hired Rosenman to draft speeches and provide counsel on legislative initiatives, and Henry Morgenthau, an old friend and neighbor, to oversee agriculture and conservation. Frances Perkins was already in place to be the administration's voice on labor and industrial matters.[41]

In everything he did as governor, Franklin prioritized conveying to citizens of the state (and around the country) his image as an active, energetic, articulate leader. He gave newspaper reporters greater access to him through regular press conferences than Smith had ever allowed while he was governor. Knowing the press would report his statements, he regularly described himself as "walking, running, and jumping" to do things. Yet Franklin did not depend just on the press to get his message and image across.

He and Howe realized the potential of the new medium of radio, which enabled Franklin to reach the public who did not have access to or time to read newspapers. In the spring of 1929, he gave the first of what eventually became known as his "Fireside Chats." He broadcast on Sunday nights when the audience was its largest and made every effort to maintain intimacy with his listeners. As Perkins recalled, "His head would nod and his hands would move in simple, natural, comfortable gestures. His face would smile and light up as though he were actually sitting on the front porch or in the parlor with them."[42] It was not just the innovative use of radio that Perkins was witnessing, but she was seeing how important acting was to Franklin's success.

The late political scientist Fred Greenstein once said the key to understanding presidential leadership was dramaturgy; that is, presidents perform different roles as chief executive. That understanding of the presidency fit Franklin perfectly. He was, as he often said, an actor, and an actor needs a script or template even if they are improvising. For Franklin, the script or template was the narrative of his presidency, a narrative in which the star—he—was strong, optimistic, vibrant, and innovative. The performance worked, as it won him an unprecedented four terms as president and a degree of popularity and impact that no other contemporary president has matched. His gubernatorial broadcasts reassured thousands, his presidential ones reassured millions. Thousands of letters flooded the governor's mansion in response to his broadcasts. He added to that success traveling by houseboat to regions of New York that no governor had visited before. Word spread about his ingenuity, energy, and accessibility. Though Eleanor made clear she had her own life and was not preoccupied with what he was doing as governor, she, too, played her part, as she remained a close confidante and frequent surrogate for her husband.

From his first day in office, Franklin acted as if he had been there before. Rosenman was impressed with his extraordinary ability to compartmentalize matters: "He would think a problem through very carefully. Having come to a decision, he would dismiss it from his mind as finished business. He never went back to it to worry about whether his decision was right." Frances Perkins was struck by how Franklin "was a walking history book."[43] She marveled at how he never lost sight of the bigger picture and how whatever he did fit in the larger scheme of American politics and history.

Franklin's ingenuity included having his closest advisors live together. Sam Rosenman, the new counselor to the governor, moved into a spare room in the executive mansion. Missy LeHand and Franklin's other secretary, Grace Tully, found rooms in the mansion, too. Together, his staff was on call twenty-four hours a day, seven days a week. The house seemed alive at all hours. Though Howe was Franklin's chief of staff, he continued working out of Franklin's New York City home. Howe visited Albany at least once a week. Unlike prior governors, Franklin was adept at recruiting experts to join his administration. He asked Jim Farley, secretary and later chair of the state Democratic Party, to broaden and strengthen the party throughout the state. With the help of Henry Morgenthau, Franklin fashioned tax relief to help farmers. It was an innovation that brought Franklin national attention as a friend to farmers who were suffering from low prices for their produce.

Thanks to the legislature's deliberate indifference, Franklin had little to show in terms of accomplishments after his first few months as governor. So he went where he could do more, and luckily get more attention. After the legislative session ended in April 1929, Franklin went on a series of speaking engagements, beginning with his remarks at the Gridiron Dinner in Washington, where he joined President Hoover and Chief Justice William Howard Taft as a speaker. When his turn came, Franklin told the audience that in the early days of the republic effective oratory was the key to political success. "Elections were won or lost, parties were driven out or swept into power entirely as the public speakers on one side or the other proved most able and convincing," he lectured them. "It was," he said, "the golden day of the silver tongue. With rare exceptions, the great public man had also to be classed as a convincing orator." He ventured further to say that radio, not newspapers, would provide the crucial connection between voters and candidates. He saw radio as a return to something lost: "The pendulum is rapidly swinging back to the old condition of things. . . . I think it is a conservative estimate to say that whereas five years ago 99 out of 100 took their arguments from the editorials and the news columns of the daily press, today at least half of the voters, sitting at their own fireside, listen to the actual words of the political leaders on both sides and make their decision based on what they hear rather than what they read. [I believe] that in reaching their decisions as to which party they will support, what is heard over the radio decides as many people as what is printed in the newspapers."[44]

Reporters in attendance serenaded him in response, "Oh, Franklin, Franklin Roosevelt/Is there something in a name? When you are tired of being Governor/Will you look for bigger game?" Everyone got the reference to Teddy and Franklin's shared ambitions. Later that spring, he received an honorary degree and Phi Beta Kappa membership at Harvard, where he and Eleanor stayed for five days, visiting with old classmates and friends and reminiscing about living in the undergraduate dorms where, in fact, he had never resided. He was in no rush to return to Albany, where he knew he could accomplish little.[45]

Instead, with Howe's pushing him, Franklin used his time away from Albany to become the new face of the Democratic Party both in New York and across the nation. He increasingly put himself forward as both the head of the Democratic Party in New York and the Democrats' best chance to retake the White House. Besides accepting honorary degrees from Fordham, Hobart, Harvard, and Dartmouth, he dedicated Tammany Hall's new headquarters at Union Square on July 4, 1929. He warned his fellow partisans about the dangers of the concentration of economic power in unelected elites. "They are becoming increasingly more powerful in the influence they are building in state and nation, an influence that someday will have to be met," he declared. The audience cheered him as "the next president of the United States."[46] Both Franklin and Howe prepared for his run for reelection as governor in 1930 as a crucial step in giving his audience what they wanted.

VI

On October 28, 1929, the stock market crashed, losing one-fifth of its total value due to an unprecedented volume of sales. Franklin had expected the bubble to burst but not as soon as it did.

Franklin's first response was not to overreact. He did not want to get ahead of the facts. He wired New York papers that he believed "that industrial and trade conditions are sound." He told a church group soon thereafter that "the little flurry downtown" was the punishment that unscrupulous investors deserved. In what would become a signature move, he proposed some support for the unemployed through the expansion of public works.[47] A week later, Democrats picked up three seats in the state assembly, though Republicans maintained their control of both chambers.

Franklin was not convinced the sky was falling. First, many Americans remained complacent. They had not experienced any fallout from the stock market collapse. Businesses and banks did not immediately close. President Hoover repeatedly declared that the economy was strong and downplayed any negative effects. Second, there had been a steady drumbeat of gloom and doom since before Hoover took office, so that when some prominent businessmen, such as the investor Joseph Kennedy, pulled out of the markets, their actions were dismissed as just more of the same negativity they had been preaching for years.

Many other prominent businesspeople and economists thought the crash was nothing serious. John D. Rockefeller's reaction was that it provided Americans a wonderful opportunity to invest in the market. Charles Schwab of Bethlehem Steel declared, "Never before has American business been as firmly entrenched for prosperity as it is today." President Hoover followed their lead in pronouncing that "the fundamental business of the country—that is, the production and distribution of goods and services—is on a sound and prosperous basis."[48]

Franklin was not as confident as business leaders like Rockefeller and Schwab that all was well. Reflexively, he distrusted Hoover. Nor could he appear gleeful or triumphant given the dangers that the crash portended. Yet his duty was to protect the people of New York—and its economy—from disaster. He and Howe honed a carefully cultivated middle position, in which Franklin, in speeches and press conferences, emphasized how the crash demonstrated the need for social and economic reforms that he had been pushing for more than a decade.

Frances Perkins convinced Franklin otherwise. As soon as the market had crashed, he asked her to do some research and tell him what was happening. She informed him through weekly updates on dwindling payrolls in the state and industry layoffs. In January 1930, President Hoover declared that employment was on the rise in the nation, but Perkins "knew the 4 percent [increase] reflected only Christmas hiring, not permanent jobs, something the U.S. Bureau of Labor Statistics should have made clear to him. She also knew that Hoover, a quick study and a good mathematician, would have known he was using the statistics improperly." Without consulting Franklin, she issued a press release declaring, "The President of the

United States has deceived the people about this matter of employment. It is worse, not better. It's a cruel deceit, because people will
believe it. Mother will be mad when father comes home and says he
can't get a job because the President said that employment is going
up. The tragedy of families who still hope that father will get a job is
just terrible when this kind of thing happens."[49] Franklin approved;
she had struck the right note, which was to contrast Franklin's actions in New York with those of Hoover in Washington.

Frances arranged meetings with several prominent economists,
such as the University of Chicago's Paul Douglas, who advised Franklin, and whom Franklin recommended advise other governors, on
how to revive employment. Thanks to her indefatigable study of the
crisis and the expert advice he was receiving, Franklin was well
ahead of where most governors were in assessing the magnitude of
the crisis and possible solutions.

When, two months later, on May 1, President Hoover told the U.S.
Chamber of Commerce that the worst was over with, Franklin
pushed back. In a speech at the Annual Jefferson Day Dinner of the
National Democratic Club in New York, he chided Hoover for ignoring the basic laws of supply and demand. "If Thomas Jefferson were
alive," he said, "he would be the first to question this concentration
of economic power" in banks and big business. Following Franklin's
speech, Montana senator Burton Wheeler, an old Democratic war-
horse, delivered the keynote address, in which he told the attendees,
"As I look about for a general to lead the Democratic Party, I ask to
whom we can go. I say that, if the Democratic party of New York will
re-elect Franklin Roosevelt governor, the West will demand his nomination for president and the whole country will elect him."[50]

Franklin made it clear that this was a time for action: Drawing
on the kinds of progressive policies Wilson had championed as governor, including workers' compensation, Franklin urged the state
assembly to consider the plight of farmers whose prices and incomes
were falling. He endorsed the state's taking over hydroelectric power
and advocated for new laws protecting labor and for creating a board
to advise on minimum and equitable wages; restricting the use of in-
junctions by management against labor unions; and establishing a

commission to advise on old-age security. He knew these were likely dead-on-arrival propositions, but persisted in marshaling allies wherever he could find them. Though Smith and Tammany Hall were still unhappy after the 1928 presidential election, Franklin accepted their invitation and urged them to carry on the work of progressive visionaries such as Smith: "Upon you rests the responsibility for the education of the voter in the aims and principles of the Democracy, not only of the city and state but of the nation."[51]

Whereas Smith had largely focused on urban issues when he was governor, Franklin focused on expanding the party's base outside New York City. In two years, Franklin staked his claim on being one of the most progressive governors, if not the most progressive governor, in the country. Even when they failed, his actions drew national attention and praise.

VII

As the national economy limped into 1930, all eyes were on Franklin Roosevelt. It was widely known that his reelection campaign was a dry run for the upcoming presidential race in 1932. Besides the economic drama unfolding there, New York was a microcosm of the country, with its upstate farmers facing the same drop in prices for their goods as farmers across the nation and its urban workforce being laid off or fired at the same rates as their counterparts elsewhere.

The damage wrought by the stock market crash was not just financial. The market had steadily risen for seven straight years, based largely on the assumption that it was closely tied to the success of American business; as the market rose, business supposedly rose and vice versa. With the market collapsing, many realized that banking, agriculture, and many businesses were sure to follow.

Howe believed that the economic downturn made Franklin's reelection easier, though they both believed he needed a landslide to seal his stature as the party's leading candidate for president. In Washington, President Hoover understood that, too, and made it a priority to undermine Franklin's reelection and presidential ambitions.

Hoover and Franklin began circling each other like prizefighters in the ring. Each was renowned as an innovator and problem-solver, and they both had the chance to shine—or fail—in developing solutions to the growing crisis. In Washington, Hoover, long touted as the "great engineer" because of his success at fixing problems, backed the Smoot-Harley tariff, which tried to protect American jobs and profits by doubling the average duty on imports. Hoover was wrong, as the tariffs proved regressive, forcing price rises, which hurt an already ailing and increasingly unemployed workforce.

As Hoover fumbled around for solutions, Franklin kept hammering the President. He delivered speeches and made proposals for increasing governmental involvement in ameliorating the devasting effects of the Great Depression. He relentlessly attacked the concentration and unaccountability of corporate wealth. Big business thrived while smaller businesses increasingly failed.

Frances Perkins helped Franklin to better understand that the plights of New York were not isolated or detached from the problems the country was facing. At her suggestion, he issued a special message to the New York State Legislature requesting a commission to investigate unemployment insurance. As she explained, the commission was called "Stabilization of Employment" because "Roosevelt had already developed what became a consistent attitude, namely, an emphasis on the positive. He did not like to appoint a committee against anything."[52] Because she had thought of the commission, Franklin placed Perkins in charge of it.

That same year at the national governors' conference, Franklin criticized President Hoover's responding with nonsensical economic politics to the crash and declared, "More and more, those who are victims of dislocation and defects of our social and economic life are beginning to ask [why] government cannot and should not act to protect its citizens from disaster."[53]

Franklin was concerned that increasing spending on public works (as he had done to a modest degree), as Hoover was promising as a means of combatting unemployment, would produce deficits beyond the nation's capacity to afford. Franklin's gubernatorial opponent, Charles Tuttle, the U.S. attorney for the Southern District of

New York (a Hoover appointee), tried to tarnish Franklin as weak for not doing enough to rein in New York City's Mayor Jimmy Walker, renowned for his good looks, defiance of Prohibition, and taking bribes from businessmen for local contracts. While promising a thorough investigation, Franklin kept his focus on Hoover's weak response to the depression. "Never let your opponent pick the battleground on which to fight. If he picks one, stay out of it, and let him fight all by himself," he told Rosenman.

Accordingly, Franklin focused on the economy. He repeatedly attacked Hoover for shifting responsibility for fixing the depression onto the states and not making the federal government the primary engine for reviving the national economy.[54] Hoover's response was that private charity, not government, should be responsible for easing economic distress, and he denounced government assistance for the unemployed, believing it would make them dependent on government and lose their initiative to work.

With three weeks left in the campaign, Hoover sent three cabinet members to stump against Franklin. It backfired, as their visit fit into Franklin's narrative that Hoover was scared of him because he was a genuine contender for the presidency. Their attempt to make Franklin responsible for the corruption linked to Tammany Hall backfired, too, since it united Franklin with Tammany Hall. He ignored the attacks until his final rally, which was held in Carnegie Hall. His response was brief but pointed, vowing to remove any corrupt officials, "regardless of whether [they were Democrats or Republicans]. That is honesty. That is justice. That is American. That is right." He ridiculed the three cabinet secretaries who had the temerity to tell New Yorkers what was good for them. Franklin said one was a carpetbagger and the other two had failed in their efforts to be elected governor of New York. "The people did not believe in them or their issues then, and they will not believe in them or their issues now." He told them to go back to Washington to deal with the nation's pressing economic problems. "Rest assured," Franklin said, "we of the Empire State can take care of ourselves."[55]

Howe and Franklin made his reelection run not just a referendum on Hoover, but also on Roosevelt's support for labor, seniors, "hospitals, public works, cheap electricity, regulation of public utilities, [and] prisons,"[56] which were all Eleanor's constituencies. Whatever resistance she had had to helping Franklin she had put aside, and she became one of his most active surrogates, relishing her role in speaking on his behalf, inspecting state institutions, and reporting what she learned to Franklin and Howe.

The campaign's message was that people, not big business, came first. Franklin's Fireside Chats expressed great sympathy for the people suffering in New York, and he managed to provide some financial support for ailing farmers, businesses, and the unemployed. Indeed, through his use of radio and increasing popularity, Franklin was occasionally pressuring the state legislature into action. Yet any help he provided was relatively minor. Washington had the big bucks and was the source of the big problem, as he declared throughout the campaign. In a series of speeches, Franklin outlined the stakes for the state and the country. The issues were not just local but national. He rode the voters' dissatisfaction to a smashing victory, the largest landslide in the state's history, and the widest margin of victory ever in a gubernatorial reelection, winning by more than 730,000 votes over his challenger, twice the previous record in New York history. The *New York Times* declared, "The tremendous vote for Governor Roosevelt was regarded as increasing greatly his chance for the Democratic nomination for President in 1932, for which he is known to be aspirant."[57] Sam Rosenman credited the victory to "the warmth of the man and the orator, who knew how to convey his personality and charm to the people he met and the people he talked with over the air."[58]

In his first public statement after Franklin's victory, Jim Farley, who pivoted from chairing his reelection to leading his presidential campaign, said, "I do not see how Mr. Roosevelt can escape becoming the next presidential nominee of his party."[59] The race was on.

CHAPTER FOUR

Sailing into the
Presidency (1932–1933)

BEFORE 1932, NEW YORKERS HAD not handled economic crises well as presidents. The first was Martin Van Buren, Andrew Jackson's handpicked successor who became president in 1837. Once in office, Van Buren had to address the fallout from the economic turmoil triggered by Jackson's policy of making hard money (gold or silver) the only currency in America. Few small businesses were able to pay for services or debts in hard money, and their failures to pay their debts on time unleashed a cascade of failing commercial ventures and banks.

Van Buren opposed federal intervention to ease economic conditions. He backed instead a system of independent treasuries that performed the responsibilities of the national bank, which Jackson had effectively closed, and Van Buren, like Jackson before him, expected state banks to take the lead in addressing the national downturn. But state banks could do little to heal a national economic crisis, and Van Buren lost his reelection bid to William Henry Harrison, a military hero, who died a month into office, having done nothing to address the depression.

The second depression happened during New Yorker Grover Cleveland's first term as president. Cleveland's pledge to reduce tariffs did not help him in a tight reelection battle with Benjamin Harrison during an economic downturn in 1884. Cleveland's defeat made him the first incumbent after Van Buren to lose in a general election.

The Great Depression, following soon after the stock market crash, was the first to happen on the watch of a Republican president. Herbert Hoover believed, like Van Buren and Cleveland, that states and the private sector were primarily responsible for solving the nation's economic problems. It was the Democrats, this time led by Franklin Roosevelt, who urged more aggressive federal intervention to ease the pain.

Politicians, the American people, and economists were divided on what to do. Economics was hardly a science during Van Buren's administration, and in the Cleveland years it lacked the sophistication to pinpoint the causes of or solutions to the depression. With the help of Frances Perkins and a team of economic advisors, Roosevelt proposed to adopt at the national level the economic and labor programs that he had implemented as governor and that had built on, or extended, the progressive ideals of Woodrow Wilson. Hoover denounced Roosvelt as naïve, ignorant of economics, weak, and overly fond of big government. Voters had to choose between Hoover's vision of rugged individualism as the core American ideal or the constitutional revolution Roosevelt promised.

I

On January 23, 1932, Franklin D. Roosevelt announced his intention to run for the presidency. As part of the announcement, campaign chair Jim Farley told reporters that Franklin already had the support of 678 delegates in the Democratic national convention scheduled for June 27–July 2. Roosevelt thus had a majority of delegates but was still 72 delegates short of the two-thirds required for the nomination.

As the front-runner for the Democratic Party nomination, Roosevelt did not rest on his laurels once he was reelected New York governor in 1930. There were other Democrats eager for the nomination, including John Nance Garner, the speaker of the house of representatives, and Al Smith, but Roosevelt was the fastest off the mark in organizing supporters in the states holding the earliest primaries. In landslides, he won New Hampshire, North Dakota, Georgia, Iowa, and Maine.

To surpass the required threshold of delegates, Franklin used the same organization that had run his reelection campaign. Louis Howe saw his job as nothing less than to "build a President."[1] He had the organization increase its letter-writing campaign to voters and the party faithful, while Franklin called and wrote letters to Democratic leaders around the country. Farley became known as the "political drummer" as he rallied support for Franklin's presidential campaign.[2] Franklin took Sam Rosenman's advice to follow Al Smith's strategy in 1928 to enlarge his team of advisors. Rosenman told Roosevelt, "You have been having good experiences with college professors. If we can get a small group together willing to give us some time, they can prepare memoranda for you. You'll want to talk with them yourself, and maybe out of all the talk some concrete ideas will come."[3]

Already consulting academics regularly as governor, Roosevelt added several Columbia University professors to the campaign, though he and others counted Rosenman, a compact, bespectacled, Phi Beta Kappa graduate of Columbia,[4] among the first. On Rosenman and Howe's suggestion, Franklin hired Raymond Moley, a Columbia law professor who specialized in the criminal justice system, to coordinate policy positions and papers for the campaign.

Moley's first hire was Columbia economist Rex Tugwell, whom he asked to analyze agricultural issues for the campaign. Moley next hired another Columbia professor, Lindsay Rogers, whose first act was embarrassing the campaign by composing a speech for Roosevelt on tariffs that was nearly identical to a paper he had written for Al Smith—and from which Smith had extensively quoted—on the same subject. Smith delighted in telling the press Roosevelt was merely copying the paper Rogers had written for him.

Though Moley was impressed early on by "one of the loveliest facets of Roosevelt's character—he stood by his people when they got into a jam,"[5] Rogers left the campaign immediately to work for Smith, whom he believed had the better chance to win the nomination in

1932. Moley hired several more Columbia colleagues, including Adolf Berle, a law professor who was reputedly an expert on everything, and James Angell, an economist who was the son of the president of Yale University. Berle had coauthored with Harvard economist Gardiner Means a seminal treatise in 1932, *The Modern Corporation and Private Property.*[6] Their timing could not have been better in providing careful analysis of capitalism and concluding that the economic power of the United States was concentrated in the hands of the largest two hundred corporations.

New York Times columnist James Kieran dubbed Roosevelt's academic advisors the "Brains Trust," which was shortened to Brain Trust.[7] Moley, Berle, Rosenman, and Tugwell were among the first members, along with Roosevelt's law partner D. Basil O'Connor, called "Doc." Roosevelt relied on the Brain Trust for the rest of his political career.[8] Berle's coauthor, Gardiner Means, was one of many economists and lawyers who later joined the Brain Trust.

Of the brainy crew, Moley was especially impressed with Tugwell. He recalled that "Rex was like a cocktail. His conversation picked you up and made your brain race along."[9] Moley placed Berle, both an economist and a lawyer, in charge of issues relating to corporations and the economy. Nearly every night after dinner, Roosevelt sat with his team of advisors. As Moley described, "The Governor was [a] student, a cross-examiner, and a judge. He would listen with rapt attention for a few minutes and then break in with a question whose sharpness was characteristically blurred with an anecdotal introduction or an air of sympathetic agreement with the speaker.... The questions ... would become meatier, more informed—the infallible index to the amount [Franklin] was picking up in the evening's course. By midnight ... the visitor ... would look a trifle wilted; and the Governor ... would be making vigorous pronouncements on the subject we had been discussing, waving his cigarette holder to emphasize points."[10]

Tugwell was especially good at briefing Franklin, particularly after discovering Franklin knew little about economics. Tugwell's tactic was to reduce what he had to say to the simplest, graphic terms, compressed to five minutes. Usually, Franklin was able to master the

subject in less time than that. Tugwell later described his first meeting Roosevelt as "somewhat like coming into contact with destiny
itself."[11] "I never saw Roosevelt listen to anyone as long as he did to
you," Moley told Tugwell.

Franklin's primary competition for the party nomination was Al
Smith, once again. Though Smith had said he would not campaign
outright but would be ready to serve as the nominee if the convention desired, he set out to cultivate support from urban voters and
eastern, conservative Democrats.

Roosevelt regarded the strongest looking dark-horse candidate
to be house speaker John Nance Garner, a favorite son of Texas.
Roosevelt's campaign used whatever means it had to dampen support for the Smith candidacy without alienating Smith's supporters.
At the same time, it established cordial relations with the Texas delegation, hoping that Franklin would be its second choice if, and
when, Garner's star faded.

One person that the Roosevelt campaign did not expect help
from was Eleanor. She later wrote that she did not recall "when
[Franklin] decided to run for the presidency, but I knew from Louis
Howe that he, Howe, had decided and had been working in his own
way to prepare the ground."[12] She had absented herself from the campaign, because she believed becoming first lady would end her social
activism, and the campaign had to turn instead to Mary Dewson, a
social worker and former ally of Smith, to rally women's support.

Countering Smith's support in the cities and on the east coast,
Franklin aligned himself with Southern and Western leaders, and
his team outmaneuvered Smith in settling on Chicago as the host
city. Throughout the tense negotiations and sharp elbowing, Franklin took great pains to maintain as much peace as he could with the
Smith forces, since he did not want Republicans to benefit from any
splits among the Democratic ranks. Pushed by reformers to make
eliminating corruption at Tammany Hall a priority, Franklin hedged,
often infuriating them.

Conservative columnist Walter Lippmann took the lead in hammering Franklin for being too eager to please and not tough enough
on the corruption in Tammany Hall, or the administration of Jimmy

Walker, New York City's popular playboy mayor whom opponents charged with heading a corrupt administration. Smith's supporters tried to use the charges of corruption against Roosevelt to make inroads among Southern Democrats. William Randolph Hearst, the head of the nation's largest newspaper chain and proponent of yellow journalism, which emphasized scandal over substance, broadcast harsh critiques of Roosevelt, particularly his involvement with the ill-fated League of Nations.

Hearst backed Garner as the candidate best suited to put "America first," a slogan that, along with his nickname Cactus Jack, caught fire during the campaign. When Franklin told an audience at the New York State Grange that he did not favor, or support, America's participation in the League of Nations, former Wilson advisors and Wilsonian Democrats were not pleased.

As the convention grew closer, the pressure to remove Walker intensified. Six days before the start of the convention, Franklin tried to finesse the problem by sending Walker the charges made against him by Samuel Seabury, who was leading the New York Assembly's investigation into Walker's antics. (Moley was working for Seabury as an advisor.) In response to Franklin's request that he explain himself, Walker said he would not send a reply until after the convention. The problem lingered.

Yet Franklin's well-honed critique of the Hoover administration's failed economic policies won enormous support from Democratic voters and delegates. The collapse of more than two thousand banks hurt Hoover's popularity further, as did his persistent denials that unemployment was a serious problem and his assertion that "federal aid would be a disservice to the unemployed."[13] When Hoover asked Congress to appropriate $2 billion for the Reconstruction Finance Corporation, which was intended to help out failing banks and businesses, Hoover got pilloried for prioritizing banks and big business over destitute Americans.

Franklin took the fight to the airwaves. In April, he broadcast a speech he had drafted with the help of Moley and Rosenman, declaring, "These unhappy times call for the building of plans that rest upon the forgotten, the unorganized . . . for plans like those of 1917 that build from the bottom and not from the top down, that put their faith once more in the forgotten man at the bottom of the economic pyramid."[14] (The notion of "the forgotten man" caught on, later used in President Trump's 2017 presidential inaugural address.) Franklin made the speech the next week at the Democratic Party's Jefferson Day Dinner in St. Paul, Minnesota. When Smith and other candidates complained about his pandering to "the working people of the country," Franklin stepped up his rhetoric on the need for radical change: The "country demands bold, persistent experimentation," he declared at Oglethorpe University in Georgia. "It is common sense to take a method and try it: If it fails, admit it and try another. But above all try something."[15]

When the Democratic convention began on June 27 at the newly constructed Chicago Stadium, it was clear Franklin's message was not getting through to everyone. His Brain Trust was less experienced than the advisors to other major candidates. Ed Flynn said, "We were green at national politics. When Farley and I set off for Chicago we confessed to each other that we felt pretty new at this game."[16]

Yearning to avoid the conflicts that had divided the party in 1924 and sunk its chances to prevail in the presidential election that year, Franklin's team proposed that the convention drop the two-thirds threshold, but its plan faltered when Huey Long, the controversial, populist governor of Louisiana, gave a rousing speech backing the proposal. The uproar boxed the Roosevelt campaign in, and it found itself forced to back the proposal. Because Long was notorious for the extent of corruption within his administration, Smith and others railed against his proposal, which they considered unfair because it had been made at the last minute. They prevailed but not without the Roosevelt campaign's learning "a lesson in national politics then and there," Ed Flynn said, "cit[ing] this as an example of the inexperience of the men who were handling Roosevelt's campaign in Chicago. Louis Howe was probably the most experienced of us all."[17]

Franklin's team was blessed, however, with the capacity to learn from their mistakes and to adapt. On day two of the convention, they outmaneuvered the Smith campaign to secure the selection of Senator Thomas Walsh of Montana, an ally, as the permanent chair of the convention. It was a sign of things to come, even though the "Stop Roosevelt" movement was hardly over. The Smith campaign succeeded in writing into the party platform a pledge to end Prohibition. Its architects believed this placed Franklin in an awkward situation because of his support among the anti-Prohibition crowd. Franklin tried to deflect the strategy by telling his supporters to vote as they wished.

Already believing Franklin had betrayed him in becoming his own man as governor and in attempting to block him from another nomination, Smith hammered Franklin for not taking a stand: "Now," he told the *Atlanta Constitution*, "ain't the time for trimming." (A popular critique of Franklin was that he was a "trimmer," that is, he trimmed his sails to suit different constituencies.)[18] Franklin's strategy kept his coalition together, though by early on the morning of July 1, after the third ballot had been taken, he was still eighty-seven votes short of the two-thirds required for nomination. Many people wondered whether his momentum had been stopped.

After intense negotiations between Farley and the leaders of the other campaigns, Roosevelt got assurances from several delegations, but none put him over the top. By the evening of July 1, Farley and Howe decided to intensify their lobbying of the Texas delegation, and they opened discussions with John Nance Garner's campaign manager, Sam Rayburn, given that Rayburn was a close friend of Senator William McAdoo of California, who had served as Wilson's treasury secretary and was an unsuccessful dark horse in the 1932 convention. McAdoo had assured Rayburn that "We'll vote for Jack [Garner] until hell freezes over if you say so."

When Franklin called Rayburn, Rayburn said that Garner would only throw his support to Franklin if Franklin selected him as his running mate. Garner did not want to leave the speakership but told Rayburn, "We don't want to be responsible for wrecking the party's chances.... Hell, I'll do anything to see the Democrats win one more national election."[19] With his own chances sinking fast, Garner did not need any other push by the end of the third ballot, and he agreed to run for vice president. On the fourth ballot, later that evening, the impact of Garner's agreement was apparent when California switched its support to Roosevelt. Soon following was Texas, which put Franklin over the top and sealed the ticket of Roosevelt-Garner.

Franklin then stunned the convention. Traditionally, successful nominees were not present at the convention and waited weeks until after their nomination to make public statements or speeches acknowledging their victory. In keeping with his penchant for showmanship and the campaign's strategy of boldly breaking customs and norms, moments after securing the nomination Franklin sent a telegram informing the convention that he intended to fly to Chicago to deliver his acceptance in person the next day. It was audacious, not just for breaking the custom of delaying an acceptance speech but also because flying was rare in those days. In the meantime, he met with Rosenman, Moley, and Howe, to finalize the speech. Though it reiterated the same themes Roosevelt had sounded throughout the Democratic primaries, the team understood that the speech was more than just another campaign event. They understood that it was both important as a defining moment of the campaign and historically significant as the nominee's first official words. They honed their message like a diamond.[20]

Carefully positioned before the convention, Franklin pledged that his party be one of "liberal thought, of planned action, of enlightened international outlook, and the greatest good to the greatest number of our citizens." He promised further that his administration would support aggressive governmental action to address the depression's causes and provide effective relief for the millions of Americans in distress. He finished with a peroration that electrified the delegates and the millions listening on the radio: "I pledge you, I pledge myself, to a new deal for the American people.... Give me your help, not to win votes alone, but to win in this crusade to restore America to its own people."[21]

This was not the first time the phrase "new deal" had been used by Franklin. Frances Perkins recalled that "new deal" was "a happy phrase he had coined during the campaign,"[22] which drew on the title (and theme) of economist Stuart Chase's book published earlier that same year, A New Deal.[23] (Chase later joined Roosevelt's "kitchen cabinet" in 1937.) Newspapers seized on the phrase the next day when reporting Franklin's nomination and acceptance speech. It quickly became synonymous with FDR.

II

Franklin Roosevelt had first learned of Herbert Hoover when most of the world did: In 1914, Germany invaded Belgium and left the country in ruins. Then based in London, Hoover, already a successful mining executive, worked with other London-based American businessmen to establish a committee to return home more than one hundred thousand Americans who had been stranded in Europe because of the war. Hoover later said that "I did not realize it at the time, but on August 14, 1914, my career was over forever. I was on the slippery road of public service."[24]

By October of that year, Belgium had nearly run out of food, and its citizens were starving. The American ambassadors to both Great Britain and Belgium persuaded the British to import food into the country on the condition that none of it went to Germany or German forces. As head of the Commission for Relief in Belgium, Hoover oversaw the CRB's collection and rationing of local food and other imported supplies to Belgian citizens. By mid-November, food supplies had reached all parts of occupied Belgium, and there was no catastrophic famine as the rest of the world had feared.

Hoover became known worldwide as the "Great Humanitarian," who had fed 10 million people who lived in the middle of a war zone for five years. In 1917, President Wilson placed him as the head of the U.S. Food Administration. Hoover then guided the effort to conserve resources and supplies and to feed America's European allies. Hoover became a household name, and "to Hooverize" meant to economize on food.[25] Under Hoover's direction, Americans began observing "Meatless Mondays" and "Wheatless Wednesdays" and planting War Gardens to grow their own food. Within a year, the United States had doubled its food shipments to Europe. After the war, Wilson named Hoover as the head of the European Relief and Rehabilitation Administration. In this position,

Hoover sent 34 million tons of American food, clothing, and supplies to war-torn Europe.

In January 1920, Franklin Roosevelt wrote Hugh Gibson, an American diplomat, that he had just had "some nice talks with Herbert Hoover before he went [back home] west for Christmas. He is certainly a wonder and I wish we could make him President of the United States. There could not be a better one." Gibson shared the letter with Hoover, who relayed through Gibson back to Franklin that he was, in fact, a Republican.

Later that year, Hoover tried but failed to secure the Republican nomination for president. When Roosevelt became the Democrats' candidate for vice president, Hoover wrote him, "My dear Roosevelt: The fact that I do not belong to your political tribe does not deter me from offering my personal congratulations to an old friend. I am glad to see you in the game in such a prominent place.... If you are elected you will do the job properly."[26] They kept up a cordial correspondence until 1932.

By the time the two men ran against each other for the presidency, Hoover had grown to dislike Roosevelt intensely. He frequently described Franklin as a political "lightweight," while Roosevelt lost respect for Hoover because of his mismanagement of the depression and propensity to equate political with personal attacks. Hoover resented Roosevelt for looking down at him: Hoover had been in the first graduating class at Stanford in 1895, not yet the world-renowned institution it would become, while Roosevelt dressed and spoke like the Groton and Harvard man that he was. Though both were renowned as problem-solvers and innovative thinkers, Hoover regarded Roosevelt as "the easiest to beat" of the Democratic contenders. Hoover's disdain for Roosevelt intensified during the election.[27]

In 1932, the public held Hoover in even lower esteem than Hoover held Franklin. Roosevelt was the front-runner because of Hoover's mishandling of the economy and inability to connect with the common man. When Hoover had become president in 1929, twenty-four thousand banks were open for business in the United States, but in 1933, ten thousand had closed, and several states were suspending normal bank operations. Hoover's proposed solution that nations, which had abandoned the gold standard, return to it, seemed antiquated and pointless, harkening back, as it did, to the gloomy days of Grover Cleveland. It paled in contrast to the flurry of proposals coming from Roosevelt.

The two candidates were each beholden, to a great extent, to their respective parties' attitudes about the virtues and vices of big business and big government. Hoover was thus tied to his party's fundamental belief in the inherent virtues of big business, volunteerism, and charity. Hoover believed that people had to pick themselves up by their own bootstraps, as he himself had done. He and his surrogates berated Roosevelt as a child of privilege, inexperienced, and spoiled. Hoover had earned his way by working hard, and he believed, as he urged voters to believe, that Franklin had not earned his way in the world but benefitted from family connections. Much of that attack, like so many of Hoover's, backfired, as Franklin's well-known struggle with polio had created more sympathy than scorn among the electorate and his policies were working, as several governors had adopted them, too.

There was no contest between Hoover's dour, irritable disposition and drumbeat of individual rather than collective responsibility on the one hand and Franklin's message captured in his campaign song, "Happy Days Are Here Again." Franklin took his message on the road, particularly in the West, which his campaign shrewdly judged would allow Franklin both to demonstrate his physical strength and to rally supporters, who were ravenous for innovative thinking.

If there was any doubt about the candidates' relative appeal, Hoover removed it when he made another blunder: In the middle of the summer, more than forty-three thousand people gathered to protest the federal government's failure to pay bonuses owed to World War I veterans. Called the "Bonus Army," the crowd included more than seventeen thousand veterans, families, friends, and allies. Hoover refused to pay the bonuses. He told reporters and the crowd that he did not think the government could afford to make the payments, that veterans should not be given special treatment, and that giving in to the pressure would establish a terrible precedent. Hoover offered instead to pay the veterans' expenses to return home, which most accepted. But a separate group refused to leave federal buildings near the White House, which they frequently picketed.

Refusing to leave the White House before the squatters were removed, Hoover ordered the capital police to disperse them, but when the confrontation between them and the police became violent, he ordered General Douglas MacArthur, then the army's chief of staff, to use federal troops to remove the squatters from federal property. Against the counsel of his aide, Dwight Eisenhower, MacArthur ordered Major General George Patton and his units to sweep the protestors' camps, and they did, with bayonets, machine guns, and tanks. Hoover was pleased, but millions of Americans were appalled, especially by the burning of the shantytowns called "Hoovervilles" on site near the White House. The tactics outraged millions of voters. In Albany, Franklin told Harvard Law School professor Felix Frankfurter, whom he had added to the Brain Trust, "Well, Felix, this will elect me."[28]

Franklin had a keen understanding of the image he needed to project and the rhetoric he needed to use to become an effective leader. He was clear-eyed, unsentimental, and confident in appraising people.

Roosevelt explained to Tugwell that "Huey [Long, the popular governor of Louisiana] was the second most dangerous man in America."[29] The first [most dangerous] is Douglas MacArthur. You saw how he strutted down Pennsylvania Avenue. You saw that picture of him in The Times after the troops chased all those vets out with tear gas and burned their shelters.... There's a potential Mussolini for you. Right here at home. The head man in the army. That's a perfect position if things get disorderly enough and good citizens work up enough anxiety." He told Tugwell that he had known MacArthur during the First World War. "You've never heard him talk, but I have. He has the most portentous style of anyone I know. He talks in a voice that might come from an oracle's cave. He never doubts and never argues or suggests; he makes pronouncements. What he thinks is final.... If all this talk comes to anything—about government going to pieces and not being able to stop spreading the disorder—Doug MacArthur is the man. In his way, he's as much a demagogue as Huey. He has as much ego, too. He thinks he's infallible—if he's always right, all people need to do is to take orders. And if some don't like it, he'll take care of them in his own way."[30]

Tugwell, like Moley, considered Franklin's emotional intelligence an aspect of his great acting ability. He had seen firsthand Franklin's performances as "a consummate actor."[31] On first meeting Roosevelt, Tugwell was struck by Franklin's physical appearance. On watching Roosevelt closely that day, Tugwell told Moley that Franklin's face "was mobile and expressive. It might have been an actor's." Tugwell recalled that Moley agreed. "[Moley] said it was an actor's, and a professional actor's at that. How did I suppose he'd created and maintained the image of authority" even when sitting in his wheelchair. Tugwell asked Moley if the man he had met was the real Roosevelt. Tugwell remembered Moley's response. "Yes, he said, in the sense that all this paraphernalia of the governorship had become part of him. It was a real talent; it was a lifetime part that he was playing. . . . He'd figured out what he ought to be like in order to get where he wanted to get and do what he wanted to do, and that was on display. [Moley] added, thoughtfully, that no one would see anything else."[32]

Moley expanded on his impressions of Roosevelt in a letter to his sister. He wrote, "The idea people get from his charming manner— that he is soft and flabby in disposition and character—is far from true. When he wants something a lot he can be formidable—when crossed he is stubborn, resourceful, relentless. I used to think . . . that his amiability was 'lord of the manner,' 'good to the peasants' stuff. It isn't that at all. He seems quite warm and friendly—less because he genuinely likes many of the people to whom he is pleasant [than] because he just enjoys the pleasant and engaging role, as a charming woman does. And being a born politician, he measures such qualities in himself by the effect they produce on others."

Moley said the demeanor might mislead people into thinking Roosevelt was weak. To the contrary, he told his sister, "Nobody in public life since T.R. has been so robust. . . . The man's energy and vitality are astonishing. I've been amazed with his interest in things. It skips and bounces through seemingly intricate subjects, and maybe it is my academic training that makes me feel that no one could possibly learn much in such a hit or miss fashion. I don't find that he has read much on economic subjects. What he gets is from talking to people. When he stores away the conversation, he never knows what part is what he said himself or what his visitor said."[33]

Franklin had burnished his talent as an actor, just as Abraham Lincoln had done seventy years before, by closely studying people. Lincoln prided himself on his ability to size people up quickly, and Franklin did the same. Lincoln loved the theater, especially comedies; Roosevelt did, too. Whereas Lincoln enjoyed acting out Shakespearean scenes with the people around him, Roosevelt invited the comedy team of Bud Abbott and Lou Costello to the White House several times while he was president, and he tried but failed to get Congress to approve a project that would have brought live theater to people in remote areas around the country. While Roosevelt did not love comedies because Lincoln loved them, wartime presidents, such as Wilson, Lincoln, and Roosevelt, often found solace in the same places.

From both Lincoln and Teddy, Roosevelt had learned the importance of image, as Lincoln had benefitted from carefully cultivating the reputation as "honest Abe" and a "rail-splitter" while Teddy's lust for life and bravado had been the secret to much of his success as a candidate and leader.

From Woodrow Wilson and Endicott Peabody, Franklin had learned how preachiness could turn people off, including allies. No one enjoyed being lectured to. Like Wilson and Al Smith, Franklin was a progressive, but one who, unlike them, understood, from listening to his constituents, how much most of them distrusted government. Franklin thus tailored his messages to his audiences, telling them what they wanted to hear and echoing their hopes and dreams. From his own personal and political successes, Franklin found that charm and empathy were more effective at reaching people than browbeating and arrogance, that confidence was contagious, and that hope was addictive and nurtured the ability to endure almost anything, whether it was polio or unemployment.

From Louis Howe, he learned that image counted more than authenticity on the campaign trail and that stubbornness was the enemy of compromise, which was the politician's lifeblood. From Teddy, Howe, and Al Smith, he learned how to court the media, and he learned, by doing, the potential of the new media—radio—for reaching broader audiences. Last but hardly least, Franklin learned from his own mistakes and the mistakes of others. Overconfidence made one lazy and reckless, while blaming people for their problems was the surest way to ensure they voted for the other candidate. He rarely left charges unaddressed, and he worked the crowds because he knew that it was one of his most effective ways of connecting with people. And his message was carefully honed and endlessly repeated and broadcast. He left nothing to chance in his quest for the presidency.

These lessons were on display during Franklin's first presidential campaign in 1932. Elections energized Franklin. His campaign was not perfect, as his prevarications on the League of Nations and investigating corruption at home in New York reinforced some voters' concerns that Franklin lacked sincerity. But Franklin did not have to be a consummate actor to know Hoover was out of his depth, a point he kept hammering, knowing all the while that this would frustrate Hoover and push him into further blunders.

Franklin had to decide, however, whether to press his advantage by campaigning around the country or to sit tight. He recalled that Harding had stayed home through most of the 1920 presidential campaign and still handily defeated the Davis-Roosevelt ticket in spite of Franklin's touring the country. Coolidge, too, said little during his successful run for the presidency in 1928. John Davis and Al Smith barnstormed and lost. Franklin's advisors implored him to keep a low profile throughout the campaign and ride the wave of disenchantment with Hoover and the economy into the White House. (In this regard, Lincoln was a model for Roosevelt, as Lincoln, too, did no public events when he ran for the presidency in 1860, knowing that, if he could avoid making any mistakes, the White House was his.) Ed Flynn cautioned Roosevelt that the "most important thing in a political campaign is to make as few mistakes as possible."[34]

Franklin's advisors agreed that because Franklin was already the popular governor of New York, he could claim that he was staying

close to home to do the job he had been elected to do. But Franklin
ultimately balked, knowing that Hoover was loath to leave the con-
fines of the White House. Franklin had promised boldness as a
candidate, and campaigning across the country would be bold, contrasting with the overly cautious Hoover, who was too timid to use
his powers, and the might of the federal government, to combat the
nation's woes. Franklin had to do more than just win. He needed
Democratic majorities in both chambers of Congress, and he needed
a mandate to implement his bold plans.

Once Franklin made up his mind, only Howe could change it,
and Howe agreed with Franklin. Indeed, nothing in the campaign
happened unless Howe approved. Barely leaving his room at the Congress Hotel during the convention, Howe's vision firmly shaped the
campaign's strategy. As one of Howe's research assistants recalled,
"Louis' plans had been so thorough and he believed things were so
good for Franklin that he sat down with the Governor in February
[1932], mapped out a campaign trip, with pins stuck in the map
where campaign speeches were to be made, and planned the type of
speech for each section!"[35]

Ed Flynn once said Roosevelt "seemed to have a sixth sense that
enabled him to do the right thing at the right time." Franklin's instincts told him to campaign, and campaign he did. As Roosevelt
biographer Jean Smith noted, "Roosevelt made twenty-seven major
addresses between August and November, each devoted to a single
subject. He spoke briefly on thirty-two additional occasions, usually
at whistle-stops or impromptu gatherings to which he was invited.
Hoover, by contrast, made only ten speeches, all of which were delivered in the closing weeks of the campaign." Franklin traveled to
Western states like no other presidential candidate had, visiting
Topeka, Salt Lake City, Seattle, and Portland. To large crowds, he proclaimed, "My policy is as radical as American liberty. My policy is
as radical as the Constitution."[36] The positive reviews in the press of
his speeches and rallies confirmed his gut, fortified his base, and motivated him to keep at it.

The harder Roosevelt campaigned, the more offended Hoover became. Hoover's only political campaign before 1932 was his successful

run for the presidency in 1928. As Coolidge's handpicked successor, all Hoover had to do was say little and wait for the inevitable outcome. For most of 1932, Hoover thought it beneath him to engage with Franklin. But the pummeling on the campaign trail, in the newspapers, and among the public, who called shantytowns "Hoovervilles" and pockets turned inside out "Hoover flags," forced Hoover's hand. No longer able to remain silent, he came out swinging—and yet again hurt himself. His disdain for Roosevelt—and arrogance in thinking it silly anyone would disagree with him on economic and business policy—further turned the public against him. He argued that the only way to be rid of the depression was to return to the principle that had built the nation and the economy in the first place—rugged individualism,[37] but most Americans had had more than enough of that. They needed help.

Hoover ignored their pleas. For him, the presidential election was "more than a contest between two men. It is a conflict between two philosophies of government." Hoover placed his philosophy on the side of the framers, whom he believed had created a constitution that prioritized individuals and the private sector. The government's job was largely to stay out of the way on economic matters and concern itself primarily with national security. He considered Roosevelt's philosophy as rooted in an unrealistic vision of government as a force for good rather than constraint. As Hoover declared, "You cannot extend the mastery of government over the daily life of a people without somewhere making it master of people's souls and thoughts." Like Coolidge before him, Hoover worried that government would never stop once it took over the economy; it would end, he charged, in tyranny. "Economic freedom cannot be sacrificed," he said, "if political freedom is to be preserved."[38]

Franklin ended his campaign on familiar territory, Madison Square Garden, in the heart of New York City. He had traveled more than fifteen thousand miles in the campaign. Now, back on his home turf, he reassured the crowd that, throughout the campaign, he had "consistently set forth the doctrine of the present-day Democracy. It is the program of a party dedicated to the conviction that every one of our people is entitled to the opportunity to earn a living, and to develop himself to the fullest measure consistent with the rights of his fellow man."[39]

On the evening of Election Day, November 8, 1932, Franklin was careful, as Flynn advised, to say as little as possible and make no mistakes. He kept his first public comments short: "It looks friends like a real landslide this time. But we have not yet had the returns from the West Coast and for that reason I am making no official or public statement yet."[40] Surprisingly, Roosevelt inserted his special thanks: "There are two people in the United States more than anybody else who are responsible for this great victory. One is my old friend and associate, Colonel Louis McHenry Howe, and the other is that splendid American, Jim Farley."[41] Farley had already been widely hailed as the campaign manager, but Howe never forgave Roosevelt for destroying his cherished anonymity.

The next morning, the returns, Hoover's concession, and the congratulations of the chair of the Republican National Committee arrived. The race was not nearly as close as it had been in 1929: Roosevelt beat Hoover by more than 7 million votes and he crushed Hoover in the Electoral College, 472 to 59. He carried forty-two of the forty-eight states, including winning Hoover's home state of California. Hoover became the sixth incumbent president to lose reelection (the previous ones were John and John Quincy Adams, Grover Cleveland, Benjamin Harrison, and William Howard Taft). The rout did not end there, as Democrats added 97 seats to their House majority and established control of the Senate, 60–35. The significance of these numbers was lost on no one: Roosevelt and his party controlled both the presidency and Congress. They had the public warrant—and the power—to make the promised New Deal a reality.

Against the backdrop of his resounding victory, the president-elect issued a statement, composed with the help of Farley and Howe: "I am glad of this opportunity to extend my deep appreciation to the electorate of this country which gave me yesterday such a great vote of confidence. It is a vote that had more than mere party significance. It transcended party lines and became a national expression of liberal thought. It means . . . that the masses of the people . . . firmly believe that there is great and actual possibility in an orderly recovery through a well conceived and actively directed plan of action. It shows in this country unbounded confidence in the future of sound agricultural and honorable industry." He concluded by putting into words the precise import of that moment: "This clear mandate shall not be forgotten and I pledge you this and I invite your help in the happy task of restoration."[42]

III

Under the rules of the original Constitution, the president-elect had four months to prepare for his inauguration and start on March 4, 1933. The idea behind the large gap between election and inauguration was to allow time for the news of the election to travel across the country, for the president-elect to communicate and meet with the people he wanted for his cabinet, and to travel to the capital and prepare to move into the White House. In 1932, this period had no special name, but, later in 1963, it became known as the presidential transition.

In practice, most presidents found the time lag to be more of a burden than a benefit: It gave an incumbent president too much time to make trouble for the winner, as John Adams had done by trying to stack the federal judiciary against Thomas Jefferson in 1800 and as James Buchanan had done by ordering the federal government to do nothing to impede Southern states, which were planning to secede and preparing to bombard Charleston Harbor in anticipation of Lincoln's inauguration.

Sometimes, presidents of different parties might establish cordial, if not terribly helpful, working relationships with their successors, as Taft had done for Wilson. In some cases, the incumbent had already checked out of the White House by Election Day. Coolidge, for example, backed his commerce secretary for president in 1928, but he was so deep in mourning over the death of his son Cal that he did nothing of consequence to help Hoover's transition. In characteristic fashion, he said nearly nothing during the 1932 election and less afterward.

Franklin had four months to prepare an administration he had promised the world would be bold and innovative. To achieve that goal, he—and his Brain Trust—undertook the arduous tasks of gathering information and advice that Franklin needed as president, laying the groundwork for policies that he hoped to put into effect once he took office, and assembling the staff and leaders in his administration. He took an eleven-day Caribbean cruise, which he expected would be his last vacation for the foreseeable future. He traveled back and forth from New York to Washington several times. He met with business and political leaders, and experts on economics and foreign affairs. He authorized the Brain Trust to begin drafting legislative proposals designed to stimulate recovery, and the Brain Trust in turn consulted with experts and Democratic allies.

During the transition period, Franklin did not settle on particular policies and, in fact, did not know most of the details his advisors were pondering. He shared few plans with the public and the press. Indeed, he did not have any yet, as his advisors were not sharing with him details of proposals they were drafting.

Few things went as well or as smoothly as Franklin hoped. His first challenge was Eleanor. Though she celebrated on election eve with Franklin, his advisors and friends, her concerns about losing her independence as first lady worsened. Franklin knew she was anxious and had said to her the evening of his historic election, "I wish I knew what you are really thinking and feeling." She did not answer, explaining years later, she "did not want my husband to be president." She conceded, "It was pure selfishness on my part, and I never mentioned my feelings on the subject to him." "As I saw it," she recalled, "I knew what traditionally should lie before me. I had watched Mrs. Theodore Roosevelt and had seen what it meant to be the wife of the President, and I cannot say that I was pleased at the prospect. The turmoil in my heart and mind was rather great that night, and the next few months were not to make any clearer what the road ahead would be."[43]

Franklin relished presenting the image of a happy family to the world, but the image was no longer a reality: Eleanor no longer slept in the same bed as he and had often been absent during his long days on the campaign trail. Under Louis Howe's tutelage, she had grown to like her role in representing Franklin when he was governor, reporting on her interactions with different constituencies and advocating for progressive causes. Howe, who was now the president-elect's chief of staff, understood her strengths and public appeal, and he gently encouraged her to continue to do the same things she had done before but on a grander scale. The love and trust she had developed with Howe did Franklin's work for him. Howe helped her transform the position of first lady to advance the interests nearest to her heart— mobilizing women, advocating progressive solutions to social and economic problems, and helping the destitute.

One thing neither Howe nor Eleanor could do, however, was delay Franklin's departure from the New York governorship. He desperately wanted to stay until the last possible moment, because he needed the money, but Democratic leaders in the state, spurred by Al Smith, demanded that Franklin step down to focus on his new duties. His staff agreed, and he begrudgingly did as they asked.

The biggest obstacle Roosevelt had to face during the transition was Herbert Hoover. Spurred by his virulent dislike for Roosevelt and stubborn insistence that he alone understood how to resolve the Great Depression, Hoover could not bring himself to concede his defeat. He was convinced that Franklin had fooled the voters, or that they were fools, perhaps both. His priority was to ruin Roosevelt's presidency.

IV

Though he had lost the election, Hoover had four months to convince Franklin to drop the idea of a New Deal, and to poison the public's view of Roosevelt. With his advisors in agreement, Hoover was already planning to run again in 1936, at which time he expected to have the dilettante's disastrous record to run against.

Hoover was convinced that the depression had resulted from an international debt crisis in which various countries, including the United States, France, and Britain, overextended their credit and lacked the resources to pay their bills. When the debts owed to the United States from Britain and France came due, Hoover suspended them. It was an unpopular policy, but Hoover planned to blame

Franklin. Hoover insisted Franklin meet with him, after which Hoover planned to tell America that Franklin either now agreed with him or refused to take any actions to address the international debt crisis. After exchanging telegrams, Franklin warily agreed to meet Hoover at the White House on November 22, 1932.

Hoover prepared for the meeting as if his life depended on it, while Franklin prepared for Hoover to bait him. Hoover's initial gambit was hiring a stenographer to record the meeting. This act showed Roosevelt that Hoover mistrusted him. Franklin planned to say little, in any event.

The two men had not seen each other in years, but when Hoover saw Roosevelt leaning on braces, emaciated, and tired, he was stunned. He had underestimated Roosevelt's physical handicap. Recovering his resolve, Hoover launched into nearly an hour-long lecture on international debt. Franklin nodded his head and murmured "yes," "I understand," "ok," all of which led Hoover to think that Franklin was agreeing with Hoover's plan to give Roosevelt access to the administration during the presidential transition period through a "joint board" including Roosevelt as a member in return for Franklin's giving Hoover a free hand to set policy.[44]

When Hoover contacted Franklin the next day to follow up on what he thought was now their joint plan, Franklin informed him that he was rejecting Hoover's proposal. Rather than avoiding Franklin's fooling him, Hoover had fooled himself. Franklin made clear that Hoover, not he, was the President for the next few months and should feel free to pursue the policies of his choice, and then Franklin would make his own choices after he was inaugurated.

Hoover was not done. He tried again in December, hoping to interest Franklin in appointing a delegation to a World Economic Conference in London. Franklin demurred, telling Hoover later in a telegram that it was not his place to make such appointments. It was the President's job, Hoover was still president, and he could appoint whom he liked.

Outraged, Hoover released their respective telegrams to the public. Hoover hoped it would show Franklin's duplicity and refusal to compromise. Hoover voters were delighted, but Roosevelt's supporters, who vastly outnumbered Hoover's, were angered by Hoover's churlishness.

Hoover's next move was to deny Franklin the opportunity to meet with his secretary of state, Henry Stimson, to discuss the deteriorating peace in Europe, including the troublesome rise of Nazism in Germany and the installment of its new chancellor, Adolph Hitler, in 1933. With Stimson also wanting the meeting, the stalemate was broken when Hoover's ambassador to France, Walter Edge, threatened to resign unless Hoover allowed a meeting with the president-elect to take place. After Franklin telegrammed Hoover again, Hoover relented, but he could not stop trying to find ways to embarrass Roosevelt and relitigate the election.

Hoover's antipathy toward Roosevelt and fervent belief that Roosevelt and the Democrats spelled ruin for the country were so strong that Hoover barely took a pause after February 15, seventeen days before the inauguration, when Giuseppe Zangara, an unemployed house painter, fired at two open limousines, one with Franklin Roosevelt and the other with Anton Cermak, the mayor of Chicago. Zangara got off five shots, none hitting Franklin but one striking Cermak, whom Franklin cradled en route to the hospital. Cermak died two weeks later.

Three days after the assassination attempt, Hoover handwrote a long personal letter to FDR and delivered it to Roosevelt's hotel. It warned Roosevelt of an impending catastrophe which only could be averted by Franklin's declaring for, and adopting, Hoover's economic policies and abandoning his plans altogether. Franklin did not respond for twelve days, after which he sent a short note politely declining Hoover's advice.

With the inauguration five days away, Hoover intensified his efforts to get the president-elect to renounce his plans for the New Deal and instead agree to restore public confidence in Hoover's policies. With hundreds of banks failing, the Federal Reserve Board requested Hoover order a suspension of bank transactions for at least a week. Hoover refused. Instead, he agreed to forward the request to Roosevelt and his team. They declined to act, prompting Hoover to write yet another letter pleading with Roosevelt to renounce the New Deal and endorse Hoover's policies instead. This time, Roosevelt did not bother to answer.

In the meantime, the Federal Reserve Board, created at the end of President Wilson's first year in office, increased its pressure on Hoover, who was doing almost nothing to help with the recovery other than badger Roosevelt and his team. The board drafted a letter for Hoover to sign, which would authorize the bank holiday. Hoover refused. He thought it more important that Roosevelt be the one responsible for authorizing the holiday, thus vindicating Hoover. When Roosevelt demurred, Hoover let the press and the public know that Roosevelt was declining to order a bank holiday. Since Hoover was still president, he just made himself look silly.

V

While navigating the obstacles Hoover placed in his path and the painful aftermath of the assassination attempt, Roosevelt managed to assemble his cabinet. Of course, he knew that when Teddy Roosevelt first became president in 1901, he had inherited McKinley's cabinet, but, after his election as president in his own right in 1904, Teddy replaced most of its members with influential Republican leaders who shared his vision of the federal government as an important engine of social justice.

When Wilson had become president in 1912, he chose his cabinet members based on their support for him during the election and his, or some other trusted ally's, appraisal. Yet Franklin knew that neither Teddy nor Wilson had a harmonious relationship with their cabinet in their first years in office. Each had to make significant changes later and was unable to avoid high-profile disagreements with cabinet members throughout his time in office. Franklin recalled all too well that Wilson's secretary of state Williams Jennings Bryan was not a team player or loyal to Wilson; his resignation was made to embarrass the President.

Franklin's priorities in filling a cabinet were support for his campaign and progressivism, useful expertise and experience, and loyalty.

Rather than follow Lincoln's model of placing his political rivals in his cabinet, Roosevelt left them out. He wished to avoid adding the political intrigue of his cabinet members to the problems his administration had to solve. He needed unity, competence, and obedience.

As the first Democrat elected president in twelve years, Roosevelt—and his advisors—were inundated with recommendations and résumés. For more than a decade, Democrats had been in political exile, and they were eager to be back in charge. Roosevelt had been here before, back when he was scrambling, like so many other Democrats, for positions in the then-incoming Wilson administration. He could not stem the tide of résumés, but he could place the people he most trusted in charge of handling the flood of applications.

Besides appointing Howe and other close advisors to key positions within the White House, Franklin named Farley postmaster general, a position that might have seemed innocuous to the public but allowed Farley to dispense more than one hundred thousand jobs as patronage. Franklin hired Missy LeHand and Grace Tully as his secretaries, and Steve Early and Marvin McIntyre as press secretary and appointments secretary, respectively. Both had been original members of the Cuff Links Club, a group of associates Roosevelt had given special cuff links in recognition of their service to him when he was running for the vice presidency in 1920.

For the first and preeminent position within the cabinet, Franklin went with his gut: He chose popular Senator Cordell Hull of Tennessee as secretary of state. Hull had been an ardent Wilsonian, who had been elected to the House in 1906 and to the Senate in 1930. Though his knowledge of foreign affairs was limited, and several senators questioned his idealism, Hull had earned Roosevelt's trust as an early supporter and for having influence within the Senate and beyond. As Franklin noted, "Cordell Hull is the only member of the Cabinet who brings me any political strength that I don't have in my own right."[45]

Franklin had little choice in offering the post of treasury secretary to Carter Glass, whom he had known since he served as Wilson's treasury secretary and as the architect of the Federal Reserve Act, and who was the senior senator on the Appropriations Committee and had long been the party's senior spokesperson on finance. Franklin was apprehensive, because Glass did not share his economic vision: Glass favored hard currency, fiscal restraint, and a sound dollar, none of which Franklin, a pragmatist, agreed with under the economic circumstances of 1932-33. After pondering the offer for a while, Glass declined because of poor health.

Relieved, Franklin next asked William Woodin, a Republican industrialist who had contributed heavily to Franklin's campaigns. Though Woodin was as uneasy as Glass had been with Franklin's relative indifference about inflation, his devotion to Franklin made his decision easy. He accepted. Franklin heaved a sigh of relief.

For attorney general, Franklin's first choice was another friend in the Senate, Thomas Walsh of Montana, who had chaired the 1924 and 1932 Democratic conventions. Franklin liked his longstanding opposition to corporate malfeasance. With Walsh at the Justice Department, Franklin sent a strong signal that his administration opposed special interests. But, two days before the inauguration, Walsh, who had just married a much younger woman, died of a heart attack.

Moving quickly, Franklin offered the job to Homer Cummings, whom he had planned to name governor-general of the Philippines but who had a distinguished background as a prosecutor and faithful Democrat, who had chaired the Democratic National Committee in 1919 and 1920.

Franklin did not get his first choice for war secretary, either. He settled on Utah's Governor George Dern, who had campaigned hard for Roosevelt in the West. Initially, Roosevelt wanted Dern at Interior, but conservationists complained he had no record as a conservationist. Instead, Franklin nominated him to head the war department, a position and department that he knew little about. Yet Roosevelt trusted him, and the administration's policy of isolationism and the department's small budget indicated it would not be hard for Dern to oversee.

Of the remaining five slots—navy, agriculture, interior, commerce, and labor—the selection of the labor secretary was the only one that went according to plan. In getting Virginia governor Harry

Byrd's support at the Democratic convention, Howe had cut a deal
to put one of Virginia's two senators—Carter Glass and Claude Swanson—in the cabinet, so Byrd could have their seat. When Glass
declined, Roosevelt then tapped as navy secretary Virginia's other
senator, Claude Swanson, who agreed to join Roosevelt's cabinet.
That gave Roosevelt two senators in the cabinet, which he expected
to cultivate good relations with the Senate—and it did.

Next, Roosevelt hoped to appoint Henry Morgenthau, a friend
and neighbor, as secretary of agriculture, but farm groups objected
to his appointment to the Farm Board, which was slated to be a centerpiece of one of the linchpins of the New Deal—the Farm Credit
Administration. In response, Roosevelt begrudgingly accepted
Henry Wallace, who had once been a Republican but changed
parties to support Roosevelt and the New Deal. Wallace's appeal included his coming from Iowa, another Western state that had voted
for Roosevelt, and his having won acclaim for his experiments to increase agricultural productivity.

At Commerce, Roosevelt initially wanted Jesse Strauss, the head
of Macy's and a strong financial backer of his. The fact that his uncle
had been commerce secretary under Teddy Roosevelt provided a
nice link between the old and new Roosevelts. But too many old-line
Wilsonians argued that Daniel Roper of South Carolina should be
given the appointment for Roosevelt to ignore.

Since Roosevelt had known Roper for years—as the head of Wilson's reelection campaign in 1916 and as the leader of both the U.S.
Tariff Commission and the Internal Revenue Service in Wilson's second term—Roosevelt entrusted Roper to head Commerce.

Interior was an unexpected challenge for Roosevelt. When Dern
proved unacceptable there, Franklin turned to Hiram Johnson, a senator from California, who had been a major supporter of Roosevelt's
in the election. But Johnson declined, preferring to remain in the
Senate. Roosevelt then asked Bronson Cutting, a Republican senator
from New Mexico, but he, too, declined. Several advisors pressed Harold Ickes of Chicago on Roosevelt, but Roosevelt did not know him.
With little time left before inauguration, Ickes got the nod by default,
having lobbied Howe and other advisors to be commissioner of In-

dian Affairs. Howe, who thought Ickes lacked tact and was prone to indelicate remarks, said it was "the first break that the Indians have had in a hundred years."[46]

For Labor, Roosevelt took his time, though there never was any doubt about his choice. Waiting until just a month before the inauguration, he went with the person whose expertise, political value, and loyalty were beyond question—Frances Perkins. Despite protests from leading Democrats that she would face trouble in being confirmed as the first woman nominated to a cabinet post, Franklin liked that prospect and stood behind her.

The Senate unanimously confirmed each one of his cabinet nominees. It was the first time in modern history the Senate had done so. Much to Roosevelt's surprise, Hoover had arranged for the cabinet's confirmation before Roosevelt was sworn in. It was an unmistakable sign, combined with the overwhelming extent of his victory, that Roosevelt was positioning himself not just to be an even more popular and consequential president than his cousin Teddy but also any Democrat who had preceded him in office. But the prospect and the reality of governing were two different things, as both he and the nation soon learned.

CHAPTER FIVE

The Rise of the
New Deal (1933–1936)

PRESIDENTS UNDERSTAND A SIMPLE TRUTH: that symbolism is as important as, if not more important than, anything else to their success. Presidential historian Richard Neustadt famously suggested that a president's most potent power was his ability to persuade. But persuasion depends on many factors, such as a president's popularity and rhetoric, which are shaped by how well they manage their image.

Perhaps no president better mastered this aspect of the presidency than Franklin Roosevelt. He won the office based on an image he and Howe cultivated, projecting the relentless optimism and determination many still associate with his presidency.

In fashioning the symbolism for his own inauguration, Franklin looked backward. His model was Andrew Jackson, one of the founders of the Democratic Party and its first elected president. Although Jackson had been president a century before Franklin Roosevelt, the Democratic Party in the 1930s still regarded him among the pantheon of great presidents. (Lincoln, too, had modeled himself on Jackson, who was the first president to publicly oppose the idea of secession.) After Jackson, only four Democrats had been elected president. Of those presidents, Franklin knew Wilson best:

Despite the defeat of Wilson's grand idea of a League of Nations, he was still a model for Franklin to emulate as he had steered the country through the First World War and persuaded Congress to enact a series of progressive reforms, including the Federal Reserve Act.

Wilson looked back to Jackson, too, as Wilson was the first Democrat after Jackson to win two consecutive terms as president. In the 1930s, Andrew Jackson still shone as the founder of the modern Democratic Party. He was the last Democrat before Roosevelt who promised radical reform of the federal government. And Jackson, Franklin understood, had been a winner, having won the most votes each of the three times he ran for the presidency. (Cleveland has this distinction as well.) Jackson won a mandate more clearly and more decisively than any prior Democrat elected before Franklin. As the first Democrat elected president, Jackson symbolized the rise of American democracy. The "forgotten man" whose dignity Franklin promised to restore was the successor to the "common man" whom Jackson had championed. Jackson saw himself as the servant of the American people, as did Franklin Roosevelt a century later.

Jackson was the first president to defend the vision of the President as the only national figure elected by all Americans and thus having greater claim than other elected officials to represent all the people of the United States. As such, Jackson rode the first wave of populism unleashed in American history. Franklin saw himself as Jackson's successor, riding the next wave, indeed a bigger wave, of populism than either Jackson or Wilson represented. Franklin's inauguration symbolized the manifestation of the popular will for change and the restoration of the American dream for every American, especially those forgotten and crushed by the Great Depression.

I

A century before Franklin's inauguration, to the day, Andrew Jackson was sworn in as president a second time. He declared that day, "The eyes of all nations are fixed on our Republic."[1] It was equally true at Roosevelt's inauguration.

Franklin began the morning with a prayer service at St. John's Episcopal Church, directly across Lafayette Square from the White House. His predecessors had often invoked religious imagery in their inaugural addresses, but Franklin intended to show how central religious faith was to him and to the restoration of the American dream. Roosevelt saw himself as the "instrument" of the Lord's will. For some, this seemed opportunistic or hubris, but for Roosevelt and Endicott Peabody it was the truth of his presidency.

Franklin invited Peabody to preside over the service. He had been a steady presence and influence in Franklin's life throughout the decades following his graduation from Groton. Besides officiating at Franklin's wedding, he had been one of the first people outside the immediate family to reach out when Franklin contracted polio, maintain a steady correspondence with Franklin that was filled with encouragement and spiritual and sometimes political advice, and regularly visit him.

Peabody contacted "Dear Franklin" on small occasions, such as birthdays and awards ceremonies at Groton, and big occasions, such as his State of the Union addresses and announcements of major initiatives. Some letters went so far as to assure the President of his support within the Groton community, particularly its faculty, and Peabody's readiness to set the record straight on Franklin's accomplishments and religiosity. Franklin dutifully called his mentor "Dr. Peabody" and took his counsel and encouragement to heart. In an interview with the *New York Times* during his first term as president, Roosevelt admitted, "As long as I live, the influence of Dr. and Mrs. Peabody means and will mean more to me than that of any other people next to my mother and father."[2] (Eleanor surely felt the sting of that statement.)

Spirituality was the most common theme of their correspondence. After Roosevelt had reached out to more than one hundred thousand clergy asking for their advice on and support for the government's new social security and public works programs, Peabody wrote "to assure you of my lasting conviction that you have one supreme purpose in mind, the guidance of this country in such a way that all its citizens who are minded to do honest work shall have a chance to secure a living free from anxiety and with an opportunity for the development of which they are capable." In a time of "unsteady faith," Peabody continued, the country was fortunate to have "a spiritual leader at the head of the nation [who] brings fresh power to the individual and to the cause of Christ and His Church." "I have thought," Peabody told the President, "the guiding principle of a man's life should be the motive which Jesus revealed as his fundamental purpose: 'For their sakes, I sanctify myself that they also may be sanctified through the truth.'" He concluded with gratitude that Franklin had "such an opportunity to carry out this great purpose in your own life with a view to inspiring a mighty company of your fellow country-men."

On the first morning of his presidency, Roosevelt listened as Peabody read selections from the Book of Common Prayer, concluding with his asking God "Thy favor to behold and bless Thy servant Franklin, chosen to be President of the United States."[3] Franklin had personally selected the other prayers and hymns for the service. He made a point of remaining on his knees in prayer well after the service ended. The image of a righteous, humble man was fundamental to the success of his presidency. Reuniting with Peabody underscored the extent to which their relationship was a constant reminder for Roosevelt about the centrality of his religious faith, honed with the help of Peabody, to the performance of his presidential duties.

After the service, Franklin and his entourage traveled to the North Portico of the White House, arriving shortly before the appointed time of 11 a.m. All but two presidents-elect had visited with their predecessors in the White House before proceeding to the ceremony, but Franklin had no interest in prolonging his interaction with Hoover. (Nor did he want the press taking photographs of him struggling on the steps up to and down from the White House.)

Hoover arrived with a smile on his face, though it did not last long: After Hoover asked Roosevelt in vain if he could give a position to Hoover's administrative assistant, the two men traveled in silence the two miles to the Capitol. Once the ceremonies were over, they parted and never saw each other again.

After Vice President John Nance Garner was sworn into office, Franklin leaned on the arm of his son James as he walked 146 feet to the rostrum. It was one of the few times Roosevelt allowed photographs of his walking rather than sitting or standing. It was impossible to miss the symbolic value of Roosevelt showing the world what he had overcome to be President of the United States.

Swearing Roosevelt into office was Charles Evans Hughes, the chief justice of the United States. A former two-term governor of New York, associate justice of the Supreme Court, and secretary of state, Hughes had been appointed chief justice by President Hoover in 1934. Tall, bearded, invariably serious and boring in public, Hughes embodied the Republican establishment. He waited patiently on the dais for Roosevelt to arrive at the spot where he would be sworn in. Once Roosevelt arrived, Eleanor appeared with the Roosevelt family Bible (dating back to 1650) on which he had twice taken the oath as governor. Then, pursuant to an understanding worked out beforehand with Hughes, Franklin recited the full text of the oath Hughes administered, promising that "I, Franklin Delano Roosevelt, do solemnly swear that I will faithfully execute the office of the President of the United States and will, to the best of my ability, preserve, protect, and defend the Constitution of the United States." Roosevelt spoke slowly and distinctly to underscore to the public his heartfelt commitment to the Constitution and to them. He wanted them to think of him as their champion, and most Americans believed he was.

II

According to Franklin's account, he wrote the first draft of his inaugural address in one sitting, late on the evening of February 27. Jim Farley recalled being struck by how much Roosevelt had altered the speech that he and Howe had revised. Franklin had streamlined the draft, which he peppered with religious references. The final product reflected the input of others, including Felix Frankfurter, who had told Roosevelt the week before the inaugural, "I look forward to having your Inaugural modify greatly the defeatist attitude so sedulously cultivated recently.... Our greatest need is to resume employment and the way to resume employment is to resume employment. The budget will be balanced when business recovers rather than this foolish theory of magic that business will recover by balancing the budget."[4]

On the day before the inauguration, Roosevelt had had little choice but to go to the White House for the president-elect's traditional call on the outgoing president. Though the meeting had been pitched as a ceremonial occasion, Hoover planned a surprise: He invited both the chair of the Federal Reserve Board and his treasury secretary to attend the meeting, so that they, too, could lobby Franklin to renounce the New Deal. Sensing the trap, Franklin placed a call to Ray Moley, who had just lay down for a nap across the street, to come to the White House immediately. Hoover pressed Franklin to make a joint announcement on the bank holiday. At this point, Moley appeared and immediately joined ranks with Roosevelt in declining Hoover's offer. His patience wearing thin, Roosevelt refused and rose to leave, saying that he hoped Hoover would not feel any obligation to return the call. Hoover dismissed him, "Mr. Roosevelt, when you have been in Washington as long as I have been, you will learn that the President of the United States calls on nobody." Franklin left with Moley, telling him later that if he had not left then, he would have hit Hoover. Safely back at his own hotel, Roosevelt tinkered with his address further, this time adapting a quote Howe had inserted into the draft on February 28, "The only thing we have to fear is fear itself."[5]

By the time Franklin stood at the podium the next day, Hoover was a thing of the past and Franklin was ready for his own rendezvous with destiny. With the traditional twenty-one-gun salute complete, Franklin began, "This is a day of national consecration. I am certain that my fellow Americans expect that on my induction into the Presidency I will address them with a candor and a decision which the present situation of our Nation impels."[6] Beautifully crafted, the first two sentences presented FDR exactly as he hoped the American public would see him—as humble, transparent, god-fearing, and duty bound to serve the American people. Such powerfully succinct statements were rare in inaugural addresses, but

Roosevelt both drew on what he knew had worked among the larger crowds during the campaign and had as his model Andrew Jackson in his simple, direct, unvarnished rhetoric.

Over the course of more than two decades campaigning, Roosevelt had perfected the pitch. Being at ease came naturally to Franklin, as did such direct appeals, contrasting with the unease (and lack of sophistication) of Jackson, who could overcompensate for his lack of education, as reflected in his own tortuous first sentence in his first inaugural address.

Besides Jackson's directness and plainness of speech, three other influences on Roosevelt's rhetoric were evident. First, in Roosevelt's two preceding gubernatorial inaugurations, he had adopted a basic format for his inaugural and other major speeches. He began each with a religious or spiritual reference, thus consecrating, to use his word, the occasion. Next, he marked the occasion itself, pronounced his vision for the office and the future, and included messages of hope.

A second, related influence was the Bible. Many presidents used the Bible, none more poetically and profoundly than Abraham Lincoln. Yet Roosevelt had so many biblical references in his speech that the National Bible Press published an edition with appropriate verses. Frances Perkins was struck by the extent of Roosevelt's religious references, beginning with his acknowledgment of the day as a national "consecration," his alluding to "the lilies of the field," and invoking the plague of locusts and Jesus expelling the moneylenders from the temple and denouncing the "practices of the unscrupulous money changers." Though finding that Roosevelt's speech fell short of Lincoln's masterful second inaugural address, Farley observed that the "same cadences suggestive of the King James Bible were audible in the moving prose." Franklin's mother told Farley that "a thought to God was the right way to start off."

The heavy emphasis on religious imagery and terms in the speech was no accident. It illustrated the insight of Robert Sherwood, a speechwriter and prize-winning playwright, that "religious faith was the strongest and most mysterious force that was in him."[7] Similarly, Frances Perkins suggested that Roosevelt "knew what religion was and he followed it. It was more than a code of ethics for him. It was a real relationship of man and God, and he felt as certain of it as of the reality of his life."[8]

Third, Franklin did not mention any former presidents or statesmen. It was a not-so-subtle reflection of his determination to break the norm followed by nearly every other president while it also reflected his practice of not mentioning or acknowledging various sources that he used in his speeches. At the same time, his rhetoric helped to create the effect that he wanted: Once he had finished, Ray Moley turned to Frances Perkins and said, "Well, he's taken the ship of state, turned it right around."[9]

Franklin Roosevelt's address was not long. More important than the length was the tone. Roosevelt knew that millions were listening on the radio. His message thus had to be crystal clear, serious, short, and memorable. Besides casting what he deemed to be the appropriate image on his first day as president, Roosevelt had three basic objectives for his address: First, it attacked the damaging psychology of the depression. Second, it explained the constitutional foundations for the New Deal. Third, he effectively declared war against the depression through his pledge to mobilize the American people, as they had never been mobilized before, and to harness their energy, patriotism, and determination to build the recovery the country sorely needed.

Roosevelt was back at the White House greeting friends and family when he received the news from the Senate that the cabinet had been approved. Roosevelt's cabinet was the first to be sworn into office all at once, with each cabinet officer taking the oath of office from Justice Benjamin Cardozo. By late afternoon, they were officially in place, the swiftest assembling of a presidential cabinet in history. It was just one of the norms that Roosevelt and his team broke, not just to ensure that the administration got moving quickly, but also to demonstrate their "revolutionary" mission.

Franklin chose not to attend any of the evening affairs, sending Eleanor instead. As she and others celebrated around the city, Franklin and Louis Howe quietly discussed the events of the day and their plans for tomorrow. There is no record of their conversation, though it is likely they reminisced some about the twenty-two-year-long journey they had taken to the White House. At ten-thirty, Franklin went to bed, knowing, as he had just told the American people, that the next day would be his administration's first full day to proceed with "treating the task [ahead] as we would treat the emergency of a war."[10]

III

While there was no war waging when Franklin became president, he drew on his experiences during the First World War to do something no other president had done before—he declared war on the economic conditions. He declared it in his inaugural address. He said as much to confidants and reporters. "The nation," Roosevelt said, must move "as a trained and loyal army willing to sacrifice for the good of a common discipline." "I shall ask the Congress for the one remaining instrument to meet the crisis—broad Executive power to wage a war against the emergency, as great as that power that would have been given to me if we were in fact invaded by a foreign foe." Roosevelt followed the martial rhetoric with bringing into the administration many former Wilson administration officials, who shared both his commitment to progressive ideals and experiences in helping to lead the nation through the First World War.

Roosevelt promised an active first hundred days in office. During the transition, his Brain Trust had drafted more than a dozen laws that fulfilled Roosevelt's objective to attack the depression as if the United States were at war with it. In his inaugural address, Roosevelt declared, "The Nation asks for action, and action now." Over the next hundred days, he unleashed his proposals on Congress.

Roosevelt and Howe were so consumed with action that they never fully settled into the White House. Eleanor took charge of moving Howe into the Lincoln Bedroom, where he lived through most of Roosevelt's first term. But settling was not their way. Instead, the White House became the locus of an unprecedented level of activity, productivity, and creativity.

The President made sure that his influence was felt throughout the administration, as he placed key advisors strategically in positions of power. He placed Moley as an assistant to Cordell Hull at the State Department; Rex Tugwell as an aide to agriculture secretary Henry Wallace; Robert Jackson, whose support for Roosevelt had drawn him into Democratic politics, in the Justice Department; Lewis Douglas, a former conservative member of Congress, as his budget director; and General Hugh Johnson to lead the National Recovery Administration. When Roosevelt made requests of different departments, as he did throughout the first one hundred days as well as the remainder of his term, he made sure that one or more trusted advisors were involved in fulfilling them.

Roosevelt likened himself to the "captain" or "quarterback," who ran plays and made adjustments as game conditions changed.[11] He delegated substantial responsibility to his staff and advisors, and he generally (but not always) left the details to them.

Yet, if Franklin were the captain or quarterback, there was little doubt that the coach was Louis Howe. Just as with the campaign, every piece of important business went through Howe. He was the first person whom Roosevelt saw in the morning and the last person he saw at night, and he had the first and last words with both the President and his staff. He did not do substance, but he knew the President's temperament and needs better than anyone else, including Eleanor. Howe was the gatekeeper who spoke to Franklin and even got to work closely with the President. As a result, he brought order to the chaos of the Roosevelt White House. As Ray Moley recalled, "We stood in the city of Washington on March 4th like a handful of marauders in hostile territory."[12] It was Howe's job to keep them from destroying what they had been sent to save.

Inspired by the nation's desperation and both his and Wilson's flurry of activities at the outset of each other's gubernatorial turns, Roosevelt's first one hundred days were marked not just by the accomplishments but by Roosevelt's own management style of delegating different tasks to different advisors. It was a style reminiscent of both Lincoln and Teddy Roosevelt, both of whom ignored hierarchy within their own administration to get the results they wanted. Like them, Roosevelt went directly to the people he knew could get the job done. The result was an array of overlapping, sometimes conflicting legislation, in the areas of relief, recovery, and reform, whose purpose was to extend the progressivism.

Speed and substance, not consistency or efficiency, were the order of the day. Moley later said that Roosevelt had no coherent plan during the first hundred days; to think that he did was to make the mistake "to believe the accumulation of stuffed snakes, baseball pictures, school flags, old tennis shoes, carpenter's tools, geography books and chemistry sets in a boy's bedroom could have been put there by an interior decorator."[13]

As the dust settled after Roosevelt's first hundred days in office, the results were historic—the enactment of fifteen landmark bills, a larger number than any administration in history had gotten through Congress in the same amount of time. The laws reflected Franklin's vision of the presidency as both "a place of moral leadership" and an engine for compromise. The combination was essential, in Franklin's view, for solving the national depression. Chiding Eleanor, he once told her, "You'll never be a good politician. You are too impatient."[14] As the quarterback, Franklin recognized that change was not possible without educating the public on the need for change and keeping it invested in the success of his administration.

Yet he also believed that a compromise was better than nothing at all. Eleanor was eager to improve the world as much and as fast as possible, while Franklin learned from Teddy and his own experiences that, as president, he had to take great care not to get too far ahead of the general electorate. He could command only so long as the public continued to invest in the promise and substance of the New Deal.

Contrary to critics, Roosevelt's New Deal was not a socialist's or communist's dream. Anyone who understood politics understood that socialists and communists were near opposites, with the former believing that citizens should share economic resources equally and the latter believing that the government should own all property and economic resources. In the one, government controls everything, while in the other the public (supposedly) does.

Far from being either one of these, Roosevelt was not even ultra-liberal, at least judging by today's standards. In his first one hundred days, he consistently zigged toward the conservative. He pleased conservatives to no end through several actions—adopting Hoover's plan for a bank holiday; placing the young, brilliant conservative Lewis Douglas in charge of the economic program; seeking Congress's approval to give him the power to reduce both veterans' benefits and government employees' salaries; and ending the gold standard (to undo the harmful effects of too many people hoarding gold during the depression) and the deflation that had taken hold during Hoover's term. For the most part, his administration's actions produced the desired effects—depositors deposited their cash and gold, which triggered a rise in prices, and the expectations of further increases in prices prompted people no longer to hoard their money and to purchase goods instead. The higher demand fueled production. When there was resistance in the Senate to giving him such authority, Roosevelt astutely cut a deal—not allowing the Senate to vote on a popular proposal to legalize weak beer until it approved his economic proposals.

On financial matters, Roosevelt's Brain Trust—the modern equivalent of the kitchen cabinet, which Jackson had made famous—was his principal sounding board that oversaw the details of the legislation championed by the administration. He intended, for example, to issue two proclamations on the day of his inauguration, and he directed Moley and Tugwell to work out the details of legislation giving authority to the President in declaring bank holidays and other matters. Perkins advised Roosevelt on public works projects and labor reform, to which Franklin largely deferred. If compromises were to be made, Franklin made them, and he expected his staff to follow up accordingly.

Roosevelt's first hundred days were a blanket rejection of Hoover's "three demands" or "declarations," insisting that Roosevelt not do anything that entailed "first, inflation of the currency; second, failure to balance the budget; third, prospective projects which will overtax the borrowing power of the Government."[15] While the national economy began to rebound, Hoover and his allies relished every misstep of the Roosevelt administration and never relented in their belief that Hoover, not Roosevelt, had the right ideas to combat the depression,

particularly in resisting and curbing government growth and in rely-
ing on the private sector and charity to save the national economy.
They did not root for Roosevelt to fail; rather, they expected him to
fail, spectacularly. When Congress approved all fifteen of the administration's proposals in its first hundred days, they just got shriller.

The enactment of the fifteen bills reflected Roosevelt's mastery of
the legislative process. A closer look at several of his actions reveals
how he worked with key members of his staff and Congress to do
what he believed he had been elected to do.

On the morning of the inauguration, Roosevelt asked Attorney
General Cummings to research whether the dormant provisions of
the Trading with the Enemy Act could be used as a basis for his ordering a bank holiday. He asked incoming treasury secretary
Woodin to work with Raymond Moley to draft emergency legislation permitting the banks to reopen in orderly fashion, later known
as the Emergency Banking Act.[16] On Sunday, Roosevelt met with his
cabinet to review the two actions. At eleven in the evening of March
5, Roosevelt issued a proclamation recalling Congress back into session at noon on March 9. By that time, the speaker of the house, at
Roosevelt's urging, had requested the House vote on a bill that had
not yet been drafted but which the chair of the Banking Committee
read from a typewritten draft handed to him. Before he finished
reading, there were calls for a vote. House leadership agreed to hold
the vote without debate, and the House, by voice vote, unanimously
approved the bill without it. When the Senate convened to consider
the bill, it had been formally drafted and copies were made available
for senators who wished to read it. With little debate, the majority
voted down requests for amendments and approved the bill 73–7, the
opposition coming from progressives, who believed the bill did not
go far enough in asserting federal control of the banking industry.

From its beginning to the moment Roosevelt signed the bill, the
entire lawmaking process to authorize Roosevelt to proclaim, as he
did, a bank holiday had taken six hours. Under regulations drafted
by the treasury secretary with the help of Moley and approved by the
President, banks wishing to reopen needed a license approved by the
secretary of the treasury. Within a month, eight out of every ten

banks reopened with the approval of the treasury secretary's formal approval. Approving the reopening of the largest bank on the west coast, the Bank of America, took slightly longer, as Roosevelt, after consulting with the treasury secretary and his economic advisor Moley, instructed the secretary to call on the director of the Federal Reserve in San Francisco to either agree to open the bank or take responsibility for keeping it closed. When the treasury secretary spoke with the director, John Calkins, the two had harsh words. But when the secretary asked Calkins whether he would accept responsibility for keeping the bank closed, Calkins declined. "Well then," Woodin said, "the bank will open," and it did.[17]

Next, Roosevelt signed the Emergency Banking Act and then asked congressional leaders to agree to cut the salaries of government workers and veterans' benefits, which consumed a fourth of the federal budget. They agreed, and Roosevelt announced on March 10 his request for Congress to approve a bill giving him the authority to balance the federal budget. After two hours of heated debate, the House approved the bill, 266–138, with Republican senators giving Roosevelt the majority he needed for the bill's approval.

Roosevelt kept the pressure on Congress, which responded by eventually approving a series of bills his team drafted to protect mortgages, farmers' income, and federal regulation of securities. It enacted the Agricultural Adjustment Act (shaped by Henry Wallace, among others), and it supported Roosevelt's push of inflationary policy. It enacted the National Industrial Recovery Act (shaped by Frances Perkins, among others), which gave the administration the power to set wages and hours. It approved the creation of the Tennessee Valley Authority, the Civilian Conservation Corps, the Federal Emergency Relief Agency, the Homeowners' Loan Corporation and Farm Credit Association; dropping the gold standard; and enacting the Glass-Steagall Act (separating investment and commercial banking, the combination of which was, for many, a major problem causing the depression), the Railroad Construction Act, and the National Recovery Act and public works projects, which Frances Perkins and her team at the Department of Labor envisioned and administered. Roosevelt managed to include the largest appropriations bill yet in American

history, including billions of dollars in public works appropriated to
the Public Works Administration.

While Howe knew Franklin was busy orchestrating the first hundred days, he put Eleanor to work as well. In May 1933, he asked her
to take him on a drive, though he did not explain the purpose. As
they neared the encampment of bonus marchers near Fort Hill, he
asked her to leave the car and walk among the veterans. For more
than an hour, as Howe dozed in the car, Eleanor toured the camp,
talked with numerous veterans, sang World War I songs, and assured
them that she understood their frustration at not receiving the bonuses they had been promised at the end of the war. It was the first
time that Eleanor acted as the White House's emissary. It was not lost
on anyone, especially Franklin, Howe, and Eleanor, that the veterans
cheered her remarks.

IV

Not everything went as planned during the first hundred days. To
spur recovery, Franklin managed fallout from his delegations, failed
plans, and incompetent, disloyal, or unhelpful aides. In working for
Wilson and as governor, he often had to deal with similar problems,
but as president, they came faster and in greater numbers and guises.

What many young lawyers who were flocking to Washington
lacked in experience, they made up for with zeal. As Sherwood Anderson recalled after a visit to the Agriculture Department in the
early days of the Roosevelt presidency, "You cannot be with [old
friends now in the administration] without a feeling of the entire sincerity of many of these men."[18] One administrator complained, "A
plague of young lawyers settled on Washington. They all claimed to
be friends of somebody or other and mostly of Felix Frankfurter and
Jerome Frank. They floated airily into offices, took desks, asked for
papers and found no end of things to be busy about. I never found
out why they came, what they did or why they left."[19]

Partisans on both sides recognized Frankfurter's outsized influence, "a kind of alderman-at-large for the better element," one

writer observed. General Hugh Johnson, a member of the Brain Trust who drafted speeches for Roosevelt and drafted plans for the New Deal, saw Frankfurter as "the most influential single individual in the United States."[20] Diminutive, brilliant, ambitious, and progressive, Frankfurter would have liked the description. (Indeed, he cultivated good press whenever he could.)

After graduating first in his class at Harvard Law School, Frankfurter served in three administrations—first as an assistant to Henry Stimson when he was U.S. attorney in the administration of Teddy Roosevelt, then as a law officer in the Bureau of Insular Affairs under Stimson in the Taft administration, and in that same office as well as a labor relations expert under the secretary of war in the Wilson administration. In 1914, he joined the faculty of Harvard Law School, where he taught classes in constitutional law. Over the next few decades, he advocated for various liberal causes, defended judicial restraint, advised Democratic politicians, and cultivated a network of friends and former students, including the thirty-second president of the United States.

Frankfurter's constant stream of letters peppered Roosevelt with suggestions regarding policy, appraisals of possible nominees to important governmental offices including the courts, recommendations regarding policy and other matters passed on from other experts, critiques of Supreme Court decisions, news from abroad, and recommendations for many of his former students in positions throughout the administration, including Dean Acheson as undersecretary of the treasury and the team of Benjamin Cohen, Tommy Corcoran, and James Landis, who helped to draft the nation's first securities law, the Truth in Securities Act in 1933. Corcoran and Cohen became known as the Gold Dust Twins based on a popular 1930 advertisement for soap that advised housewives "to let the Gold Dust Twins do your work." Over the next several years, the two worked closely with Roosevelt to address a wide range of economic and social problems.

The name "Gold Dust Twins" had also been associated with two economists, George Warren and Frank Pearson, whose work persuaded Roosevelt that if the government bought gold at increasing prices, not only would the country win a greater share of the world's trade, but domestic commodity prices would soar as the gold value of the dollar fell. Devaluing the dollar would, they argued, restore the balance between the prices of consumer goods and raw materials. Their larger ambition, New Deal historian William Leuchtenberg explained, "was to achieve a commodity dollar—one which would have a constant buying power for all commodities—by keying the dollar to the price index through manipulating the gold content."[21]

Roosevelt viewed opposition to the plan as disloyal and favored by bankers and Wall Street financiers who wanted the administration to fail. He wrote Wilson's former chief of staff Colonel House that "the real truth [is] that a financial element in the larger centers has owned the Government since the days of Andrew Jackson—and I am not wholly excepting the administration of W.W. The country is going through a repetition of Jackson's fight with the Bank of the United States—only on a far bigger and broader basis."[22] Jackson had waged that battle because he believed the National Bank, enacted as the depository of federal tax dollars and empowered to make loans, was corrupt and beholden to big businesses determined to make profits at the expense of the common man.

Roosevelt followed Jackson's policy of dismissing administration officials who supported the National Bank by terminating financial advisors who opposed his policy of buying gold, including not just James Warburg and his old Harvard professor Oliver Sprague, but also Dean Acheson, who was enforcing the policy despite his disagreement with it. It would not be the only administration policy that failed to work.

As someone who had studied and practiced law and surrounded himself with top-notch lawyers and legal scholars, Franklin understood that the federal courts still had a say about the major pieces of the New Deal. To ensure the courts made the right decisions, he initially asked Felix Frankfurter to serve as his solicitor general, the administration's advocate before the Supreme Court. Frankfurter declined. (He did not hide his ambition to be appointed to the Supreme Court.) In his place, Roosevelt named James Biggs, one of the worst appointments he ever made. Often called "the tenth justice" because

of the close working relationship between him and the Court, the solicitor general was charged with the responsibility of defending the
administration's policies. Biggs was an ardent progressive, whom
Franklin knew from his service to Wilson's attorney general as a special prosecutor and assistant.

Yet the appointment was a surprise: Most New Dealers did not
know Biggs, though he was known among those who had worked
in the Wilson administration. Once on the job, he quickly failed to
distinguish himself, losing ten of the seventeen cases he argued before the Supreme Court. The losses were all major defeats for the
New Deal.

By the end of Biggs's first—and only—term as solicitor general,
in 1935, then Associate Justice Harlan Fiske Stone, who had been
dean of Columbia Law School when Roosevelt was a student, said,
"Biggs was not fit to argue a cow case before a justice of the peace, unless the cow was fatally sick."[23] Years later, Bill Clinton's solicitor
general, Seth Waxman, recounted that the "justices sent word infor-
mally to Roosevelt that Biggs should not be permitted to argue any
case the United States hoped to win. Attorney General Homer Cummings stepped in to ensure that important cases would be handled
by attorneys outside the Solicitor General's office. By the time a more
capable successor took office, the New Deal was in deep legal trouble."[24] Biggs returned to North Carolina after resigning in disgrace
on March 14, 1935.

Three days later, Roosevelt named a replacement—Stanley Reed.
Hoover had named him general counsel in December 1932 to restore
order at the Reconstruction Finance Corporation after it had earned
Congress's ire by failing to comply with its directives to publicize the
names of companies that it had been helping to remain economically
viable. Reed had earned Roosevelt's respect and gratitude when he
successfully took charge of implementing the administration's policy
in October 1933 to purchase gold above market prices to drive down
the value of the dollar and then helped Attorney General Homer
Cummings to defend before the Supreme Court the decision of the
United States to void all public and private contracts permitting re-
demption in gold.

Though the Court ruled against the administration, it decided that the government did not have to pay any damages since none of the contract holders had been damaged. Reed's job was now playing catch-up in the cases pending and coming before the Court involving constitutional challenges to various aspects of the New Deal.

Despite the administration's investment in the gold buying plan, it failed miserably. Wholesale commodity prices fell in November and December, and farm prices fell even further. By the beginning of 1934, the President had abandoned the plan altogether. While Franklin wondered aloud that "it was funny how sometimes [commodity and farm prices] seemed to go against all the rules," economists around the world declared the plan a bust. John Maynard Keynes called the theories underlying the plan "puerile," said the books setting forth the theories would have been rejected as silly even if proffered by an undergraduate, and observed that the dollar's gyrations "looked to me more like a gold standard on the booze than the managed currency of my dreams."[25]

Roosevelt had told the American people more than once that he would "try anything" and some plans would fail, but that it was better to try something than nothing at all. Yet, in following the advice of the Gold Dust Twins, Roosevelt lost precious time in pushing other solutions, such as investing in public works more.

Nor was this the only failed New Deal plan. Despite its great promise, the National Recovery Act was not working out as intended. It was the product of several advisors with competing views and consisted of two main provisions. The first proposed cooperation among trade groups, with codes of fair compensation aimed at curbing overproduction by loosening antitrust regulation (ironically, initially put into place in Teddy Roosevelt's administration). The second established a Public Works Administration, which was tasked with financing nationwide infrastructure projects that would modernize the national economy and reduce unemployment. Moley, who would later leave the administration after a falling out with Roosevelt, described the act as "a thorough hodge-podge of provisions" and as "a confused, two-headed experiment."[26] Moley admired Roosevelt and worked tirelessly for him in his first term, but he was, at heart,

a conservative, whose patience with the liberal turn of the administration eventually ran out.

Roosevelt had hoped that General Hugh Johnson would whip the
program into shape, but the failure of the Public Works Administration to provide economic stimulus doomed the National Recovery
Act's objectives from the start. Rather than blame the act itself, Roosevelt blamed Johnson. If Roosevelt could or did not discard programs
that were failing, he discarded the people running them. Roosevelt
did not care about the turnover; positive results were the only things
that mattered.

In the last two years of his first term, the bill came due. First, several allies within the administration resigned in protest over
Roosevelt's insistence on expanding the scope of federal regulation.
Among the more prominent was Lewis Douglas, who resigned in
1935 because of Roosevelt's persistent failure to achieve (and apparent
indifference to) a balanced budget. By the next year, Moley resigned
in protest over what he perceived to be the administration's radical
shift to consolidating federal authority over the economy and other
matters and to vast overregulation.

Meanwhile, several prominent conservative Democrats abandoned their support for Roosevelt's New Deal, including Al Smith,
who joined the American Liberty League, begun by the prominent
du Pont family. At the time, Roosevelt observed, "All the big guns
have started shooting—Al Smith, John W. Davis, James W. Wads-
worth, du Pont, Shouse, etc. Their organization has already been
labeled the I CAN'T TAKE IT CLUB."[27] Not surprisingly, Hoover
joined the bandwagon of critics, deriding the New Deal as a "challenge to liberty."[28]

In his Fireside Chat at the end of September 1934, Roosevelt addressed critics who thought he had gone too far in the direction of
centralizing federal regulation of the economy. He declared, "In our
efforts for recovery we have avoided, on the one hand, the theory
that business should and must be taken over into an all-embracing
Government. We have avoided, on the other hand, the equally un-
tenable theory that it is an interference with liberty to offer
reasonable help when private enterprise is in need of help."[29]

As Louis Howe had hoped, the public heard Roosevelt and agreed with his message: In the midterm elections two months later, the Democratic Party gained thirteen seats in the House and nine in the Senate, giving them more than a two-thirds majority in each chamber. Historian Charles Beard described the elections as "thunder on the left." Hearing the same thunder, Roosevelt advisor Harry Hopkins said it showed that Roosevelt was able to get all he wanted—"a works program, social security, wages and hours, everything—now or never."[30]

V

While the administration continued to combat the depression and its aftermath through policy, it had to mount defenses of the key components of the New Deal, whose constitutionality was being repeatedly challenged in the Supreme Court. Nearly all the Court's members had been appointed by Republican presidents, and most of the justices, along with James McReynolds, whom Wilson had appointed, were making mincemeat of the New Deal. In 1933, Franklin Roosevelt did not know that he would become the first American president to complete a full term without making a single Supreme Court nomination. But, with each blow against the New Deal, the Court's conservative justices reminded the President that he was stuck with them.

Initially, that prospect had not bothered Roosevelt. In his first few days in office, he wanted to create bridges between his administration and the Court. He had Benjamin Cardozo, a Hoover appointee on the Court, swear in his cabinet. On his second day in office, Roosevelt was invited to accompany Frankfurter, who was going to pay a visit to the Court's eldest member, Oliver Wendell Holmes, Jr., whom Teddy Roosevelt had appointed in 1904. The visit went well.

Roosevelt had no power to change the attitudes of the Court's majority of hard-line conservatives whom Roosevelt and Cummings rightly suspected would strike down the New Deal when it came before them. They hoped that, as a political conservative, Reed had insights into how best to persuade the Court's hard-liners—James McReynolds, Willis Van Devanter, Pierce Butler, and George Sutherland, sometimes joined by Owen Roberts and Chief Justice Hughes—to leave the laws alone. But the Court was stacked against the New Deal.

Despite that, the administration managed to win its first two cases defending the progressive laws before the Court. In the first, *Home Building & Home v. Blaisdell*,[31] the Court upheld a Minnesota law that extended the time mortgagers had to redeem their mortgages. In *Nebbia v. New York*,[32] the Court upheld a New York law allowing the state to regulate the price of milk. In both cases, the Court was upholding progressive measures designed to dampen the devasting effects of the depression. *Nebbia* made New Dealers hopeful, since it adopted a more lenient test for assessing the constitutionality of state laws regulating the economy.

The administration lost, however, every one of the next ten cases involving challenges to the New Deal. The rulings were devasting— and not all by slim margins either. The first major blow came in January 1935, in a case called *Panama Refining Company v. Ryan*.[33] The specific law at issue was the provision of the National Industrial Recovery Act, passed in June 1933, vesting the President with the authority "to prohibit the transportation in interstate and foreign commerce petroleum . . . produced or withdrawn from storage in excess of the amount permitted . . . by any State law."

To add insult to injury, the Court issued three unanimous opinions striking down portions of the New Deal on May 27, 1935, a day that became known as Black Monday. In the most important of these, the Court ruled unanimously that the NIRA was unconstitutional because it exceeded the power given to Congress to regulate interstate commerce. In his opinion for the Court, Chief Justice Hughes argued that the act had given the federal government unlimited power and sanctioned a "completely centralized government."[34]

What soon followed were several back-channel communications from the justices urging Roosevelt to be more realistic. Privately, Justice Louis Brandeis, a Wilson appointee to the Court, told Cohen and Corcoran (who had clerked for Justice Holmes in 1926–27), that he thought Roosevelt "has been living in a fool's paradise" and directed them "to go back and tell the President that we're not going to let this government centralize everything. It's come to an end."[35]

Within two days, Frankfurter visited Roosevelt. He advised the President to bide his time before clashing with the Court. He suggested Roosevelt should allow the Court to make more adverse rulings and then come out in favor of a constitutional amendment authorizing the federal government to do what it had been doing.

Roosevelt could not hold his fire, however. On May 31, 1935, he held a news conference to protest the Court's striking down the National Recovery Act. He claimed that "the implications of this decision are much more important than any decision probably since Dred Scott," which had upheld the constitutional entitlement of slave owners to keep their slaves without any federal interference. Disputing Hughes's suggestion in his opinion that no national crisis had given the government the authority "to enlarge constitutional power," Roosevelt pointed out that even more extreme laws had been enacted (and upheld) during the First World War. He stressed that the crucial issue was how to view the "interstate commerce clause," which empowered Congress to regulate commerce among the several states. He believed (as did the vast majority of New Deal lawyers) that the clause had to be understood and construed "in the light of present-day civilization" and not "in the horse-and-buggy age when the clause was written."[36]

The losses were hardly over. In yet another blow to progressive legislation, in its last decision published in 1936, the Supreme Court struck down a New York minimum wage law. This was yet again a decision justifying itself on the grounds that the law, in attempting to regulate wages, violated a fundamental right of the parties to make contracts free from any governmental interference or regulation. Significantly, Chief Justice Hughes dissented, as did Justices Stone, Brandeis, and Cardozo. Interior Secretary Harold Ickes wondered whether now the country would finally be outraged. Indeed, it was, as the decision angered both Democrats and Republicans, who approved as part of their party platform that same year a pledge declaring the decision flat wrong and requiring overruling.

In dissent, Justice Harlan Fiske Stone, appointed to the Court by President Coolidge in 1924, had declared that "it was not the job of the courts to resolve doubts about whether the remedy by wage reg-

A young Franklin with his mother Sara in New York, 1893.
Franklin D. Roosevelt Presidential Library and Museum.

Franklin's school portrait at Groton, aged 18. *Franklin D. Roosevelt Presidential Library and Museum.*

Portrait of Endicott Pea[...] headmaster of the Groton S[...] and mentor to Fra[...]

Franklin and Eleanor at
Hyde Park in 1906.
*Franklin D. Roosevelt
Presidential Library
and Museum.*

A family portrait with Franklin,
Eleanor, Anna, and James
at Hyde Park in 1908.
*Franklin D. Roosevelt
Presidential Library
and Museum.*

Press photo of assistant secretary
of the navy Franklin Roosevelt, 1913.
Library of Congress.

Flag Day celebration in Washington, D.C.,
Woodrow Wilson, William J. F
Josephus Daniels, Breckenridge
and William Phillips are pic
along with Franklin, who is on the far
Franklin D. Roosevelt Presia
Library and Mu

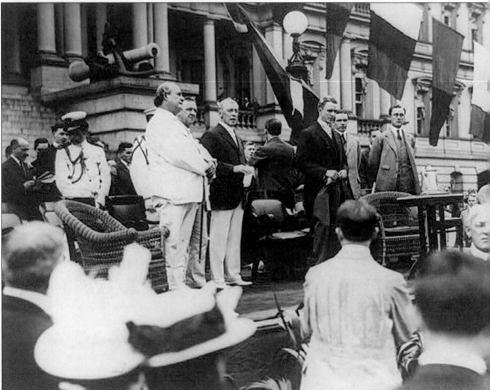

A rare picture of Franklin
and Teddy together.
Newspaper-printed photograph
of Franklin D. Roosevelt and
President Theodore Roosevelt
h William H. Van Benschoten
in center. Taken May 4, 1915
during the libel trial.
*National Archives and
Records Administration.*

klin with secretary
lover Missy LeHand
wife Eleanor in 1929.
*onal Archives and
rds Administration.*

Franklin with two boys (Hugh Love, Walter Carpenter, Jr.) in Warm Springs, Georgia, November 193
Franklin D. Roosevelt Presidential Library and Museum.

Franklin swimming in Warm Springs, October 1929. *National Archives and Records Administration.*

New York governor Franklin D. Roosevelt shakes hands with predecessor Al Smith in 1930.
Franklin D. Roosevelt Presidential Library and Museum.

President-elect Roosevelt rides with President Hoover to the inaugural ceremonies, March 4, 1933.
Franklin D. Roosevelt Presidential Library and Museum.

Portrait of Louis McHenry Howe, 1932.
*Franklin D. Roosevelt Presidential
Library and Museum.*

Louis McHenry Howe shaking
hands with Franklin.
*Franklin D. Roosevelt Presidential
Library and Museum.*

FDR delivering Fireside
Chat Number 6,
September 30, 1934.
*Franklin D. Roosevelt
Presidential
Library and Museum.*

Frances Perkins
and President
Franklin D. Roosevelt
sharing a light moment.
*Franklin D. Roosevelt
Presidential Library
and Museum.*

Eleanor casting her vote,
November 3, 1936 at Hyde Park.
*National Archives and Records
Administration.*

Franklin watches the parade
for his second inaugural from a
replica of Andrew Jackson's home,
the Hermitage, January 20, 1937.
*Franklin D. Roosevelt Presidential
Library and Museum.*

Franklin in his wheelchair
with Ruthie Bie, a daughter of
one of Hyde Park's caretakers,
and Franklin's dog Fala,
1941 at Hyde Park.
*National Archives and Records
Administration.*

Franklin with
Henry Morgenthau
and unknown man
at Warm Springs, Georgia.
*Franklin D. Roosevelt
Presidential Library
and Museum.*

Franklin with Winston Churchill
in Casablanca, Morocco, January 1943.
*Franklin D. Roosevelt Presidential
Library and Museum.*

Poster by James Montgomery Flagg, 1944.
*Franklin D. Roosevelt Presidential
Library and Museum;
gift of Joseph Jacobs.*

Joseph Stalin, FDR, and Winston Churchill at the Tehran Conference, Iran, November 29, 1943.
Franklin D. Roosevelt Presidential Library and Museum.

Lord Lothian, FDR, Winston Churchill, and Canadian prime minister Mackenzie King
at the Second Quebec Conference, September 1944.
Franklin D. Roosevelt Presidential Library and Museum.

Eleanor with Clementine Churchill during a radio broadcast at the Second Quebec Conference.
Franklin D. Roosevelt Presidential Library and Museum.

Winston Churchill, FDR, and Joseph Stalin at the Yalta Conference,
Livadia Palace, Yalta, USSR, February 9, 1945.
Franklin D. Roosevelt Presidential Library and Museum.

The last known photograph of FDR, taken the day before he died in Warm Springs, Georgia, April 11, 19
The photo was taken by Nicholas Robbins to aid Elizabeth Shoumatoff's portrait.
Franklin D. Roosevelt Presidential Library and Museum.

ulation is efficacious as many believe, or is better than some other, or is better than even that blind operation of uncontrolled economic forces. The legislature must be free to choose unless government is to be rendered impotent." In short, he said, "governance" was for Congress not the Court.[37] The New Deal's losses before the Court did more than delight Roosevelt's conservative critics. It motivated them to attack the New Deal even more.

During his battle with the Supreme Court, Franklin found solace from two sources. The first was his cousin Margaret "Daisy" Suckley, with whom he had spent some time recovering in Hyde Park after the Court struck down the National Industrial Recovery Act, which had given the President the power to regulate certain industries. Knowing Franklin was fighting hard to salvage the New Deal, she urged him not to let the opposition "get you angry by what they say in the papers! It takes half the wind out of their sails if you don't answer back." She thought that the public "expect[ed] just about perfection of you, and don't want you even to be capable of losing your temper!" She knew, "it's pretty hard on you," but reassured him that "you are so right about not answering attacks no matter how provoking." She had struck the right chord, as he wrote back, "You alone have known that I was a bit 'down cast' these past weeks. I couldn't let anyone else know it—but somehow I seem to tell you all those things and what I don't happen to tell you, you seem to know anyway!"[38]

Franklin took further solace from President Lincoln. He took to heart Lincoln's reflections during the darkest days of the Civil War when Lincoln vowed to himself "to do the best I know how, the very best that I can; and I mean to keep doing it until the end. If the end brings me out all right, what is said against me will not amount to anything. If the end brings me out all wrong, then angels swearing I was right would make no difference." Roosevelt told Daisey that he believed that Lincoln, like himself, "no matter how philosophic he was in public," was hurt by the attacks.[39] Yet, Roosevelt reminded himself, Lincoln "had kept his peace—that was and is the great lesson." Roosevelt later shared the same sentiment with Tugwell: "You won't always be right, but you mustn't suffer from being wrong. That's what kills people like us."[40]

On June 4, 1935, Roosevelt struck back with a vengeance. He sent a message to Congress listing nine new laws that he told them he must get approved that session. The message was the opening act of what many called the Second New Deal. While he got nearly everything he wanted from Congress, it was not without a series of fights. In the period from June through August, he won congressional approval for five new laws, including, most importantly, the Social Security Act, which he signed into law on August 14, 1935. Though he had not initially cared about labor's need for collective bargaining, Frances Perkins had carefully brought him along. Roosevelt had not thought of the law, or taken any efforts to frame it, but rather, as she recalled, "all the credit for [the National Labor Relations Act] belongs to [New York Senator Robert] Wagner," who had been advocating workers' right for years.[41] After the Senate passed Wagner's bill in mid-May, Roosevelt remained lukewarm to the measure, which rejected traditional objections to collective bargaining and strikes as violations of antitrust laws opposing restraint of trade. With Perkins steadfastly urging he do so, Roosevelt signed it into law on July 5, 1935.

He spent most of the rest of the summer—and a lot of his political capital and goodwill as president—badgering Congress to enact a tax bill raising the rates on corporations and the wealthy and a bill limiting holding companies to no more than one operating company and subsidiary, except if the newly established Securities and Exchange Commission determined that the holding company could not stand alone or that it was not so large as to endanger local companies in the same business. Roosevelt got the bills he wanted, but at the cost of making it easier for a conservative coalition in opposition to form, widening the breach between his administration and the business community, and squandering some goodwill of many of his fellow Democrats.

The Supreme Court losses were among Roosevelt's biggest disappointments during his first term. He waited in vain for a vacancy to arise, but none did, making him the first president in American history to complete a full term without at least one Supreme Court vacancy to fill. He even had a candidate in mind if one did, Senate Majority Leader Joseph Robinson. But without a vacancy, Roosevelt felt frustrated. Attorney General Cummings did not mince words when he said, "Mr. President, they mean to destroy us.... We will have to find a way to get rid of the present membership of the Supreme Court."[42] Roosevelt agreed, and he asked Cummings to develop a plan to ensure more favorable rulings from the Court. Getting rid of Biggs was one thing, but throughout the next election cycle he began exploring other options, which he kept under wraps until (as they all expected) he won reelection in 1936.

VI

It was not just the Supreme Court that frustrated Roosevelt. He came into the presidency with a longstanding, deep-seated interest in foreign affairs, intensified during his seven years helping to coordinate the war effort during the First World War. Having witnessed Wilson's grand plans for world peace crash and burn, he was no idealist in foreign affairs. Yet he relished the President's role on the world stage and was aware of serious problems unfolding in Europe. While Roosevelt was battling for the New Deal, Adolph Hitler, the leader of the Nazi Party, became chancellor of Germany in 1933; and there was no doubt, for Roosevelt and other leaders, that Hitler's ascent meant trouble for the world, given his intense hatred of the Jewish people and the sanctions Germany had to endure after the First World War, including massive war debts. Within a month of Hitler's ascent, the Nazis burned down the German parliament's building and then blamed Communists as the culprits. As Roosevelt's first hundred days were beginning, Hitler launched a national boycott of Jewish businesses and Jews in the professions. With other leaders—Joseph Stalin in Russia, Benito Mussolini in Italy, and Japan's Emperor Hirohito—investing heavily in their military, it was hardly naïve to think, as Roosevelt did, that it was just a matter of time before another world war erupted.

Yet, if it seemed as if foreign affairs were not Roosevelt's priority during his first few years in the White House, this was because it was not. Pragmatist that he was, Roosevelt followed the isolationist line that Congress (and much of the public) demanded he follow in his first term. The result was that Roosevelt found himself straddling a tightrope. On one side, Secretary of State Cordell Hull griped that Roosevelt did not keep him in the loop with his periodic meetings with envoys, ambassadors, and other world leaders who occasionally visited the White House. And, on the other, European leaders were pushing Roosevelt for more American help, something he could not provide without congressional approval.

In the meantime, Hull's opening speech at the London Economic Conference in mid-July 1933 unintentionally caused a stir when he suggested that nations had to put the welfare of the world ahead of their own self-interest and that any country that failed to provide aid to the "distressed" in other countries "will merit the execration of mankind."[43] These were hardly the comforting words of isolationism. When Roosevelt sent Moley to address these concerns, his "reception in London was surpassed only by those given to kings," Hull noted with jealousy.[44] When Roosevelt declared later that summer that he opposed any international agreement to fix exchange rates as a way to stabilize the international economy, it brought the conference to an end.

Hull blamed Moley for Roosevelt's decision dooming the conference and undermining his authority by bypassing him to talk with the President and other international leaders about foreign affairs. "That piss-ant Moley," Hull complained. "Here he curled up at my feet and let me stroke his head like a hunting dog, and then he goes and bites me in the ass!"[45] He demanded Roosevelt dismiss Moley and communicate directly only with him. Forced to choose between Moley and Hull, Roosevelt felt he had no choice. When he transferred Moley to another department, Moley was displeased.

In June 1936, the break between the two finally came: In a small gathering at the White House, Roosevelt began taunting Moley about his conservatism, Moley replied sharply, and the two shocked the small crowd of insiders with the angry quarrel that followed. Moley resigned soon afterward. Roosevelt lost one of his most loyal lieutenants, but he did not miss Moley's frequent dissents. Nor, apparently, did the State Department, where after his departure "there has been a unanimous sigh," reported Sumner Welles, the undersecretary.[46]

While it was in Roosevelt's nature to keep his own counsel, he begrudgingly began having lunch at least once a week with Hull, both to mend their relations and ensure Hull followed his lead in walking the tightrope of being isolationist while doing whatever he could, behind the scenes and through intermediaries, to learn about the growing discord in Europe and the war that he and other Wilsonians knew was coming.

Because of his experiences in the Naval Department during the First World War, Roosevelt felt that he did not need much help on matters of foreign affairs. He knew how bad things could get but also what he needed to do to remain in power. He was aware of the national conviction that Wilson had mistakenly named Germany as the primary reason for the First World War and thus did not want to get ahead of unfolding events abroad or the national opposition to war.

With news of growing discord and violence in Europe, many Americans did not want any part of it. In the first half of 1935, antiwar protests became popular, fueled in part by the awareness of the precious costs the nation had had to endure because of the First World War. Roosevelt's instincts were not to sit on the sidelines. But with the next presidential election just around the corner, Roosevelt understood that he could not risk alienating isolationists in his own party.

Roosevelt expressed his concerns about both his and the country's predicament to Edward House, known by the honorific Colonel (though he had no military experience) and as Wilson's closest advisor. In 1935, he confided to House that he was "greatly disturbed by events on the other side—perhaps more than I should be." He told House he often pondered how "the weight of America could be thrown into the scale of peace and of stopping the armament race." He ran various ideas by House, who agreed that "a blockade would fall under the Executive's power after establishment of the fact."[47] Other advisors buried the idea, however.

In 1935, Franklin relented to public pressure to propose that Congress enact a neutrality law that prohibited shipment of munitions to warring nations. Though Roosevelt withdrew his proposal because it did not go far enough in ensuring genuine impartial neutrality, public pressure intensified for Roosevelt and Congress to do something. While he succeeded in getting Congress to give him some discretion to sanction Italy, which had invaded Ethiopia, he agreed to sign a neutrality law that effectively barred any United States involvement in any military actions abroad.

The best he could was to monitor events. Having learned German as a youth and used it while he was assistant secretary of the navy, Roosevelt listened to Hitler's speeches, which he had translated for Howe and Moley, and he continued to work behind the scenes to help give England support in its stand against Germany.

VII

For much of Roosevelt's first term, Louis Howe worried that the more powerful Roosevelt got, the more he might be disposed to listen less to him and more to the many others clamoring for his attention. But what made matters much worse for Howe was that he was dying. As early as 1935, his health had deteriorated to such an extent that he could not leave his bedroom in the White House. As the year wore on, his respiratory and heart problems and his stamina worsened.

Yet Roosevelt still relied on his advice, and Howe never quit badgering him, continuing until the end to complain of Roosevelt's pigheadedness to his face. When he could no longer do so easily, he sent subordinates to Roosevelt's office with the instructions "Tell the president to go to hell." Once, when Roosevelt left an exasperated Howe to go for a swim, Howe called after him, "I hope to God you drown!" Eleanor, devoted more to him than even Howe's own wife, equipped his bedroom with an oxygen tent, though he continued to confound everyone by loudly asking for cigarettes and smoking when he could.

By August 1935, his health had gotten so bad that he was moved to the naval hospital, where his wife and the Roosevelts regularly visited him. One reporter granted access to him at this stage reported that "as he talked, with dry twists of humor, the hospital atmosphere faded away. Howe, in his pajamas gaily striped, made it clear that there was the busy office of the President's Number One Secretary." He ordered newspapers and reports regularly brought to him, and he continued to draw organizational charts, draft political tracts, and suggest topics for campaign speeches. Among his last words were "Franklin is on his own now."[48] On April 18, Louis Howe died.

Three days later, Roosevelt arranged for a state funeral to be held in the East Room of the White House. Franklin and Eleanor accompanied the body to Howe's home in Massachusetts, where Howe was buried. The *New York Times* reported that Franklin "appeared oblivious to everything around him, both during the service and when he returned to his car."[49] Both Eleanor and Franklin never stopped expressing gratitude for Howe's impact on their lives. Franklin called him the "master mind" of the 1932 and 1936 presidential campaigns. Eleanor later said that Howe was one of the seven most impactful people in her life.

Franklin and Eleanor knew that, with Howe's passing, the only person who had successfully mediated between the two of them was no longer there to make peace between them. With his passing, there was no one to take his place. Historian Blanche Wiesen Cook wrote that Howe "was the one friend who had consistently served their partnership...no one else spoke the kind of blunt truth to power they both relied upon. [Howe] had considered ER essential to FDR's success."[50] After Howe's death, Cook wrote, "communication grew harder for each of them," and "once on their own, ER and FDR began to fly apart."[51] Years later, Eleanor said, "For one reason or another, no one quite filled the void.... There are not many men in this world whose personal ambition is to accomplish things for someone else, and it was some time before a friendship with Harry Hopkins...again brought Franklin some of the same satisfaction he had known with Louis Howe."[52]

VIII

A new set of advisors came into prominence in the White House and the 1936 campaign, including former journalist Stanley High, whom Sam Rosenman described as the best phrasemaker he had ever worked with. The Gold Dust Twins, Cohen and Corcoran, had come aboard, bringing with them remarkable expertise in both drafting legislation (a skill largely missing in the first configuration of the Brain Trust) and lobbying bills through Congress. Other legal and economic talent rose to prominence, including New York lawyer Robert Jackson, who had joined the administration in 1934 as assistant general counsel in the Treasury Department's Bureau of Internal Revenue, the predecessor to the Internal Revenue Service, and whom Roosevelt moved to assistant attorney general in charge of the Tax Division in the Justice Department in 1936, and William O. Douglas, a brilliant, irascible Yale Law School business law expert, whom Roosevelt appointed to the Securities and Exchange Commission in 1936.

Yet, before he died, Howe and Farley had put the infrastructure of the President's reelection campaign into place. They had understood that the coalition that had brought Roosevelt to the White House no longer held together, as Roosevelt had alienated both the business community and conservatives.

This time around, it was a different coalition consisting of independents (Howe had founded A Good Neighbor League as a model for international accord but also to recruit independents interested in helping the campaign), organized labor, Catholics, Jews, and the growing numbers of urban Democrats. African Americans remained loyal to the party of Lincoln, especially because Roosevelt resisted backing any civil rights legislation and New Deal programs, such as the National Recovery Act, were not helping them. Roosevelt still won 29 percent of the African American vote, supported by the relief New Deal programs provided and the administration's appointing historic numbers of African Americans to federal offices.

Roosevelt's 1936 campaign pushed two themes: The first was its continued attacks on Hoover and his policies. It was hard to argue that most people were better off under Hoover than they were under Roosevelt. The other theme was Roosevelt's campaigning as the leader of the nation not a political party. He mentioned the Democratic party by name no more than three times during the campaign.

Within the party, no one appeared to be a serious threat. Huey Long, the popular governor of Louisiana, had begun mounting a campaign to unseat Roosevelt from the left, promising redistribution of wealth and other, more liberal policies than Roosevelt had supported. But, on September 8, 1935, a Baton Rouge physician assassinated Long. The reason has never been clear; even Long said when struck, "I wonder why he shot me." Farley said he believed "Roosevelt would have lost if Long had lived and been a candidate."[53]

John Nance Garner agreed to continue as vice president, despite his quip to Roosevelt and Tugwell that "the vice presidency is not worth a bucket of warm spit."[54] Yet Garner took the job not once but twice, reflecting not only his devotion to public service but also because he considered himself a moderating force on Roosevelt. His presence on the ticket kept the great state of Texas in the Democrats' column.

Roosevelt had his not-so-secret weapon, too, Eleanor. As first lady, she had set records for both the number of letters she was writing and traveling more than four thousand miles as the President's surrogate. The ample news coverage of her speeches, visits with veterans and other constituencies, articles, and engaging, sympathetic smile was a boon to Franklin's presidency. She was a bridge between the President and groups he otherwise might have ignored. She routinely met with Walter White, the leader of the National Association for the Advancement of Colored People, to keep him posted on what the President was doing (particularly in the realm of civil rights) and to solicit his views on social, economic, and racial problems continuing to confront the country. She embodied the campaign's chief slogan, "Four Years Ago and Now," which relentlessly contrasted the differences between life now, with its sunnier, more hopeful, can-do orientation, and four years ago under Hoover.

From the outset of 1936, Roosevelt was in campaign mode. Rather than model his campaign on those of Wilson or Roosevelt, he again harkened back to Jackson. In a speech honoring Jackson on January 8, Roosevelt said Jackson had faced the same kind of issue he was addressing, namely, "the right of the average man and woman to lead a finer, a better and happier life."[55]

Jackson had built all three of his presidential campaigns on his commitment to fight for the "common man," who was being gouged by the banks and big business. Roosevelt, drawing on an argument first made by Jackson, maintained that he was president of all the people, and thus he acted in their best interests, and that he, like Jackson, was engaged in a fight for "social justice." For Jackson, that meant understanding the Constitution as empowering the popular majority whose will he pledged to follow. Jackson's perceived radicalism, Roosevelt said, exposed him, as it did Roosevelt, to "relentless hatred.... But the people of his day were not deceived. They loved him for the enemies he had made."

When he spoke of Jackson, Roosevelt sounded as if he were speaking of himself, when he told the audience, "An overwhelming proportion of the material power of the Nation was arrayed against him. The great media for the dissemination of information and the molding of public opinion fought him. Musty reaction disapproved him. Hollow and outworn traditionalism shook a trembling finger at him. It seemed sometimes that all were against him—all but the people of the United States." Thus, Roosevelt said, history was repeating itself, as the government was devoted "to the recovery and well-being" of every citizen. Like Jackson, he was determined to protect popular democracy, which, he said, depended on spreading the truth and facts, which were often obscured by "the smoke screen of charges and countercharges."[56]

Roosevelt's speech did nothing to lower the overheated rhetoric blowing from the other side as well as some fellow Democrats. Al Smith proclaimed that Roosevelt had given up "the free fresh air of America" for "the foul breath of communistic Russia."[57] Eager to pile on, Republicans searched in vain for a candidate who could take the fight to Roosevelt. Instead, they chose Kansas governor Alf Landon, an affable political liberal who had been the only Republican governor reelected in the preceding election cycle. Landon agreed with much of the New Deal but objected to Roosevelt's increasing consolidation of power and disdain for the welfare of business. Landon proved to be a terrible speaker and worse campaigner, who was reluctant to leave his front porch. When he got the news that farmers' incomes had quadrupled under Roosevelt, corporate sales were improving steadily, and the *New York Times* Index of Business Activity had reached a historic high in 1936, Landon gave up campaigning any longer.

Roosevelt's victory in 1936 outdid his historic landslide win in 1932. The night before Election Day, Farley wrote to Franklin that he could expect to lose only two states. In fact, Landon only won Maine and Vermont, losing his home state of Kansas to Roosevelt. Roosevelt won the electoral vote, 523–8, the largest margin of victory in a presidential election and the largest number of electoral votes for an incumbent president until Ronald Reagan's 525 total in 1984. Roosevelt's coattails were even longer, as the party added four seats to its majority in the Senate (bringing the total to 76–22) and twenty-five more seats to its majority in the House.

The year did not end, however, without another devasting personal loss for the President. At the end of the year, Roosevelt set sail for Latin America, where he hoped both to recuperate from the election and have more than twenty countries to join him for a conference to sustain peace in the region. While in Buenos Aires, Roosevelt's bodyguard of eight years, August Adolph Gennerich, collapsed and died of a sudden heart attack.

Gus, as he was called, had been by Roosevelt's side since he was governor of New York and had shielded Roosevelt from the assassin who killed Mayor Cermak in Florida. A fixture in Roosevelt's inner circle, Roosevelt affectionately called him "my humanizer" and his "ambassador to the man in the streets."[58] Like Howe, Gus had served as a sounding board for both Roosevelts. And, as he had done for Howe, Franklin held a state funeral for Gus in the White House.

It was a reminder that Franklin was, as Howe had said, "on his own now."

CHAPTER SIX

Learning the Limits of Power (1936–1940)

Throughout the campaign for a second term, Roosevelt had seen the major issue as not the New Deal, or even the turmoil in Europe, but rather himself. As he told Moley, "I am the issue."[1] Having gone through two campaigns for governor and two now for president, Roosevelt had been well prepared for attacks during the campaign from Father Charles Coughlin, a popular radio host known as the "Radio Priest," who promised greater "social justice" than Roosevelt delivered and assailed Roosevelt for abandoning the gold standard and as subservient to Jewish influence and money; Huey Long, who promised radical income redistribution; and Dr. Francis Townsend, who proposed a scheme to give every retiree $200 to spend every month. They all thought Roosevelt weak and insincere. The Republican nominee, Alf Landon, left the campaign largely to surrogates, who failed to dent Roosevelt.

During the 1936 campaign, Roosevelt pledged to keep fighting the war against the depression and "nine crazy years" of Republican misrule, but he said little about two other wars: The first was in Europe and the Far East. Germany had violated its agreements made at the end of the First World War, Italy backed Germany's aggressions, and Japan left the League of Nations, committed atrocities in Manchuria, and savagely put down an internal revolt.

Roosevelt was largely silent about the second war unfolding in America, although during the campaign, he condemned the Court at rallies for its obstructing the New Deal, even suggesting that if the Court failed to uphold the Agricultural Adjustment Act, another New Deal centerpiece, "there might even be a revolution."[2] In cabinet meetings, he was less circumspect, repeatedly railing against the Court for its backward-looking bullheadedness. Roosevelt refused to concede defeat.

On the day of his second inauguration, this second conflict was apparent on the stage, as two of the major protagonists would be standing together and staring directly at each other, as the chief justice of the United States, Charles Evans Hughes, administered the oath of office, for a second time, to Franklin Roosevelt.

I

On March 3, 1932, Republican senator George Norris of Nebraska, a loyal Roosevelt ally, had proposed the Twentieth Amendment, which shortened the presidential transition to little more than two months after Election Day. Ratified a few months before Roosevelt's inauguration, it did not apply to Roosevelt's first term, but it did to his second. The short transition worked well for Roosevelt, since his administration had little turnover (except for Kansas governor Harry Woodring becoming head of the War Department after George Dern had died in August of the preceding year) and was pushing its plans for the Second New Deal even harder than it had pushed those for the First New Deal.

As Roosevelt and his vice president took to the stage on the morning of January 20, 1937, the occasion was historic for both. Roosevelt was the first president to be inaugurated under the Twentieth Amendment, and Nance was the first vice president to be sworn in on the same stage as the president. But the weather was anything but celebratory, as the people on stage were deluged by a heavy rain, no one having thought that covering the stage would be a good idea given the dark skies over the nation's capital.

With his hat a soggy mess and twice having to pause to sweep the rain from his eyes, Roosevelt spoke from a water-logged script. Just as he had in his first inaugural and his speech accepting his second nomination as the Democratic candidate for president, he reaffirmed that the nation was still at war against the depression. Though declaring "We are moving toward an era of good feeling" (a reference to James Monroe, who more than a century before had christened the era as one of good feelings), Roosevelt delivered the core of the speech in four sentences, delivered like jabs in a prizefight. He told the world, "I see millions of families trying to live on incomes so meager that the pall of family disaster hangs over them every day. I see millions denied education, recreation, and the opportunity to better their lot and the lot of their children. I see millions lacking the means to buy the products of farm and factory and by their poverty denying work and productiveness to many other millions. I see one-third of a nation ill-housed, ill-clad, ill-nourished."[3]

More than a few people present felt an undercurrent of tension between Roosevelt and the old chief justice. Hughes slowly read the oath he expected the president to take and with particular emphasis on its closing words to "promise to support the Constitution of the United States." Attuned to the moment, Roosevelt repeated the oath slowly and with even greater force. Later, he said that he wanted to scream at Hughes that "yes, but it's the Constitution as I understand it, flexible enough to meet any new problem of democracy—not the kind of Constitution your Court has raised up as a barrier to progress and democracy." The battle had become personal for Roosevelt.

But rather than scream at the chief justice, Roosevelt lectured him: "The essential democracy of our Nation and the safety of our people depend upon not the absence of power, but upon lodging it with those whom the people can change or continue at stated intervals through an honest and free system of elections." Of the bloodshed and racism spreading across Europe, Roosevelt said nothing, sticking with the congressional mandate of neutrality, except perhaps for his acknowledgment near the end of his speech, "In every land, there are always at work forces that drive men apart and forces that drive men together." America, he stressed, was "one people."[4]

When the speech was done, Roosevelt and Eleanor moved into an uncovered car for the fifteen-minute ride back to the White House. When they arrived, they both looked as if they had been swimming. They changed clothes to meet their thousands of guests and to watch the inaugural parade from stands that were a replica of Andrew Jackson's home, the Hermitage, a reminder of the link between the two Democratic presidents.

It was not lost on Roosevelt that the two presidents shared disdain for the Court. Jackson had used five Supreme Court appointments to transform the Court from a liberal bastion to one that was more disposed to curb federal power and protect state sovereignty. Roosevelt wanted to do just the opposite, appoint justices who would protect innovative exercises of power.

II

Charles Evans Hughes was no one's fool. His record of public service and professional accomplishments was stellar: Two years after Franklin's birth, Hughes graduated first in his class at Columbia Law School. He subsequently served as a partner in two Wall Street firms, the second changing its name to Hughes, Hubbard, and Reed; the governor of New York from 1907 to 1910 (resigning in the middle of his second term); an associate justice of the Supreme Court (1910–1916); the Republican nominee for president in 1916 (barely losing to Wilson); secretary of state (1921–1925); and a World Court judge (1928–1930). He was conservative, but the men who served with him agreed he was a man of principle. Tall, aristocratic in bearing, with a photographic memory and impeccable temperament and manners, Hughes held himself to the highest standards and worked tirelessly, regardless of his position. Hoover regarded him as the most self-contained man he had ever met.

In early 1937, Hughes had every reason to think that Roosevelt was hardly done fighting for the New Deal and challenging the Court's integrity. He may have heard the rumors circulating among the political elite that Roosevelt was planning a bolder attack. Nor was Hughes the only justice feeling unsettled as Roosevelt prepared to enter his second term. They rightfully expected the attacks to continue. On January 6, Roosevelt had declared in his State of the Union that the executive and legislative branches "helped to make democracy succeed by refusing to permit unnecessary disagreement. [That] spirit of cooperation was able to solve the difficulties of extraordinary magnitude."[5]

When Franklin spoke of the Court, he expressed hope "to bring legislative and judicial action into harmony" to meet "the present national needs of the largest progressive democracy in the modern world." In a letter written after the event to his ambassador in Spain, Roosevelt noted that "none of the nine highest members of the judicial branch were present for the occasion, but I have received some intimation that they at least read the remarks that pertained to them. I hope so!" He told aides that he expected that the problem with the Court could be "solved without getting away from our underlying principles." It was impossible to tamp down the rumors among White House insiders that Roosevelt was planning something—and not just a continuation of his verbal attacks on the Court.[6]

Barely two weeks after his second inaugural, Roosevelt made his first public move at the annual dinner he hosted for the Supreme Court in the White House. Roosevelt was charming, as he spoke amiably with not just the justices but also the senators and cabinet members who were attending. Knowing what was coming, Attorney General Homer Cummings told Sam Rosenman that he felt that evening "too much like a conspirator," while William Borah, Democratic senator from Idaho, observed, as he watched Roosevelt charm the room, "That reminds me of the Roman Emperor who looked around his dinner table and began to laugh as he thought how many of those heads would be rolling on the morrow."[7]

Three days later, lightning struck. Roosevelt's special message to Congress on February 5, 1937, shocked the nation: It proposed to add six new justices to the Court, one for every justice who had served at least ten years but did not retire within six months after turning seventy.

Nothing like this had ever been proposed before, much less done. While the Constitution did not mandate a specific number of seats on the Court, it left in Congress the authority to expand or contract the Court's size, which Congress had kept at nine since 1869. Expecting a firestorm, Roosevelt was uncharacteristically nervous in making the announcement, though he enjoyed theatrics. The plan ensured plenty of drama over the next weeks and months, overshadowing the administration's progress in extending the New Deal.

There was little doubt the plan was constitutional. Since the Constitution vested Congress with the power to shape the Court's size, it necessarily had the discretion to determine the Court's numbers of seats. A plan that would have approved merely abolishing a seat that was already filled would undoubtedly have raised serious concerns about whether Congress was trying to bypass the impeachment process in removing a justice.

But Roosevelt's plan removed no one; instead, it purported to expand the Court, something Congress had done more than once since the founding, including when the Republican Congress increased the Court's size to ten seats for Lincoln, reduced it to seven when Andrew Johnson was president, but added two more for President Grant to fill in 1869.

Nevertheless, opposition to the plan based on concerns about the Court's workload and Roosevelt's ambitions was swift and overwhelming, even among fellow Democrats. Business leaders, powerful politicians, the press, and the public were divided in their support. Most newspapers and many members of Congress opposed the plan. The opposition likened Roosevelt to Hitler, Mussolini, and Joseph Stalin. When the plan was read aloud at a Democratic caucus, Roosevelt's vice president, Garner, held his nose and turned thumbs-down to great applause. He told his colleagues that the plan "was an encroachment on the prerogatives of the members of the legislative branch no President ought to engage in."[8]

Old friends condemned Roosevelt. An ally, Sam Rayburn of Texas in the House of Representatives, persuaded Roosevelt to have

the plan introduced in the Senate rather than the House because he
and the rest of the Texas House delegation opposed it.

There were some Roosevelt allies among the electorate and in Congress that supported the idea. They likened Roosevelt to Washington, Jefferson, and Jackson, because of his bold and courageous vision. Hyperbole was in the air as the battle raged across American newspapers, prompting Interior Secretary Harold Ickes to say that he did not "recall any single issue affecting the Government has caused the spilling of so much printer's ink or led to so many fervent discussions."[9]

Determined not to let the opposition take control of the narrative, Roosevelt went to the airwaves to rally support. On March 4, at a victory dinner celebrating his reelection, Roosevelt attacked the Court's opposition to the New Deal. He explained, "We live in a nation where there is no legal power anywhere to deal with its most difficult problems—a No Man's Land of Final Futility. [The Court had created] doubts and difficulties for almost everything. [We] have promised to fight—help for the crippled, for the blind, for the mothers—insurance for the unemployed—security for the aged—protection of the consumer against the monopoly and speculation—protection of the investor—the wiping out of slums—cheaper electricity for the homes and farms of America." "If," he added, "we would keep faith with those who had faith in us, if we would make democracy succeed, I say we must act—NOW!"[10]

Franklin's attacks recalled Teddy Roosevelt's defense of the President as a "steward" of American democracy. Just as Teddy had argued that the only constraint on the President's power was popular opinion, Franklin was asserting that so long as the presidency and Congress had the backing of the American people, the Court should step aside. It was a matter of following the majority's will, as Jackson had proclaimed a century before.

Five days later, Roosevelt continued assaulting the Court, though this time with less anger and fervor, in his first Fireside Chat in six months. Citing the Court's string of 5–4 decisions, which Roosevelt described as sending "all the affairs of this great Nation back into hopeless chaos," he asserted that it was essential "to have a government with power to prevent" a return to the dire circumstances the country faced in Hoover's last few months as president. Yet, he said, "the unanswered challenge of a Nation ill-nourished, ill-clad, ill-housed" required the Court to change its responses to the government's innovations. It was time for the Court to end acting like "a policy-making body" or "third House of Congress" and begin acting again like "a judicial body." His proposal would "save the Constitution from the Court and the Court from itself. There is nothing radical or novel about this idea. It seeks to maintain the bench in full vigor." He concluded by reassuring Americans of "my solemn assurance that in a world in which democracy is under attack, I seek to make American democracy succeed."[11]

Roosevelt's exhortations failed to win the public, or Congress, to his side. He lobbied senators one-on-one and in small groups but to no avail. Public opposition to the plan grew to 59 percent from 51 percent. Roosevelt's public approval rating fell five points during the Court fight, which effectively ended the second honeymoon period he'd been expecting.

Congressional Democrats groused that Roosevelt had not consulted them before releasing the plan. As Senator Alben Barkley of Kentucky complained, Roosevelt had proven to be "a poor quarterback" in leading the fight against the Court. "He didn't give us the signals in advance of the play," he said. Representative Edward Cox of Georgia complained that the proposal "asks for something that no man in all this world ought to enjoy. [It] constitutes the most terrible threat to constitutional government that has arisen in the entire history of the country." Senator Burton Wheeler, a staunch defender of the New Deal, broke with Roosevelt, declaring that "the usurpation of the legislative functions by the courts should be stopped. But to give the executive the power to control the judiciary is not giving the law-making power back to that branch of government in which it rightfully belongs, but rather is increasing the danger inherent in the concentration of power in any one branch of government."[12]

When the matter finally got a hearing in the Senate, its support was shrinking. The Senate Judiciary Committee issued a report declaring the proposal "an invasion of judicial power such has never before been attempted in this country."[13] Never before or since has there been such a focused nationwide discussion of both the Court's power and the power of Congress to constrain it.

Roosevelt underestimated not just the popular support for the Court but the influence of the old chief justice. Perhaps Roosevelt thought that, as a failed presidential candidate, the old man could not match his public pleas. While Roosevelt would likely have beaten Hughes on the campaign trail, their contest of wills was not waged on the campaign trail. Roosevelt failed to appreciate that, in pushing the proposal, he was playing on Hughes's field not his own. Roosevelt had the temerity to challenge Hughes where he was bound to be his strongest—when defending the Court.

While Roosevelt was attempting to strong-arm members of Congress to back his plan, extensive machinations were underway to thwart it. Immediately after the plan had been announced, Senator Burton Wheeler, the chair of the Senate Judiciary Committee, wrote Chief Justice Hughes to inquire about whether Roosevelt had been correct in claiming that the Court needed more justices because of its purportedly heavy workload. Over the weekend before the Senate Judiciary Committee hearings began on March 21, the chief justice met privately with powerful Democratic senators William Borah, Thomas Connally, and Burton Wheeler. On Saturday, March 18, Senator Borah visited Justice Brandeis at home. Brandeis told Borah that Chief Justice Hughes wanted to see him. Brandeis called Hughes to introduce the two, and Hughes invited him to his home. On arriving at the chief justice's house, Borah said, "the imposing Chief Justice greeted me warmly." Borah relayed Brandeis's message that the chief justice had "a letter" for Borah. "When do you need it?" Hughes asked. Borah said Monday the 21st. Hughes asked him to return the next day. When he did, Hughes handed him his seven-page letter, saying, "The baby is born." After Borah read the letter in Hughes's presence, the chief justice asked him, "Does that answer your question?" Borah happily answered yes.[14]

Before Borah left, Hughes asked him to sit with him. He explained that his interest was in the Court "as an institution" not "who are to be the members of the Court." Bluntly, Hughes said that Roosevelt's plan "would destroy the Court as an institution." "If we had an

Attorney General in whom the President had confidence, and in whom the Court had confidence, and in whom the people had confidence," Hughes further explained, "the story might have been different. But the laws have been poorly drafted, the briefs have been badly drawn and the arguments have been poorly presented. We've had to be not only the Court but we've had to do the work that should have been done by the Attorney General."[15]

In 2023, such a meeting would be inappropriate, but it was not unusual for the era. Borah did not mention the meeting when he appeared before the committee the next day. He told the committee, "I have here a letter from the Chief Justice of the United States, Mr. Charles Evans Hughes, dated March 21, 1937, written by him and approved by Mr. Justice Brandeis and Mr. Justice Van Devanter."[16]

Described by two journalists as "a masterpiece of exposition," the letter initially addressed the purported justifications for the plan. Hughes pointed out that the Court had no backlog, that it was hearing oral arguments within weeks of cases being filed, and that expanding the numbers of justices would produce delays in the Court's decision-making. He went further to dismantle the possibility of the Court's splitting into panels to hear cases. He concluded the letter by saying that, while he had not had time to consult the matter with the full Court, he had consulted with Justices Brandeis and Van Devanter, who, he wrote, "approved" his "statement." Signaling that the Court's most liberal justice (Brandeis) was joining one of its most conservative (Van Devanter) in opposing the plan, Hughes deftly created an image of a unity cutting across ideological divides that Roosevelt could not challenge. The effect of the letter was devastating. The plan died in committee.[17]

In the popular press at the time, the proposal's defeat was attributed to a shift in Justice Owen Roberts's votes in two cases involving the constitutionality of economic regulations. The former special prosecutor charged with investigating corruption in the Harding administration, Roberts was widely viewed as one of the Court's lightweights. While the opinions in the cases had come out after the plan had become public, Roberts's shift had occurred before the plan became public. Nevertheless, the shift was a factor in the public's perception that the plan was unnecessary, and it was popularized as the reason for the plan's failure in the ditty, "the switch in time that saved nine."

Two other developments doomed the plan. One was the announcement on June 2, 1937, of Justice Willis Van Devanter's intention to resign. In having the opportunity to fill the vacancy nearly five years into his presidency, Roosevelt finally had the chance to consolidate a liberal majority on the Court. When the next month Senate Majority Leader Joseph Robinson died of a heart attack, the plan lost its most ardent, vocal, and effective defender in the Senate.

Roosevelt did not help his cause with his next moves. A day after Robinson's death, he wrote a letter to Senator Alben Barkley of Kentucky, whom he addressed as "Dear Alben" and urged to continue pushing for the passage of the Court-packing plan.[18] The letter backfired. Many Democratic senators were insulted that Roosevelt was attempting to weigh in on a matter that was solely within their discretion. Barkley, too, was embarrassed when, shortly after he had won the majority leader position by a single vote within the Democratic caucus, Senator Burton Wheeler joined several Republican and Democratic colleagues to kill the proposed bill in committee. Barkley's colleagues derisively referred to him as "Dear Alben," the greeting in Roosevelt's letter and, throughout the rest of his time in the Senate, he was called Franklin's "errand boy."[19]

Roosevelt made things worse when he blamed Robinson for the plan's failure and refused to attend Robinson's funeral in Arkansas. Robinson had been popular in the Senate, and his Senate colleagues, as well as Vice President Garner, were insulted by Roosevelt's churlishness. On returning to Washington, Garner told the President, "You are beat Cap'n. You haven't got the votes." On July 21, one week after Robinson had died, the Senate rejected the plan, twenty in favor, but seventy against. The Court-packing plan was officially dead.

III

Nature, not the Court-packing plan, did Roosevelt's work for him. The dam burst with Van Devanter's resignation on the same day as the Senate Judiciary Committee voted against the plan. Over the course of Roosevelt's second term, four other justices left the Court, enabling him to have five Supreme Court appointments, the third most made in a single term. Only two presidents—Washington and Taft—had more.

Roosevelt had plenty of time to consult with staff and Democratic senators about the kind of justice he wanted. He had four criteria: The first was personal knowledge of the individual's constitutional commitments. Second, Roosevelt prized loyalty, which he could best measure through actual performance; and the performance he valued was a strong belief in the constitutionality of the New Deal. These two factors largely excluded lower court judges, whom he likely had not known well or worked closely with. The third consideration was a nominee who would have an easy, smooth confirmation in the Senate. A swift confirmation ensured he could have a solid liberal majority on the Court sooner than later and without expending needless political coinage. A final factor was a political benefit to the nomination, besides ensuring the nominee's commitment to the New Deal and the likelihood of swift confirmation.

Roosevelt's first choice had not been a secret to Washington insiders: He had favored Senator Joseph Robinson of Arkansas. He had stood out for all the right reasons—as majority leader, he had worked closely with Roosevelt and been his most loyal and ardent defender of the New Deal in the Senate; he would benefit from the tradition of senatorial courtesy, the longstanding tradition of the Senate's giving special deference to the nomination of a colleague; and he had come from Arkansas, a state which had voted twice for Roosevelt and helped to secure his base in the old South.

Though Robinson was no longer available, Roosevelt used him as a template in choosing his first Supreme Court nominee. He wanted someone who had Robinson's strengths, and he found him in the person of Hugo Black, twice elected to the Senate from Alabama. He was sure to benefit from senatorial courtesy; he had voted for all twenty-four of Roosevelt's New Deal programs; his support for the New Deal drove Southern conservatives mad; he came from a state that had voted twice for Roosevelt, and the nomination could shore up Roosevelt's support in the old South; and Roosevelt knew

Black well from having worked closely with him in pushing New Deal legislation through the Senate and in his chairing several Senate investigations into possible governmental reforms. Roosevelt made the announcement in early August 1937 just after his Court-packing plan had died in the Senate.

The nomination stunned many Court observers and New Dealers. Frankfurter groused to anyone who listened that the appointment made little sense—an Alabamian, who was not a prominent judge or academic and who'd attended a small college (Ashland) no one had ever heard of, was hardly qualified for a seat on the country's highest court. Not surprisingly, former President Hoover declared that, if confirmed, Black's appointment would mean that the Court was now "one ninth packed." Some colleagues protested that Black "was a prosecutor not a judge."

The *Washington Post* joined the chorus of critics complaining that Black lacked the requisite judicial temperament for a justice and was unqualified because of "his lack of training on the one hand and extreme partisanship" on the other.[20] Later, Justice Harlan Fiske Stone, concerned about Black's brashness in heaping abuse on his colleagues in his dissents, asked Frankfurter "to render [Black] great assistance. He needs guidance from someone who is more familiar with the workings of the judicial process than he is. With guidance, and a disposition to follow it until he is a little surer of himself, he might do great things."[21]

With rumors beginning to circulate that Black had been a member of the Ku Klux Klan, Roosevelt and Black pushed the Senate hard for a swift confirmation. Five days after his nomination to the Court, Black was confirmed by the Senate 63–16 on August 17, 1937. As Black explained afterward, "I wasn't taking any chances. I knew that my enemies in big business and the press would inflame the public against me so much that they might get a judge to enjoin me from taking the oath."[22]

Two weeks later, the *Pittsburgh Post-Gazette* published the first of six articles documenting Black's membership in the Ku Klux Klan. Even before the news had become official, polls showed the public largely opposed to nominating anyone, including Black, who had been a member of the KKK. But with the news now spreading across the country, Black quickly hired a Catholic secretary and an African American messenger who was also Catholic. The small gestures helped but did not stem the rising tide of outrage.

Because it was Black's problem, Roosevelt let Justice Black fix it. As the opening of the Court's term in October 1937 approached, Black had two more responses he hoped would silence his critics. The first was his most dramatic: He delivered an eleven-minute address on the radio. Reaching more than 40 million listeners, Black cast himself as the victim, and went further to explain that "some of my best and most intimate friends are Catholics and Jews." He told the listening audience that he had made "the sole executor of his will" his closest friend, Herman Beck, who was Jewish. Beck, he explained, had persuaded him to join the Klan, which, he said, had in those days been "a fraternal organization" that was not "anti-Catholic, anti-Jewish, or anti-Negro." (Black was never asked how he could describe the Klan as not being antisemitic when it had barred his friend Beck from joining.)[23] Next, Black hired his first law clerk, Jerome Cooper, who, newspapers around the country reported, was Jewish.[24] While the public outrage eventually died down, Black's reputation as a civil libertarian took years to forge.

Within a year of Black's appointment, George Sutherland resigned. Van Devanter and Sutherland had been two of the "Four Horsemen," the name given to the conservative justices who voted consistently to block the New Deal. William Howard Taft had attested to Van Devanter's credentials when he appointed Van Devanter to the Court, but later, as chief justice, Taft complained that he was lazy and lacked the intellect to be a competent justice. In contrast to Van Devanter, a former United States senator from Utah, Sutherland had come to the Court with a reputation as a thoughtful, principled conservative. He often spoke for the Court's other conservative justices and argued that judges were the best guardians of individual liberty. His departure ensured Roosevelt's further consolidation of a liberal majority on the Court.

This time, Roosevelt chose Solicitor General Stanley Reed of Kentucky, whom he had briefly considered for the seat to which he had appointed Black. Though not a Democrat, much less a New Deal Democrat, Reed had impressed Roosevelt with his advocacy before the Court for the constitutionality of the New Deal. Since Reed, like Black, had come from the South, Roosevelt figured the appointment might appease the base he hoped to grow there. Pleased with Reed's credentials, temperament, and absence of any skeletons in his closet, senators confirmed him within ten days of the announcement of his nomination.

In July, Justice Benjamin Cardozo, widely revered for his legal acumen, died after a decade on the Court. Roosevelt asked Felix Frankfurter for a list of possible candidates, none of whom impressed Roosevelt. It likely was for show, as Roosevelt soon nominated his longtime advisor.

His hesitancy in nominating Frankfurter proved justified when opposition quickly formed. Opponents claimed a variety of reasons for opposing the nomination, including antisemitic reluctance to have another Jew added to the Court (Brandeis had been the first), fear that Frankfurter was foreign born, concerns that there were still no justices from west of the Mississippi, belief that Frankfurter's connection to Roosevelt was too close and personal, and that he was too liberal for the Court given his work for the American Civil Liberties Union. Some groups worried he was a Communist. The opposition was so quick and strong that the chair of the Senate Judiciary Committee, Henry Ashurst of Arizona, felt he had no choice but to schedule a hearing and invited Frankfurter to testify.

When he appeared to testify before the Senate Judiciary in 1939, Frankfurter was only the second Supreme Court nominee to appear in person at his own confirmation hearing, the first having been Harlan Fiske Stone in 1925. With his counsel (and former student) Dean Acheson sitting beside him, Frankfurter calmly and carefully addressed senators' concerns that he was too liberal (he expertly distinguished between his work as a lawyer and his duties as a judge), and that he was anti-Christian and a Communist (he was neither). On January 17, 1939, nearly five months after his nomination to the Court, the Senate confirmed Frankfurter by voice vote.

Less than a month later, Justice Louis Brandeis announced his retirement because of poor health. Having heard the concerns during the fight over Frankfurter's nomination that the Court had no justice west of the Mississippi, Roosevelt turned to a Westerner whom he liked, William O. Douglas, who had advised him on commercial matters and had taught commercial law at Columbia and Yale Law Schools. Widely regarded as one of the nation's most brilliant business lawyers, Douglas had been appointed by Roosevelt to the Securities and Exchange Commission in 1936 and later made chair. Robert Maynard Hutchins, the president of the University of Chicago, called Douglas "the best law professor in the nation."[25]

Only fourteen years out of Columbia Law School when nominated to the Supreme Court, Douglas was not just a brilliant commercial lawyer. He was a leading voice in the legal realism movement, which viewed law as merely a device politicians, lawyers, and judges manipulated to reach the results they wanted. As a pragmatist, Roosevelt appreciated a jurist who would cut through legal nonsense and do justice in real cases.

While Douglas had a penchant for ticking people off, senators wanted a speedy confirmation. The Senate Judiciary Committee's hearing on Douglas lasted five minutes. The Senate confirmed him 62–4 on April 4, 1939. A week later, Roosevelt swore him into office. He was thirty-nine years old, the fifth youngest justice ever appointed to the Court. He still holds the record as the Court's longest serving justice.

On November 16, 1939, Pierce Butler, the last surviving Harding appointee, died. Butler had been not just one of the Four Horsemen but also the Court's only Catholic and only Midwesterner. In finding a replacement, Roosevelt did not look far: Earlier in the year, Attorney General Homer Cummings, who had helped to lead the administration's defense of the New Deal, returned to private practice. To replace him, Roosevelt picked an old ally, Frank Murphy, who had proven his mettle as governor-general and later high commissioner of the Philippines, mayor of Detroit, and governor of Michigan. He was Catholic, too. Nearly one year to the day since Roosevelt had nominated Murphy as attorney general, he nominated him to the Court. Ten days later, on January 14, 1940, the Senate confirmed him as an associate justice.

With five appointments, Roosevelt transformed the Supreme Court. Never again did it strike down any portion of the New Deal.

IV

The defeat of the Court-packing plan cost Roosevelt dearly. The loss, along with his refusal to attend Robinson's funeral, coincided with a drop in his approval rating. It showed the world that Roosevelt was not invincible and his political judgment was far from perfect. (It might have showed, too, the costly absence of Howe as a moderating force on Roosevelt.) Conservative Democrats increasingly felt more emboldened to break ranks and challenge his actions. The costs were manifest where they hurt most—in impeding his efforts to expand and reinvigorate the New Deal.

When Roosevelt introduced his Court-packing plan, he had five other bills pending before Congress, including wages and hours legislation, low-cost housing, reorganization of the executive branch, a revised farm program, and the creation of seven new TVA-type regional authorities. When Congress adjourned for recess in August, it had approved none. Instead, the most significant New Deal measure it approved had been introduced and pushed by Senator Robert Wagner of New York—the eponymously named Wagner Labor Relations Act, which established the legal right of most workers to join unions and to bargain collectively with employers and which barred employers from unfair labor practices. Determined to get the legislation through Congress, Roosevelt recalled it into a special session in August. As Roosevelt biographer Jean Smith wrote, "the session proved a disaster. Despite unprecedented Democratic majorities in both Houses, not one additional piece of legislation was enacted. Only a year after his overwhelming election victory, FDR had lost control of the party."[26]

As Farley recalled, "The Supreme Court fight lived on in the President's memory. His attitude was that he had been double-crossed

and let down by the men who should have rallied loyally to his support. For weeks and months afterward I found him fuming against
the members of his own party. Outwardly he was as gay and debonair as ever; inwardly he was seething."[27] Privately, Roosevelt
boasted that he would get even with the traitors in his party. Democrats in Congress did not take the threat seriously, as many began to
think Roosevelt needed them more than they needed him.

With Democrats bickering among themselves, Roosevelt failed
to learn a lesson from another of his predecessors, James Monroe:
True, Monroe in 1820 had won reelection by the largest margin of
any president until Roosevelt in 1936. This was the high point of what
Monroe and his supporters had characterized as "the era of good feelings," because there was no opposition party. The name proved to be
a misnomer, as Monroe's party splintered during his second term,
opening the door for John Quincy Adams, a Democratic-Republican,
to prevail ultimately within the House to take the presidency in 1824.

Similarly, the fractures within Roosevelt's Democratic Party took
their toll. The first place they were evident was disagreement over
how to handle a series of sit-down strikes that crippled several major
businesses, including General Motors, the world's largest manufac-
turing corporation, and several smaller steel companies known as
"Little Steel." General Motors suffered a near-collapse as a strike in
Flint, Michigan, the only plant that made dies for its cars, ground
production to a halt and, with that, did the same for the entire line
of its automobiles.

Though General Motors once produced one-half of the automobiles in the United States, it was no longer true: Having produced
50,000 cars in December 1936, the company made only 125 during
the first week of February 1937. Roosevelt, Labor Secretary Perkins,
and then Michigan governor Frank Murphy agreed to not use force
to break the strike. When Vice President Garner pressed Roosevelt
to press Murphy to use force, if necessary, Roosevelt resisted. Instead,
Roosevelt and Murphy degenerated into a shouting match. While
their tempers flared, the strike lasted another seven weeks.

After initially counseling Roosevelt to use caution, Perkins suggested he place a phone call to the president of General Motors.

Gently, Roosevelt urged him to meet with the workers' committee. After General Motors agreed to recognize the United Auto Workers as labor's bargaining agent at its sixteen factories in fourteen states, the strike ended. "Big Steel," the name given to the country's largest steel manufacturer, the United Steel Corporation, got the message and averted a strike by recognizing the steelworkers' union and agreeing to pay hikes, a forty-hour workweek, and overtime.

Things went worse for "Little Steel." Republic Steel not only refused to recognize the union's bargaining power but also used force, which badly backfired. At the end of May 1937, at Ford's huge River Rouge plant, several United Auto Workers organizers were brutally beaten. The worst violence in modern labor history then erupted on Memorial Day 1937, when Chicago police opened fire on protestors, killing ten and wounding thirty people. The violence spread to Ohio, where five more workers were shot and killed. Though Republic Steel folded, several other corporations, including International Harvester, Westinghouse, and the four largest meatpacking industries in the country, refused to bargain with their workers.

Polling was beginning to show most Americans opposed striking. Congress soon approved a resolution condemning striking as illegal. Roosevelt steadfastly refused to take sides, provoking John L. Lewis, the preeminent labor leader in the country, to condemn Roosevelt and withhold any future support for the New Deal.

As labor unrest and its fallout were reaching a stasis by the summer of 1937, Roosevelt—and his ragtag team of economic advisors, scattered across his administration—took some solace in the surprising upturn in the economy. Production increased above pre-depression levels for the first time, the Dow Jones Industrial Average had increased almost sixfold, the steel industry was operating at 80 percent capacity, payrolls were making sold gains, and unemployment had shrunk to 12 percent. In response to the good economic news, Roosevelt optimistically set out to balance the federal budget and significantly slashed federal spending.

By October, the country found itself in the grip of recession. On October 9, the New York Stock Exchange had its worst day since 1929—and kept falling for the rest of the month, wiping out the gains

of August. Industrial activity reached historically new lows; steel production by the end of the year had fallen to 19 percent of capacity;
businesses were failing; and gold was being sold abroad. As Jean
Smith wrote, "Between Labor Day and Christmas, more than two
million people lost their jobs, and another 2 million in the first three
months of 1938. If the rate of decline continued through the year, the
United States would lose almost two-thirds of its gains since 1933."[28]

Roosevelt's advisors split over the proper response. Treasury Secretary Morgenthau, Commerce Secretary Roper, and Farley argued that
Roosevelt should stay the course and finish balancing the budget, but
a slate of others—Interior Secretary Ickes, Harry Hopkins, Frances Perkins, and Agriculture Secretary Wallace—urged increases in federal
spending. Marriner Eccles, head of the Federal Reserve, believed that
the administration's spending cuts had triggered the recession. Corcoran and Cohen in the White House, Douglas then at the SEC, and
Robert Jackson (whom Roosevelt elevated to replace Reed as solicitor
general), blamed big business for the nation's economic woes.

That kind of thinking persuaded Roosevelt to name Thurmond
Arnold, a Yale law professor, to replace Jackson to lead the Justice
Department's Antitrust Division. Arnold expanded the division
from eighteen lawyers in 1933 to more than three hundred and initi-
ated over the next five years 44 percent of all the anti-monopoly
actions undertaken by the Justice Department since the passage of
the Sherman Act in 1890. Morgenthau found himself virtually alone
in the administration in blaming the strikes for the recession.

Roosevelt chose a middle course between those who wanted to
use federal money to revive the economy and those who were anti
big business: He did nothing. When Morgenthau chided him that
he was "just treading water," Roosevelt replied, "Absolutely." Though
urged by British economist John Maynard Keynes to spend money
as stimulus, Roosevelt appeared uninterested in theories on how to
revive the economy.[29] As historian James MacGregor Burns suggested, it was apparent that "Roosevelt's deficiencies as an economist
were as striking as his triumphs as a politician."[30] Roosevelt had no
patience for theory; he was only interested in a concrete plan. As he
searched for one, economic conditions worsened.

Harry Hopkins pushed Roosevelt off the ledge. While Roosevelt was vacationing in Warm Springs, Hopkins invited himself down to persuade the President to abandon any hope of balancing the budget and instead to back spending proposals Hopkins had brought with him. After considerable lobbying, Roosevelt agreed.

The process Roosevelt used in developing his request to Congress on April 14 for a special appropriation of $1.4 billion to combat the recession was typical: He assigned advisors of different views to come up with solutions. The practice often drove wedges between advisors and sewed needless tension among them, many of whom quit in frustration. As described by William Leuchtenberg, Roosevelt "often appointed advisers of clashing temperaments and beliefs to the same policy issue, leading to internal confrontations and squabbling. The benefits of the system were that [Roosevelt] received political and policy advice from a range of advisers. It also left the President with an array of options and allowed him to forge a consensus within his administration." Leuchtenberg saw the further advantage for Roosevelt in such a scheme as allowing him "a degree of flexibility in the policymaking process, which harmonized with Roosevelt's often experimental approach to the New Deal." Leuchtenberg considered one cost of Roosevelt's management style to be that it made the administration appear to be "moving in several directions, many of them contradictory, all at once."[31]

Into the mix stepped Felix Frankfurter, who urged Roosevelt to listen to John Maynard Keynes, who had published groundbreaking treatises on employment and depression, including *A Treatise on Money* in 1930. In 1934, Frankfurter arranged for the two to meet. Thereafter, the two stayed in contact, though there is little evidence Keynes had any impact on Roosevelt's thinking about the economy in his first term.

The same year Roosevelt was elected to a second term, Keynes published his magnum opus, *The General Theory of Employment, Interest and Money*, which increased his influence and reputation throughout the Western world, including the United States. The timing of the publication could not have been better, at least for Keynes. Keynes's greatest impact on Roosevelt's thinking, and that of several advisors, including Hopkins, arose near the end of Roosevelt's second term, as he followed Keynes's recommendation of deficit spending designed to recharge the ailing economy. By the end of 1938, the economy showed some signs of recovery, as employment, payrolls, and production began to rise.

The good news was short-lived, as it turned out that the funding given by Congress at the end of 1938 was the last law Congress enacted as part of the New Deal. Complicating matters for Roosevelt was the growing movement among some Democrats to view him as a lame duck. Already angered by his high-handedness and stubbornness and no longer appeased by his charm or the economic numbers as 1939 dawned, they began abandoning the New Deal.

Even in Roosevelt's first term, Democrats complained, without any hint of irony, that there was no party organization or loyalty. In July 1935, Hopkins met with the Democratic Steering Committee to broker peace, but the members excoriated Roosevelt for ignoring the committee, disrespecting them and their staffs, and not seeking their input on appointments. Hopkins reported back that they had threatened reprisals unless the President paid more attention to their concerns and contributions.

Moreover, the basic thinking behind the New Deal was not aging well. Government spending had not been meant to be a long-term fix. It was meant to prop up, or reenergize, the national economy, but with the expectation that the private sector would increasingly take up the slack as the depression began to recede. But, for both defenders and opponents of the New Deal, the private sector was not in the position to do that. The federal government could not put everyone to work for the rest of their lives, and the private sector held no guarantees of employment, much less long-term employment.

The government could subsidize certain activities, such as farming, but it could not do so forever, and once it began cutting back its support, there were no guarantees that farming would remain as productive and lucrative as it had been. Nor was it clear that the private sector would take over the same policies that the government was pursuing in the New Deal. Indeed, no new industries were forming, and the New Deal (with the notable exception of agricultural policy) offered few if any incentives for innovation.

Adding insult to injury, the increasing prosperity of the nation led people back to the old values of individualism and self-reliance, which conflicted with the New Deal's fundamental commitment to the betterment of society. Harry Hopkins had foreseen the problem, commenting, as early as 1937, that Americans had become "bored with the poor, the unemployed, and the insecure."[32] Republicans capitalized on the growing numbers of Americans obsessing over individualism.

The realization of the New Deal's limits and failure to serve as a long-term solution for the country split Democrats. Just as Moley had done in 1938, Adolph Berle, a member of the original Brain Trust, resigned. An anti-Keyensian, Berle left embittered over the rising influence of officials whose economic thinking he believed was archaic. Consequently, Hopkins began working with several of the remaining true believers in the administration, such as Farley, to root out disloyal Democrats and conservatives.

Roosevelt went further to openly challenge Democratic senators whom he thought had betrayed him. In June 1938, he told the American people that the great divide in Washington split along two lines: Liberals believed that government could solve problems "through democratic processes instead of Fascism and Communism," while, he said, conservatives did not recognize the legitimacy of the government's trying to fix new problems. He said that the conservative philosophy "believes that individual initiative and private philanthropy will solve them—that we ought to repeal many of the things we have done and go back . . . to the kind of government we had in the Twenties."[33]

There was no going back for Roosevelt, as he campaigned against Democratic senators who had turned against his agenda. The administration's support helped Claude Pepper win a Senate seat in Florida, but Roosevelt failed to oust more than one of the ten Democratic senators he actively campaigned against.

In the fall of 1938, it was clear Roosevelt no longer had the magic touch, as Republicans picked up eighty-one seats in the House, eight seats in the Senate, and thirteen governorships. Several prominent liberal governors, including Frank Murphy in Michigan, lost reelection. While Democrats still won most of the elections nationally, statewide, and locally, their iron grip on power had clearly loosened. Whether it was the fault of the recession, the unstable economy, or Roosevelt, no one could say for sure, but, as the leader of the party, Roosevelt had to take some blame.

Yet Roosevelt was quick to point out after the midterms that he was the first two-term president since Monroe who had not lost control of Congress before the end of his second term. He reminded Democratic members of Congress that they could only remain in power if they remained united. Thus, he doubled down on the increasing liberal tilt of his policies and appointments. Roosevelt was not infallible, but it was folly to bet against him.

Roosevelt never gave up hope big business would cooperate with at least some of the New Deal, even as fellow Democrats joined Republicans to retract other aspects of it. When he vented his frustration to Eleanor in 1939 that he did not understand why many leaders of big business persistently refused to cooperate with the administration, she said it was because they were afraid of him. His high approval ratings gave some relief but not enough to mend fences with Democrats who had become disillusioned with his policies and mounting congressional investigations into New Deal spending, corruption, and Communist spies.

V

In a conversation with Treasury Secretary Henry Morgenthau, Eleanor once said, "There were only two people who stood up to Franklin, you and Louis." Morgenthau responded, "No, you're wrong. There were three—Louis, myself, and Eleanor Roosevelt."[34]

Whether she wanted to be or not, Eleanor was a member of Franklin's inner circle. Just as she had done in the first term, she continued to bring new visitors with new ideas into his presence. Besides continuing to serve as the President's eyes, ears, and legs, she understood that Franklin got information primarily from people not

books. The more different kinds of people and diverse views she
could bring to him, the better informed he would be.

To the public, Eleanor exuded confidence and was uniquely effective as first lady. When she first assumed the role, she had declined a
weekly column, but with Howe's support and encouragement, she
began one called "My Day." Initially, the purpose was to publicize her
public activities, but Franklin, Howe, and she realized it could be used
as an asset for his reelection. Before the end of the year, *Women's Home
Companion* had discontinued the column because it thought that it
had become too political. That did not stop Eleanor. She persisted in
writing the column, and by 1938, it appeared in sixty-two newspapers
across the country. As both her and the column's popularity soared,
she used it for plainly political purposes—backing Roosevelt's reelection, the Court-packing plan, new civil rights laws, and the United
States' obligations abroad. Franklin agreed that the column made Eleanor an even greater asset to his reelection and popularity than she had
been, as it allowed her to reach 4 million people, many of whom Franklin could not reach otherwise. She transformed the role of the first lady
by becoming such a public face for the administration.

Despite Eleanor's best efforts, Franklin persistently refused to
support civil rights legislation. When she asked him to support Senator Wagner's anti-lynching bill, introduced in January 1934, he
refused, even after meeting privately with Walter White, the secretary of the NAACP. After telling White he could not support the
legislation, Franklin explained, "I did not choose the tools with
which I must work. But I've got to get legislation passed by Congress to save America."[35] When the bill came up for a vote four years
later, Franklin refused to take a public stand on it. The NAACP invited Eleanor to attend the closing of its twenty-sixth annual
convention in 1935, but the President told her not to go. He explained that any support he showed for civil rights legislation would
undercut his popularity in the old South. Yet he had previously supported abandoning Woodrow Wilson's segregation of governmental
employees and appointed African Americans in larger numbers
than any previous administration had, including the first African
American to sit on the federal bench.

Eleanor was widely acknowledged as the administration's con-science. Her impact was evident when she resigned her membership in the Daughters of the American Revolution in response to its barring world-renowned opera singer Marian Anderson from performing in a concert at Constitutional Hall in Washington because she was Afri-can American. Working with Interior Secretary Ickes, Eleanor enlisted Franklin's support and arranged for Anderson to perform at the Lin-coln Memorial. More than 75,000 people attended her performance. Six weeks later, the President invited Anderson to sing at the White House, at a dinner given for King George VI and Queen Elizabeth.

Similarly, the nation saw photographs and read of Eleanor fetch-ing a glass of water for Mary McLeod Bethune, a prominent African American educator, at a fund-raising event for Bethune-Cookman College, a historically black college in Florida, and deliberately plac-ing her seat in the aisle between the white and black sections at a segregated conference in Birmingham, Alabama. As Pauli Murray said, "You would have to have lived in that era to know what kind of impact this had."[36]

While some aides, including Ickes, thought Eleanor did more harm than good, the President said, "I can always say, 'Well, that's my wife; I can't do anything about her.'"[37] Eleanor acknowledged that "he might have been happier with a wife who was completely uncrit-ical. That I was never able to be.... Nevertheless, I think I sometimes acted as a spur, even though the spurring was not always wanted or welcomed. I was one of those who served his purposes."[38]

In February 1939, she told the American Youth Congress, "I be-lieve in the things that have been done. They helped but did not solve the fundamental problems [confronting the country]. I never be-lieved the Federal government could solve the whole problem. It bought us time to think."[39] It was not just her idealism that Eleanor brought to the President's table but also an absence of the arrogance, partisanship, and abstract thinking of many of his advisors. Engaged with the problems of real-world people, she brought an invaluable perspective to policy discussions with the President.

Yet, even when Roosevelt could not back civil rights laws, he en-couraged Eleanor, "You go ahead; you do everything you can do....

But I just can't do it."[40] She formed an alliance between White and the two Senate sponsors of the anti-lynching bill. Her advocacy, along with her visible support for the civil rights of African Americans, helped to nurture public support for the measure. In 1937, supporters of a strong bill in the House forced it out of the Judiciary Committee, where the committee chair, Hatton Summers, a Democratic representative from Texas, had hoped to bury it. In the aftermath of the horrific blowtorching of two African Americans in Mississippi, the House rallied to Eleanor's cause and passed the measure 227–120.

In January 1938, Franklin came out in favor of the bill, which Southern senators filibustered. They worried that it would lead to the elimination of Jim Crow, while others attributed the law to a Communist conspiracy to destroy America. By February 21, Roosevelt could no longer afford to keep pushing it. The cost was too high: The filibuster produced inaction on legislation to provide emergency relief to people hurt by the recession. Only by relinquishing his opposition to the filibuster was he able to get final New Deal legislation concerning the creation of the U.S. Housing Authority and the Farm Security Administration freed for a vote in the Senate.

While Roosevelt assured Americans in his 1939 State of the Union, "We can and should avoid any action, or any lack of action, which will encourage, assist, or build up an aggressor,"[41] Eleanor protested. Franklin's persistent defense of his inaction abroad as deferring to "political realities" at home "annoyed me very much," she said "by trying to convince me that our course was correct. Though he knew I thought we were doing the wrong thing, he was simply trying to salve his own conscience.... It was one of many times that I felt akin to a hair shirt." Yet Franklin kept encouraging her to voice her concerns because it allowed him to understand liberals' objections to his positions both at home and abroad.

Eleanor felt keenly the truth of the adage that "no good deed goes unpunished." Some of her advocacy provoked vicious, misogynistic insults and criticisms. At other times, she felt betrayed, as she did with Harry Hopkins.

Eleanor always denied the rumor that she first brought Hopkins to the attention of Franklin, whom in fact he had placed in charge of relief programs when he was governor of New York. Yet Eleanor and Hopkins had once been close friends, and she helped Hopkins through the death of his first wife and nursed him through a serious bout with stomach cancer in 1939. But at the end of that year he left Eleanor behind as he inserted himself into the President's inner circle.

As Eleanor's daughter Anna Roosevelt recalled, "Here was Harry who was Mother's protégé to start with, and suddenly Harry became Father's protégé." Eleanor herself confessed to a friend that "I haven't gotten used to people who say they care for me but are only interested in getting to Franklin."[42]

VI

As Roosevelt proposed various federal solutions to the weakened economy, his critics likened him to the dictators threatening to divide Europe up among them—namely, Hitler, Mussolini, and Stalin. The comparisons both angered and hurt Roosevelt, as he cherished the American system of government. For all the vitriol he had directed at the Supreme Court, he always accepted its judgments, and he often twisted himself into knots to appease Congress. He knew it was up to him to persuade Congress to relinquish the Neutrality Act or at least give him more authority to protect American interests and allies abroad. With Hitler boasting of a new German arms program, Roosevelt announced on October 11, 1938, $300 million to fortify American armaments.

As Roosevelt and his foreign policy advisors floated various options for helping allies, Germany, Italy, Japan, and Russia were each on the move. Four months after Germany invaded the Rhineland in 1936, civil war erupted in Spain, which became a proving ground for the newly developed weapons of both Germany and Italy. In early 1936, Roosevelt wrote his ambassador in Paris that "the whole European panorama is fundamentally blacker than at any time in your life or [mine]." He predicted "these may be the last days of peace [before] a long chaos."[43]

Over the next two years, Congress amended the Neutrality Act twice. In January 1937, a joint resolution was approved that kept the main features of the Neutrality Act but added a "cash and carry provision," which gave the President discretion to allow benign nations to purchase any items from the United States so long as they were not arms, they were paid for with cash, and they were carried away on non-American ships.

In 1938, Germany marched into Austria. At a conference in Munich later that year, Hitler secured the agreement of Britain and France to his annexation of Sudetenland. Six months later, Germany extended its domination of all of Czechoslovakia. In response, Congress, at Roosevelt's urging, amended the Neutrality Act further to allow arms trades with France and Great Britain on a cash and carry basis.

In mid-April 1939, Roosevelt asked both Hitler and Mussolini if they would promise not to attack thirty-one nations he listed by name. In response, Hitler appeared before the Reichstag to mock Roosevelt by listing each name to howls of laughter. Hermann Göring, Hitler's chief lieutenant, wondered aloud about whether Roosevelt had some brain malady, while Mussolini speculated Roosevelt must have been suffering from paralysis.

After signing a nonaggression pact with Russia in 1939, Hitler's army invaded Poland on September 1. Two days later, Britain and France declared war against Germany. With Italy invading Albania, Japan extending its full-scale invasion of China and going to war against the Soviet Union on the Manchurian-Mongolian frontier, and the Soviet Union invading Finland on November 30, 1939, a second world war was underway in all but name.

VII

Before Germany invaded Poland in September 1939, Roosevelt had been thinking ahead: As early as the 1930s, he had encouraged scientific leaders seeking funds for researching atomic weaponry, but Congress declined.

Feeling the urgency of impending war and German ingenuity, three scientists—Enrico Fermi, formerly of Italy, Leo Szilard from Hungary, and Albert Einstein—drafted a letter in October 1939 to the President expressing their confidence such a weapon could be assembled. Einstein warned Roosevelt of the need for "watchfulness and, if necessary, quick action," pointing out that Germany had acquired uranium from Czechoslovakia. He explained that such bombs could be "carried by boat or exploded in a port" and destroy "the whole port altogether with some of the surrounding territory." Roosevelt told economist Alexander Sachs, who had brought the letter for Roosevelt to read, "What you are after is to see that the Nazis don't blow us up."[44]

Several scientists, led by the president of the Carnegie Institution, Vannevar Bush, convinced Roosevelt to establish a new scientific committee within the Council of National Defense. Bush advised Roosevelt that, because Germans had discovered fission in 1938, time was of the essence for the United States to catch up and fortify its armaments. (Roosevelt modeled the new committee on a similar effort that had been undertaken under the Council for National Defense during World War I.) The new committee's charge was to study and develop new "mechanisms and devices of warfare." Thus began a race to develop a nuclear weapon that could end the war if necessary.

Spreading hostilities in Europe and Asia, coupled with concerns about Germans' developing a new weapon that could obliterate its enemies, led Roosevelt to send Undersecretary of State Sumner Welles to Europe in early February 1940 ostensibly on a peacekeeping mission, just like the one Wilson had sent Colonel House to conduct in 1916.

Roosevelt had known Welles for years; he had encouraged him to attend both Groton and Harvard and later helped Welles land a position in his State Department. The architect of the Good Neighbor Policy, Welles was one of a coterie of advisors whom Roosevelt trusted more than Hull on matters of diplomacy. Ickes reaffirmed Roosevelt's lack of confidence in Hull, whom he regarded as having been responsible for his department's "undemocratic...outlook," which was "shot through with fascism" and antisemitism.[45] Roosevelt appointed several ambassadors, including Josephus Daniels in

Mexico and Joseph Kennedy in England, who reported directly to the President, though neither maintained his confidence for long.

Roosevelt trusted Welles, whose acumen in foreign affairs proved itself time and again. He first traveled to Italy, where he met with Mussolini, whom, he told Roosevelt, was untrustworthy, ponderous, and woefully out of shape. Next, Welles visited Berlin, where he met Hitler and his foreign minister Joseph von Ribbentrop. Roosevelt had never met Hitler, and Welles's appraisal was the first Roosevelt had received from a trusted source: "He has, in real life, none of the effeminate appearance of which he has been accused. He looked in excellent physical condition and in good training. His color was good, and while his eyes were tired, they were clear. He was dignified both in speech and movement, and there was not the slightest comic effect from moustache and hair which one sees in his caricatures."

It was not the appearance Roosevelt had expected, though, as Welles's message went on, the danger was manifest: "His voice in conversation is low and well-modulated. It had, only once, in our hour and a half's conversation, the raucous stridency which is heard in his speeches—and it was only at that moment that his features lost their composure and that his eyes lost their decidedly 'gemutlich' look. He spoke with clarity and precision, and always in a beautiful German, of which I could follow every word."[46] After speaking with Hitler, Welles was convinced that the only way to avert war in Europe was to disarm Germany.

The other German leaders Welles met reinforced his concerns. He thought Ribbentrop had "a very stupid mind. The man is saturated with hate for England, and to the exclusion of any other dominating mental influence. [He] was guilty of a hundred inaccuracies in his presentation of German policy during recent years. I have rarely seen a man I disliked more."

Welles met as well with Rudolf Hess, who impressed him as a man "of a very low order of intelligence," and with Hermann Göring, whom he regarded as seriously overweight and as unintelligent as he had found most of the other German leaders he met.

In Paris, Welles found French officials comprised of nothing but "ice water" but at least agreeing with his critical appraisals of Germany's leaders, especially Hitler. In London, British leaders expressed skepticism of the utility or value of Welles's visit and made clear that war, not diplomacy, was the only way to ensure a lasting peace. On returning to the United States in April, Welles made certain Roosevelt understood the grim outlook in Europe and for America's chances to stay out of the impending world war.

Over the span of the first five months of 1940, Germany bombarded Denmark and Norway and invaded France, which quickly surrendered. The only major United States ally left free of domination in Europe was Britain, which Germany bombed throughout the summer. Hitler warned Latin American countries that, once Germany defeated Britain, they would have to rely on Germany to provide any further markets for food and economic assistance.

In early January 1940, Roosevelt announced that he would not seek renewal of Japan's treaty with the United States, which had governed American trade with Japan for decades. Through Secretary Hull, Roosevelt rejected Japan's invocation of its own Monroe Doctrine, a policy made by President James Monroe that warned European powers not to interfere in the affairs of the Western Hemisphere, which the United States considered its sphere of influence. "There is no more resemblance between our Monroe Doctrine and the so-called Monroe Doctrine of Japan than there is between black and white," Roosevelt declared. Though Hull communicated America's intentions "to defend itself against any aggression which may be undertaken against it," Japan made clear it intended to do the same in its sphere in the world. In July, Roosevelt directed that the law restricting exports to belligerent nations should be extended to aviation fuel, and he added scrap iron and steel in September. Japanese officials were displeased, labeling the move "unfriendly."[47]

After the fall of France, Roosevelt was eager to increase funding of scientific research into the building of atomic weapons. In the opening months of 1940, he persuaded Congress to appropriate several billion dollars for defense measures, including an aircraft production program with the ambitious goal of building fifty thousand planes in a year.

Roosevelt had never made any headway with the British prime minister Neville Chamberlain, who stubbornly insisted on continuing to appease Hitler until he was forced to resign in the summer of 1940. The new prime minister was his conservative colleague Winston Churchill.

Roosevelt welcomed the change as he had given up on Chamberlain after he had rejected cohosting with the United States an international conference on the crises in Europe. When Chamberlain said he wanted to recognize the legitimacy of Italy's conquest of Ethiopia, Roosevelt was apoplectic. Chamberlain told Churchill that he did not trust Roosevelt: "It is always best and safest," he said, "to count on nothing from the Americans but words."[48] Though Chamberlain reversed course, Roosevelt had ceased taking him seriously.

Roosevelt was pleased to learn Churchill was the opposite of Chamberlain in nearly every important way. Once in office, Churchill announced to the world that if Germany wanted war, England would use every means possible to defend themselves and defeat the Nazis. Churchill told Roosevelt it was time for the United States to step up to the defense of its oldest ally in the world, Britain. He pleaded for military aid, especially destroyers that would defend Britain's coastline. In August 1940, Roosevelt devised a plan to give Britain fifty American destroyers in exchange for long-term leases on naval bases in the western Atlantic. Congress ratified the Lend-Lease Act in March 1941.

VIII

There was no one in Roosevelt's administration who was an obvious heir apparent, and, even if there were, Franklin well remembered how the efforts of both Andrew Jackson and Theodore Roosevelt to handpick their successors had failed.

To begin with, Roosevelt's relationship with his vice president, John Nance Garner, had turned toxic. The split over the Court-packing plan was hardly the beginning. In the early days of the New Deal, Garner had warned the President that he did not support a welfare state. In 1936, he vigorously opposed Roosevelt's giving any support for unions, which he thought were encouraging workers to violate the property rights of owners. He groused incessantly that Roosevelt listened more to his liberal advisors than to congressional leaders, who genuinely loved Garner.

While Jim Farley gave Garner credit for getting New Deal programs through Congress during the first five years of the Roosevelt administration, there were reports as early as 1937 that Vice President Garner had become the "conniver in chief," who was leading the opposition not just to the Court-packing plan but any further New Deal measures. When Garner became aware of the efforts of Hopkins and other administration officials to purge the administration of conservatives opposed to the New Deal, he made no secret that he no longer supported Roosevelt or his programs. On December 17, 1938, Garner and Roosevelt met to see if they could reach any reconciliation. None was possible.

Indeed, in 1938, the Texas state Democratic convention had endorsed Garner for president. By March 1939, both houses of the Texas legislature followed suit, and in June, Garner endorsed the formation of a Garner-for-president committee. In late December, Garner said that he would accept the Democratic nomination for president based on the assumption Roosevelt would not run for a third term.

Roosevelt's decision on whether to run had all the frustrating elements of his usual management style. First, he kept people guessing for as long as possible. People had good reason to refer to him as the "Sphynx."[49] Not divulging his intentions sooner than he had to enabled him to control the party machinery and the party faithful whose support he needed to secure the nomination. It kept Congress off-balance, as its members were unsure whether they were dealing with a lame duck or not. Foreign nations, too, could not lightly disregard his opinion and input so long as there was a possibility that he would still be president in the next few years.

Second, Roosevelt's dallying had the effect of splintering his opposition. As early as February, Senator Walter George of Georgia urged Roosevelt to run for a third term, but Roosevelt rebuffed him: "I am chained to this chair from morning to night ... day after day, week after week, month after month. And I can't stand it any longer. I can't go on with it." Roosevelt might well have meant what he said at that moment, but, as biographer James MacGregor Burns explained, "his tactic was quite in keeping with his usual political and administrative leadership—to strengthen his own position by the method of divide and conquer. Now he carried the tactic to a new level; not only did he encourage the rest of the candidates to contend with each other, he enlarged the field so that there would be a host of rivals wrestling for delegate votes."[50]

In accepting Farley's resignation, he encouraged Farley to assemble his own presidential campaign. In 1940, he encouraged Hopkins to run, appointed him secretary of commerce to strengthen his résumé, and even advised him on campaign strategy. He did the same with former Indiana governor Paul McNutt, whom he appointed to lead the Federal Security Agency and encouraged to run. He told Secretary of State Hull that he hoped Hull might succeed him as president, told Senator Alban Barkley some White House officials were hoping he would run for president, suggested to New York governor Herbert Lehman that he deserved the vote of his state delegation at the convention, and encouraged others within his circle, including Robert Jackson and Henry Wallace, to consider running, too. He did not encourage Eleanor to run, but she urged him not to.

Third, Roosevelt preferred to focus on only one major problem at a time. This had been true of his Court-packing plan, and it was true of his approach to foreign affairs and to a possible third term. These problems were interrelated, but he came at each with a singular focus that could, at times, pose complications for the others and his image. Consistency was less important to Roosevelt than his finding the best solution—for him—to the problem at hand. As the coalitions that had secured Roosevelt's victories in 1932 and 1936 were fracturing, Roosevelt cobbled together a new coalition, consisting of die-hard New Dealers, liberals who supported widening and strengthening the safety net for the unemployed, sick, and impoverished. Its blue-collar members could be found in the cities not in the rural areas, whose support had been critical for Franklin's electoral successes in 1932 and 1936.

In late June, Republicans nominated Wendell Willkie, a success-ful New York lawyer and businessman, as their candidate for president. Willkie agreed with Roosevelt on the most important issue—the likelihood of war—an agreement Roosevelt helped to sew through his appointments of two prominent Republicans to lead the War and Navy Departments just three days before the start of the Re-publican convention: as secretary of war Henry Stimson, who had served in the cabinets of both Taft and Hoover, and as secretary of the navy Frank Knox, an influential newspaper editor and one of Teddy's Rough Riders. Given that both men were widely respected within the Republican establishment, the appointments were de-signed to help Roosevelt's fall campaign.

From Roosevelt's perspective, he had no option but to do what he did. He told confidants that he would only run for a third term if matters in Europe got worse and if Democrats supported his run for a third term. Yet all the while Roosevelt was lining up supporters to serve as delegates for the Democratic convention scheduled to begin July 15. For Roosevelt recognized something the opponents to his seeking a third term had not acknowledged: While it was true that Washington and Jackson had not sought a third term, which they each likely could have won, the people they had chosen to follow them—John Adams and Martin Van Buren, respectively—to effec-tively be their third terms—had failed miserably in their attempts. Of course, Franklin well remembered, too, that Teddy's attempt to pick a successor had failed miserably. That was not a chance Roose-velt had any intention of risking.

Before the convention began, Roosevelt met with Hull and Farley separately. At a July 3 lunch with Roosevelt, Hull noticed a change in Roosevelt, who downplayed the likelihood of his becoming a can-didate but spoke in a "sort of impatient, incredulous tone" of the growing pressure within the party to nominate him for a third term. After the meeting, Hull was sure Roosevelt planned to run again.

Farley was less cordial when he and Roosevelt met in early July. He was angry with Roosevelt over his persistent failure to tell Farley his plans for the upcoming election and for what he considered to be Roosevelt's deceit in not being straight with Farley about his views on whether a Catholic, like Farley, had any realistic chance of winning the nomination or the presidency. Yet, keen on winning the Catholic vote, Roosevelt appointed several Catholics to high-profile positions, including Joseph Kennedy as ambassador to Britain in 1938. It did not take long before Roosevelt tired of Kennedy's antisemitism and appeasement of Germany.[51] Wanting to remove Kennedy in 1940, Roosevelt hesitated because of his likely appeal to Catholic voters. At a dinner at the White House in October, he secured Kennedy's support for his reelection in exchange for Roosevelt's pledge to support him for the presidency in four years and his son Joseph for the governorship of Massachusetts in 1942.

With the convention less than two weeks away, Roosevelt invited Farley to Hyde Park in what turned out to be their last meeting together. He told Farley, "Jim, I don't want to run and I'm going to tell the convention so." Farley responded, "If you make it specific, the convention will not nominate you," and pushed again his case for Roosevelt not to seek a third term. "What would you do if you were in my place?" Roosevelt asked. Farley said, "Exactly what General Sherman did many years ago—issue a statement saying, I would refuse to run if nominated and would not serve if elected." Roosevelt responded, "Jim, if nominated and elected, I could not in these times refuse to take the inaugural oath, even if I knew I would be dead within thirty days." Despite the earnestness Farley saw in Roosevelt's eyes, the two men understood each other. Farley understood Roosevelt was going to run, and Roosevelt understood Farley would not stand down. They both realized their longstanding friendship and partnership was at an end.[52]

Farley was hardly the only one who thought Roosevelt's decision a betrayal. He, Garner, and Hull met early in 1940 to feel one another out on how best to deny Roosevelt the third term they suspected he craved. Roosevelt tried to get intermediaries to talk Farley out of running, but he stayed in the race. Hull was possibly the one that concerned Roosevelt the most, because he knew Farley and Garner would be willing to unite behind him. Hull was uncomfortable being a candidate and remaining as secretary of state, and Roosevelt knew that Hull would not fully commit to being a candidate if it meant losing Roosevelt's support. But Hull received virtually no support within the convention or the party, and he ultimately could not bring himself to run.

Once Germany invaded France in May 1940, the die was cast. Roosevelt trusted no one more than himself to lead the country through the coming conflict. He knew none of the other Democrats running could beat him at his own game. That same month, without taking anyone into his confidence, he announced he was running again.

At the convention, Frances Perkins was on site to monitor the circumstances. Shortly after it began, she called Roosevelt to inform him that "the situation is just as sour as it can be," and she urged him to come to Chicago to ensure his support among the delegates remained strong. Roosevelt declined, but Perkins suggested at least Eleanor should go, and, at Franklin's urging, she called the first lady.

Eleanor's first reaction was to dismiss the suggestion Franklin would not win renomination as absurd, but she said she would be willing to consider giving a speech at the convention so long as it was okay with Farley. Touched by her call asking for his permission, Farley said, her "coming will not affect my situation one way or the other. From the President's point of view I think it desirable, if not essential, that you come."[53] She arrived in time to witness Roosevelt's winning the Democratic nomination with the support of nearly 90 percent of the delegates.

Despite cheers throughout the convention hall to renominate Franklin, Farley demanded a roll call vote, ensuring that Roosevelt not receive the acclimation he wanted. None of the defeated had much of a political future after such trouncing. Franklin and Eleanor pleaded with Farley to remain part of the team, but he resigned from his position of leadership in the party. Garner retired to his home in Uvalde, Texas.

While Roosevelt met several times with his aides during the first few months of 1940 to discuss possible Democratic candidates for president, those meetings also served as opportunities for him to explore possible running mates. Once he had the nomination in hand, he called his secretary of state to offer him the vice presidency. Hull declined.

Roosevelt then called Harry Hopkins to say that he wanted his progressive secretary of agriculture, Henry Wallace, to be his running mate. The case for Wallace was not obvious: While, by all accounts, he had done an excellent job in leading the Department of Agriculture, been an ardent supporter of the New Deal, and openly backed Roosevelt's running for a third term, he had never run for public office before, had written embarrassing letters addressing the President variously as "Flaming One" and "Wavering One,"[54] and his father had been secretary of agriculture for two Republican presidents—Harding and Coolidge—which thus raised concerns among some Democratic voters about Wallace's core political leanings.

A slew of candidates emerged as contenders, with Hopkins having urged Roosevelt to choose William O. Douglas instead, and the speaker of the house, William Bankhead, a conservative from Alabama, insisting Roosevelt had offered him the job. Eleanor agreed with the others that "Wallace won't do."[55] Franklin disagreed and threatened that if the convention did not choose Wallace, he would decline his nomination to run for a third term as president.

The race tightened between the liberal Wallace and the conservative Speaker Bankhead of Alabama. With the delegates fiercely divided, Farley led Eleanor to the stage. Commanding the respect of the delegates, she began with a tribute to Farley: "I think nobody could appreciate more what he has done for the party and I want to give him here my thanks and devotion." Her praise and affection soothed Farley as well as the convention itself. She went on to tell the delegates that "this is no ordinary time. No time for weighing anything except what we can best do for the country as a whole."

Without mentioning Wallace's name, she asked the convention to accept Franklin's choice for vice president. "No man who is a candidate or who is President can carry this situation alone. This is only carried by a unified people who love their country and who will live for it . . . to the fullest of their ability."[56] The convention chose Wallace on its first ballot. Wallace begrudgingly agreed when Eleanor pleaded with him not to take to the stage to make a public statement.

Further putting aside her objections to Roosevelt's run for a third term, Eleanor gave speeches, met with leaders of different coalitions, and scheduled events that she thought would help to make her husband more appealing to the groups whose support he needed to win.

In early June 1940, she invited the leaders of the American Youth Congress to meet with the President. Among the surprisingly sharp questions directed at him, one complaint that he and Congress were doing nothing to help the American people brought him up short. After a pause, the President asked his inquisitor, "Young man, I think you are very sincere. Have you read Carl Sandberg's *Lincoln*?" After the young man said no, Roosevelt added, "I think the impression was that Lincoln was a pretty sad man, because he could not do all he wanted to do at one time. . . . He had to compromise to make a few gains. Lincoln was one of those unfortunate people called a 'politician.'" He turned the question around, adding "Maybe you would make a much better President than I have. . . . If you ever sit here, you will learn that you cannot, just from shouting at the housetops, get what you want all the time."[57]

The comments were revealing. On a day of special significance, Roosevelt was thinking of Lincoln, demonstrating, yet again, how he regarded Lincoln as a model. He likely invoked Lincoln to appeal to Republicans, though the appeal was broader. It was obvious, too, that Roosevelt felt only presidents could appreciate what the job required. He could not hide his own elitism.

The fall election was tense for both candidates. Though one poll in August showed Willkie leading in enough states to have a majority of Electoral College votes, Roosevelt was dubious. Meanwhile, Willkie berated Roosevelt for seeking a third term, for being a warmonger, and for being duplicitous. He cited examples of Roosevelt's isolationism, appeasement, and preparing for war all at the same time. Roosevelt bided his time until the middle of October when he announced he would deliver five speeches in two weeks.

Though he had a team of speechwriters, including Rosenman and the playwright Robert Sherwood, Roosevelt usually wrote the final draft by hand. As Rosenman explained, Roosevelt "had worked so hard and continuously on [a speech] that he knew it almost by heart.... He could look away from the manuscript so much that many people did not even know he was reading."[58]

In Philadelphia, Roosevelt reminded the audience that he accepted the Democratic platform's pledge "not [to] participate in foreign wars." In Cleveland, he shared his vision of America, with several paragraphs beginning with the words "I see" followed by his description of what lay ahead for the country. He concluded, "I see an America devoted to our freedom—unified by tolerance and religious faith—a people consecrated to peace, a people confident in strength because their body and spirit are secure and unafraid."

On November 2, in Buffalo, Roosevelt told the crowd, "Your President said this country is not going to war." Near the end of the campaign, he appeared at Madison Square Garden, where he lambasted senators for voting against the repeal of the arms embargo. Yet, in Boston, he pledged again that "this country is not going to war."[59] With that promise, Roosevelt won 449–82 in the Electoral College. The popular vote was narrower, with Roosevelt winning 27 million votes to Willkie's 22 million. Roosevelt's winning margin in the popular vote was the smallest of any winner since 1916.

In his first post-election news conference, Roosevelt was surprisingly testy. As the campaign was nearing its conclusion, he had made whatever pledges he could to help himself, telling a staffer, "When that term is over, there will be another president." Though Roosevelt did not mention the pledge again, a reporter did. After reading the statement back to him, the reporter asked Roosevelt, "Did you definitely mean that?" Roosevelt shot back, "Oughtn't you to go back to grade school and learn English?" "That was your meaning?" the reporter insisted. "Read it," the President said. "I am not teaching you English. Read it." "I have read it, sir," the reporter responded. Roosevelt persisted, "Read it again."[60]

People had good reason to distrust Roosevelt's pledges not to run again or reassurances to Americans, "Your boys are not going to be sent into any foreign wars."[61] While in September 1940 Hitler put on hold his plan to invade Britain amphibiously, he ordered massive bombing of London and other British cities in October. Churchill was elated with Roosevelt's victory, writing him the next day, "I did not think it right for me as a foreigner to express my opinion upon American policies while the election was on. But now I feel you will not mind my saying that I prayed for your success, and I am truly thankful for it." He pressed Roosevelt further for help in securing the armaments necessary to rebuff the German assault. Roosevelt's naval secretary foresaw no chance for the country to avoid entering the war. Following the collapse of France, the army's chief of staff, General George Marshall, told Roosevelt that he expected Britain soon to suffer the same fate.

On December 7, Churchill wrote a letter to Roosevelt outlining Britain's long-range strategy but acknowledging that Britain could no longer pay for its supplies. Receiving the letter while on vacation with Harry Hopkins, Roosevelt mulled over a response for two days. "Then," as Hopkins said later, "one evening, he suddenly came out with it—the whole program. He didn't seem to have any clear idea how it could be done legally. But there wasn't any doubt he'd find a way to do it." At a hastily arranged press conference held on December 17, Roosevelt proposed a new initiative in which the United State would lend, not sell, the supplies it needed to fight Germany. The reason for the plan, he explained, was simple: "Suppose my neighbor's home catches fire," he said, if "he can take my garden hose and connect it up with a hydrant, I may help him to put out his fire. Now, what do I do? I don't say to him before the operation, 'Neighbor, my garden hose cost me $15—I want my hose back after the fire is over.... In other words, if you lend certain munitions and get the munitions back at the end of the war, [you] are all right."[62] In his December 29 Fireside Chat, Franklin said that in facing threats to its national security the United States must be "the great arsenal of democracy."[63] His next big challenge was to make that true.

CHAPTER SEVEN

War Comes to
America (1940–1941)

O N THE SAME DAY THAT he took the oath of office as the first President of the United States on April 30, 1789, George Washington
wrote James Madison, "As the first of everything, in our situation will
establish a Precedent, it is devoutly wished on my part, that these
precedents may be fixed on true principles."[1] But, for Franklin Roosevelt, precedents, like tradition, could and even needed to be broken.

In his first two terms, Roosevelt's New Deal revolutionized the
role of the federal government in regulating the national economy
and serious social problems. As Roosevelt prepared for his third inauguration in 1941, the economy was no longer his highest priority.
Defending democracy was. Roosevelt had to harness the revolutionary zeal at home to protect democracy here and abroad.

Roosevelt knew Americans rejected the most radical movement
in averting war—Wilson's proposed League of Nations. While the
world never accepted Wilson's objective of ending war once and for
all, the threat of world domination was not new to human history,
even if it took new forms in the years ahead. Roosevelt met the new
threats in the only ways he knew—the classic ways of negotiating,
forging alliances, and ultimately war. The more the world changed,
the more its problems seemed worse than ever. That basic dynamic

led Roosevelt to look back, now that he was leading the nation into world war, not to Jackson but to Abraham Lincoln, whose leadership during the Civil War became a model for Roosevelt as his generation struggled to defeat the forces threatening to destroy the world as they had known it.

I

Franklin Roosevelt entered his third term more seamlessly than he had his first or second. Neither he nor the nation needed a transition; the election settled that. He had his staff largely intact and a new vice president already at work, and he had assembled his war cabinet well before his inaugural set for January 20, 1941. Besides having made Frank Knox secretary of the navy and Henry Stimson secretary of war in 1940, Roosevelt allowed each of them to bring their trusted lieutenants, aides, and advisors with them. Roosevelt had elevated Robert Jackson to be attorney general in 1940, and he asked Harry Hopkins to leave his position as commerce secretary to move into the White House in 1940 as his second-in-command. Always eager to please Roosevelt, Hopkins effectively became Howe's replacement and more, often serving as a surrogate for the President.

In 1942, Congress approved Roosevelt's proposed Joint Chiefs of Staff, modeled on the British system. Its members were the heads of all the military branches—Admiral William Leahy, who was chief of the new council and special military advisor to the President, General George Marshall as army chief of staff, Admiral Ernest King as chief of staff of the United States Fleet and chief of naval operations, and General Henry "Hap" Arnold as chief of staff for the air force, which, at the time, was housed in the army. Roosevelt knew each from his days in the Naval Department in World War I.

Roosevelt tasked Hopkins, Rosenman, and Early to draft his last Annual Message to Congress of his second term. Roosevelt usually took the first cut at drafting his speeches and then had his team, if he allowed them to look at them at all, fine-tune them. When it was the trio's turn to draft, it often took them days, if not weeks, to fine-

tune Roosevelt's speeches, with Franklin giving direction and feedback and often revising the speeches up until the last moment—if
not during the addresses themselves. The message he delivered on
January 6, 1941, was among his boldest yet.

Modeling his speech on Woodrow Wilson's Fourteen Points,
which had set forth on January 8, 1918, the principles Wilson believed should guide peace negotiations to end the First World War,
Roosevelt set forth the Four Freedoms that he believed should guide
the new war effort: "The first is freedom of speech and expression—
everywhere in the world. The second is freedom of every person to
worship God in his own way—everywhere in the world. The third
is freedom of want—which . . . means economic understandings
which will secure to every nation a healthy peacetime life for its in-
habitants—everywhere in the world." And, finally, he said, "The
fourth is freedom of fear [so that] no nation will be in a position to
commit an act of physical aggression against any neighbor—anywhere in the world."[2] These were ambitious aims, which required
collaboration with Britain, the last nation standing between Nazi
Germany and European domination.

Americans of a certain age, including Franklin Roosevelt, knew
firsthand the ravages of war and did not want to repeat them. The
nation had survived one world war, incurring the deaths of more
than 110,000 Americans and the serious wounding of 300,000 more.
But could it survive a second? When Roosevelt met Churchill in 1941,
80 percent of the American people opposed the United States' entry
into the war.

The Nazi regime was a destroyer of democracy, and the last standing democratic regime in Europe seemed hardly any match for it.
England fought with whatever it had and could borrow. Edward R.
Murrow, covering the war for CBS, reported when Churchill took office, "Now the hour had come for him to mobilize the English
language, and send it into battle."[3] Many other words followed, but
they would all be for naught if he could not get Roosevelt to unleash
America's "arsenal of democracy." Roosevelt did not invent the
phrase; it came to his attention from Justice Frankfurter, who had
heard it from Jean Monnet, a French diplomat stationed in Washing-

ton. John McCloy, whom Stimson brought into the administration as assistant secretary of war, had used the same phrase in a speech drafted for Roosevelt, who declared "I love it" when he first read it.[4]

Roosevelt, like Churchill and Lincoln, used language to unite, mobilize, inspire, and soothe people. Yet they also used language like a weapon to defeat the opposition, build public support, and, if necessary, go to war. Whether it was a strategy or the result of having a Congress opposed to squandering American lives and resources on another grand scale, Roosevelt adopted Lincoln's singular focus; whereas, for Lincoln it was "to save the Union," Roosevelt's was to save democracy.

Roosevelt also took another page from Lincoln, who said, more than once during the Civil War, that he had no policy. The statement is often misunderstood as meaning Lincoln had no idea what he was doing. Rather, it meant that Lincoln adapted to the exigencies of the moment; he perceived himself as responding to a crisis rather than having a well-thought-out plan or solution in mind from the outset.

The same was true of Roosevelt: In his first years in office, his problem had been that he had too many policies, which confused Americans and often obscured his purposes. His strategy, like that of Lincoln, was to wait for events to reveal the best way forward. Less than a year after his third inaugural, they did.

Though Congress's approval of the President's reorganization of the White House in 1939 allowed him to hire six additional assistants, his staff remained largely intact and as loyal as ever. By the beginning of his third term, Steve Early as press secretary, Grace Tully as Roosevelt's principal personal secretary, and Marvin McIntyre as a presidential secretary, had each become a fixture in the White House. All would serve his entire presidency.

Missy LeHand, who had moved into the White House in 1940, been a member of Roosevelt's inner circle for more than twenty years, and been his confidante and surrogate wife for nearly as long, suffered a debilitating stroke in 1941, left the White House in 1942, and died in 1944. Though she had pleaded with Roosevelt as a lover that he should give her more (and acknowledge her publicly), he never did. Instead, he changed his will so that half of its assets would be used to cover her expenses until she died.

Where would Roosevelt look for guidance in preparing for war?
He looked to the past. In looking to Lincoln (whom he quoted more
than any other president), Roosevelt emulated the brevity and clarity
if not the elegance. His cousin Teddy had modified the Monroe Doctrine not only to oppose European colonization of the countries in
the Western Hemisphere but also to pledge American resolve to protect life, property, and order in those countries. Franklin effectively
tried to globalize the Monroe Doctrine, beginning in 1941 and extending through the remainder of his presidency.

War was hardly the only item on the nation's agenda. For the third
time, the chief justice swore the same man into the presidency. This
time around, Roosevelt conveyed none of the animosity he had shown
the last time the two had stood on this stage. Both men understood
there were bigger challenges than their personal or constitutional differences. Hughes perhaps knew better than anyone that Roosevelt had
transformed the Court through each of his five appointments; and as
Calvin Coolidge's secretary of state, he was familiar with the griev-
ances of Germany and the fragile alliances to stop it.

Yet of the two men standing on the stage of Roosevelt's third inaugural, only one had been completely immersed in a world war. He
was the one leaning on the podium as the weight of the world de-
scended on his shoulders. He was the one who had worked daily
with the one former president who had been tasked initially with
keeping the country out of conflict and then charged with leading it
through the First World War. As Roosevelt spoke that day, he understood that task was now his.

Someone watching Roosevelt's third inauguration might have
had a different impression than someone listening. Not yet sixty,
Roosevelt appeared frail and thin, as his son James, dressed in his
colorful marine uniform, led him slowly to the front of the stage
where he met the chief justice. Hughes was hardly more robust, as
his wife's illness and his nearly eighty years were wearing him down.
Unknown to those listening or watching, he had already spoken with
Roosevelt about the possibility of retiring soon so that he could help
his ailing wife. Anyone looking on could have been forgiven if they
felt unease at the state of the nation's affairs as they watched the two

frail men who were entrusted with preserving American's Constitution and way of life.

Roosevelt's purpose that day was to rally the American people to the defense of democracy. It was now the nation's highest priority. If there was any doubt about where Roosevelt would look for guidance and inspiration, he quickly revealed it, as his first three sentences referenced America's past. This time, it was not Jackson that Roosevelt used for inspiration and authority. Instead, he mentioned America's two greatest presidents, George Washington and Abraham Lincoln, each twice. First, he reminded Americans of the stakes confronting the American people under each presidency: "In Washington's day the task of the people was to create and weld together a nation. In Lincoln's day the task of the people was to preserve the Nation from disruption from within." In 1941, the stakes for the people were arguably more serious—"to save the Nation and its institutions from disruption from without."[5]

America's democracy was very much alive and well, he reassured Americans. He sang the praises of democracy as "the most humane, the most advanced, and in the end the most unconquerable of all forms of human society." He reminded Americans that democracy's "vitality was written into our Mayflower Compact, the Declaration of Independence, into the Constitution of the United States, and the Gettysburg Address." While Lincoln had promised the American people that ending the civil war would bring forth "a new birth of freedom," Roosevelt put his own spin on those words when declaring that the people who had come to America sought "a life that should be new in freedom."[6]

Yet Roosevelt spared no words in condemning isolationists like the aviator Charles Lindbergh and his wife Anne Morrow. Lindberg had become a folk hero as the first person to fly solo across the Atlantic Ocean. Although he had been recruited in 1936 to visit Germany to help gather intelligence on its military air power, Lindbergh and his wife returned home as fans of and apologists for Hitler. With his Hollywood good looks, he was a matinee idol for many Americans. He had used his fame to become the preeminent spokesperson for America First, an isolationist movement fed by antisemitism and hostility

to immigrants and other minorities. Against the advice of his own
State Department, Roosevelt warned Americans of complicity with
German's fifth column operating within the United States: "There are
also American citizens, many of them in high places, who, unwittingly
in most cases, are aiding and abetting the work of these agents." When
told not to include the phrase "many of them in high places," Roosevelt
angrily responded, "In fact, I'm very much tempted to say 'many of
them in high places, especially in the State Department.'"[7]

"The destiny of America," Roosevelt declared, "was proclaimed in
words of prophecy spoken by our First President in his first inaugural in 1789—words almost directed, it would seem, to this year of
1941: 'The preservation of the sacred fire of liberty and the destiny
of the republican model of government are justly considered...
deeply... finally, staked on the experiment entrusted to the hands
of the American people.'" America had never faced a threat like it
did in 1941, but Roosevelt reassured Americans that "in the face of
great perils never before encountered, our strong purpose is to protect and to perpetuate the integrity of democracy."[8]

Before Roosevelt's speech, more than 60 percent of the American
people had signaled their support for the Lend-Lease Act. After the
speech, the number went up. In characteristic Roosevelt fashion, the
speech struck a balance between the forces of isolationism at home
and the forces abroad pushing the country toward war. Most Americans wanted assurance the nation would not enter another world war.
He gave them that while he was preparing to do just the opposite.

II

In the weeks preceding Abraham Lincoln's first inaugural, several
Southern states threatened to secede and attack federal forts. Both
as president-elect and president, Lincoln took great care to ensure
that if any shots were fired, they came from Southern forces. He was
determined that, if war broke out, no one could argue that American
forces had fired the first shot. Wilson, too, obstinately refused to
allow United States entry into the First World War until after Ger-

many made it an issue no more, as it did when its submarines persisted in attacking American ships.

Roosevelt was equally determined not to be the aggressor in any conflict with Germany, Italy, or Japan. With Lincoln and Wilson in mind, he told his cabinet that he was "not willing to fire the first shot." Several months later, in a speech at the Navy Day banquet, Roosevelt returned to the same point, this time noting that the "shooting had started" (Germany had sunk the American ship *Kearny*) and "history recorded who fired the first shot. In the long run, [all] that will matter is who fired the first shot."[9] Lincoln had done everything he could to remind the world—and the people in the South—that they had begun the war, and now it was Roosevelt's turn to state the obvious—Germany, not the United States, had begun the war.

For most of 1941, Roosevelt had the same objective. Gallup polls showed at least 80 percent of the public opposed entry into the war. Aware that the United States was unprepared for war, either in the weaponry it had (or did not yet have), personnel, and training needed for victory, in December Roosevelt floated the idea that fulfilling England's armament needs meant good jobs at good pay for Americans, but told reporters, "I am talking selfishly, from the American point of view—nothing else."[10]

In preparing for war, Roosevelt tasked three different men to visit England, carry messages to Churchill, and report back their assessments of British resolve and resources. The first, Sumner Welles, had gone the year before. The second was Harry Hopkins, about whom Robert Sherwood later said, "The extraordinary fact was that the second most powerful individual in the United States government . . . had no legitimate official position nor any desk of his own except a cardboard table in his bedroom. However, the bedroom was in the White House." Sherwood explained Hopkins's special relationship with the President arose from the fact that "Hopkins made it his job, he made it his religion, to find out just what it was Roosevelt really wanted and then to see to it that neither hell nor high water, nor even possible vacillations by Roosevelt himself, blocked its achievement."[11]

On January 3, Hopkins was at work on Roosevelt's State of the Union speech when Press Secretary Steve Early called to congratulate

him. "Why?" Hopkins asked. Early told him that Roosevelt had just
held a press conference announcing he was sending Hopkins to England. Roosevelt had no trusted ally in place to work with Churchill
and the British. Ambassador Joseph Kennedy had been recalled in
1940 ostensibly to help Roosevelt shore up Catholic support for his
reelection. In fact, he had become a liability because of his outspoken
antisemitism and opposition to a third term for Roosevelt and to helping the British defense against German rocket attacks. Hopkins had
asked Roosevelt at the end of 1940 to authorize him to visit England
to gather firsthand information on the conditions of England's military and to convey American support for the British people. Though
Roosevelt initially turned the offer down, he relented, given the increasing threat that the Nazis posed to England and Churchill's
urgent requests for aid. Once Roosevelt decided to send Hopkins, no
time was wasted. Late in the afternoon on January 3, Hopkins met
with Secretary of State Hull, who briefed him for the trip.

On the evening of January 4, 1941, Roosevelt met with Hopkins.
Roosevelt handed him two letters. The first authorized Hopkins to
"act as my personal representative. I am also asking you to convey a
communication in this sense to King George VI." The letter requested Hopkins convey to Roosevelt what he learned during his trip.
The second letter was an introduction to the King of England. That
same evening, Hopkins left for England. By the time he arrived in
London on January 9, it had already been subjected to five months
of bombing from Germany. British morale was low, and its armaments lower.[12]

Before Hopkins traveled to England, Roosevelt delivered his State
of the Union message on January 6, 1941. Shortly thereafter Roosevelt met privately with Wendell Willkie, a meeting Roosevelt set up
after meeting with England's chief intelligence officer in the United
States, William Stephenson, who suggested that sending Willkie
would ensure the British people that the Americans were united in
their support for England. When Roosevelt realized just before the
meeting, their first after the election, that his desk had no papers on
it, he told his aides Rosenman and Sherwood, "Just give me a handful [of papers] to strew around my desk so I will look very busy when

Willkie comes in." The meeting went well, though Willkie near the end asked the President why he retained Hopkins as an advisor given how unpopular he had become as he climbed over more experienced and more longstanding aides to curry Roosevelt's favor. Roosevelt answered, "Someday you may well be sitting here where I am now. And when you are, you'll realize what a lonely job it is, and you'll discover the need for somebody like Harry Hopkins who asks for nothing except to serve you."[13]

Four days later, on January 10, 1941, House Majority Leader John McCormack of Massachusetts introduced the Lend-Lease Act in the House and Senator Alban Barkley introduced it in the Senate. The new law would allow the United States to lend or lease war supplies to any nation deemed "vital to the defense of the United States." Though facing loud opposition from isolationists in both the House and the Senate, Roosevelt had what he needed to get the bill approved: three-quarters of the American people were firmly behind it, his former foe Wendell Willkie testified in its favor after returning from England, Winston Churchill released England's financial statements to show it could not afford buying any armaments and broadcast his reassurance to the American people that it was the weapons, not the lives of Americans, that his country needed to survive.

More than 80 percent of the House and nearly two-thirds of the Senate voted in favor of the bill. Its passage coincided with Congress's repealing the "cash" provision of the Neutrality Act but retaining the requirement that Britain could take whatever it carried home in its own ships. On signing it, Roosevelt delivered a message to the dictators of Europe and Asia. "Yes," he acknowledged, "the decisions of our democracy may be slow to arrive at. But when that decision is made, it is proclaimed not with the voice of any one man but with the voice of one hundred and thirty million. It is binding on us all. And the world is no longer left in doubt."[14]

On the same day the Lend-Lease Act was being introduced in Congress, Hopkins met with Churchill in England. Churchill's aides were initially underwhelmed with Hopkins's "deplorably untidy" appearance.[15] Hopkins tried to gage whether former Ambassador Kennedy's impression that Churchill did not like Roosevelt was inaccurate. After he realized it was, Hopkins explained his mission to Churchill. "He assured me," Hopkins wrote Roosevelt, "that he would make every detail of information and opinion available to me and hoped that I would not leave England until I was fully satisfied of the exact state of England's need and the urgent necessity" of the aid Churchill requested from the President.[16]

Over the next two weeks, the two were inseparable. Hopkins shared with Churchill both his and Roosevelt's admiration for Churchill's oratory, and Churchill repeatedly reassured Hopkins that the British agenda was not to find treasure or acquire more territory but rather to protect the basic freedoms of each British citizen to worship the God of their choice and lead their life as they wished, free from persecution and with security from "the secret police [who would] disturb his leisure or interrupt his rest." The British, he explained, wanted the same kind of government that Americans had, a system based on the consent of the governed, the freedom of speech, and equality. "But war aims other than these we have none," Churchill said. Hopkins reassured Roosevelt that "Churchill is the government in every sense" and that the British desperately needed American aid to survive the German assault. "I cannot emphasize too strongly," he wrote, that Churchill "is the one and only person over here with whom you need to have a full meeting of the minds."

Though reassured by Hopkins's reports, Roosevelt, as a man of keen emotional intelligence, was wary that Hopkins might have come under Churchill's spell, especially when, at one of their final dinners, Hopkins got the world's attention when he rose to say, "I suppose you wish to know what I am going to say to President Roosevelt on my return." Churchill's gaze was riveted on Hopkins, who then quoted from the Book of Ruth, "Whither thou goest, I will go; and where thou lodgest, I will lodge; thy people shall be my people, and thy God my God." He added his own words at the end, "Even to the end." Churchill cried.[17]

Years later, Churchill recalled his 1941 meeting with Hopkins: "Thus I met Harry Hopkins, that extraordinary man, who played, and was to play, a sometimes decisive role in the whole movement of the war. His was a soul that flamed out of a frail and failing body. He was a crumbling lighthouse from which there shone the beams that led great fleets to harbor."[18]

Hopkins returned to the United States on the same day the House approved the Lend-Lease Act. Once it did, Roosevelt placed Hopkins in charge of the law's implementation. The new appointment shifted responsibility over pre-Lend-Lease arrangements from the Treasury Department, where it normally would have been, to Roosevelt's inner circle.

The third man Roosevelt sent to meet Churchill was his friend former New York governor Averell Harriman, whom Franklin had known since they both attended Groton. Like Hopkins, Harriman had no formal title when Roosevelt sent him during the spring of 1941 to be responsible for being the liaison between the United States and British officials. Though he initially called Harriman a "defense expediter," Roosevelt used him, as he had used Welles, Hopkins, and Willkie, to bypass the State Department. When pressed to explain what job Harriman had, Roosevelt told reporters, "I don't know, and I don't give a—you know."[19]

Like Hopkins and Welles, Harriman was more than just a loyal foot soldier for Roosevelt. Each was a surrogate, intermediary, and advisor. Harriman became as close to Churchill as Hopkins did, perhaps more so, as Churchill even encouraged Harriman, a well-known playboy, to have an affair with his daughter-in-law Pamela after her marriage to Churchill's son fell apart. (In 1971, they married.)

III

Roosevelt's presidency coincided with Germany's solution to what it euphemistically called "the Jewish problem." The truth, which became clearer the longer the war lasted, was that the Third Reich's rampage through Europe was about more than domination. It was about blaming the Jews as the reason for Germany's defeat in the First World War (and every other ill Germany had experienced) and exterminating them from the face of the earth. Just months after Roosevelt's first inauguration, *Time* magazine featured Joseph

Goebbels, the Nazi propaganda minister, on its cover. While dismissing Hitler as a "Vegetarian Superman," it noted how both he and Goebbels restored the German people's morale by "explaining away all Germany's defeats and trials in terms of the Jew." It ended by quoting Goebbels's refrain, "The Jews are to blame."[20]

As Edward R. Murrow reported, Hitler's becoming chancellor in 1933 had just been the beginning of a reign of terror that the world even now has trouble reconciling. That same year, under Hitler's command, Germany established the first concentration camp at Dachau and the secret police known as the Gestapo and mandated laws barring Jews from holding civil service, university, and state positions. The state burned books by Jews and other dissidents, and stripped East European Jewish immigrants of their citizenship.

In 1934, Hitler named himself both leader (führer) and reich chancellor. In 1935, the Third Reich barred Jews from serving in the armed forces, enacted anti-Jewish racial laws that prohibited Jews from marrying non-Jews, and defined a Jew as anyone who had three Jewish grandparents, or two Jewish grandparents but identified himself as Jewish as well.

The next year, the year the Olympics were held in Germany, the Reich barred Jewish doctors from practicing medicine in German institutions, opened a second concentration camp, and joined with Italy to form the Rome-Berlin Axis. In 1937, a third concentration camp was opened, and the next year the Third Reich officially extended its policies to ridding its schools of Jews, confiscating businesses and property owned by Jews, and beginning to brutalize Jews, as exemplified on November 9–10, Kristallnacht ("The Night of Broken Glass"), an anti-Jewish pogrom in Germany and Austria and Sudetenland that destroyed two hundred synagogues, looted seventy-five hundred Jewish businesses, and deported thirty thousand Jewish males to concentration camps, where most of them died.

As Roosevelt's presidency unfolded, he and Eleanor increasingly found themselves surrounded by Jewish advisors and friends, who made sure they were aware of the growing menace of the Third Reich. They became more comfortable with, and relied increasingly on, such advisors as Morgenthau, Bernard Baruch, and Sam Rosenman.

Yet both Roosevelt and Eleanor understood the Jewish people were not just a problem for the Third Reich but for Americans as well. Roosevelt often had to bend over backward to appease isolationists, many if not most of whom harbored a not-so-secret dislike for Jews and other minorities.

Isolationism had deadly consequences, however. In one well-known incident in 1939, a German transatlantic liner, *St. Louis*, left Germany with 937 passengers, most of whom were Jews escaping Nazi Germany. When the ship arrived in Cuba on May 13, the Cuban government allowed entry for only 28 passengers who had American visas. Those who did appealed to both Roosevelt and Secretary of State Hull to let the rest in but to no avail. Roosevelt and Hull (and Hull's assistant, the antisemitic Breckenridge Long) explained that saving Jews was not a priority for the American government and that allowing them entry into the country risked taking jobs away from Americans.

When Hull spoke with Treasury Secretary Morgenthau, Morgenthau suggested that perhaps the Coast Guard should at least locate the ship to ensure its passengers were alive. Hull agreed so long as the search did not make the news. Refusing to take no for an answer and knowing that returning to Germany meant certain death for his Jewish passengers, the ship's captain, Gustav Schroeder, found four European countries—England, France, Belgium, and the Netherlands—who took all but 254 passengers, who later died in the Holocaust. Hitler and Goebbels used the incident to demonstrate that no other countries wanted the Jews.

On September 11, 1941, Eleanor bypassed Hull to work directly with another State Department official to allow Jewish refugees aboard a Portuguese ship to receive United States visas and disembark in Virginia. Breckinridge Long complained to the President that he should not allow the first lady to bend the rules, which forbade such immigration, but Roosevelt took no public stance on the issue.

If anything changed in 1941, it was Franklin's awareness, made possible through the persistent intervention of Eleanor, Jewish advisors such as Morgenthau, leaders in the Jewish community such as Rabbi Steven Wise, Jewish organizations, and liberal cabinet members such as Harold Ickes and Robert Jackson, that Jewish refugees desperately needed help. He took the initiative to sound out other prominent Jewish citizens, such as Isaiah Bowman, the president of Johns Hopkins, for advice on how to save Jewish refugees.

No one pushed Roosevelt harder to find a humane answer to the relocation of Jewish refugees than Eleanor. She confessed to him that "the German-Jewish business makes me sick." She had come a long way from her derision of the Jewish people in her teens and twenties. Sometimes her lobbying got through to the President. In 1938, he denounced not just the horrific Kristallnacht but Mussolini's decree expelling all post-1919 Jewish migrants and barring them from owning or participating in any business activity within the country. As he told a news conference in September of that year, "The news of the past few days has deeply shocked public opinion in the United States. . . . I . . . could scarcely believe that such things occur in a twentieth-century civilization."[21]

While the President issued a formal protest by recalling the American ambassador from Berlin, he went no further and, pointedly, did not follow the example of his cousin Teddy, who had delivered to the Russian government formal complaints in 1903 and 1906 about its pogroms against Jews. When reporters pressed Franklin on which other countries Jews could emigrate to, he could not think of any. He was thinking instead of Gallup polls indicating that 94 percent of Americans disapproved of Germany's mistreatment of the Jews but 83 percent opposed increasing quotas allowing more European immigrants into the United States.

Among the most vocal critics of Roosevelt's responses to German policies regarding Jews was Charles Lindbergh, who had become the most prominent advocate for isolationism in the country. After meeting Hitler, Lindbergh praised the führer and expressed the view that the greatest threat to democracy and the United States came from the Soviet Union not Germany. On September 11, 1941, in a visit to Iowa, Lindbergh delivered a speech blaming the Jews for pushing the United States into war. The speech strengthened Roosevelt's resolve to look for other ways to help Jews fleeing Germany. One was shifting the responsibility for addressing the issue away from Hull and the State Department to the cadre of Eleanor, Hopkins, Harriman, and Morgenthau.

Even so, as historians Richard Breitman and Allen Lichtman determined, "for most of his presidency Roosevelt did little to help the imperiled Jews of Germany and Europe. He put other policy priorities well ahead of saving Jews and deferred to fears of an anti-Semitic backlash at home. He worried that measures to assist European Jews might endanger his political coalition at home and then a wartime alliance abroad."[22]

A sad confirmation was the President's response in 1942 to Eleanor when she asked him to read a letter written by a German Jewish physician who was being held at a concentration camp in France and who urged the United States to come to the rescue of him and other Jews held in confinement. Refusing to get involved, the President sided with Long, who, he told Eleanor, had informed him that there were Nazi saboteurs and Fifth Columnists among the Jewish refugees seeking entry to the United States.

Yet it is an overstatement to say Roosevelt did nothing. In their study of Roosevelt and the Jews, Breitman and Lichtman concluded that "at times Roosevelt acted decisively to rescue Jews, often notwithstanding contrary pressures from the American public, Congress, and his own State Department. Oddly enough, he did more for the Jews than any other world figure, even if his efforts seem deficient in retrospect. He was a far better president for Jews than any of his political adversaries would have been."[23]

As deficient as his attitudes about saving Jews may have been, Roosevelt was educable. To be sure, he was never perfectly so, as reflected in his obstinate refusal to be educated about economic theory and practice. Yet, in this respect, Roosevelt had something in common with Lincoln, whose attitudes about race evolved over time. Not until nearly two years into the Civil War did Lincoln decide that the Union's preservation required the abolition of slavery.

In his ninth year as president, Roosevelt was still overwhelmingly concerned with the political clout of the isolationists. Like Lincoln, Roosevelt would change his mind after political and military developments made it inevitable. He was never a leader of the worldwide movement to save the Jews, but, in time, he let his military lead the way. He was convinced that the best way to end the Nazi threat was to convincingly defeat it. In the meantime, the Third Reich proceeded with its "final solution" to exterminate Jews.

IV

In the summer and fall of 1941, several developments significantly informed Roosevelt's foreign policy. The first was the military's recognition that it was not ready to go to war. Though Roosevelt, meeting with his Joint Chiefs in January 1941, speculated there was a one-in-five chance Germany or Japan would attack the United States, he was advised that the United States lacked the means to respond in kind. General George Marshall reminded the President that the army only had six divisions. Based on the Joint Chiefs' advice, Roosevelt acknowledged that "the Army should not be committed to any aggressive action until it was firmly prepared to undertake it; that our military course must be conservative until our strength had been developed."[24]

Roosevelt understood that the nation's best course of action was to keep England supplied while working to fortify American armed forces and armaments. Thus, when, in early June 1941, a German submarine attacked an American ship, which had not been near the war zone, Roosevelt issued a strong condemnation, froze German and Italian assets, removed German diplomats from the country, but went no further. He pointedly did not follow Wilson's decision of April 18, 1916, when he sent an ultimatum directly to German leaders in response to German submarines' attacks on merchant vessels in peaceful waters. Roosevelt bided his time until the military's planned expansion of the United States fighting force was accomplished. In 1941, the projection was it would be at full force in two years.

Ten days later, on June 22, 1941, Germans launched an assault against the Soviet Union. No one was more shocked than Stalin, who considered any attack to be pure lunacy, even though Roosevelt and other world leaders had warned Stalin Hitler was that crazy.

With the American people and Roosevelt's military advisors split over the proper response to the attack, Roosevelt was cautious. He mostly refrained from public comment, though he vowed at a press conference on June 24 "to give all the aid that we possibly can to Russia."[25] While Franklin gave no public speeches or any Fireside Chats on the subject, he asked Undersecretary of State Welles to deliver a public statement, which Roosevelt helped him to draft. It condemned the attack, concluding that "any defense against Hitlerism... from whatever source... will benefit... our own defense and security."[26]

In response to pressure from Eleanor and several African American leaders including A. Philip Randolph, president of the Brotherhood of Sleeping Car Porters, Roosevelt issued Executive Order 8802 on June 25, 1941. It banned "discrimination in the employment of workers in defense industries and in Government, because of race, creed, color, or national origin."[27] It was the first presidential directive on race since Reconstruction.

With a stroke of a pen, Roosevelt undid Wilson's mistake in refusing to end segregation in many sectors of the federal government, though the order did not extend to military service.

Roosevelt dispatched Harry Hopkins at the end of July to meet with Stalin. While he did not share former Ambassador Kennedy's impression of Stalin as "Uncle Joe," Hopkins was impressed. He reported to Roosevelt that in their first talk Stalin had said, "Give us anti-aircraft guns and the aluminum and we can fight for three or four years."[28] Through his role in implementing the Lend-Lease Act, Hopkins got Stalin what he needed.

When Hopkins fell ill, Roosevelt sent Harriman to represent the United States at the Three-Power Conference to be held at the end of September in Moscow. The other attendees included high-ranking Soviet officials, such as Stalin, and the British ambassador. After two days of negotiation, the three countries signed an agreement, the First Protocol, which promised the Soviet Union four hundred aircraft, five hundred tanks, and ten thousand trucks a month, until June 1942, in addition to other supplies. In a memo recording his impressions of Stalin, Harriman acknowledged that "it is hard for me to reconcile the courtesy and consideration that he showed me with the ghastly cruelty of his wholesale liquidations." Nonetheless, Harriman wrote, "others, who did not know him personally, see only the tyrant in Stalin. I saw the other side as well—his high intelligence, that fantastic grip of details, his shrewdness and the surprising human sensitivity that he was capable of showing, at least in the war years. I found him better informed than Roosevelt, more realistic than Churchill, in some ways the most effective of the war leaders." "At the same time," Harriman concluded, "he was, of course, a murderous tyrant. I must confess that for me Stalin remains the most inscrutable and contradictory character that I have known."[29]

As of August 1941, Roosevelt and Churchill had not yet met in person, though they had been in daily, sometimes hourly, contact for months. Roosevelt knew Churchill was desperate to meet, as conveyed by Hopkins, Harriman, and Welles. To arrange for such a meeting, Roosevelt orchestrated a massive ruse, with the help of Sumner Welles: Franklin told the cabinet and the press that he and some staff were taking the presidential yacht (first purchased by President Hoover) for a cruise along the New England coast, and he arranged for a stand-in to be sitting on the deck and waving a long cigarette holder to observers along the way.

In fact, Franklin and several advisors, including Hopkins and Marshall, were on a different boat heading in a different direction. They were on two cruisers headed to Agentia Harbor on the southern coast of Newfoundland. They were soon joined there on August 9 by the British battleship *Prince of Wales*, whose passengers included Churchill and a staff twice as large as Roosevelt's entourage.

For the next four days, Churchill, Roosevelt, and their respective staffs met to forge what became known as the Atlantic Charter. With Churchill and his staff meticulously prepared to discuss details and Roosevelt keeping them off-balance with his asides and insistence on maintaining informality throughout, they eventually reached agreement on eight key points, which they termed their Joint Agreement. On August 14, the two men held a press conference to announce the eight promises of the Atlantic Charter—agreeing to commit to "seek no aggrandizement, territorial or other"; "to see no territorial changes that do not accord with the freely expressed views of the people concerned"; to "respect the right of all peoples to choose the form of government under which they will live [and] to guarantee sovereign rights and self government restored to those who have been forcibly deprived of them"; "[to] [provide] further [access] on equal terms, to the trade and raw materials of the world"; to improve "labor standards, economic advancement, and social security"; to ensure that "after the destruction of the Nazi tyranny," "all men in all the lands may live out their lives in freedom from fear and want"; to achieve a "peace [that] should enable all men to traverse the high seas and oceans without hindrance"; and to make essential "the abandonment of force" and "the disarmament of [belligerent or aggressor] nations."[30]

The eight points were based on Woodrow Wilson's vision and Roosevelt's Four Freedoms speech. The Atlantic Charter provoked skepticism and resistance back in England and the United States and with Joseph Stalin, who feared it threatened Soviet domination of the Baltic republics. Nonetheless, Roosevelt and Churchill agreed it was a necessary step for the two nations to take in response to the expanding war in Europe.

V

The British and the American delegations left their August 1941 meeting with different impressions. The British were discouraged in not getting more in terms of American assurances. As one Churchill aide wrote, "I think the general opinion in our party would be that the Americans have a long way to go before they can play any decisive part in the war. . . . Both their Army and their Navy are standing like reluctant brothers on the brink." For his part, Roosevelt was overconfident in his assessment of what the meeting achieved. Thinking he had bested Churchill in their negotiations, Roosevelt was told by an aide, "You may want to look out, Mr. President, Churchill may be pulling your leg by letting you win the first round."[31]

Roosevelt was not the trusting type, and he was not going to share with even his closest allies the extent of America's unpreparedness to go to war. The most Roosevelt could do was to provide financial assistance and some military equipment to the British. Roosevelt trusted Stalin far less than he did Churchill; indeed, he did not trust Stalin at all. Nor had have any kind words for the Soviet Union; he denounced Stalin's "dictatorship as absolute as any dictatorship in the world."[32] The lack of trust worked in the other direction, too, as Soviet leadership failed to take seriously Sumner Welles's warnings earlier in the year that the Nazis intended to invade the Soviet Union.

Always pragmatic, Roosevelt took incremental steps rather than big leaps into the international fray. In early October 1941, he asked Congress to revise the neutrality law to allow the arming of all U.S. ships. Congress balked, given polling showing Americans nearly evenly split on whether American ships should be delivering war materials to England. Advised by congressional leaders that "it would be disastrous" to revise the law "if one of our transports proceeding to or from Britain were to be sunk, when manned by U.S. naval officers and men," Roosevelt waited.

Franklin had devoted earlier Fireside Chats to the sinking of other American ships, but the Germans' sinking of the destroyer *Kearny* on October 17 dramatically shifted public opinion. On October 31, shortly before Congress was to give its final approval to modifications of the Neutrality Act, another German attack sunk the American destroyer *Reuben James*, killing 115 Americans. This time, Roosevelt chose not to repeat the bellicose tone of his earlier Fireside Chat and of his naval address on October 27, 1941. Instead, he said nothing. Silence helped, as Congress narrowly enacted the revisions to the Neutrality Act into law in November.

Roosevelt had yet to focus closely on the Japanese threat to American security. His advisors were split over not only how the United States should respond to the Third Reich's murderous intentions but also whether to maintain the so-called Stimson Doctrine, drafted in 1932 as a response to Japan's decision to quit the League of Nations because of American objections to its conquest of Manchuria. Forged by Hoover's then–secretary of state, Henry Stimson, the doctrine declared that the United States would not recognize any territorial arrangements imposed on China by force.

Roosevelt's military advisors assured him, however, that the economic war he was fighting against Japan was likely to keep them from directly attacking the United States. When Treasury Secretary Morgenthau pressed Roosevelt at a cabinet meeting to consider using even more economic leverage to keep Japan in line, Roosevelt "gave us quite a lecture why we should not make any move because if we did, if we stopped all oil, it would simply drive the Japanese down to the Dutch East Indies, and it would mean war in the Pacific." Admiral Harold Stark backed Roosevelt's thinking in a memorandum dated July 12, 1941, declaring that "an embargo would probably result in a fairly early attack by Japan on Malaya the Netherlands East Indies, and possibly would involve the United States in an early war in the Pacific." Stark assured the President and Secretary of War Stimson that he should keep his focus on the possibility of war in the Atlantic, since "collapse in the Atlantic would be fatal; collapse in the Far East would be serious but not fatal."[33]

On July 6, Roosevelt announced that the government would freeze Japanese assets in the United States. At the same time, the President told the nation, there would be a freeze on Chinese assets and a military order placing the Philippine armed forces under American command. He recalled General Douglas MacArthur to active duty to command United States forces in the Philippines. "If there is to be trouble in the Far East," he told his military aide Pa Watson, "I want Douglas to be in charge."[34] Army command was less than enthused with MacArthur's recall, and it took so much time in delaying MacArthur's reinstatement that Roosevelt had to intervene along with General Marshall to expedite it.

Tensions between the United States and Japan worsened when Japan, with the consent of Nazi-occupied France, took control of the northern portion of Indochina, adjacent to the Chinese province of Yunnan, as a source for Japan to get the resources the American government had denied them. Roosevelt responded on August 1, 1941, with a complete embargo on all types of iron and steel intended for Japan and the announcement of a $100 million loan to China through the Export-Import Bank.

Two days later, Japan joined the Berlin-Rome axis. The three nations agreed to come to the aid of one another if attacked by a third party. Since the treaty excluded the Soviet Union, it plainly applied to only one country—the United States.

Though American support for war with Japan increased to 67 percent at the beginning of September, the United States lacked the means to back its policies with force. Japan's navy outnumbered the collective forces of the United States, England, and the Netherlands. On September 6, after meeting with the Japanese emperor Hirohito, Prime Minister Fumimaro Konoye met secretly to inform the American ambassador to Japan, Joseph Grew, a lifetime diplomat, that the two countries might find some area of agreement concerning the Japanese invasion of China and American opposition to Japan's expansion of its empire. Japan's leaders wanted the embargo to end, while Roosevelt was uneasy allowing Japan free rein to do as it pleased in trying to expand its empire. Grew sent Roosevelt what he considered to be "the most important cable to go from his hand since the start of his diplomatic career," and he followed up with a short letter informing Roosevelt that time was of the essence to avert war and that failing to appreciate that the prime minister could best be dealt with by avoiding ironclad commitments before any meeting risked war.[35] Roosevelt told aides that he doubted Prime Minister Konoye could make any concessions that the military would accept.

The State Department ignored Grew's counsel. Hull was convinced that any meeting with the Japanese prime minister, "without an advance agreement could only result in another Munich or in nothing at all."[36] He confided to his diary that, while the President would have "relished a meeting" with the Japanese prime minister, Hull convinced the President that any such meeting "would be a disaster."[37] On October 16, Konoye resigned.

The appointment of General Hideki Tojo as his replacement confirmed that war was imminent. Roosevelt wrote Churchill and Stalin that "I am a bit worried over the Japanese situation."[38] Roosevelt conveyed that he did not expect any Japanese attack or further movement south in China until after the Soviet Union had been defeated. While Roosevelt told Admiral Stark he could not rule out the possibility of a Japanese attack against the United States or England, both Stark and General Marshall did not consider an attack to be imminent. Grew soon followed with further communiqués that the Japanese "cannot be gauged by any Western measuring rod" and said it would be folly to think "that our economic pressure will not drive Japan to war." If war came, Grew informed the President and the State Department, it would likely "come with dangerous and dramatic suddenness." In early November, the Joint Chiefs advised Roosevelt that war with Japan should be avoided because it "would greatly weaken the combined effort in the Atlantic against Germany."[39]

The Joint Chiefs' concerns about the unpreparedness of the American military shaped Roosevelt's thinking throughout the year. On November 7, he asked each member of the cabinet for their opinion on the threat posed by Japan and the United States' retaliatory options. Everyone agreed Congress should give the President a declaration of war if he asked for one. Hull and the cabinet agreed the United States should prepare, but Roosevelt and his military advisors wanted to minimize conflict with Japan. He ordered Hull to "do nothing to precipitate a crisis."[40]

Later that month, Tokyo presented its final offer for averting war with the United States—a six-month cooling-off period between the two nations. Although the military supported the proposed modus vivendi, it was never sent to Japanese authorities. When Roosevelt met with his war council (Secretaries Hull, Stimson, and Knox, General Marshall, and Admiral Stark) on November 25, everyone agreed it would make no difference. Aware Japan had set a deadline of November 29 for a response to its proposal, Roosevelt said, "We are likely to be attacked perhaps as soon as next Monday because the Japanese are notorious for attacking without warning. The question is how to maneuver them into firing the first shot without too much danger to our-selves."[41]

On November 17, Hull brought Japan's special ambassador, Saburo Kurusu, and ambassador to the United States, Nomura Kichisaburo, to visit Roosevelt at the White House. They agreed on nothing more than the main points of contention between the two nations. On November 20, Roosevelt drafted a new proposal that asked for the two sides to agree on modus vivendi—or maintaining the status quo—for the foreseeable future.

On November 26, Hull met with Japanese representatives to present the United States' final proposal for averting war with Japan. That same day, Secretary of War Stimson informed Roosevelt that Army Intelligence reported that five Japanese divisions had embarked on ships and had been sighted south of Formosa in northeast Argentina. Roosevelt "fairly blew up" at Stimson "and said [that] changed the whole situation, because it was evidence of bad faith on the part of the Japanese that while they were negotiating for an entire truce—an entire withdrawal—they should be sending this expedition down there to Indochina."[42] American military authorities put the military on high alert, while Japanese authorities were preparing for war.

On December 3, 1941, Roosevelt learned that the Japanese Foreign Office had ordered key embassies to destroy their codebooks and that it had informed German officials "that war may suddenly break out ... quicker than anyone's dreams." Desperate, Roosevelt tried one last effort to avert war by sending the Japanese emperor a message on December 6 re-proposing his offer of modus vivendi. Later that evening, a naval officer brought the lengthy Japanese response that had gone to the State Department. Getting the gist quickly without needing to read the entire document, Roosevelt told Hopkins, "This means war." Hopkins remarked it was a shame that "we could not strike the first blow and prevent any sort of surprise." "We can't do that," Roosevelt responded. "We are a democracy and a peaceful people."[43] He followed the example set by both Abraham Lincoln in 1861 and Wilson in 1917 in waiting for the enemy to fire the first shot and thus to initiate war.

VI

Just before eight o'clock the next morning, Japan fired the first shots. Less than an hour later Navy Secretary Knox called the President to relay a message from Admiral Husband Kimmel in Pearl Harbor: "Air raid on Pearl Harbor. This is not a drill." Hopkins, who was at lunch with the President, thought "that surely Japan would not attack Pearl Harbor." Roosevelt responded such an attack was "just the kind of thing the Japanese would do." A half hour later, Roosevelt received confirmation of both the attack and its destruction. Grace Tully recalled, "With each new message [the President] shook his head and tightened the expression of his mouth." Yet Eleanor recalled that after the news broke the President, "in spite of his anxiety, [was] in a way more serene."[44]

Before learning all the damage done, Roosevelt knew the attack settled whether the United States would get involved in the war. As soon as the attack was confirmed, Roosevelt ordered Admiral Stark to execute the orders prepared in advance of an outbreak of hostilities earlier that year; took calls from Churchill and members of Congress; and issued new orders regarding the disposition of troops, surveillance of Japanese citizens in the United States, and tightening security at the White House. He ordered storing the originals of America's founding documents, including the Declaration of Independence and the Constitution, at Fort Knox in Kentucky.

The President replaced Kimmel with Chester Nimitz and named Admiral Ernest King, the commander of the Atlantic fleet, as chief of naval operations. He could not stop from repeatedly asking Naval Secretary Knox, "Find out, for God's sake, why the ships were tied in rows."[45]

Roosevelt met with his cabinet at eight-thirty that evening. Surveying the grim faces sitting around the table, Roosevelt began solemnly, "This is the most serious meeting of the cabinet that has taken place since" Lincoln's meeting with his cabinet on March 15, 1861, immediately after Southern forces attacked federal forts in Charleston Harbor, South Carolina. Indeed, they were meeting in the same room. To Frances Perkins, Roosevelt "could barely bring himself to describe the devastation" to the cabinet. "His pride in the Navy was so terrific," she said, that it was obvious that the President "was having a dreadful time just accepting the idea that the Navy could be caught off guard."[46]

At ten that evening, the congressional leadership joined the cabinet. When pressed by Senator Tom Connally of Texas, "How did it happen that our warships were caught like sitting ducks at Pearl Harbor? How did they catch us with our pants down?," the President whispered, "I don't know, Tom, I don't know." He asked the leaders when he could speak to a joint session of Congress the next day, December 8, and they agreed he would speak at twelve-thirty. The Senate minority leader, Charles McNary of Oregon, assured the President that "Republicans will go along with whatever is done." The GOP House leader, Joseph William Martin, Jr., of Massachusetts, told Roosevelt, "Where the integrity and honor of the Nation is involved there is only one party."[47]

An hour later, Roosevelt met privately with the journalist Edward R. Murrow and Columbia Law School classmate William Donovan, who had been leading the clandestine Office of Information, later named the Office of Strategic Services. Roosevelt asked each for their candid assessment on how they thought the American people would react if he asked Congress for a declaration of war. They assured him the public would be in favor. Perhaps for the first time that day, he let himself be angry, pounding the table with the exclamation that American planes had been destroyed "on the ground, by God, on the ground."[48]

The full story of the destruction took several weeks to come to light. Ultimately, the President learned that nearly 20 American ships, 188 airplanes, docks, and airfields were destroyed or seriously damaged, and more than 2,000 lives were lost. A subsequent report in 1946 by the Joint Committee on the Investigation of the Pearl Harbor Attack determined that, in the two weeks prior to the December 7 attack, seven of the eight commanders in the Pacific had put their commands on war footing.

The exception was Hawaii, because Admiral Kimmel and General Walter Short, who were in charge of the defense of military installations in Hawaii, had not taken Washington's warnings seriously. After months of hearings and detailed field investigations, the Joint Committee determined, "The commanders in Hawaii were clearly and unmistakably warned of war with Japan. They were given orders and possessed information that the entire Pacific area was fraught with danger. They failed to carry out these orders and to discharge their basic and ultimate responsibilities. They failed to defend the fortress they defended—they were taken by surprise."

The Joint Committee concluded that "the ultimate and direct responsibility for failure to engage the Japanese on the morning of December 7 with every weapon at their disposal rests essentially and properly with the Army and Navy commands in Hawaii whose duty it was to meet the enemy against which they had been warned."[49] Kimmel was demoted to rear admiral and Scott to major general, and both retired from active service in 1942.

In 1999, nearly fifty-eight years after the bombing of Pearl Harbor, the Senate approved a nonbinding resolution exonerating both Kimmel and Short, whom many in the military thought were made scapegoats for the destruction on December 7, 1941. President Bill Clinton refused to sign the resolution and to restore them both to their wartime ranks. No subsequent president has done so, either.

While the damage was being assessed at Pearl Harbor and before the emergency cabinet meeting he had convened, Roosevelt dictated to Grace Tully the message he intended to deliver the next day at a joint session of Congress. With one change made by Hopkins, Roosevelt kept it short, less than five hundred words.

The President arrived at the Capitol accompanied by Eleanor and President Wilson's widow, Edith. When Roosevelt entered the House chamber, the Congress rose for a prolonged standing ovation. In a speech that had only twenty-five sentences, the President was interrupted by applause twelve times. He spoke for six and a half minutes, and his message was clear: "Yesterday, December 7, 1941, a date which will live in infamy—the United States was suddenly and deliberately attacked by the naval and air forces of Japan." He continued, "No matter how long it may take us to overcome this premediated invasion, the American people in their righteous might will win through to absolute victory. I ask that Congress declare that since the unprovoked and dastardly attack by Japan on Sunday, December 7, 1941, a state of war has existed between the United States and the Japanese Empire."[50]

Thirty-three minutes later, the Senate voted unanimously to declare war against the Empire of Japan, and the House voted 388–1.

The sole dissenter was Congresswoman Jeannette Rankin of Montana, who had voted against a declaration of war in 1917. The next day, Germany and Italy declared war against the United States. On December 11, Roosevelt asked Congress to declare a state of war against both Germany and Italy. This time, it did unanimously in both chambers.

VII

Like Wilson before him, Franklin Roosevelt did not have the luxury as president of focusing only on the war. Domestic affairs demanded attention, and nature and human mortality did not pause.

No one knew better than Franklin Roosevelt that presidents rarely control the timing of Supreme Court appointments. The only president who had was George Washington, who was given the opportunity to fill an entirely empty Court. Having appointed five Supreme Court justices by 1941, Roosevelt already had made the fourth largest number of Supreme Court appointments by any president in history. In 1941, he had three more opportunities, bringing his total to eight, the most of any president other than Washington, who had ten.

At the end of January 1941, James McReynolds, to everyone's relief, resigned from the Supreme Court. He was the last surviving Wilson appointee and the last of the Four Horsemen. Though he had arrived at the Court with the impressive credentials of having graduated first both in his college class at Vanderbilt and from the University of Virginia Law School, served for four years as an assistant attorney general in Teddy Roosevelt's Justice Department, practiced antitrust law at one of New York's most prestigious firms, and been Wilson's first attorney general, he was universally despised as a person. He was racist, antisemitic, crude, and a genuinely horrible colleague.

Though McReynolds sometimes could be charming in private (and remarkably generous to charities and orphans), Chief Justice William Howard Taft considered him as "one who delights in making others uncomfortable," and as "fuller of prejudice than any man

I have ever known." Stories of his vile temperament became legend,[51] as demonstrated by his not accepting any "Jews, drinkers, blacks, women, smokers," or married persons as law clerks, and his refusal to speak to Justice Brandeis for the first three years of his tenure on the Court and to sign the ceremonial colleagues' letter commemorating Brandeis's retirement.

McReynolds pointedly read a newspaper at Justice Cardozo's swearing in, refused to attend Cardozo's funeral, often hid behind a brief when Cardozo spoke, and refused to speak directly to him. When President Hoover had appointed Cardozo to the Court, McReynolds and Justices Butler and Van Devanter pleaded with the President "not to afflict the Court with another Jew." McReynolds rejected Taft's request that he accompany Taft at a ceremonial event in Philadelphia because, "as you know, I am not always to be found when there is a Hebrew abroad."[52]

He was as bad, if not worse, in his interactions with African Americans, as he verbally abused his servants and turned his chair around to show his back to the great civil rights lawyer Charles Hamilton Houston when he argued before the Supreme Court. When McReynolds died in 1946, no justices attended his funeral.

Though it was not going to be hard for Roosevelt to find someone more liberal and collegial than McReynolds, the President took his time and did not nominate a replacement for six months, until June 12, 1941. The criteria changed only slightly from before—he wanted a justice who was firmly committed to the constitutionality of the New Deal, would be easily confirmed, came from the South as did McReynolds, and would be disposed to uphold the administration's wartime policies.

Roosevelt's appointments demonstrated his acumen in picking people for the Court that would rule exactly as he wanted them to. Washington and Jackson had appointed people they personally knew and thus were not surprised by their performance on the Court. Cousin Teddy had proclaimed he wanted justices "opposed to big railroad men and other members of large" businesses but was apoplectic when his first appointee, the widely revered Oliver Wendell Holmes, did not back the administration in the biggest

railroad-busting case at the time. "I could carve out of a banana a justice with more backbone than that," he declared.[53]

McReynolds's opposition to progressive government disappointed Wilson, though many suspected he had elevated
McReynolds to the Court to get him out of the cabinet. Roosevelt
never regretted a single appointment he made to the Court; he knew
most of his appointees personally and thus had firsthand experience
with their temperaments and commitment to his administration.

Nonetheless, Roosevelt took his time. He had already transformed
the Court and knew that any new appointees would reinforce its
course. He may have been distracted by the war in Europe or might
not have wanted to make a move until he picked a new chief justice.

In June 1941, Charles Evans Hughes announced his departure
from the Court. After informing Roosevelt of his intention to resign
because of his and his wife's poor health, he suggested that the President name as chief justice then Associate Justice Harlan Fiske Stone,
who had been dean of Columbia Law School when Franklin studied
there. Thus, in early June, Roosevelt knew he had three vacancies—
the chief justiceship, Stone's seat if Franklin named him chief justice,
and McReynolds's seat.

On the same day in June, Roosevelt filled all three: He agreed to
nominate Stone, a Republican who had been an ardent supporter of
the New Deal. Stone's appointment thus allowed Roosevelt to benefit
from reaching across the aisle for the new chief justice. To fill Mc-
Reynolds's seat, Roosevelt nominated another Southerner, his good
friend Senator Jimmy Byrnes of South Carolina, who had been an
ardent defender of the New Deal. And, for Stone's seat, he nominated
his attorney general Robert Jackson, who had served Roosevelt
loyally for nearly a decade in the Justice Department. Roosevelt
named Francis Biddle, a prominent Philadelphia lawyer, as the new
attorney general.

Though Robert Jackson only served on the Supreme Court for a
little more than a decade, he made a lasting impact as the finest
writer yet to serve on the Court. Byrnes left earlier; less than a year
after he joined the Court, he resigned to become administrator of
Roosevelt's Office of Economic Stabilization followed by a stint as di-

rector of economic mobilization through the end of the war. (Byrnes wanted to become secretary of state, an appointment that happened only after Harry Truman became president.) Roosevelt replaced Byrnes with the only sitting judge he ever nominated to the Court, Wiley Rutledge of the United States Court of Appeals for the District of Columbia. The Senate approved each nomination with a voice vote, and, after having further stacked the Court, Roosevelt returned his attention to the wars in Europe and the Pacific.

CHAPTER EIGHT

Waging War (1942–1944)

As America assessed the damages and mourned its dead after the attack on Pearl Harbor, Adolph Hitler was "delighted" and declared from his headquarters, "We can't lose the war at all. We now have an ally which has never been conquered in 3,000 years."[1] Years later, Winston Churchill confessed that he had felt at the time "the greatest joy. The United States was in the war, up to its neck and in it to the death. So we had won after all.... England would live; Britain would live; the Commonwealth of Nations and the Empire would live.... Many disasters, immeasurable cost and tribulation lay ahead, but there was no doubt about the end.... Being saturated and satisfied with emotion and sensation, I went to bed and slept the sleep of the saved and the thankful."[2]

The Nazi invasion of the Soviet Union had allied the Soviet Union with Britain, and the Pearl Harbor invasion cemented the alliance among the United States, Britain, and the Soviet Union. Their alliance soon included China, the "Free French" movement, and twenty other countries.

Yet the Allied Powers were hardly harmonious. Besides fighting to preserve their respective sovereignty, they fought for different reasons. The United States and Britain fought to preserve democratic principles, but China and the Soviet Union were not democratic regimes, and neither made any pretense that they were. Their leaders came from different backgrounds and championed different ideologies.

Educated in Japan, Chiang Kai-shek had been the leader of the Republic of China and the National Revolutionary Army since 1928. While Chiang wished to unify China, the Japanese invasion forced him to join forces with Chinese Communists led by Mao Tse-tung. Though Roosevelt regarded China as one of "the four policemen" of the world, he did not wish to get involved with the internal fighting among factions in China and preferred to meet with Chiang's wife, who was more polished, urbane, and diplomatic than her husband.

The "Free France" movement was led by one of Roosevelt's least favorite people in the world, French general Charles de Gaulle, a decorated veteran of the First World War who had established a "government-in-exile" in London in 1940. The antipathy between the two men was mutual, as Roosevelt suspected de Gaulle of having imperial ambitions of his own and de Gaulle never forgave Roosevelt for having failed to keep his promise in 1940 to bypass Congress and send troops to fortify de Gaulle's Free France movement.

Churchill and Roosevelt were natural allies, but they were not friends: Initially, Churchill was bent on schooling Roosevelt, eight years his junior, and pushing the younger man—and his country—to follow his lead. So eager was Churchill to have the United States join the war in Europe that he insisted, two days after Pearl Harbor, that he come to Washington to confer with the President. Reluctantly, Roosevelt agreed.

Arriving in the United States on December 22, 1941, Churchill came for a week but stayed for three. The two men and their staffs conferred at length about strategy, including how soon the Americans could join the fight and how best to structure their collaboration. Roosevelt agreed to reject Wilson's approach in 1917 to enter the war as an "associated" power rather than a fully committed ally.

Though the Americans and the British understandably each wanted a unified command structure, they initially could not agree if it should be led by an American or a Brit. After Harry Hopkins arranged an informal meeting between Churchill and George Marshall,

Churchill agreed that Marshall should be that man. Churchill and Roosevelt agreed further to establish a Combined Chiefs of Staff, which would be headquartered in Washington. Churchill agreed, too, with Roosevelt's suggestion that the Allied Powers be referred to as the United Nations.

Churchill and Roosevelt (and their staffs) constructed an agreement on principles that all the anti-Axis powers agreed to, including the promise "to defend life, liberty, independence, and religious freedom, and to preserve human rights and justice in their own lands as well as in other lands." On military strategy, the agreement contained two pledges—the first that each of the signatory countries pledged "to employ its full resources, military, or economic, against those members of the Tripartite Pact and its adherents with which such Government is at war" and the second "to cooperate with the Governments signatory hereto and not to make a separate armistice or peace with the enemies."[3]

The more time Churchill and Roosevelt spent together the more often Hopkins warned Roosevelt to resist Churchill's charm. It was good advice, which Roosevelt largely ignored. His war council went ballistic when, without their awareness, Roosevelt agreed to various requests from the prime minister, including turning over to the British the Americans' proposed reinforcements initially allotted to MacArthur in the Pacific. After being chastised by his staff, Roosevelt relented, and Churchill acquiesced to Roosevelt's change of opinion.

Hopkins was hardly the only advisor to caution Roosevelt in negotiating with Churchill. After meeting with the President, Marshall, Hopkins, and Hap Arnold (one of the first military aviators, who eventually led the air force), War Secretary Stimson recorded in his diary, "This incident shows the danger of talking too freely in international matters of such keen importance without the President carefully having his military and naval advisors present. . . . I think he had pretty nearly burnt his fingers and had called this subsequent meeting to make up for it. Hopkins told me at the time I talked with him over the telephone that he had told the President that he should be more careful about the formality of his discussions with Churchill."[4] Churchill completed his visit with an unprecedented address to a joint session of Congress, in which he charmed the nation and members of Congress with reminders of his close ties to the United States through his mother who was an American, his steadfast commitment to democracy and the Gettysburg ideal of the people, by the people, for the people. He denounced Germany and Italy as "evil," acknowledged the war would be "long and hard," five times used the word "together" in characterizing the positions of Great Britain and the United States, praised America's "Olympian fortitude," and ended with Congress and the American public in his thrall.[5]

Churchill's address did not mention the third country that both he and Roosevelt hoped would join their two countries in their quest to "beat the life out of the savage Nazi," the Soviet Union. By this time, Roosevelt had yet to meet the craftiest and deadliest of his allies, Joseph Stalin. While Churchill and Roosevelt were attending elite boarding schools, Stalin had dropped out of a seminary to devote himself to the Bolshevik Revolution. Sent into exile multiple times, he was an acolyte of Vladimir Lenin and followed him into power. Lenin and his deputy Trotsky worried about Stalin's ambitions and antisemitism, but neither could stop him from dismantling the system of collective leadership Lenin had set into place for when he was no longer the party leader.

By the time Lenin died of a brain hemorrhage at the age of fifty-four in 1924, he had failed to get Stalin removed as the leader of the Politburo, and Stalin was already well on his way to removing Jews, including Trotsky, from leadership positions within the Party. Though Stalin denounced antisemitism, he ordered the execution of more than half a million Russians, many Jews, during the Great Purge of 1936–37. Betrayal was a way of life for Stalin, and his regime was ruthless in exiling and executing any political opponents.

Even with the United States' entry into the war, the challenges confronting the Allies were staggering: The simple truth was that the Americans were outnumbered and outgunned. Waiting in the Pacific and farther east for the Americans was the third most powerful navy in the world, which had already partially crippled the United States' own navy.

Across the Atlantic, Americans faced the combined might of the Rome-Berlin Axis, which had ravaged Europe—occupying the Baltic states, Ukraine, European Russia, Poland, Greece, Norway, Denmark, the Netherlands, Belgium, and the nominally independent states of Slovakia, Croatia, Hungary, Rumania, and Bulgaria. In a few occupied territories, resistance, or partisan, forces complicated Nazi rule, including France, Yugoslavia, and the Soviet Union.

Yet Hitler's mistake in attacking the Soviet Union was taking its toll. Famously, Napoleon had made the same mistake in 1812, ending in the defeat of his army as it got bogged down in the brutal Russian terrain and winters. German forces, which were also bogged down in Russia, were unavailable to assist fellow soldiers spread increasingly thin across Europe and North Africa. While desperate to take advantage of Germany's dilemma, Roosevelt knew that if the United States were to prevail, it had to increase production at unprecedented rates. As a pragmatist, he knew the United States had to work with what it had to win the war, even if that meant joining forces with two countries—Great Britain and the Soviet Union—that oftentimes brutalized their own people.

I

With war declared against Japan and the Berlin-Rome Axis, Roosevelt assessed the challenges ahead. He commanded more public and congressional support than Wilson ever had. He was not impatient for war, as his younger self had been in 1915 and 1916, but he was as frustrated at the stubborn refusal of so many in Congress to help the country prepare for war. Despite his best efforts, the best estimates in 1942 indicated that the American military might need as much as two years to be prepared to go to war on multiple fronts—one in the Atlantic, another in the Pacific, one on the ground in Europe, and one in the air over the Atlantic and the Pacific as well as over Japan and Europe. It was naïve to think America's casualties would be less than those of the First World War.

To lead the country in war, Roosevelt adapted his leadership style in several ways. First, he recognized the need to consolidate as much power over the deployment of the armed forces as possible. Roosevelt had seen Wilson frustrated and burdened with the byzantine bureaucracy of the executive branch during the First World War, and he was determined not to have a repeat of any of that. On December 18, Congress enacted its first War Powers Act, which updated war-related legislation from the First World War and gave Roosevelt unprecedented power over the military needs of the nation, from production to censorship to the deployment of personnel and weaponry. As he told the nation, he was "the final arbiter in all departments and agencies of the Government."[6] He was determined to ensure that red tape did not cost needless lives, resources, and time. He created the War Production Board and revamped several war agencies and personnel assignments to help streamline and expedite production.

Second, Roosevelt needed advisors who had excellent judgment, decisiveness, and experience. Unlike Churchill, Roosevelt was not disposed to second-guess or micromanage the armed forces once they were in harm's way. Besides Stimson and Knox, the leadership of each of the branches had experience dating back to at least the Spanish-American War.

Roosevelt had known Admiral Stark, appointed chief of naval operations in 1929, since the First World War, when he led America's submarine forces and Franklin was assistant secretary of the navy. Though Roosevelt had not removed him immediately after the Pearl Harbor attack, he was not confident Stark could be the strict disciplinarian that the navy needed. Besides appointing Admiral Chester Nimitz as head of the Pacific Fleet, Roosevelt promoted Admiral Edward King (a veteran of several wars) to be the commander in chief of the entire United States Fleet. In 1942, Roosevelt moved Stark to London, where he worked with the British as the head of the Atlantic Fleet.

To oversee assembly of armaments, Roosevelt wanted someone like the financier Bernard Baruch, whom Wilson had placed in control of production in the First World War. Without any obvious choice, Franklin placed his longtime friend, Donald Nelson, an executive with Sears, as the director of the War Production Board. When the board's performance began to suffer because of infighting among Nelson's deputies, Roosevelt ordered Nelson which to fire. When production was not moving as fast as members of Congress wanted, Hopkins directed Nelson's deputy, Donald Wilson, formerly the president of General Electric, to run the board as efficiently as possible.

There was widespread consensus among military advisors that the right man to serve as chief of staff was George Marshall, who had earned accolades for coordinating planning and training during the First World War. Roosevelt agreed, and on September 1, 1939, he appointed Marshall chief of staff, a position he held throughout the war. Though Roosevelt expected him to lead the army, he increasingly delegated all military authority to Marshall, including placing him in charge of the largest military expansion in the nation's history.

But Roosevelt decided not to appoint him as the supreme commander of Operation Overlord, the Allies' planned invasion of Europe. He did not want Marshall to relocate to London. Roosevelt appreciated that Marshall pulled no punches in advising him. He told Marshall, "I don't feel I could sleep at ease if you were out of Washington."[7] Instead, Roosevelt sent Dwight Eisenhower, whom Marshall had promoted to his staff because of his knack for developing battle plans.

Within a year, Eisenhower helped to streamline the command for the army air force, which was under the immediate control of General Hap Arnold. In 1943, Roosevelt elevated Eisenhower to be the supreme Allied commander, making Eisenhower's job both strategic and political, as he was responsible for coordinating any invasion with the military leaders of the other Allied Powers. While Roosevelt had to rely on his military advisors for reliable accounts from the field of battle both in the sea and on land, he had Hopkins and Eleanor function as his eyes and ears in visiting production plants, monitoring their output, and reporting on conversations with the workers.

Roosevelt saw his role as giving the military what it needed to win the war. As Admiral King told Robert Sherwood a year after the war, "Churchill, fancying himself as a great strategist, and being so powerful personally, ruled his Chiefs of Staff with an iron hand, forcing them at all times to compliance with the policy as he and the War Cabinet laid it down." In contrast, King explained, Roosevelt "trusted his Chiefs of Staff and thus gave them more personal authority and immeasurably more freedom of action and of speech than was enjoyed by their British opposite numbers."[8]

Roosevelt, like Lincoln and Churchill, understood the importance of rhetoric. Just as he had mobilized the government and the American people to combat the depression, he now had the responsibility (and opportunity) to mobilize them into soldiers, sailors, pilots, medics and nurses, code-breakers, and ship and aircraft builders. Like never before, the nation rallied to the cause, with women, from one coast to the other, volunteering to work in defense plants, code-breaking, and war-related organizations such as the United Service Organizations (known as the "USO").

It was not just his experiences during the First World War that convinced Roosevelt of his unique role in rallying the troops. Roosevelt was familiar with Lincoln's fine-tuning of the objective of the Civil War as events unfolded. At the outset of the Civil War, Lincoln, in 1861, declared that preserving the Union was the most important objective. By 1863, he said preserving the Union required abolishing slavery once and for all. Later that same year, in his address at Gettysburg, Lincoln linked the war's purpose to the ideals of liberty and equality set forth in the Declaration of Independence.

While Lincoln kept his messages clear, direct, and even poetic, Roosevelt tailored his messages differently. Most importantly, he took advantage of radio and television to communicate more often and more directly with the American people than Lincoln ever could. Lincoln understood that people had short attention spans but benefitted from messages they could remember and quote aloud themselves. Roosevelt, like Lincoln, believed he was more than a father figure to the nation; he was also a teacher. He needed Americans to understand the challenges ahead, even if that required more than a few homilies.

In his first wartime State of the Union, delivered on January 6, 1942, President Roosevelt spelled out the war's objectives, including increasing the production of airplanes, tanks, and antiaircraft guns. He did not mince words in explaining that sacrifice was necessary: "Our task is unprecedented, and the time is short. We must strain every existing armament-producing facility to the upmost. We must convert every available plant and tool to war production. That goes all the way from the greatest plants to the smallest—from the huge automobile industry to the village machine shop." He readied the American people for increased "taxes and bonds and bonds and taxes. It means cutting luxuries and other non-essentials. In short, it means an all-out war by individual effort and family effort in a united country." He concluded, "Only this all-out scale of production will hasten the ultimate all-out victory.... Lost ground can always be regained, lost time never."[9] Though not as poetic as Lincoln at his best, Roosevelt's rhetoric got the job done as he rallied public support for the grueling work of the war.

In a Fireside Chat on February 23, 1942, he explained that the country faced "a new kind of war. It is different from all other wars of the past, not only in its methods and weapons but also in its geography." Asking Americans to have world maps in front of them, he pointed out where and why the Allies needed fortification to keep the channels of communication and aide open in the months ahead. Harkening back to prior statements in the run-up to the war, he concluded with the reminder that "the Atlantic Charter applies not only to the parts of the world that border the Atlantic but to the whole world; disarmament of aggressors, self-determination of nations and peoples, and the four freedoms: freedom of speech, freedom of religion, freedom of want, and freedom from fear."[10]

Yet, Roosevelt's limitations were showing. His preoccupation with popularity and public support came at the expense of civil rights. He never thought the time was right to enlist the government on the side of protecting the civil rights of minorities.

Within two weeks of his State of the Union in January 1942, the Third Reich, at a conference outside of Berlin, formalized its "Final Solution of the Jewish question." Nazi Germany had been killing Jews since 1941, but it quickly set up six killing centers, the largest being Auschwitz-Birkenau, which averaged killing more than six thousand Jews each day from 1943 to 1944. The conference signaled the final phase of the Holocaust, culminating in the death of 6 million Jews (and other minorities), nearly two-thirds of the Jewish population in Europe. Roosevelt did not acknowledge the policy publicly. Nor did he alter his administration's policy denying entry into the country for many Jews fleeing Nazi Germany.

II

Four days before reminding Americans of the war's objective to protect the four freedoms across the world, Roosevelt had gone a step too far in trusting military leaders. General John DeWitt, the overall army commander on the West Coast, convinced Roosevelt that a fifth column was operating in that region. DeWitt took as confirmation the report of the Roberts Commission (named for Justice Owen Roberts, its chair), which had been charged with investigating the Pearl Harbor attack and found that the assault was made possible in part because of Hawaii-based espionage agents, including American citizens of Japanese descent. That was more than enough for DeWitt and Secretary of War Stimson, as well as California's Governor Culbert Olsen and Attorney General Earl Warren, who supported Roosevelt's Executive Order 9066 authorizing the forced removal of all people deemed a threat to national security from the West Coast to "relocation centers." Notably, most of these people were of Japanese and Asian descent.

At the time, there was concern among administration officials that there was, in fact, no legitimate or credible evidence of a threat posed to national security by American citizens. Many prominent administration officials, including Attorney General Frances Biddle and Treasury Secretary Morgenthau, opposed Roosevelt's order. J. Edgar Hoover, then in his seventeenth year as FBI director, called the evacuation "utterly unwarranted." When Biddle said the executive order was "ill-advised, unnecessary, and unnecessarily cruel," the President responded "this must be a military decision."[11]

Two years later, in 1944, the Supreme Court agreed and, in delivering a severe blow to its own legitimacy and credibility, upheld the constitutionality of the measure. Many years later, a congressional inquiry found no legitimate basis for the order, and in 1985, President Ronald Reagan signed a reparations bill into law. It was not until 2018 that the Supreme Court overturned its decision upholding the detention order.

Besides discounting concerns about civil rights, Roosevelt hid his physical limitations from the public throughout his presidency. Once the United States entered the war, the press was loath to showcase any of his declining health for fear that it would cripple American morale. World leaders such as Churchill were struck, upon meeting Roosevelt, by his gaunt and sickly appearance. Indeed, as the war wore on, Roosevelt's health worsened, though only the people closest to him or who visited him in person could see his physical deterioration.

After returning from lunch with the President in August 1944, Harry Truman told the press that Roosevelt "looked fine and ate a bigger lunch than I did," but confided to his military aide Harry Vaughan, "I had no idea he was in such feeble condition." When asked by a Senate colleague what the President was like, Truman responded, "He lies."[12]

Indeed, Roosevelt's lies were catching up with him. Truman was hardly the first senator to complain of Roosevelt's duplicity. Franklin had made campaign promises he did not keep, he misled or lied to friends and colleagues about his intentions to run for a third term, he broke promises to foreign and civil rights leaders, such as de Gaulle, and many others, and he was never as straight and candid with the American people as he repeatedly proclaimed he was. He lied to nearly everyone, especially Eleanor, about his lady friends.

Yet, as both Truman and Churchill had done, other leaders kept the facts of Roosevelt's declining health to themselves. As Churchill told Stalin in 1943, "In wartime, truth is so precious that she should always be attended by a bodyguard of lies."[13]

Others, such as Press Secretary Steve Early, depicted Roosevelt as imbued with a wealth of experience and good judgment. Virtually all agreed that, in the months after the Pearl Harbor attack, Roosevelt tried, like two previous wartime presidents, Wilson and Lincoln, to elevate his administration above politics. He tried to avoid the trap into which Wilson had fallen in calling for a Democratic Congress in the 1918 election. For instance, in February 1942, Roosevelt told the American people, "When a country is at war we want Congressmen, regardless of party—get that—who have a record of backing up the Government of the United States, in an emergency, regardless of party."[14] Such remarks had little impact given Roosevelt's many years of partisanship. Republican senator Robert Taft of Ohio repeatedly reminded the public to distrust Roosevelt and to see that, whether in fighting inflation or work stoppages, Roosevelt's solution was invariably to increase the federal government's control over the American economy and people.

To help himself and his administration against partisan attacks, Roosevelt asked Jimmy Byrnes, once a power in the Senate, to leave the Court to be the director of his Office of Economic Stabilization. The President and first lady often went out of their way to make rationing seem the democratic way to guarantee equal supplies for everyone. Byrnes rallied his friends and allies in the Senate to back the President's anti-inflationary policies, eventually getting compromises that gave the President some of what he wanted, but the policies did not stem the rise in prices in agriculture and other products.

When the rise in prices fueled demands in wage increases, Roosevelt turned to Labor Secretary Frances Perkins, who put together a management-labor conference in Washington that reached agreement on wartime labor policy and the machinery to enforce it, including the establishment of the National War Labor Board.

When the administration next faced concerns about abolishing the forty-hour workweek, Roosevelt went back to the drawing board, enlisting the help of both Byrnes and Perkins, to develop a seven-point anti-inflation program. The purpose of the program was to make the cost of war fall less hard on consumers of limited means, but Republicans in Congress complained that Roosevelt's supposed solutions to problems were making government bigger and less efficient.

Yet Roosevelt's management style was wearing thin, too. His appointment of special envoys to undertake various tasks, his preference to assign the same task to several people, his bypassing cabinet secretaries whenever he felt the need, his insistence on saddling cabinet secretaries and agency heads with deputies who despised, or could not get along with, them, and his reluctance to say no were just some of the quirks that irked people working for him.

Cabinet officials found that their meetings with the President were often nothing more than "pep sessions," without any important decisions being made, or worse. Secretary Stimson found attending was both a waste of time and a source of exasperation: "His mind does not follow easily a consecutive chain of thought, but he is full of stories and incidents and hops about in his discussions from suggestion to suggestion and it is very much like chasing a vagrant beam of sunlight around a vacant room."[15]

Roosevelt's peculiar management style was obvious to nearly everyone who spent time with him. After observing Roosevelt at a press conference, the writer John Gunther described his performance: "In twenty minutes Mr. Roosevelt's features had expressed amazement, curiosity, mock alarm, genuine interest, worry, rhetorical playing for suspense, sympathy, decision, playfulness, dignity, and surpassing charm. Yet he said almost nothing. Questions were deflected, diverted, diluted. Answers—when they did come—were concise and clear. But I never met anyone who showed greater capacity for avoiding a direct answer while giving the questioner the feeling he had been answered."[16]

Roosevelt delighted in keeping people off-balance, unsure or confused about his plans, and giving himself time to change his mind, for these all ensured he would be the center of attention, a position he never willingly relinquished. He once explained to Henry Morgenthau, "Never let your left hand know what your right hand is doing." When Morgenthau asked which hand he was, the President replied, "My right hand. But I keep my left hand under the table." In his diaries, Morgenthau wrote that "this is the most frank expression of the real FDR that I ever listened to and that is the real way that he works." In May 1942, Roosevelt acknowledged, "You know I am a juggler, and I never let my right hand know what my left hand does.... I may be entirely inconsistent, and furthermore I am perfectly willing to mislead and tell untruths if it will win the war."[17]

A young navy lieutenant who ran Roosevelt's secret wartime White House intelligence center—the Map Room—observed that "Roosevelt had the habit of saying he was in agreement with whoever he was with and making them feel they had his full support, and he might well go off in another direction an hour later."[18] Roosevelt biographer Geoffrey Ward believed "Roosevelt had a fairly creative relationship with the truth. He could convince himself that what he was saying was the truth for the moment. He was a master at pleasing the visitors to his office."[19]

Eleanor had a different take: She thought Franklin's "real weakness" was that "he couldn't bear to be disagreeable to someone he liked."[20] After observing Roosevelt's inability to tell Wallace that he was being dropped from the ticket in 1944, Eleanor wrote, "He always hopes to get things settled pleasantly and he won't realize that there are times when you have got to do an unpleasant thing directly, and, perhaps, unpleasantly." Various aides agreed with that assessment. Jim Farley often spoke of how Roosevelt "forever put off things distasteful." Ray Moley remarked that "perhaps in the long run, fewer friends would have been lost by bluntness than by the misunderstandings that arose from engaging ambiguity."[21]

As the war wore on, one thing was becoming evident to those working closely with the President: He had trouble making decisions. Stimson was not the only cabinet member to grouse about Roosevelt's not showing enough decisive leadership in the cauldron of war. It might have been the pressures of war along with his poor health. It could also have been the fallout from the death of Franklin's mother, Sara, four months before the attack on Pearl Harbor. Roosevelt felt her absence keenly: Locked into his makeshift wheelchair for hours on end, without an outlet or confidant with whom he could blow off steam, left him feeling more alone than he had yet experienced as president.

III

In the early morning hours of April 18, 1942, sixteen American bombers, led by Lieutenant Colonel James Doolittle, suddenly appeared over Tokyo. In less than a minute, they dropped bombs, as Doolittle reported, on "Tokyo's oil refineries, oil reserves, steel and munition plants, naval docks and other military objectives."[22] They killed fifty people and wounded four hundred.

Because the bombers did not have enough fuel for the pilots to return home, they bailed out where they could. Most landed in portions of China not controlled by the Japanese Empire. Of the sixteen crews, fourteen survived intact; one crew member was killed in action; eight aviators were captured by the Japanese in Eastern China, three of whom were executed; and all but one of the sixteen planes were destroyed in crashes. One pilot landed in the Soviet Union and was released a year later. A month after the attack, the President awarded Doolittle, on behalf of the entire crew, the Congressional Medal of Honor.

The raid caused the empire to lose face, pinned down fighter planes on home fields, and prompted the Japanese government to accelerate its plans for extending its perimeter. In reprisal for China's giving safe harbor to several pilots, Japan killed more than 250,000 civilians and 70,000 soldiers in China.

Though he had authorized the mission, Roosevelt played coy with the press afterward and gave no indication it had all been part of a plan to demonstrate Japan's vulnerability to air attacks. While the damage done was relatively small, the raid was a symbolic victory for Americans, whose morale needed fortifying after a series of Japanese air strikes in December and January that destroyed Allied ships and expanded Japanese control in Burma, Malaya, southern Thailand, and portions of Borneo, Bali, Timor, and the Philippines, and made inroads into the oil-rich Indies.

In the aftermath of the raid and with lessons learned from underestimating the firepower of Japan's navy and aircraft, the combined British–United States Joint Chiefs of Staff made a few crucial adjustments in the war in the Pacific. The first was to establish a new command structure. Forced out of the Philippines on February 22, 1942, where he had been headquartered, General Douglas MacArthur was greeted in Australia with great fanfare and adulation. He still had the confidence of the President, who appointed him the supreme commander, Southwest Pacific Area.

Admiral Nimitz became the commander in chief for the Pacific Ocean Area, which included most of the rest of the Pacific that did not fall within MacArthur's jurisdiction. The new command structure was more streamlined than before and worked well due to the cooperation and mutual respect that the two men had for each other.

The second adjustment followed the realization that the future of naval warfare was at hand: As had been the case with the Doolittle Raid, Allied aircraft, including American pilots and planes, had the tactical advantage in a fight at sea in bombing and strafing the enemy's ships while the vessels never made direct contact. This realization was put to the test at the Battle of Wake Island (December 8–23) and the Battle of the Coral Sea, culminating on May 7 and 8, when the United States lost more tonnage than the Japanese but successfully repelled Japan's southward advance and were able to keep the sea lanes open. This moral victory, too, proved that the Japanese Navy was not invincible.

The third adjustment was made based on the realization that the Allies did not need to be stronger than the Japanese fleet (though they would soon be); they needed to be smarter. As the Japanese Navy spread itself thin across the great expanse of the Pacific, American cryptographers deciphered Japanese messages to discover a plan of attack in the Pacific. To determine the specific location for the attack, Americans sent a false message that Midway was running low on fresh water. When American cryptographers read Japan's next message indicating the locale was low on fresh water, they confirmed the locale for the next attack was Midway, roughly equidistant between North America and Asia and the home of Naval Air Facility Midway Island. They decoded other Japanese messages to discover the date of the attack and the Japanese order of battle.

Admiral Nimitz prepared naval forces for their counteroffensive, while arrangements were made for Allied fighter pilots to bomb the four carriers leading the Japanese attack. Over the course of five days, the United States lost one carrier and one hundred planes while Japan scuttled one of its carriers and lost the three others, more than two hundred planes, and, perhaps most importantly, their naval advantage in the Pacific. The empire was left with only one carrier for the duration of the war. On June 13, Churchill cabled Roosevelt to extend his "heartiest congratulations on the grand American victories in the Pacific which have very decidedly altered the balance of the Naval war."[23] History would prove Churchill right.

IV

For more than a year after Congress declared war against the Rome-Berlin Axis, there was more talk among Allied commanders than actual fighting in Europe, but they soon reached consensus on three matters that reshaped the war.

The first was agreement among the Allies on the best place and time to launch an American assault into Nazi-occupied Europe. For much of 1942, Marshall, Stimson, and Eisenhower believed the best strategy was to attack Germany directly. They opposed Churchill's idea of sending troops into North Africa to block any German move to capture the Strait of Gibraltar, which served as a British fortress overseeing naval traffic in the region. The Joint Chiefs rejected the plan as aimed at helping the British more than bringing the war to a speedy end. But when he met with Churchill in Hyde Park in June 1942, Roosevelt rejected the Joint Chiefs' advice and agreed with Churchill's plan for North Africa.

A meeting with Stalin's Foreign Minister Vyacheslav Molotov near the end of May 1942 further convinced Roosevelt to continue with the North African invasion plan, later called TORCH, since it met with the approval of Stalin, who had long urged the Americans to open a second front in the war in Europe that would draw German forces away from Russia. Putting aside his objections to an invasion in North Africa, Eisenhower agreed to plan the invasion for that fall.

On November 8, 1942, the Western Task Force launched its three-pronged attack in Morocco. More than eighteen thousand American troops, under the command of Major General Charles Ryder, captured Casablanca, with the help of British air cover and the first major airborne assault by the United States.

But French forces were confused over whom to attack or follow, and their nominal leaders refused to take sides in the confrontation. Eisenhower, with the approval of Roosevelt and Churchill, appointed François Darlan, already in charge of Vichy forces, as the French high commissioner in North Africa, though he was assassinated weeks later and replaced by a weak figurehead. Nonetheless, the Eisenhower-Darlan agreement meant that the officials appointed by the Vichy regime in North Africa would remain in power (and thus persist in still discriminating against Jews). Left out was the Free France movement, even though it was supposed to be the French government in exile and had wrested control of other French colonies from the Nazis.

Though German troops, on Hitler's orders, seized control of what remained of unoccupied France, all of Morocco and Algeria were under Allied control by November 12, 1942. In exchange for Roosevelt's agreement that the United States remain neutral in the Spanish Civil War, Generalissimo Francisco Franco responded to Roosevelt's declaration that "the presence of American military forces in North Africa presages in no manner whatsoever a move against the people or Government of Spain," with his own declaration, "I accept with pleasure and I thank you for the assurances which Your Excellency offers the Government and the people of Spain. I can assure you that Spain knows the value of peace and sincerely desires peace for itself and all other peoples."[24]

A summit followed each significant advancement in the war in Europe. The first, following the Allies' success in Morocco, was January 14–24, 1943, where Churchill, Roosevelt, and de Gaulle met in Casablanca. Stalin was unable to attend, in order to lead his Red Army's offensive against the German Army's siege of Stalingrad.

Roosevelt's trip to Casablanca, Morocco, requiring forty-eight hours in the air, marked the first time a sitting president had flown. (Though the location for their meeting was a secret, Roosevelt took delight on New Year's Eve in watching the movie *Casablanca* at a screening in the White House.) After witnessing firsthand on the drive to and from the airport the poverty and squalor of the nearby British colony of Gambia in West Africa, Roosevelt became a harsh critic of British colonialism.

The meeting secured some important agreements. The first involved the next plan of attack. By the time of the summit, the news on both fronts was positive: The British, under the command of Field Marshall Bernard Law Montgomery (popularly known as "Monty"), had broken German field marshal Erwin Rommel's famed Africa Korps of tanks and pressed into Libya; the Red Army had mounted a successful counterattack at Stalingrad and isolated the German Sixth Army Group; and the Allies had captured the Pacific island of Guadalcanal and pressed their island-hopping campaign forward.

Against this backdrop, Allied commanders divided: Marshall pushed for a cross-channel invasion, Admiral King (whose stubbornness prompted Eisenhower to express hope in his diary that he would be shot) urged focusing more on the Pacific, while the British insisted on invading Sicily, effectively the underbelly of Europe, as the next step.

Roosevelt, with his advisors divided, deferred to the British on the next plan of attack. The British came with a larger staff, more detailed plans, and a much better communications network. Roosevelt was persuaded to adopt the sequence of their priorities—first seizing control of Sicily, then moving into Burma in southeast Asia, followed by a preliminary invasion of France, but also doing whatever was necessary to stop submarine attacks in the Atlantic.

Though Marshall was less than enthused, he agreed with the British that their priorities should be achieved by 1944. Roosevelt left the conference determined that his staff never again come underprepared to such conferences.

The second agreement was the result of a last-second inspiration Roosevelt had during the press conference held at the end of the summit. Without talking to Churchill beforehand, he announced that the Allied Powers had agreed that the war would end only when the enemy unconditionally surrendered. (Lincoln had demanded the same from the Confederacy to end the Civil War.) "Unconditional surrender" became a popular rallying cry for the Allies, while it reassured Stalin that Churchill and Roosevelt would not negotiate any peace that failed to protect Soviet interests.

After the press conference, Roosevelt told Averell Harriman, his new ambassador to Russia, that Roosevelt was determined not to repeat Wilson's mistake in issuing his Fourteen Points in advance of the armistice, which Germany blamed as a basis for the postwar settlement. Though Eisenhower later questioned the wisdom of insisting on Germany's unconditional surrender, Churchill, on learning the news, declared that "I agree with everything that the President has said." Later, Churchill explained, "Any divergence between us, even by omission, would on such occasion and at such a time have been damaging or even dangerous to our war effort."[25]

The parties could not agree, however, on the future of France. Though Roosevelt initially preferred to name General Henri Giraud, not de Gaulle, as the nominal head of the new French regime, he met resistance from his own advisors as well as the British and de Gaulle, who, in keeping with his flair for the dramatic, arrived late with much pomp and circumstance. On January 22, Roosevelt met de Gaulle for the first time, a meeting that each later regarded as a failure. De Gaulle's objective at the conference was to hasten France's return as a great power, but the war had taught Roosevelt that no good came from any empire and he thus opposed the restoration of the French Empire. Though they never reached any agreement, the two men posed for photographs at the end of the summit to support the impression they had.

Roosevelt never treated de Gaulle as an equal. In talking with his son Elliott, who had also come to Casablanca, Franklin said, "De Gaulle is out to achieve a one-man government in France. I can't imagine a man I would distrust more. His own Free France is honeycombed with police spies. He has agents spying on his own people. To him, freedom of speech means freedom from criticism—of him." Of course, Roosevelt was not immune to thinking he and the republic were one and the same. But, after the conference, Roosevelt could not stop himself from expressing insulting comments de Gaulle resented. For his part, de Gaulle appraised Roosevelt accurately: "Roosevelt meant the peace to be an American peace, convinced he must be the one to dictate its structure, that the states which had been overrun should be subject to his judgment, and that France in particular should recognize him as its savior and its arbiter." He added "that like any star performer [Roosevelt] was touchy at the roles that fell to other actors. In short, beneath his patrician mask of courtesy, Roosevelt regarded me without benevolence."[26]

When the conference ended, Churchill went to the airport to ensure Roosevelt's safe departure. After helping Roosevelt onto the plane, Churchill told an aide, "If anything happened to that man, I couldn't stand it. He is the truest friend; he has the farthest vision; he is the greatest man I have ever known."[27]

Churchill and Roosevelt attended two more conferences near the end of the year. The first was held November 22–26, in Cairo, Egypt. Churchill, Roosevelt, and Chiang Kai-shek attended, and the subject was the future of postwar Asia. Roosevelt had asked for the meeting since the spring and summer of 1943, because of concerns about a series of issues—low morale and high inflation in China, growing tensions between Chiang Kai-shek and the American commander in that part of the world, General Joseph Stillwell (who called Chiang "peanut"), and difficulties in getting needed supplies into China— that threatened to sever the relations among the Allies.

The conference itself was designed to give China a symbolic boost of confidence in its place as one of the four great powers in the world, and Roosevelt offered to return to China territories it had lost to Japan in exchange for China's siding with the Americans to check British, Japanese, and Russia expansion into Asia. Though Churchill had little role in the negotiations, the three countries released the Cairo Declaration on December 1, 1943, pledging to continue the war against Japan and ejecting Japanese forces from all the territories it had conquered, including Korea, the Pacific Islands, and the Chinese territories.

Cairo was a warmup for the next conference, scheduled in Tehran for November 28–December 1. The war on both fronts had clearly turned in favor of the Allies due to significant victories in the Pacific, North Africa, and Italy. Germany was on the defensive, and the Japanese Empire was finding itself now the inferior force in the Pacific. A related factor was the United States' unprecedented production of military equipment: Between 1941 and 1945, the United States produced 300,000 military aircraft. In the peak of 1944, American factories built 96,318 planes—more than the yearly total of Germany,

Italy, Britain, Japan, and the Soviet Union combined. Henry Ford's enormous Willow Run plant produced a B-24 plane every sixty-three minutes. By the end of the war, the United States had manufactured 2.4 million trucks, 635,000 jeeps, 88,400 tanks, 5,800 ships, and 40 billion rounds of ammunition.

Production had progressed on another front for the United States—the development of two kinds of atomic bombs. In April 1942, Roosevelt had authorized the Manhattan Project, a top-secret research and development operation, overseen by Secretary of War Stimson, who named General Leslie Groves as its director. Groves in turn designated Berkeley physicist J. Robert Oppenheimer as the project director, and over the next two years they assembled a staff of world-renowned physicists, many of whom had emigrated to the United States just before the war.

In June 1942, when Churchill met with Roosevelt at his home in Hyde Park, the two leaders generally agreed on sharing of information about the project's development, though the Americans, often with Roosevelt's approval, ignored the policy when it suited their needs. When, on December 2, 1942, Enrico Fermi, an Italian physicist who had been awarded the Nobel Prize in Physics in 1939, reported that his team, working beneath the football field at the University of Chicago, had split an atom for the first time, Oppenheimer recruited Fermi for the project, and Fermi became the associate director of the lab located in Los Alamos, New Mexico. Roosevelt ordered Stimson to keep such developments secret, even from the British and other Allies.

Against this backdrop, the three leaders who met in Tehran—Churchill, Roosevelt, and Stalin, in person for the first time—arrived with the conviction that the outcome of the war would be in their favor. They saw their mission as not just plotting the Allied invasion in Europe but also positioning themselves and their respective countries for the postwar era.

Roosevelt's strategy was to keep Churchill and Stalin off-balance. He told Churchill he wanted to meet alone with Stalin, which upset the prime minister. Stalin persuaded Roosevelt to stay at the Russian embassy in Tehran. Naively, Roosevelt agreed. He had no idea Stalin had bugged his apartment, which allowed Stalin to stay a step ahead of Roosevelt in their face-to-face meetings.

When the three leaders met, they agreed on the necessity of opening a second front in Western Europe against the Third Reich and reaffirmed that the cross-channel invasion would occur in the late spring of 1944. Otherwise, Stalin disagreed with the initiatives proposed by Churchill and instead found a ready ally in Roosevelt, who wanted to maintain the peace among the three but considered it more important to convince Stalin that the United States would help to ease the burdens on the Soviet Union.

Stalin kept pressing the utility of forcing Germany to fight on a second front. "The Red Army," he explained, "usually attacks from two directions, forcing the enemy to move his reserves from one front to the other. As the two offensives converge, the power of the whole offensive increases. Such would be the case in simultaneous operations from southern and northern France."[28]

When Churchill objected, Roosevelt cut him off and insisted that the military staffs study the merits of attacking southern France or launching a joint cross-channel invasion into northern France. Churchill was further annoyed by Stalin's ridiculing him throughout the conference. Roosevelt's response was merely to laugh, seemingly giddy over the prospect that the United States and the Soviet Union could work together in the future.

One of the few areas of disagreement between Roosevelt and Stalin arose over the future of Poland. Stalin wanted Poland moved as fast as possible out from under Nazi control, though Churchill and Roosevelt recognized that what he really wanted was to return Poland to Soviet control. Churchill and Roosevelt agreed on the importance of liberating Poland, but Churchill pushed to ensure Poland's freedom from foreign domination.

In private, Stalin urged Roosevelt to agree with the Soviet Union on the borders for any future Poland. But Roosevelt resisted, telling Stalin that he wished to postpone the question until later in 1944 because of the presidential election that year. He said he did not expect to be a candidate though he might if the war still raged on. "There are six to seven million Americans of Polish extraction," Roosevelt told Stalin. "As a practical man, I don't wish to lose their vote." Stalin conceded the point.[29]

The final matter that arose in the Tehran conference was the choice of commander to lead Operation Overlord. When Stalin asked Roosevelt, "Who will command Overlord?," Roosevelt replied, "That has not yet been decided." But Roosevelt had already decided it, and his answer to Stalin was an attempt to keep Stalin off-balance. In fact, the Allies had agreed the choice of commander should be made by Roosevelt, since most of the personnel involved would be Americans. For him, the choice boiled down to George Marshall or Dwight Eisenhower.

The Joint Chiefs thought that Marshall should not be chosen, because they believed he was indispensable in his role as Roosevelt's chief of staff for the war. Roosevelt agreed, but he believed that Marshall should at least be given the choice, since he had, in Roosevelt's judgment, earned that right through outstanding service. When pressed, Marshall told Hopkins and Roosevelt that he would serve the President in whatever capacity Roosevelt thought best. As Marshall recalled, he "wished to make clear [to Roosevelt] that whatever the decision, I would go along with it wholeheartedly."[30] Roosevelt had expected nothing less from Marshall. Over the course of the war, Roosevelt's respect for Eisenhower had grown, as Ike had plotted the defeat of the Germans in North Africa and Sicily, established excellent working relationships with British commanders, and discounted American special interests for the sake of the common good. Roosevelt indicated as much to Stalin and Churchill, and on his return trip from Tehran, he stopped in Tunis, where he met Eisenhower, who was overseeing "Operation Torch," the Allies' invasion into North Africa. As Eisenhower climbed into his car, Roosevelt greeted him, "Well, Ike, you are going to command Overlord."[31]

V

Throughout the war, George Marshall and Dwight Eisenhower worked together like clockwork. Though they each had come to the army by different routes, Marshall as a graduate of Virginia Military Institute and Eisenhower through West Point, they each had different skills, Marshall in coordinating complex military operations and Eisenhower in planning them; and they differed in their personalities, with Marshall straightforward, direct, and unencumbered by any artifice and Eisenhower more gregarious and contemplative. They shared something else that had brought each of them to the top of the military chain of command in World War II—they'd had the same teacher, Major General Fox Connor.

Connor made his name as both the brains behind the Army Expeditionary Force, which provided invaluable assistance to the French in the First World War, and as a mentor to many of the United States' military leaders in the Second World War. Among them were both George Marshall, who had served on Connor's staff when Connor was assistant chief of staff for the operations of the Army Expeditionary Force, and Dwight Eisenhower, with whom Connor was so impressed after meeting him at a dinner with General George Patton that he later named him to his staff when Connor took command of the 20th Infantry Brigade in Panama in 1921.

Connor later described Marshall as the ideal soldier and a brilliant military leader, and he was so impressed with Eisenhower that he not only had placed him on his staff but also gotten him into the Command and Staff School located in Eisenhower's home state of Kansas. With the help of his experiences with Connor, who assigned Eisenhower for three years to extensive readings in military history and daily exercises such as writing field orders for every aspect of command, and the notes taken by General Patton when he attended the school, Eisenhower graduated first in his class.

Connor, Marshall, and Eisenhower shared enormous respect for one another. Eisenhower regarded the greatest reward of his friendship with General Patton his introduction to Connor. In later years, Eisenhower said, "He had more influence on me and my outlook than any other individual, especially in regard to the military profession." Connor introduced Eisenhower to classic treatises and studies of military leadership and strategy. Eisenhower declared that "in sheer ability and character, [Connor] was the outstanding solider of my time." Connor, who became known as the "man who made Eisenhower," taught Eisenhower invaluable lessons in coalition building.[32]

One lesson Eisenhower said he never forgot was how, "again and again, Connor said to me, 'We cannot escape another great war. When we go into that war it will be in the company of allies. . . . We must insist on individual and single responsibility—leaders will have to learn how to overcome nationalistic considerations in the conduct of campaigns. One man who can do it is [George] Marshall—he is close to being a genius.'"[33] Robert Gates, who later served as secretary of defense for both Presidents George W. Bush and Barack Obama, said that "Connor became Eisenhower's teacher and a father figure whom he admired above all others."

Among the many lessons that Marshall and Eisenhower learned from Connor was one that they each followed during the war. It was Connor's three rules of war: "Never fight unless you have to; Never fight alone; and Never fight for long."[34]

But try as he might, Eisenhower could not keep the planned Allied invasion of France from becoming overly complex. It was not until the Trident Conference in May of 1944 that Allied commanders reached agreement that the invasion would be made onto several beachheads in Normandy, France. To ensure that the Germans would not be in full force at the locale for the invasion, Allied intelligence released false messages that led their German counterparts to focus their forces on the Pas de Calais, the closest French coastline to England. It was more than 170 kilometers from the point of invasion in Normandy.

At the same time as D-Day approached, Allied forces nearly completed their campaign to liberate Italy. In July 1943, the invasion of Sicily had led to the collapse of the Fascist Italian regime and the fall of Mussolini, who was arrested on the order of King Victor Emmanuel III on July 25, 1943. The new government signed an armistice with the Allies on September 8. German forces took control of northern and central Italy, and a civil war broke out in Italy between the puppet government of the Italian Social Republic, put into place by the Germans, and the Italian Co-Belligerent Army and partisans.

Four major offensives between January and May of 1944 by the Fifth and Eighth Armies broke the German defense, and the Fifth Army, under the command of Lieutenant General Mark Clark, took possession of Rome on June 4, 1944. Elated, Roosevelt held his first Fireside Chat of the year, hailing Clark and telling the American public that "the first of the Axis capitals is now in our hands. One up and two to go."[35] After the war, Clark was faulted for various command mistakes, including allowing Germany's Tenth Army to escape.

The liberation of Rome raised the morale and confidence of Allied commanders that Germany was next. After planning for more than a year, Roosevelt gave Eisenhower the final authority to give a greenlight to the invasion. Initially, Ike hoped to have the invasion launched on June 5, 1944, but he delayed the order because of bad weather. Then Eisenhower had to make his best estimate on when next there might be a window for the invasion. British planes dropped five thousand tons of munitions on Nazi gun batteries to weaken their defense for the upcoming invasion. Refusing to delay any longer, Eisenhower gave the go-ahead for the next day, June 6.

Allied commanders understood that planning on paper was one thing, but the reality on the ground another. The plan was for six divisions to land on the first day, and two more British and one American division were to follow up after the assault divisions had cleared the way through the German defenses.

It would be the largest amphibian invasion in the history of warfare; the Allies used more than 18,000 paratroopers and 5,000 ships and landing craft to launch more than 150,000 troops, split into five divisions, on five beaches in Normandy—Utah, Omaha, Gold, Juno, and Sword. Called the Supreme Allied Expeditionary Force (adapting the name of Connor's unit in the First World War), its troops came from eleven different countries, principally the United States, Britain, Canada, and France. Its purpose was to open a second front in the war that would relieve pressure on the Soviet Union in the east and weaken Germany's overall position in Europe, beginning with France and moving inexorably toward Germany itself.

The weather was not much better on June 6 than it had been the day before, there still being strong winds and heavy seas, which made it more difficult for landing craft to navigate their way safely to shore and for bombers to hit their targets. Planes dropped more than 13,000 bombs before the landing, almost all of which failed to clear the way for the Allies as pilots released them too early in order to avoid hitting British troops. Paratroopers were scattered across the invasion zone, and many of the Americans' floating tanks sank, drowning their crews.

The ultimate success of the invasion was largely due to the persistence, innovation, and ingenuity of Allied forces, as well as Germany's placing most of its forces in Pas de Calais and Hitler's refusal to allow Erwin Rommel to place his elite panzer formations close to the shore.

In the weeks after the invasion, Allied forces liberated France, in August 1944, and the Red Army pushed its way into German territory. Soon thereafter, American, British, and Free French forces raced against the Red Army to take Berlin. Even the German high command knew that the Third Reich's days were numbered.

VI

By the evening of June 6, 1944, the Allies controlled all five beachheads in Normandy. On June 12, Roosevelt held another Fireside Chat, telling the American people, "Germany has her back against the wall—in fact three walls at once! In the south, we have broken the German hold on central Italy.... On the east, our gallant Soviet allies have driven the enemy back from the lands which were invaded three years ago.... And on the west, the hammer blow which struck the coast of France last Tuesday morning, less than a week ago, was the culmination of many months of careful planning and strenuous preparation." "We are now on the offensive all over the world," he reassured Americans, "bringing the attack to our enemies."[36]

Roosevelt warned there would be sacrifices. War comes at a cost, and the highest cost is in terms of lives lost and shattered. The United States was slow to report the casualties on D-Day, because of the difficulties in identifying the dead and concern about giving any aid and comfort to the enemy with the figures disclosed. Years later, it was determined that, on the day of the D-Day invasion, 4,414 Allied soldiers died, including 2,501 Americans, and more than 100,000 American soldiers were wounded. By the end of the invasion, the Allies had captured some 200,000 German prisoners of war.

From Normandy, Allies invaded Eastern Europe, which was followed by six weeks of brutal but decisive combat, from December 6, 1944, to January 25, 1945, in the Battle of the Bulge, Germany's last major offensive campaign on the Western Front in World War II. More than 1 million Allied troops were involved in the battle, which the army estimated cost the lives of 75,000 Americans and more than 100,000 Germans. Neary 50,000 American soldiers were wounded. Field Marshall Montgomery wasted no time in declaring that the Battle of the Bulge was a British victory, but Churchill corrected him publicly to say that the battle was an American victory. Montgomery sheepishly apologized.

As the wars in the Far East and in Europe were turning in favor of the Allied Forces, Roosevelt and his aides tried to verify the numbers of civilians that were killed. The numbers were staggering: More civilians were dying than soldiers. The Soviet Union had incurred the most, with estimates ranging between 20 and 27 million people, followed by China, with losses of between 15 and 20 million, and then Germany with between 6 and 7.4 million. In Poland, 20 percent of the population had been killed, and in Japan between 2.5 and 3.1 million civilians died. The final figures had to wait until after the war to confirm. It would take years, even decades afterward, to arrive at reliable figures.

The more the Allies learned about German atrocities, the more horrified they were. Soon they would discover that the worst fears of Roosevelt's Jewish advisors, as well as Eleanor and leaders of Jewish organizations, had been realized.

VII

The revelations of massive Jewish exterminations came well before 1944. On December 13, 1942, Edward R. Murrow, broadcasting from

Europe, had described "a horror beyond what the imagination can grasp.... What is happening is this: millions of human beings, most of them Jews, are being gathered up with ruthless efficiency and murdered.... The phrase 'concentration camps' is obsolete.... We must speak now of 'extermination camps.'"[37]

Four days later, the United States, led by Roosevelt, joined ten other Allied countries, including England, in publicly condemning Nazi Germany's "bestial policy of cold-blooded extermination" of European Jews. The Congress and the British Parliament held silent protests to mourn the Jews. At the time, Roosevelt believed that the best and fastest way to end the cruelty was to defeat Germany. Though urged to bomb death camps in 1943 and 1944, Roosevelt decided not to, because of concerns about possibly killing the prisoners themselves and diverting military resources that were needed elsewhere to defeat Germany.

On January 16, 1944, Treasury Secretary Morgenthau arranged a private meeting with the President and two of Morgenthau's assistants. He told the President that the State Department, still under the leadership of Cordell Hull, was obstructing efforts to save the Jews in Europe. In response, Roosevelt created the War Refugee Board to coordinate governmental and private efforts to rescue as many Jews as possible. In the meantime, as they feared that the war was lost, German leaders hastened the extermination of Jews and ordered covering up evidence of their atrocities.

On July 22–23, Soviet soldiers came upon Majdanek in Poland. It was the first extermination camp that the Allies discovered and liberated. They freed five hundred prisoners and found intact gas chambers and crematoria and hundreds of incinerated bodies. Soviet officials invited journalists to record what they saw, and they shared the photographs with Allied leaders, including Roosevelt.

The decision was made not to release the photographs to the public, because they could not yet identify the dead and wanted to avoid upsetting families until the deaths of their loved ones could be confirmed. Over the next several months, Allied Forces discovered and liberated several other death camps. Though Allied leaders were conflicted over how extensively to share the evidence of the horrors they uncovered, it would all eventually become known as the Holocaust.

VIII

Americans by the thousands incurred losses during the war, including the President. In 1941, his cousin, Theodore Roosevelt, Jr., who had been gassed in the First World War, was determined to return to action. His wife asked George Marshall to allow him to reenlist as an officer. Marshall agreed, and Roosevelt was given command of a regiment in the First Army Division and promoted to one-star general. Roosevelt was known for being fearless, and he was awarded France's Croix de Guerre for bravely leading his unit during Operation Torch.

In 1942, he commanded Allied forces in Sardinia and the Italian mainland and was the chief liaison officer to the French Expeditionary Forces for General Eisenhower in Italy. In 1944, he petitioned to command one of the assault units for the invasion of Normandy and became the only general to land by sea with the first wave of troops. He was also the oldest, at fifty-six, of any of the men who stormed Normandy, and was the only person whose son landed that day, too, Colonel Quentin Roosevelt. A little more than a month later, Teddy Roosevelt, Jr., died of a heart attack in France. The President posthumously awarded him the Congressional Medal of Honor on September 21, 1944.

There were many other losses for Franklin, albeit short of death. For nearly ten years, Secretary of State Hull and Roosevelt's trusted advisor Sumner Welles had feuded relentlessly, often because of Roosevelt's practice to bypass Hull to give Welles special assignments. By 1943, however, Hull had had enough. Three years earlier, Hull had learned from William Bullitt, who had served as ambassador to Russia and France, that Welles had propositioned two male railroad workers for sex. Hull pressed Roosevelt to dismiss Welles, but the President refused, and when Bullitt confronted Roosevelt with his evidence, Roosevelt dismissed Bullitt from any further service in the State Department. Yet, both Hull and Bullitt kept pushing the story, and, in 1943, at a lunch with the President, Hull said that he must choose between Hull and Welles. Roosevelt did not want to lose Welles, whom he had known for years and thought indispensable to the administration, but he understood he needed Hull more, because Hull still was popular in the Senate.

Roosevelt met with Welles in August 1943. In a letter written the next day to his wife, Welles told her, "The President asked me to see him. He said he had never been angrier in his life at the situation in the State Department, which has now reached an impossible climax." Roosevelt complained to Welles that Bullitt had been spreading "poison" about him throughout Washington and that "Hull complains about you to every senator and newspaper man he meets." Welles told his wife, "I will never embarrass [the President,] especially in wartime. I will resign at once." Indeed, Welles offered his resignation to Roosevelt, who rejected it. Roosevelt told Welles, "I have known you since you were a little boy, before you went to Groton. I have seen you develop into what you now are. I need you for the country. After all, whom have I got? Harry Hopkins is a sick man. I thought he would die when he joined me last week. We are just moving into the first critical stage of peace talks. You know more about that than anyone, and you can be of more value than anyone." Welles again offered his resignation, but Roosevelt rejected it. Welles said that he would think the matter over on the weekend and give the President his final decision on the following Monday.[38] Over the weekend, Welles had a heart attack, leaving Roosevelt no choice but to accept his resignation.

Roosevelt never forgave Hull or Bullitt. In fact, he kept both Hull and the State Department largely removed from any further significant involvement in war-related matters, including peace talks, for the remainder of his presidency.

Nevertheless, Bullitt kept pushing the salacious story to anyone he could, including Vice President Wallace. When Wallace told Roosevelt, the President told him that Bullitt should "burn in hell." Later, Bullitt had the audacity to call Roosevelt to ask for Welles's job. Roosevelt reportedly responded, "Bill, if I were St. Peter and you and Sumner came before me, I would say to Sumner, 'No matter what you have done, you have hurt no one but yourself. I recognize human frailties. Come in.' But to you I would say, 'You have not only hurt another human being, you have deprived the country of the services of a good citizen; and for that you can go straight to Hell.'" Other versions of their exchange were similarly worded. In any event, Bullitt was done, though he apparently did not know it. Later, Roosevelt suggested to Bullitt that he had a future in politics in his hometown of Philadelphia. Bullitt got the message and announced to the public that he was running to be the mayor of Philadelphia. Roosevelt then sent a message to the Democratic bosses in Philadelphia: "Cut his throat." Bullitt lost and never served again in the government.[39]

Yet another casualty was Eleanor. Though she never wavered in her devotion to Franklin's political success, the President often found her persistent requests for him to intervene, such as in supporting civil rights and protecting Jewish refugees, to be irritating, and he would try to avoid her when he wanted to relax. When, for example, she was visiting troops in the South Pacific in 1943, the President was entertaining the Empress Zita of Hungary at Hyde Park. After Roosevelt told the empress that Eleanor would return in a few days, she commented, "She will be very tired," referring to the fact that Eleanor had been crisscrossing America and sometimes went abroad to represent Franklin. "No," he replied, "but she will tire everyone else." A far cry from the letters he had first sent Eleanor declaring his love for her, Roosevelt had largely marginalized her because she could not give him the adulation he craved and got from other women.

When Princess Martha of Norway came to stay at the White House while Eleanor was away, Eleanor's friend Trude Pratt was bitterly disappointed that she "says nothing, just giggles and looks adoringly at him. But he seems to like it tremendously—and there is a growing flirtatious intimacy which is of course not at all serious." When Trude told Eleanor of their interaction, Eleanor said "that there always was a Martha for relaxation and for the non-ending pleasure of having an admiring audience for every breath."[40]

Their son, James, believed their one moment for possible reconciliation came at the funeral of Franklin's mother, Sara, in 1943, but, as he recalled, the President only looked at Eleanor once at the end of the funeral, and only briefly, and she declined his offer to use as her own the big bedroom Sara had occupied for years. There had been too many slights from Sara and Franklin for Eleanor to try to recapture what she had lost.

Instead, Eleanor prepared herself for new reports of Franklin's betrayal, and more were coming. Unknown to her, Roosevelt had continued his affair with Lucy Mercer. He had arranged for her to attend each inauguration, where she sat unseen, and the two met during the war, including at least once in 1944 at the White House. Though surprised to see Lucy, their daughter Anna kept her father's secret and said nothing to Eleanor.

IX

There were striking parallels between Abraham Lincoln's reelection campaign in 1864 and Roosevelt's bid for a fourth term seventy years later, in 1944. First, no one doubted each was determined to run for reelection. In Lincoln's case, he had made appointments, crafted policies, and cultivated his image throughout his first term to help his reelection. True to form, Roosevelt tried to play coy about whether he was going to run for another term, but no one took seriously his protestations to the contrary and delays in making any announcement. By the fourth time, there was no one left to fool.

Second, Lincoln and Roosevelt ran against strong contenders. In 1864, Lincoln ran against the once-popular George McClellan, whom he had dismissed as head of the Union command for repeatedly failing to take the war to the rebel forces. McClellan was young and handsome, which sharply contrasted with Lincoln's homely and often ragged countenance. Roosevelt was running for the second time in a row against a popular New Yorker, this time Thomas Dewey in his second term as governor of the state. Dewey had successfully battled corruption in New York State politics as both a prosecutor and governor; and, unlike Willkie, Hoover, and Landon, Dewey was a strong campaigner, who, Roosevelt conceded, was his toughest opponent yet. The contrast could not have been sharper, with Roosevelt, looking tired, haggard, and sick, and the youthful Dewey, at forty-two, relentlessly attacking Roosevelt for his poor health.

The third similarity was that Lincoln and Roosevelt knew that their chances for reelection turned on the outcome of war. In fact, Roosevelt was the third commander in chief, after Lincoln and Wilson, to run for reelection during a major military conflict. While he might have taken solace in knowing that both Lincoln and Wilson won, he understood that they had because the wars had turned in their favor in time to count during the election. For much of 1864, Lincoln expected to lose, and it was not until the late summer and early fall of that year that Union forces had a string of successes that favored an ultimate Union victory. It was, therefore, no coincidence that Roosevelt announced his bid for another term on July 11, 1944, a little more than one month after the successful Allied invasion of France.

Fourth, both Lincoln and Roosevelt won their party's nomination with relative ease. By having the likeliest people to challenge him in his cabinet, Lincoln preempted their candidacies, and he worked closely with the Republican Party leadership to stack the convention in his favor. His repeated emphasis that it was not a good thing to swap horses while crossing a stream[41] struck a chord with the voting public, particularly after the tide of war turned in the Union's favor. Roosevelt pushed that same theme in 1944. With his opposition within the party largely coming from segregationists, Roosevelt won the Democratic nomination for president in 1944, with 92 percent of the vote on the first ballot.

Both Lincoln and Roosevelt functioned as the respective heads of their own campaigns. Lincoln had done a better job in streamlining his campaign than Roosevelt, whose poor health, coupled with the burdens of world war, deflected his energy and attention.

X

A final but important other similarity between Lincoln and Roosevelt was how they regarded their vice presidents. Both scrapped their vice presidents, because they each regarded their vice presidents at the time, Hannibal Hamlin from Maine for Lincoln and Henry Wallace from Iowa for Roosevelt, as liabilities for their reelections. Yet

each was loath to tell their vice president face-to-face of their decision. (Lincoln and Roosevelt shared the discomfort of telling people
bad news to their face.) In fact, Lincoln said nothing publicly about
dropping Hamlin, nor did he tell Hamlin beforehand that the party
was going to back another candidate for vice president in 1864.
Though Lincoln said he would let the party decide on his running
mate, the only reason that explained the ultimate choice—Andrew
Johnson—was that having someone from a border state (Tennessee,
in Johnson's case) on the ticket helped to expand Lincoln's potential
support for reelection and to signal to the deep South his determination to bring the country together in his second term.

Roosevelt had difficulty in getting the message to Wallace that he
would no longer be on the ticket. He had told confidants, "Wallace
won't do" any further,[42] but, in a comedy of errors, the message was
not getting through to Wallace. Initially, Roosevelt asked Hopkins
to break the news to Wallace, but Wallace refused to discuss the subject with anyone but Roosevelt. Roosevelt then met several times
with Wallace, hinting but never directly saying Roosevelt preferred
a different running mate. Nearly everyone at the convention knew
that Wallace was not Roosevelt's choice, but Wallace insisted on allowing his nomination to go before the convention. He narrowly lost
to Missouri senator Harry Truman.

Many people wonder why Roosevelt chose Truman, whom he did
not know well, to be his vice president and likely successor because
of his poor health. Yet there never was any secret, even before the convention, that Roosevelt had narrowed his choice for vice president
down to Senator Truman of Missouri, Supreme Court Justice William
O. Douglas, and former Justice Jimmy Byrnes of South Carolina.

The choice of Truman is less mysterious than why Roosevelt (and
many others in the party) favored Douglas. Douglas had never run
for any elected office before, and, though not a communist or socialist, he was among the most progressive people in Franklin's orbit.

There are several plausible explanations why Roosevelt chose Truman and not Douglas, Byrnes, or Wallace. First, Wallace was not a
politician, but Truman was. The 1940 presidential race was the only
election in which Wallace had yet stood as a candidate, but, even as

vice president, he was prone to say the wrong thing and to be attacked as a Communist (which he had once been). His being sympathetic to the Soviet Union was unpopular, especially in the South, and Roosevelt needed Southern support to win the Democratic nomination and the presidency again.

Second, Truman, coming from the border state of Missouri, and Byrnes, coming from South Carolina, enjoyed political support from Southern delegates at the convention. Neither Wallace nor Douglas were popular in the South, though Douglas lacked the long record of liberal positions Wallace had.

At the outset of the convention, Truman had agreed to nominate Byrnes for the vice presidency, but, as both the convention and Truman's candidacy progressed, he asked Byrnes if he could withdraw from nominating the South Carolinian. Byrnes angrily agreed—and understood it signaled his own candidacy was waning. While everyone understood Roosevelt needed Southern support, Roosevelt was reluctant to give Southern Democrats, many of whom were racist segregationists, any significant power in any administration he led. That left Douglas and Truman as the most viable candidates.

The third factor in favor of Truman was age. Wallace, Truman, and Douglas were all under sixty in 1944, but Byrnes was sixty-two. Byrnes never had a chance of making the cut, since Roosevelt, whose health, everyone knew, was precarious, wanted someone young enough to have the energy to serve as president if that became necessary.

The fact that Douglas was allowing the President and the convention to consider his possible candidacy was unusual. When Charles Evans Hughes decided to run for the presidency in 1916, he stepped down from his position as associate justice on the Supreme Court; however, Douglas did no such thing, sending signals that he did not have confidence Franklin could win again, he was waiting to run for the presidency in 1948, or he did not care enough about the appearance of any impropriety to act on it. He might have been playing coy or perhaps changed his mind, but before the convention chose a vice president, Douglas withdrew and went mountain climbing where no one could reach him.

Roosevelt appreciated several other attributes of the little-known Missouri senator. Truman had been a staunch defender of the New Deal in his ten years in the Senate, had served as a captain under the well-respected General John Pershing in the First World War (neither Wallace nor Douglas had any military experience), was popular in the Senate (and the Democratic Party), had earned high marks for chairing Senate hearings to uncover corruption within the federal government, had plenty of experience in campaigning, and had the support of one of the country's most powerful political bosses, Tom Pendergast of Missouri. Truman had the same outlook as everyone else in the Pendergast machine, which was racially, religiously, and ethnically diverse and opposed to segregation. This, too, was a position that resonated with Roosevelt. While Wallace led among the delegates on the first vote of the convention, with Truman coming in second, there was a dramatic shift in the second round of balloting that pushed Truman well over the top.

XI

To paraphrase the English philosopher Thomas Hobbes, the general election for president in 1944 was nasty, brutish, and not nearly as short as Roosevelt would have liked. The last thing he wanted was a repeat of the electorate's indifference if not antipathy to the incapacitated Woodrow Wilson's fight for the League of Nations. It was getting harder for him not only to hide his physical limitations but also to depend on the soldier vote. Congress had created such a complex system for soldiers to vote that it seemed likely many would not cast their ballots. Polling showed the public so apathetic that many of them could be expected not to vote, either.

Dewey's campaign pounded Roosevelt for his poor health and the tiredness of his ideas. Dewey hammered Roosevelt for his elitism, being out of touch, and (falsely) ordering American military vessels to take his pet dog Fala to safety. Roosevelt had battled difficult foes before, but Dewey's attacks were personal and angered Franklin to an unprecedented extent. The only possible way Roosevelt could rebut Dewey's attacks was to project the robust image he needed to prevail.

On the evening of September 23, 1944, he silenced supporters who were worried he could not withstand Dewey's nastiness, when he delivered his first political speech of the year at a dinner for the Teamsters Union and local politicians at the Statler Hotel in Washington, D.C. Having had the time to sharpen the speech, with the help of Sam Rosenman, Roosevelt sounded like his old self when he said, "The Republican leaders have not been content with attacks on me, or my wife, or on my sons. No, not content with that, they now include my little dog, Fala." He paused for good effect and then said, "Well, of course, I don't resent attacks, and my family doesn't resent attacks, but Fala does resent them.... He has not been the same dog since."[43]

But Dewey had earned his reputation as a crusading prosecutor who defeated and jailed organized crime. He responded by systematically attacking the President's record in allowing the country to be woefully unprepared for war in 1941.

It was a bold move, given that the one subject Dewey wanted to avoid during the campaign was foreign affairs. Before then, he'd had a solid record as an internationalist and was immune to any attack as an isolationist. But when Dewey learned that the Japanese diplomatic code had been cracked before Pearl Harbor, he was prepared to attack Roosevelt as a liar and traitor.

When George Marshall heard what Dewey was planning, he convinced Dewey that such attacks would help the enemy. Hull reassured Dewey that Roosevelt would not turn foreign affairs into a campaign issue, but Roosevelt did not get the message—and gave a rousing speech two weeks before the election at the Foreign Policy Association. Dewey was apoplectic, charging (rightfully) that Roosevelt had broken his commitment not to bring foreign policy into the election. He credited the last move as winning the election for Roosevelt.

Every indication was that it would be an even closer race than the one Roosevelt had against Wendell Willkie, who had died unexpectedly in October. In the closing weeks and days of the campaign, Dewey and the Republican Party intensified their attacks on Roosevelt's health and repeatedly charged, based on past Roosevelt statements, that Roosevelt was accepting Communist support. Dewey quoted Churchill, who had said in 1937 that Roosevelt "has waged so ruthless a war on private enterprise that the United States is actually ... leading the world back into the trough of the depression."[44]

Yet, with his back against the wall and newspapers reporting stories about his poor health, Roosevelt sprang back with renewed vigor and relentless attacks of his own against the dangers of risking national security and national economic health by scrapping the programs and administration that had bolstered both.

On the morning of October 20, the news about the war gave Roosevelt another big boost, as newspapers reported that General Douglas MacArthur had landed in the Philippines. He had vowed, on leaving there on March 11, 1942, "I shall return," and, lo and behold, he had, this time as the leader of the vanquishing force. Roosevelt followed this immediately with an extraordinary demonstration of his resilience, as he waved to crowds along a fifty-one-mile route through the boroughs of New York City.

As more good news about the war broke, this time the defeat of the Japanese Navy in the Battle of Leyte Gulf, Roosevelt kept moving, stopping to campaign in Chicago, Ohio, Indiana, Pennsylvania, West Virginia, Boston, and Connecticut, ending with various stops in New York State. No one could doubt his stamina now.

Roosevelt won by the narrowest margin in popular vote since Wilson in 1916. Dewey conceded early the next morning of the day after the election and sent the President a note three days later extending his congratulations. Roosevelt barely acknowledged Dewey's outreach, telling an aide, "I still think he is a son of a bitch."[45] The final tally had Franklin winning 53.5 percent of the popular vote and 432–99 in the Electoral College.

The margins of Roosevelt's victories were increasingly narrowing. While several isolationist members of Congress lost reelection (to the President's delight), everyone, including Roosevelt, understood his hold over the Democratic Party was weakening and likely would only be getting weaker in the weeks and months ahead.

CHAPTER NINE

The End of an Era (1944–1945)

Franklin Roosevelt's health was declining sharply—and nearly everyone who interacted with him saw his attention, memory, stamina, and energy faltering. In March 1944, White House physician Howard Bruenn found an alarming array of maladies, including arteriosclerosis, cardiac failure, and acute bronchitis. Aware of the President's declining health, Bruenn tried to be close by during the transition period in 1944 and the beginning of his fourth term in 1945.

The press was aware, too, of the President's weakening state, and reporters were not as sensitive and protective of his image as they had been before the fall of 1944. Newsreels of Roosevelt during his last meetings with Churchill and Stalin, held in Yalta shortly after his fourth inauguration, reinforced concerns about his well-being as they showed him slack-jawed and emaciated. Afterward, a bodyguard began twenty-four-hour duty with Vice President Truman.

Roosevelt did not help himself by largely ignoring his doctor's recommendations, while the deaths of close friends or associates were reminders undoubtedly of his own impending mortality. On July 31, 1944, he received the news that Missy LeHand had died of a cerebral embolism, never having recovered from the stroke she had three years earlier. In Franklin's stead, Eleanor, along with Jim Farley and Joseph Kennedy, attended her funeral. Rosenman remembered, "She was one of the most important people of the Roosevelt era.... She was the frankest of the President's associates, often telling him unpleasant truths or pressing about some proposed action or policy. I feel that had she could have lightened [the President's] wartime burden that his own life would have been preserved."[1]

Within weeks of the presidential election, Cordell Hull resigned because of poor health, having outlasted Welles for little more than a year. Though Roosevelt lavished praise on Hull at his retirement, he was glad to see him go. His new secretary of state was Edward Stettinius, Jr., who had been Hull's deputy. Roosevelt directed him to scour the department from top to bottom, removing anyone whom he disliked, but with the one exception of Archibald MacLeish, a distinguished lawyer and poet who, in 1944–45, wanted to serve as assistant secretary of state for public affairs so he could work on the peace after the war.

While Franklin and Eleanor constantly worried about Harry Hopkins nearing death's door in 1944, there were other deaths that weighed heavily on Roosevelt. Roosevelt's loyal senior aide Pa Watson died in early February 1945. Whereas the President did not attend Missy's funeral, he attended Watson's funeral, where he appeared frail and unsteady.

The specter of Woodrow Wilson haunted Roosevelt, who was determined not to repeat Wilson's mistake in isolating himself from his advisors, risking his presidency and legacy on impractical ideals, and being incapacitated from a stroke for more than a year before the end of his term. Wilson's wife and doctor had managed to keep his incapacity a secret from the nation, but maintaining such a secret was harder to do in 1944, with reporters invariably around and disgruntled former associates who were uninterested in perpetuating a fraud on the public.

Aware of Franklin's weakening condition was Eleanor, who kept prodding him to follow doctor's orders and take advantage of the euphoria following Germany's surrender to do more for the safety of Jews and the progress of civil rights in America. Increasingly finding her more of an irritant than a relief, Franklin distanced himself further from her.

  |

As Franklin Roosevelt entered his fourth term, his parallels with Lincoln were striking.

Both Lincoln and Roosevelt prioritized stability in their administrations and had little turnover in their cabinets. Secretary of State William Seward and Naval Secretary Gideon Welles were the two cabinet secretaries to remain throughout Lincoln's presidency; Stanton was his war secretary for all but the first months of his presidency; John Usher was secretary of the interior for all but the first year and a half of his presidency; Montgomery Blair was his postmaster general for all but the last several months of Lincoln's presidency; and Edward Bates served as his attorney general for all but the last few months.

Frances Perkins and Harold Ickes were the only cabinet secretaries that served through the entirety of Franklin Roosevelt's presidency, while he had three secretaries of war (the longest running being Henry Stimson, who served from 1940 to 1945), two secretaries of state, two treasury secretaries, four attorneys general, two postmasters general, four secretaries of commerce, and two secretaries of agriculture.

Lincoln and Roosevelt had each transformed the Supreme Court: Lincoln had made five Supreme Court appointments in his first term, the fourth most Supreme Court appointments of any president for a single term, with George Washington having made the most—seven—in his first term and Taft the second most (six in his one term). Roosevelt tied Jackson for the third most Supreme Court appointments in a single term.

Among their nineteen Supreme Court appointments, Jackson, Lincoln, and Roosevelt each appointed a chief justice of the United States. Even before he became president, Andrew Jackson was at ideological loggerheads with the current chief justice, John Marshall: In more than three decades as chief justice, Marshall had overseen the consolidation of power in the national government, often at the expense of state sovereignty. A proponent of states' rights and a weaker, smaller federal government, Jackson came into office determined to reverse the expansion of federal powers under Marshall. When Marshall died in 1835, Jackson named his former attorney general and longtime counselor Roger Taney to replace him, ushering in more than two decades of the Court's siding with states in their efforts to contain the federal government.

That changed with Lincoln. Having already transformed the Court with four Supreme Court appointments before his reelection, fate gave him one more vacancy to fill: Just weeks before the 1864 presidential election, Chief Justice Roger Taney died, but President Lincoln delayed announcing a replacement until after the election. He did not want to politicize the appointment and took time to carefully assess his best option. More than a month after the election, Lincoln settled on naming his former treasury secretary Salmon Chase, who had resigned after having tried once too often to undermine Lincoln's presidency, to succeed Taney as chief justice. By then, Chase had proven his loyalty, not just to Lincoln but to the Union. The Court that Lincoln made did not last for long, as a series of Republican presidents assembled a Court that was determined to contain the federal government's powers and to protect private property rights.

It was this Supreme Court that Roosevelt transformed in his second term, and his appointment of Harlan Fiske Stone as chief justice in 1941 harkened back to the first time a president nominated a Supreme Court justice from the opposition party, Abraham Lincoln's appointment of Stephen Field in 1863. Such moves were calculated in part to win bipartisan support for the nomination—and for the president responsible for it.

Both before and after their respective reelections, Roosevelt and Lincoln endured the ambivalence and frequent wrath of Southern Democrats, who were keen on obstructing both. (Southern Democrats still admired Jackson, whose influence extended into the New Deal era.) The Southern Democrats' influence shaped both presidents' choices of vice presidents in their final years in office, and their support was needed for Roosevelt's cabinet appointments, particularly in his third and fourth terms.

John Nance Garner was hardly the only Southern Democrat who made Roosevelt miserable. After serving in several other administrative posts, Jesse Jones, who had been a successful business executive in Texas, became Roosevelt's secretary of commerce in 1940. By 1945, Jones had become the cabinet member whom Roosevelt most wanted to fire, as he had been a constant source of irritation and obstruction. When Roosevelt named Henry Wallace to replace Jones, Jones publicly opposed the nomination, prompting a Senate hearing at which they both testified. Subsequently, the Senate narrowly confirmed Wallace.[2]

After having appeased Southern Democrats through their choices of vice presidents, Lincoln and Roosevelt ignored their vice presidents after their inaugurations. After listening to Johnson deliver a drunken speech at their inauguration, Lincoln told a confidant to keep Johnson away from him. He had no other interaction with Johnson before he was killed. Roosevelt did not know Truman well before their inauguration in 1945, and he spent no meaningful time with him in their few months together.

War and its aftermath were, not surprisingly, the major concerns for Lincoln and Roosevelt. The Confederate Army surrendered unconditionally on April 9, 1865, and Lincoln gave his only speech on Reconstruction on the evening of April 14, which proved to be his last. As Roosevelt entered his fourth term, he was the most confident he had been that the war would end, though he did not know when. They each died shortly before experiencing the peace they had forged, Lincoln not yet in the third month of his second term, and Franklin a month into his fourth term. The work of reconciliation and building a new world fell to the successors they barely knew.

II

Two weeks after winning his fourth term, Franklin lost his beloved mentor, Endicott Peabody. At eighty-seven, Peabody appeared hardy, but, as he was driving home on November 17, 1945, he had a fatal stroke. Different versions of the story have him discovered by a neighbor after crashing his car into a tree or a wall, and in others he was driving a family friend, Mary Louise Ackland, to the train station in Ayer, Massachusetts, when "his head fell back and his whole body slumped." In this retelling, he said, just before his stroke, "You know there's no doubt that Roosevelt is a very religious man." Peabody is also recounted as having made the statement during the drive, though people who knew Peabody well contested the story.

The next day, Franklin wired Peabody's widow, "I am, of course, deeply distressed and the news had come as a real shock. Eleanor sends her love with mine. The whole tone of things is going to be a bit different now on, for I have leaned on the Rector in all these years far more than most people know. You will understand this: We are thinking of you. My love and sympathy to all the children."[3]

Peabody's last visit to the White House had been on March 4, 1944, when he led the annual commemoration of Roosevelt's first inauguration. It was Peabody's second time attending Roosevelt's inauguration. William Hassett, an aide to the President, recalled the details of his last visit: "At 10:30 am in the East Room was held a religious service, commemorating the eleventh anniversary of the [1933] inauguration, a half hour service of dignity and simplicity."[4] Hassett recorded the attendees as including "the senior officers of the Army and Navy, the Cabinet, the Supreme Court, and all the other big wigs of officialdom with their wives."[5] Among the elite was "the venerable Dr. Peabody, the old Groton headmaster, whose voice was full and vibrant, despite his great age. He and Mrs. Peabody arrived for the Cabinet dinner and were overnight guests."[6] It was the last time he and Franklin saw each other.

On November 22, Eleanor noted in her "My Day" column that "in a number of places around the country, memorial services were held at the same time that funeral services took place at Groton for the late Endicott Peabody, who founded the school and was its headmaster for so many years." She wrote, "In the case of Mr. Peabody, he was always a forceful person, and his influence affected not only the boys but the parents with whom he came in contact." She continued, "As the years went on, his influence became even greater. Not every boy loved him, but I think I have never heard of a Groton student who did not respect the Rector. I am sure through this nation there are many men who today owe much that they have done in life to the personal influence of Mr. Peabody." She recounted, too, meeting that Sunday with one of Peabody's oldest friends, Bishop Julius Walter Atwood, who was Episcopalian bishop of Arizona, "who was one of Mr. Peabody's oldest friends," and whose presence and friendship with Peabody reminded her "about growing old [and the pain] to see one's friends depart on the greatest of all adventures, and to find the world growing lonely."[7]

Franklin and Peabody had exchanged correspondence throughout his presidency. Franklin wrote to blow off steam, to seek counsel, and to express gratitude for Peabody's mentorship, while Peabody's letters were "filled with words of encouragement and moral and spiritual advice which the President appreciate[d]."[8]

In his first term, Franklin had written Peabody, "I count it among the blessings of my life that it was given to me in my formative years to have the privilege of your guiding hand and the benefit of your inspiring example."[9] On matters both large and small, Roosevelt thought of Peabody's advice. It was rare for one or both not to correspond regarding major events in the ensuing years, including the attack on Pearl Harbor and Roosevelt's subsequent request for Congress to declare war against the Japanese Empire.

The President followed Peabody's example in reading Charles Dickens's *A Christmas Carol* every year to his family on Christmas Eve. It was one of many ways that Roosevelt paid homage to his mentor, and he was not yet done as his fourth inauguration approached.

III

In November 1944, Roosevelt, Churchill, and Stalin agreed the war had not yet been won. Some of the bloodiest battles were yet to be fought on both sides of the world.

Germany had no intention of giving up without at least one more major fight. They chose the densely forested region of Ardennes between Belgium and Luxembourg for their final battle to the death.

Beginning with a surprise attack on Allied forces in the region, the battle raged for six weeks, as Germany tried but failed in its last major offensive. The Allies suffered their largest casualties in the battle, which was named for the westward swelling in the front, the Battle of the Bulge. As the Allies continued to press east afterward, so, too, did the Red Army, which drove Germans out of Ukraine and White Russia and intensified their assault to acquire Poland. By Christmas 1944, the Allies were in Germany but stalled because of the weather. They were in a race with the Soviets to capture Hitler, whom Stalin had directed would be on trial for his crimes against humanity.

In the Pacific, General Douglas MacArthur's troops advanced through the Philippines. They reached the outskirts of Manilla ten days after Roosevelt's fourth inauguration on January 20, 1945. A monthlong battle ensued, leaving Manilla scorched to the ground, and in February, American planes began to bombard Japan.

With the Allies pushing into Germany and Japan, General Leslie Groves informed Roosevelt that the United States was close to having devastating weaponry unprecedented in the annals of war. Together with George Marshall, Groves explained the progress scientists had made in developing two kinds of atomic bombs. The first, which relied on the implosion of fissionable material, would be ready by the late spring of 1945. The other was an implosion-type device with a plutonium core. Grove explained to Roosevelt that the second type was capable of producing a much larger blast than the first kind, in fact twenty times larger. The second weapon would be available at the end of 1945. Roosevelt said he did not understand much of what was said, except that it sounded to him as if the weapons would not be available any time before July, by which time, he hoped, the war would be over.

IV

In 1840, William Henry Harrison, then sixty-eight, had been the oldest man yet elected to the presidency. He saw his inauguration as the best opportunity to demonstrate his vitality. The plan backfired, as Harrison soon contracted a series of ailments that killed him.

In his fourth inauguration, Franklin Roosevelt faced the same challenge as Harrison had, but his plan, too, failed. Roosevelt had been
attacked relentlessly for hiding his deteriorating health from the public. His staff believed the real test of the occasion was to silence
concerns about his health, but what the few thousand attendees and
press saw unnerved them, as they watched the President move unsteadily to the podium, try to calm his shaking hands, have trouble
reading the pages in front of him because of the wind and rain, and
walk unsteadily back to his seat.

The press pounced, as major newspapers showed photographs of
the ailing chief executive. Even though people listening on radio
might have thought the President sounded the same, news coverage
presented a picture of the deteriorating president.

Brevity served Roosevelt's purposes in not taxing his frailty. To
keep his ceremony as brief as possible, Roosevelt forbade any celebration. (Lincoln had done the same in his second inaugural
address.) As Franklin remarked at the time, "Who is there here to
parade?"[10] All able-bodied men of a certain age were fighting, or as-
sisting in the fighting, and the attendees, most of whom were
veterans, were largely limited to those invited by Roosevelt himself.

To make the event easier for himself physically, it was held at the
White House, the first and only time that was done in American history. In fact, the whole affair took twelve and a half minutes, the
shortest inauguration in presidential history.

Roosevelt asked—and Eleanor ensured—that his entire family, including all thirteen grandchildren, were present. Eleanor wrote in
her *Memoirs*, "Early in January, realizing full well this would certainly be his last inauguration, perhaps even having a premonition
that he would not be with us for long, Franklin insisted that every
grandchild come to the White House for a few days over the 20th."
Eleanor "was somewhat reluctant to have thirteen grandchildren
ranging in age from three to sixteen together, for fear of an epidemic
of measles or chickenpox, but he was so insistent that I agreed."[11]

Roosevelt began his last inaugural with his hope that "this inauguration be simple and its words brief." In his second sentence, he
succinctly framed his message, "We Americans of today, together

with our allies, are passing through a period of supreme test. It is a test of our courage—of our resolve—of our wisdom—our essential democracy." He made clear "America's purpose" now was "that we shall not fail" and that as a nation "we shall work for a just and honorable peace, a durable peace." He acknowledged that the United States Constitution was not perfect, but it "provided a firm base upon which all manner of men, of all races and colors and creed, could build our solid structure of democracy." He recounted the lessons of the war, declaring "that we cannot live alone, at peace; that our own well-being is dependent on other nations far away."[12]

In his final inaugural, Roosevelt did not quote Lincoln or Washington. Rather, he quoted "my old schoolmaster, Dr. Peabody, [who] said, in days that seemed to us then to be secure and untroubled: 'Things in life will not always run smoothly. Sometimes we will be rising toward the heights—then all will seem to reverse itself and start downward. The great fact to remember is that the trend of civilization itself is forever upward; that a line drawn through the middle of the peaks and the valleys of the centuries always has an upward trend.'"[13] It was the first time a president acknowledged a personal mentor in an inaugural address.

Speaking with Secretary of Labor Frances Perkins, Woodrow Wilson's widow told her, "He looks exactly as my husband looked when he went into his decline." Henry Wallace described Roosevelt as "a gallant figure, but also pitiable."[14] James thought his father looked like hell.

After the ceremonies, Franklin met privately with James to discuss his last will and testament. He told his son there was a letter in the White House safe with instructions for his funeral. Franklin gave James the family ring as a keepsake, and he assigned James as one of the three executors of the estate.

It was another sign that Franklin understood that, as the end of the war neared, so, too, did his impending death. Before he died, Lincoln had begun thinking of Reconstruction, but he had kept most of his thoughts about the future to himself. Franklin, too, had been thinking of the future of the United States and the world once the war ended. But, like Lincoln, he did not share his thoughts and never lived to enjoy the ensuing peace.

$$\overline{V}$$

Two days after the address, Roosevelt left on an arduous journey to meet with Churchill and Stalin in Yalta, a city on the southern coast of the Crimean Peninsula surrounded by the Black Sea. The purpose of the meeting was to decide what was to be done with Germany once the war ended.

Just before leaving, Roosevelt met with his cabinet. He told them that he would be leaving for four to five weeks, taking Secretary of State Stettinius, several State Department advisors, Harry Hopkins (whose health had temporarily been restored), Averell Harriman, and Admiral Leahy. (He also brought Jimmy Byrnes, who was still smarting from not being chosen as secretary of state, and a young specialist on the United Nations organization, Alger Hiss, whom no one had yet suspected of being a spy for the Soviet Union.)

The President told the cabinet that he had no objections if the cabinet met in his absence. He reminisced how, when Wilson suffered a stroke while campaigning for the League of Nations in 1919, then–Secretary of State Robert Lansing called a cabinet meeting without Wilson's knowledge. Enraged, Wilson fired Lansing. Roosevelt told his cabinet that he would make no commitments at the conference and that he would study any proposals made by England or the Soviet Union and share them with Congress.

The other attendees were struck by Roosevelt's appearance when he arrived in Yalta. Churchill's physician, Lord Charles Wilson, remarked that he found Roosevelt "looking straight ahead with his mouth open, as if he were not taking things in." After observing Roosevelt during the conference, Lord Maron said that "to a doctor's eye, the President appears a very sick man. He has all the symptoms of hardening of the arteries on the brain in an advanced stage, so that I give him only a few months to live."

Roosevelt's longstanding interpreter, Charles Bohlen, who had become special advisor to Roosevelt on the Soviet Union, noted that "our leader was ill at Yalta, [but] he was effective. I so believed at the time and still so believe." Churchill said that he found it difficult to engage Roosevelt, whom he said rambled at times. For his

part, Roosevelt went on at length one evening on how poorly Churchill looked and acted. General Laurence Kuter, representing the
air force, recalled Roosevelt saying that "the Prime Minister had
sat at the [conference] table and drifted off into a sound sleep from
which he would awake very suddenly making speeches about the
Monroe Doctrine. The President said he had to tell him repeatedly
that it was a very fine speech, but that it was not the subject under
discussion."

Stalin thought that Churchill and especially Roosevelt looked as
if they had not long to live.[15]

Though the Big Three met eight times in eight days, usually for
three to four hours, their agreements were limited. Most importantly
for Roosevelt, they agreed that after Germany's unconditional surrender, it would be divided into four postwar occupation zones,
controlled by U.S., British, French, and Soviet military forces. Roosevelt struggled in vain to secure some independence for Poland, but
Stalin and his Foreign Minister Molotov resisted all efforts to wrest
Poland from Soviet domination.

Bohlen, who translated Stalin's Russian for the American delegation, felt the agreement among the three on the Security Council
voting procedure to be "the one solid and lasting decision of the
Yalta Conference," without which "there would hardly have been a
United Nations." Summing up Stalin's tactics, Bohlen said, "The task
of the Soviet diplomacy . . . was to retain a tight grip on Poland without causing an open break [with Churchill and Roosevelt]. . . . Stalin
conveyed considerable astuteness . . . and a tenacity in beating back
one Western attempt after another to create conditions for a genuinely democratic government" in postwar Poland.

Stalin told Roosevelt he agreed there should be free elections in
Poland, but in fact there would be no elections until 1947. While the
Soviet Union also agreed to "The Declaration on Liberated Europe,"
initially proposed by the United States, that provided that the three
governments would help "form interim governmental authorities
broadly representative of all democratic elements in the population
and pledged to the earliest possible establishment through free elections of governments responsive to the will of the people," the

Soviets ignored it in dealing with Poland, Romania, Bulgaria, and other nations after the war.[16]

Where Stalin proved most cooperative was in the military planning for the rest of the war against Germany. Stalin further agreed to various requests from the American chiefs of staff and to Roosevelt's suggestion that Darien, the most northern ice-free port in China, be a free port after the war. Roosevelt also agreed to give two financial incentives— a merchant shipping fleet at no cost and a $6 billion reconstruction loan at low interest—to ensure the cooperation of the Soviet Union.

The conference ended on February 11, 1945, two days after the release of the Declaration on Liberated Europe. Roosevelt would not see Stalin again. In all, he met Churchill eleven times during the war, including twice with just the two of them in Quebec in 1943 and 1944. In the last meeting of the three Great Powers in Yalta, they agreed that Berlin, like Germany itself, should be divided into two different occupation zones. To his consternation, de Gaulle had not been invited to Yalta, though Roosevelt did get Stalin to agree to include France in the postwar governing of Germany, but only if France's zone of occupation was taken from the American and British zones of occupation. The three leaders further agreed that Germany would make reparations, but, unlike at the end of the First World War, Germany's debt was not to be paid in money but instead in the forced labor of German prisoners of war and the transfer of intellectual property rights to the Allies.

What was not made clear at the end of the Yalta conference was whether the Soviet Union would join England and the United States in their war against Japan. Stalin and Foreign Minister Molotov repeatedly raised concerns about how any statement to that effect would play back in Russia. What Churchill and Roosevelt knew, however, was that without the Soviet Union joining the war in the Pacific, it had no end in sight.

VI

Roosevelt did not return immediately to the United States. Instead, he traveled to the Suez Canal in Egypt, where, he told Stalin, there were "three kings waiting for him in the Near East."[17] They were Egypt's Farouk, Ibn Saud of Saudi Arabia, and Haile Selassie of Ethiopia.

Though the meeting with the Saudi king got off to a cordial start on February 14, it went downhill fast. When Stalin asked Roosevelt at their final dinner on February 10 what the President planned to give the Saudi king, Roosevelt responded that he was thinking of giving the king the 6 million Jews then living in the United States. While Roosevelt likely meant his remark as a joke, albeit an off-color one, Stalin responded with antisemitic slurs. Yet that did not dissuade Roosevelt from raising the issue of possible Jewish migration to Palestine. He was surprised when the Saudi king responded that Palestine had enough Jews already and that Jews should live instead in the countries from which they had been driven.

Hopkins said later that Roosevelt "seemed not to fully comprehend, for he brought up the question two or three times more and each time Ibn Saud was more determined than before." When Roosevelt tried to change the subject to the greening of Arabia through irrigation projects, Ibn Saud replied, "He himself could not do much ... in agricultural and public works projects if this prosperity would be inherited by the Jews." In trying to be conciliatory, Roosevelt said that he could not prevent discussion in Congress or the press but pledged "he would do nothing to assist the Jews against the Arabs and would make no move hostile to the Arab people."[18]

Roosevelt was heartbroken, telling Eleanor later he regarded the trip as a failure. What he did not mention, either to her or to the three kings, was a proposal he was considering that would require moving more than Arabs from Palestine to Iraq. The war had turned him pro-Zionist; the more hatred of Jews he heard on his travels, the more convinced he was they needed a secure homeland of their own. He left the details to be worked out by Stettinius and his advisors.

VII

On the trip back to the United States, Roosevelt stopped in Alexandria to meet Churchill. At lunch aboard Roosevelt's ship, Churchill made a proposal on postwar British research on the atom bomb. He took Roosevelt's silence as consent. When Churchill recorded their talk in his diary, he recalled Franklin's "placid, frail aspect," and wrote, "This was the last time I saw Roosevelt. We parted affectionately. I felt he had a slender contact with life."[19]

The return trip was painful, as one after another of Roosevelt's aides and confidants fell ill. Pa Watson was belowdecks, dying of congestive heart failure and a cerebral hemorrhage. Hopkins was too ill to leave his cabin, and when he eventually did, he took a plane back to the United States from Algiers. Bohlen left to keep him company. When Watson died two days later, on February 20, Roosevelt talked more despondently than he had ever before when reminiscing about the loss of a loved one. His daughter Anna kept him company, but he spent most of his time staring blankly at the sea. His spirits lifted a little when Sam Rosenman arrived from London to help the President draft his address to a joint session of Congress. He never saw Hopkins again.

Only thirty-six hours after the end of his trip, Roosevelt summoned his energy for one last major address. Triumphant but tired, he made a dramatic entrance into a packed House chamber on March 1. For the first time, he did not walk to the well of the House on the arm of an associate or son, but wheeled into place. After a standing ovation, he began with an apology, "I hope you will pardon me for this unusual posture of sitting down during the presentation, but I know that you will realize that it makes it a lot easier for me not to have to carry ten pounds of steel around the bottoms of my legs."[20] Another thunderous ovation followed.

Always watchful of the President, Frances Perkins recalled, "It was the first reference he had ever made to his incapacity. He did it with such a casual, debonair manner, without self-pity or strain that the episode lost any grim quality and left everybody quite comfortable." Though many disagreed with her assessment, she thought the President's "speech was good. His delivery and appearance were those of a man in good health."[21]

Roosevelt savored the occasion and spoke for almost an hour. At times rambling and repetitive, he declared that the Yalta conference was a successful effort by the three leading nations to find a common ground for peace. "This time," he said, "we are not making the same mistake of waiting until the end of the war to set up the machinery of peace. This time, as we fight together to win the war finally, we work together to keep it from happening again."[22] Yet another ovation followed as he left the chamber.

Roosevelt had tried but failed to hide the signs of his declining health. He hesitated in his delivery at times and appeared at others to struggle in finding the right words. He recounted his meetings with other world leaders, the progress on fashioning a lasting peace for after the war, describing for his audience some of the destruction wrought by the Nazis in Europe, the meeting in Malta of British and American staffs "to increase the attack against Japan[,]" and the warning to America (and other nations around the world) that "we must be prepared for a long and costly struggle in the Pacific."[23] He spoke of Japanese forces and leaders as if they were on the run from inevitable defeat.

Having established such a high bar for his orations, Roosevelt was bound to disappoint many people listening to his address. Reporters thought the speech read better than it was delivered. William Hassett, secretary to the President, "didn't think it a particularly good speech. The President ad-libbed at length—a wretched practice that weakens even a better effort." Sam Rosenman agreed the excessive ad-libbing ruined the speech that he and the President had hammered out on their voyage back to America.[24]

VIII

In addressing the joint session of Congress on March 1, Roosevelt made the point, "We haven't won the wars yet." He added, "It is still a long, tough road to Tokyo.... The defeat of Germany will not mean the end of the war against Japan. On the contrary, we must be prepared for a long and costly struggle in the Pacific."[25]

Though the President was proud of the progress made toward world peace at Yalta, disagreements arose over all three key Yalta agreements. Later that month, when the ranking German officer began negotiations to surrender, British and American officers excluded Russia's participation, concerned that Stalin would make "embarrassing demands" of the Germans, which they feared would prolong the war.

On March 24, Roosevelt assured Stalin there was no plot against the Soviets, but Stalin responded that the Germans were using these talks as an opportunity to shift divisions to the eastern front and sow "grounds for mistrust" among the Allies. A week later, Roosevelt told Stalin that his concerns were creating "an atmosphere of regrettable apprehension." Indeed, the negotiations for the settlement of the war in Europe fell apart, and no German forces were moved to the eastern front. Stalin did not back down, but instead complained that he had been misinformed, and that his intelligence officers had reported that the negotiations included an agreement with the Germans exchanging easier peace terms for allowing the advance of the Americans and the British to the east, where they could prevent the Red Army from occupying Germany.

Roosevelt cabled Churchill in mid-March to express his concerns about news in Poland, where, he said, it "seems to be acting up again—or, more accurately, the Russian Foreign Office." Churchill responded, "There are many stories put about of wholesale deportations by the Russians and of liquidations by the Lublin Poles of elements they do not like."[26]

Initially reluctant to confront Stalin about the rumors, Roosevelt could not stay silent long. First, in response to Stalin's concerns about the negotiations having been conducted to hurt the Soviet Union, he told Stalin that he had been misinformed, quite likely by German intelligence, which "aimed to create dissension between us." Stalin said he would send his ambassador to the United States, Andrei Gromyko, to the ceremony opening the United Nations, to which Roosevelt expressed disappointment and concern that not sending his foreign minister sent the wrong signals about Soviet commitment to world peace.

Though anxious not to offend Stalin, Roosevelt told him, "I cannot conceal from you the concern with which I view the development of events of mutual interest since our fruitful meeting at Yalta."[27] Roosevelt went further to chide Stalin that developments in

Poland indicated to the world that the Yalta agreement "failed." On April 6, Churchill urged Roosevelt to join him in making "a firm and blunt stand" against the Soviet aggression in Poland.[28] Roosevelt responded, "We must not permit anybody to entertain a false impression that we are afraid. Our Armies will in a few days be in a position that will permit us to become 'tougher' than has heretofore appeared advantageous to the war effort."[29]

Stalin responded with assurances to Churchill that he "had and have no intention of offending anyone." Viewing this as a good sign, Roosevelt wrote Stalin on April 11 that the "incident" that had initially triggered Stalin's mistrust "appears to have faded into the past without having accomplished any useful purpose." Instead, he told Stalin, "I feel sure that when our armies make contact in Germany and join in a fully coordinated offensive the Nazi armies will disintegrate."[30]

In fact, the Allied armies were accomplishing exactly what Roosevelt had hoped: By March 26, the main bodies of the United States and British military forces in Europe had crossed the Rhine, their last major obstacle in the conquest of Germany. By the end of March, all four U.S. armies fighting in Western Europe were west of the Rhine. While the First and Ninth Armies followed through to encircle Ruhr, a major industrial region in western Germany, the Third and Seventh Armies moved into central and southern Germany. Meanwhile, the Red Army reached the outskirts of Berlin on March 20. With one last offensive, the Allies would take Berlin.

Meanwhile, the Allies were slowly advancing in the Pacific. On February 4, 1945, U.S. troops completed the capture of Manila, the capital of the Philippine Islands. On February 19, 1945, American forces invaded the tiny island of Iwo Jima, 750 miles off the coast of Japan. It would take U.S. marines a month to conquer Japanese forces there and to take control of their airfields, which U.S. bombers planned to use for their ultimate invasion of Japan. At the beginning of April, United States forces began their siege of Okinawa, four hundred miles from mainland Japan.

On April 9, 1945, 89 percent of the American people expressed their support of the United Nations, contrasting sharply with their 26 percent approval of a similar body nearly a decade before, in 1937.

IX

Roosevelt's fourth term did not win him any new friends in Congress. To the contrary, Democrats were tiring of him and treating him as a lame duck (if not as if he were not going to be around much longer). Roosevelt pushed, but Congress did not budge.

On January 6, 1945, President Roosevelt delivered his first (and only) State of the Union for his fourth term. He declared, "In considering the State of the Union, the war and the peace that is to follow are uppermost in the minds of all of us. This war must be waged—is being waged—with the greatest and most persistent intensity. Everything we are and have is at stake. Everything we are and have given. American men, fighting far from home, have already won victories which the world will never forget. We have no question of the ultimate victory. We have no question of the cost. Our losses will be heavy. We and our allies will go on fighting together to ultimate total victory."[31]

When he left for a vacation in Warm Springs, Georgia, at the end of March, he had yet to propose any new civil rights legislation, much less resubmit his promised new economic bill of rights.

In his January 11, 1944, State of the Union, Roosevelt argued that the "political rights" guaranteed by the Constitution and the Bill of Rights "had proved inadequate to assure us equality in the pursuit of happiness." He asked Congress to enact a new "economic bill of rights," which would have guaranteed a right to work; "the right to earn enough to provide adequate food and clothing and recreation"; farmers' rights to fair income; freedom from unfair competition and monopolies; decent housing; adequate medical care; Social Security; and education. Congress moved on none of the initiatives.

After carefully watching his boss, Vice President Truman sarcastically characterized Roosevelt's March 1 speech to the journalist Allen Drury as "one of the greatest ever given."[32] He was displeased he had only met twice with the President, once having been at their inauguration. He had not been briefed on tensions with the Soviet Union, the development of the atomic bomb, and the International Trade Agreements Act, which he had submitted to Congress on March 26, 1945, but which had not yet been debated, much less enacted.

$$\overline{X}$$

Try as Eleanor might, neither she nor anyone else in the President's orbit could persuade him to stop smoking and drinking altogether, to rest more, and to take his medicine. Franklin worked himself to exhaustion nearly every day and rarely forebear drinking his regular cocktails, lighting a cigarette, and gabbing with friends and family to all hours.

When Prime Minister Mackenzie King of Canada came to visit the White House on March 9 and again on March 13, he found Eleanor at her wit's end on how to keep Franklin alive and saw for himself how sickly the President had become. At the same time, the tensions between Franklin and Eleanor seemed worse than ever. While the President spoke to her of his hope, once Germany surrendered, to retire and travel to the Middle East, where he thought he could broker peace, Anna recalled that Eleanor "pressured more abruptly and with less tact than she had in the past. The nerves of both of them were raw." Eleanor recognized that Franklin needed "a real rest" and the adulation of his cousins Daisy and Polly Delano to buck his spirits. Meanwhile, she recorded, Franklin "thinks he can retire by next year, after he gets the peace organization well-settled."[33]

Roosevelt rebounded to celebrate his and Eleanor's fortieth wedding anniversary at a family luncheon. Afterward, he said he would sleep until noon the next day, reminding everyone how weak he was. Roosevelt had rebounded earlier on March 9 as well when Jean-Paul Sartre came to interview him for a French publication and said afterward, "What is most striking is the profoundly human charm of his long face, at once sensitive and strong." Bohlen, who had begun substituting for Harry Hopkins, who was gravely ill at the Mayo Clinic in Minnesota, observed that Roosevelt "could call on reserves of strength whenever he had to meet [public] figures," but was succumbing to "weariness and general lassitude." He could barely shake hands he had become so weak, and his hands shook so badly he could hardly hold papers in his hands any longer.[34] By the middle of March, he had trouble maintaining the pace of life in the White House and complained of incessant pain and loss of taste.

On March 29, the day Roosevelt left for Warm Springs, the Secret Service increased its security for the vice president. Only a small entourage traveled with the President, which did not include any members of the first family or Admiral McIntire, the President's personal physician. Instead, the White House physician Dr. Bruenn, along with three secretaries; Mike Reilly, the longstanding head of the President's security detail; George Fox, medical orderly and masseur; cousins Daisy and Polly; and two friends with Warm Springs ties traveled with the President.

Lucy Mercer, now a widow after her husband Winthrop Rutherfurd's death in 1944, was expected to join them not long after they arrived in Warm Springs. In spite of the tensions between her and Franklin, Eleanor wrote a friend that "I say a prayer daily that he may be able to carry on till we have peace and our feet are set in the right direction." Bruenn recalled later Eleanor calling Franklin "during the final trip a week or two before his death and talking for forty-five minutes urging help for Yugoslavia. This resulted in rise of B[lood] [P]ressure of 50 points. His veins stood out on his forehead. Obviously the necessity to deny her request and the long telephone conversation was a major strain."[35]

When the entourage arrived in Warm Springs on March 30, Franklin was shown an important message from George Marshall. He told the President that he expected the "utter defeat" of the Nazi regime by the end of the month. Marshall added, "For all practical purposes, a central German political authority will have ceased to exist about May 1."[36] The U.S., British, and Soviet troops were close to storming into Berlin.

On that same day, William Hassett, traveling with the President as his press secretary, recorded that Roosevelt "is slipping away and no earthly power can keep him here. . . . To all the staff, to the family and with the Boss himself I have maintained the bluff, but I am convinced that that there is no help for him." Roosevelt's physician, Dr. Bruenn, recorded a different perspective: He "reluctantly admitted the Boss in precarious condition, but his condition was not hopeless. He could be saved if measures were adopted to rescue him from certain mental stress and emotional influences, which he mentioned."

Yet, after Hassett pressed Bruenn's diagnosis, Hassett came away with the impression that even "the doctor shared the layman's point of view."[37]

Roosevelt's cousin Daisy Suckley had the same impressions as Hassett. She recorded that Franklin, just before the trip down to Georgia, "looks terribly badly—so tired that every word seems to be an effort. He just can't stand this strain indefinitely." Once she joined him on the train several days later, she was struck again that Roosevelt "looked completely exhausted" and pressed Dr. Bruenn to ensure that the President got the rest he needed. Even at Warm Springs, he found him to be "depressed, both physically and mentally."

On April 7, Franklin received a letter from Eleanor—the last between them—that was positive. "You sounded cheerful for the first time," she wrote, "& I hope you'll weigh 170 pounds when you return." That evening, Daisy said, Franklin lapsed into "babyhood," requiring her help to get him into bed, to be fed, and to be entertained until he fell asleep.

Disregarding doctor's orders that he rest, Roosevelt had a new burst of energy on April 9. He dictated responses, some charming and funny, to correspondence from friends and associates. To others, such as Jimmy Byrnes, who had resigned as chief administrator of the war economy, he held his fire, as Byrnes had embarrassed himself and Roosevelt with tantrums at Yalta. As the President signed the letter accepting Byrnes's resignation, he said, "It's too bad some people are so primadonnish."[38]

Two days later, Roosevelt rallied to send two cables to "minimize" recent arguments with Stalin, though he had told his confidante, Anna Rosenberg, shortly before leaving for Warm Springs, that Stalin "has broken every one of the promises he made at Yalta."[39] Now he urged Stalin to avoid "minor misunderstandings" (a phrase he insisted on keeping over the objection of Ambassador Harriman, who insisted he drop the word "minor"). Roosevelt wrote Churchill that "I would personally minimize the general Soviet problem as much as possible as because these problems [seem] to arise every day."[40]

Roosevelt had his secretaries arrange for him to attend opening ceremonies for the United Nations in San Francisco and began excitedly dictating the speech he hoped to give there. That same day, Lucy arrived in Warm Springs.

After spending part of the day of April 11 finishing his draft of his upcoming speech for Jefferson Day dinners throughout the land via radio on April 13, Roosevelt met Henry Morgenthau for dinner. Morgenthau was upset over Roosevelt's condition: "His hands shook so badly that I had to hold the glasses into which he poured cocktails." As the evening wore on, Morgenthau recorded, "I have never seen him have so much difficulty transferring himself from his wheelchair to a regular chair, and I was in agony watching him." Morgenthau was upset further when, after dinner, Roosevelt rambled and was confusing people's names. After Morgenthau departed, Roosevelt stayed up late entertaining Lucy and the other women visiting him there. Recalled Lucy Rutherfurd, "I must say the President seemed to be happy and enjoying himself."[41]

On April 12, Franklin awoke with "a slight headache and a stiff neck." After a brief massage from Dr. Bruenn, he spent most of the morning fine-tuning his Jefferson Day speech. He heaped praise on Jefferson as a "democrat [who] was instrumental in the establishment of the United States as a vital factor in international affairs." The initial draft's last line was the admonition that "the only limit to our realization of tomorrow will be our doubts of today." He added one more line, "Let us move forward with strong and active faith."[42]

Around one-fifteen, while he sat for a portrait, Franklin suddenly said in a soft whisper, "I have a terrific headache." He immediately slumped over, and his body went limp.

When Dr. Bruenn arrived several minutes later, he found Franklin unconscious and breathing unevenly. He recognized the signs of a cerebral hemorrhage. Franklin never regained consciousness. At 3:35 that afternoon, he was pronounced dead. Lucy immediately left to avoid any embarrassment later. Franklin Roosevelt was sixty-three, three years older than Teddy had been when he died.

Epilogue

In 1941, Justice Felix Frankfurter received a letter from his friend Dumas Malone, a University of Virginia history professor. Malone showed Frankfurter a paper he had written on Thomas Jefferson. Publishers had rejected his new proposal because they thought it was more about "the present crisis" than Jefferson, but Malone asked Frankfurter whether he thought "it has any value to the present times."[1]

What followed was an extraordinary letter Malone had written as Thomas Jefferson giving advice to President Franklin Roosevelt. While Malone thought it was "mostly about Jefferson," the letter revealed Malone's keen insights into the connection between Jefferson's and Roosevelt's conception of government. The letter drew numerous parallels between Jefferson's and Roosevelt's careers and between Roosevelt's and Jefferson's views on "human liberty," their commitment to make government "more just," and foreign affairs.

Roosevelt seems to have been aware of the letter and perhaps read it, as the last speech he drafted made the precise point that Malone had made in his letter—that rather than being the patron saint of small government, Jefferson supported precisely the kind of government action that the New Deal had provided. Thus, even at the end of his life, Roosevelt recognized the importance of connecting his achievements with the founding fathers, particularly Jefferson.

Rather than being un-American as the critics charged, the New Deal fulfilled the original vision of the Constitution.

Mentors illuminate connections, and the connections between one leader and another forge legacies. For Roosevelt, his predecessors in office were mentors whose achievements, ideas, and failures guided subsequent leaders. A New Deal that was politically expedient was one thing, but quite another was a New Deal that was the culmination of the work done by and the ideals of America's earlier great presidents.

A music teacher once described learning music in this manner: A great cellist's student teaches another student, who teaches yet another, who can draw a link directly back to the great cellist. The student might not have ever met the great cellist, but he learned from him. Roosevelt followed a similar path, having learned from Lincoln, Wilson, and Jackson, all of whom had learned from Jefferson, whom Roosevelt thus could claim, as he did, as a direct source of his political and constitutional vision.

World leaders recognized Roosevelt's contributions to the American project of creating a "more perfect Union" as the Declaration of Independence had promised. Churchill declared, "I was overpowered by a sense of deep and irrefutable loss." To Eleanor, he said, he had "lost a dear and cherished friendship which was forged in the fire of war." He told Parliament, "For us it remains only to say that in Franklin Roosevelt there died the greatest American we have ever known and the greatest champion of freedom who has ever brought help and comfort from the new world to the old."[2] His aides talked him out of attending Roosevelt's funeral because they worried it would be too dangerous.

When Ambassador Averell Harriman informed Stalin of Roosevelt's death, he reported, "When I entered Marshal Stalin's office, I noticed he was deeply distressed at the news of the death of President Roosevelt. He greeted me in silence and held my hand four [sic] about 80 seconds before asking me to sit." Stalin asked Harriman "questions about the President and the circumstances which brought about his death." Later, Stalin wondered aloud, "He must have been poisoned," and asked for an autopsy, which confirmed Roosevelt died of natural causes.[3]

Charles de Gaulle, though insulted plenty by Roosevelt, declared a week of mourning in France and sent President Harry Truman an emotional and conciliatory letter, in which he proclaimed that "All France loved him." De Gaulle hoped the letter might help him to get off on a better foot with Truman than he had with Roosevelt, but Truman took an instant dislike to de Gaulle. After meeting him, Truman said his feelings toward France "were becoming less and less friendly."[4]

Dwight Eisenhower wrote in his diary that "in his capacity as a leader of a nation at war, [Roosevelt] seemed [to] fulfill all that could possibly be expected of him." Another Republican, Henry Stimson, Roosevelt's long-serving war secretary, pronounced Roosevelt as America's greatest wartime leader.

Yet, after serving two terms as president himself, Eisenhower in 1964 questioned Roosevelt's policy of unconditional surrender: "Germany was defeated after the Battle of the Bulge. By January 16, 1945, it was all over, and anyone with sense knew it was over. But then there was this statement that President Roosevelt made about unconditional surrender in 1943. This certainly had some influence. The whole spring campaign should have been abandoned." He added, Hitler "used something from the mouth of our leader and persuaded the Germans to fight longer than they should have."[5]

Admiral Baron Kantaro Suzuki, the Japanese premier, declared on learning of Roosevelt's passing that "Roosevelt's leadership has been very effective and has been responsible for the Americans' advantageous position today." He added, "For that reason I can easily understand the great loss his passing means to the American people and my profound sympathy goes to them."[6]

Of course, the war did not end with Roosevelt's death. Hitler and Goebbels were gleeful over the news and released statements describing Roosevelt as "a war criminal" and his death a "miracle."[7] By the time the news reached them, they were sequestered in an underground bunker where they had been since the middle of April to escape Soviet troops hunting for them. By the end of the month, the Allies had found them. On April 30, with his new bride seated next to him dead by her own hand, Hitler put a pistol to his head and fired. The next day, Goebbels and his wife did the same after killing their six children.

On May 7, 1945, Germany unconditionally surrendered. A day later, Americans stormed the streets to celebrate VE-Day.

But the Japanese Empire did not go quietly. Earlier, on March 9–10, 1945, the United States Army Air Force had conducted Operation Meetinghouse, which was the most destructive bombing raid in human history. When Japan persisted in refusing unconditional surrender, Truman ordered the first of two atomic bombs to be dropped on Japan, the first on August 6, 1945, on the city of Hiroshima, a munitions center, killing eighty thousand people immediately and tens of thousands later because of exposure to the ensuing radiation. The second bomb hit Nagasaki, a shipbuilding center, on August 9, 1945, killing between sixty thousand and eighty thousand people. Japan surrendered on September 2, 1945. Americans again stormed the streets, with greater fervor than before, to celebrate the end of World War II.

The estimated casualties in the Pacific were at least 25 million people. Unconditional surrender was achieved at the highest casualty cost of any war in human history.

At the time of Roosevelt's death, Americans—and the world—had not known any president but Franklin Roosevelt for more than a decade. Without him as their standard-bearer, Democrats faced a political realignment that looked increasingly bleak. After the end of World War II, Republicans intensified their attacks on the White House with the hope they could rattle the new, inexperienced President of the United States. Though Roosevelt had not known Truman well, senators did, and none were surprised that Truman could give as good as he got. He feared no one. When he ran for the presidency in his own right in 1948, pollsters and Republicans underestimated his appeal as a fighter. Though several major newspapers predicted a Dewey win, Truman won, 50–45 percent in the popular vote and 303–189 in the Electoral College. Truman disliked Dewey as much as Franklin did.

Truman's victory could not prevent the cracks in the Democrats' hold on power from enlarging: Their margins of victory had been systematically declining every four years with each presidential election since 1932. After twenty straight years of Democratic presidents, a new era of American politics dawned with the election of Dwight D. Eisenhower in 1952. Subsequently, Republicans occupied the White House for forty of the next seventy years, and Republican appointees to the Supreme Court have been a majority since 1969, a decade (and counting) longer than the three decades in which the appointees of Democratic presidents Roosevelt, Truman, Kennedy, and Johnson ruled the Supreme Court. The Democratic political machine symbolized and led by Franklin Roosevelt barely remains.

Yet Roosevelt's legacy endures. As William Leuchtenberg noted, "Washington personified the idea of Federal Union. Jefferson practically originated the party system.... Theodore Roosevelt and Wilson were moral leaders, each in his own way and for his own time, who used the Presidency as a pulpit."[8] Roosevelt also believed that the "presidency is a place of moral leadership." Each had a grand vision of the nation and each yearned for greatness.

During his presidency, Lincoln confounded many of his closest aides and associates with his reticence in sharing thoughts on pivotal matters. Yet Harry Hopkins never was bothered by how Roosevelt was an enigma to many who worked with him. Hopkins observed, "Oh—he sometimes tries to appear tough and cynical and flippant, but that's an act he likes to put on, especially at press conferences." Hopkins added, "He wants to make the boys think he's hardboiled. Maybe he fools some of them, now and then—but don't ever let him fool you, or you won't be any use to him. You can see the real Roosevelt when he comes out with something like the Four Freedoms. And don't get the idea that those are only catch phrases. He really believes them."[9]

Early in the war, Hopkins said Roosevelt "would rather follow than lead public opinion."[10] Similarly, Stephen Douglas found Lincoln was "preeminently a man of the atmosphere that surrounded him."[11] Yet, like Lincoln, Roosevelt died fighting for his ideals. Lincoln was on the cusp of designing a Second Founding of the nation, which was called Reconstruction, while Roosevelt hoped to be at the opening of the United Nations, which would realize Wilson's vision of a meaningful League of Nations.

Of the impact of the Roosevelt presidency on American politics, the Constitution, and the presidency, much has been said and written. Franklin had his faults—he was unfaithful, lied, was manipulative, and much too often unfocused and flippant—but, as he repeatedly said, he was a pragmatist and, ultimately, Roosevelt, like Lincoln, became a model for other presidents.

The enduring impact of Roosevelt's legacy is evident in nearly every area of American public life. Under his leadership, the federal government broadened its authority to regulate the national economy, business, agriculture, and the health, welfare, labor, and well-being of American citizens. As president, he helped to fashion new, enduring safety nets for the infirm, unemployed, and elderly. He proposed and got enacted landmark legislation, such as the Social Security Act, the Fair Labor Standards Act, and the Federal Deposit Insurance Corporation.

No president did more than Franklin Roosevelt to usher in the era of progressive big government, which still exists today. For Roosevelt, big government was not the enemy, but big business was. Big government could do what the private sector had failed to do or could provide needed support for the private sector, especially in times of economic crisis. The New Deal was not just an assortment of federal programs but the guarantor of essential services to those in need.

Roosevelt redefined the presidency. Grover Cleveland, Theodore Roosevelt, and Woodrow Wilson had each set the groundwork for a more powerful presidency, with Cleveland, in his second term, showing how presidents could use their veto power to shape domestic policy, Theodore Roosevelt using the bully pulpit and the force of his personality to impose his will throughout the executive branch and advancing the stewardship theory of the presidency which maintained that the only limit on presidential power was popular support, and Theodore and Wilson taking the lead in areas where Congress had yet to act. Cleveland, Wilson, Theodore Roosevelt, and Lincoln each showed how the President could achieve his policy preferences by serving as both the head of his party and chief executive at the same time. Franklin Roosevelt was the first president to wield all

these authorities and techniques as the preeminent national leader
in domestic and international affairs.

Roosevelt expanded presidential authority and visibility in enduring ways. In mastering radio and other media, he participated in
more than one thousand press conferences and between twenty-
seven and thirty-one Fireside Chats. He relied heavily on White
House staff, which he expanded, and later presidents followed suit
to consolidate their power at home and abroad.

No president after Roosevelt has relinquished the power Roosevelt invested in the presidency. Democrats have tried to extend the
New Deal through Truman's Fair Deal (which promised every American health insurance, increases in the minimum wage, and equal
rights); Kennedy's New Frontier (of what he called "unknown opportunities and perils"); Lyndon Johnson's Great Society programs,
including landmark civil rights and voting legislation, Medicare and
Medicaid, the war on poverty, broadening funding of housing for
the poor, and improving transportation throughout the land; Barack
Obama's Affordable Care Act; and Biden's Bipartisan Infrastructure
Law. Even presidents who derided big government, notably Ronald
Reagan and Donald Trump, equated it with Congress not with the
presidency. Congressional government is a thing of the past.

Roosevelt never stopped believing in the capacity of government
for good, a further indication he was not merely an opportunist. As
he crafted both a style and a vision from an awareness of his own
strengths and lessons he drew from other leaders and mentors, everything he did was designed to maximize his success, which he
equated with the nation's. When Roosevelt performed his presidential duties, he performed them with an awareness of both his
audience(s) and his effects on them.

Roosevelt was the first president to master the use of mass media.
He thus had his sons support him when he stood or walked, or
leaned on podiums, and rarely allowed himself to be photographed
or even seen in a wheelchair, all so he could maintain the image of
a strong, vital leader. As an inveterate consumer of movies and television, a friend of the humorist Will Rogers and other Hollywood
elite, Roosevelt appreciated the importance of image. In his Fireside

Chats, he purposely kept his language simple so that it could reach
the widest possible audience. For Roosevelt, radio and television fa-
cilitated democracy. It was no accident that one of his speechwriters,
Robert Sherwood, was a successful playwright.

Roosevelt appreciated that presidents were consumed with their
images, as Jackson had been with the way he dressed (he wore a
black armband throughout his presidency to commemorate his dead
wife and used his outbursts to make people afraid of him) and as Lincoln had been in having himself portrayed as "Honest Abe" and as
a rail-splitter. Whether it was his messing up his desk to impress Wendell Willkie or driving cars to impress the public and his lady friends,
Roosevelt was invariably attentive to appearances. Six months after
the attack on Pearl Harbor, he established the Office of War Information, whose function was to work with Hollywood (and other
outlets) to spread information helpful to the war effort.[12]

The performance of every president since Roosevelt has been
judged on hallmarks of his administration. One was the concept of
the first hundred days. Louis Howe developed the idea as a way to
highlight the immediate need for federal action, to frame the government's response to the crisis of the Great Depression, and the
effectiveness of the new president. Thanks to Roosevelt, the Constitution now has a Twenty-Second Amendment barring presidents
from serving more than two terms and ensuring that presidents now
lead Congress (rather than the other way around) in formulating policy or setting the national agenda. When administrations change,
from Democratic to Republican or vice versa, it has usually been evident in their philosophy and rhetoric, less so in the size or scope of
presidential responsibilities and the administrative support system
for the presidency.

Roosevelt's transformation of the Supreme Court into a progressive juggernaut sealed the constitutional foundations of expanded
federal regulation. The judicial philosophy of New Deal–era justices
provided the foundation for judicial restraint in deference to progressive legislation. This philosophy influenced not only New Deal
liberals but conservatives through much of the modern era. Indeed,
when Republican presidents and conservative justices in the twenty-

first century complain about judicial activism, they are responding to the liberalism of Democratic appointees to the Supreme Court, beginning with the nine selected by Franklin Roosevelt.

Roosevelt transformed the presidency in foreign affairs. His collaborative spirit during the Second World War is a model for other presidents to follow. His monument to the centrality of that spirit to his presidency is the United Nations. While it has not been immune to criticisms for being too weak, overly prone to the destabilizing influence of nations hostile to our own, Roosevelt considered the United Nations as among his greatest achievements, perhaps his greatest. Of the presidents who have served since Roosevelt, only one—Donald Trump—has insisted on a go-it-alone philosophy in foreign affairs. Otherwise, presidents and the nation have benefitted from collaboration in addressing international crises, even as they have insisted on imposing their moral leadership on the world.

Yet some aspects of Roosevelt's legacy are persistently questioned. Among the most criticized aspects was his slow and largely ineffective response to the Holocaust. Roosevelt had been sympathetic to the plight of European Jews throughout his presidency and had coined the phrase "crimes against humanity," a charge he repeatedly leveled against Hitler. Such support, though not as fulsome as it could have been, subjected Roosevelt to persistent taunts from antisemites who called him "Rosenfeld" and satirized the "Jew Deal."

Nine days after meeting with Rabbi Steven Wise, who favored an independent state of Israel, Roosevelt was told on December 8, 1942, of the Third Reich's plan to exterminate Jews. Roosevelt persuaded Churchill and Stalin to join him in a Declaration on Jewish Massacres, which condemned "in the strongest possible terms the bestial policy of cold-blooded extermination," condemned the Third Reich's "intention to exterminate the Jewish people in Europe," and declared their joint determination to try as "war criminals" all those responsible.

But the State Department under Cordell Hull steadfastly blocked plans to rescue European Jews, and Roosevelt largely left that policy alone. Besides circumventing the department sometimes, Roosevelt's response to the plight of Jews was that the best way to save them was to "win the war." This was cold comfort to Jewish refugees, and many

Jewish Democrats never forgave Roosevelt for not doing more to
stem the Holocaust. They chide his refusal to bomb the roads and
railways that transported Jews to concentration camps and the concentration camps themselves. More than once, Roosevelt expressed
misgivings about alienating German Americans and running the
risk of killing innocent prisoners. The Allied bombings of Nazi targets were designed to be strategic to cripple and destroy Nazi
industrial and military capacity, so the focus was on bombing railways, factories, coal production, harbors, and military troops and
armaments. The aim was to break the German will and win the war
as fast as possible. Bombing transportation lines and concentration
camps would not have hastened that end, whereas, Roosevelt believed, if his strategy worked, Germany would surrender and the
camps would be freed.

Some people question, too, why many of those interacting with
Franklin kept his declining health secret from the public. One answer is that it was not much of a secret. Shortly before he died, *Time*
magazine issued a report of Roosevelt's condition, including photographs. Other news organizations released newsreels of his physical
deterioration, which was well known in Congress. While just before
he died Roosevelt was musing on his possible retirement, he purpose-
fully hid his need for a wheelchair from the public throughout his
presidency. But if anyone was duped, they were not following the
news closely.

A second explanation is many people close to Roosevelt were intensely loyal to him. Most if not all of Roosevelt's cabinet, advisors,
staff, and friends agreed with Churchill that sharing the news of his
deteriorating health would have given comfort to America's enemies,
and would have hurt the morale of Americans both at home and
fighting abroad.

During and after Roosevelt's administration, there was a steady
drumbeat of criticisms that echoed the views of Herbert Hoover and
Republican leaders in Congress. Each of the four times Roosevelt
ran for president, the opposition denounced him and his policies as
"socialist" and "communist" (though the two are not the same).
Hoover was not alone among Republicans asserting that private char-

ity, not the government, should provide subsistence for destitute Americans. Programs akin to the New Deal have repeatedly been criticized for making their beneficiaries weaker and less self-reliant. (This criticism is at odds with the strength, courage, and heroism of America's greatest generation.)

Like Lincoln (and the framers), Franklin believed one of government's most important functions was education. He considered it crucial for achieving equality and maximizing liberty in the American constitutional order. Roosevelt's objective was not indoctrination. It was to make American citizens better informed and wiser sovereigns.

Nonetheless, Roosevelt's own patriotism is challenged, especially in the suggestion he allowed the Japanese Empire to attack Pearl Harbor in order to ensure American participation in the Second World War. The charge is wrong for several reasons: First, Roosevelt deferred, as he did throughout his career, to military authorities, who were giving him conflicting information about possible Japanese attacks. The practice led him to make other mistakes, including authorizing the detention of Japanese Americans on the West Coast.

He would never have sacrificed the fleet for any reason, including to get into a war that his military advisors informed him the nation was not equipped to enter. Moreover, the contemporaneous accounts of Roosevelt's reaction on the day of the Pearl Harbor attack are credible. While Roosevelt was an accomplished actor, he was not so good as to fool the sharp-witted, watchful aides and military officers who were familiar with his acting prowess. Last but not least, Roosevelt followed the precedent set by Abraham Lincoln and Woodrow Wilson, both of whom insisted, as Roosevelt did in 1941, that, if there were a war, the United States would not fire the first shot.

Critics imagining Roosevelt's duplicity on such a grand scale neglect his devout Christian faith. That faith did not prevent him from lying to his wife or others, but it animated his presidency. Franklin's parents and Endicott Peabody impressed on him the duty of doing good for others. Roosevelt manifested a spirit that treated every American with dignity, prioritized the general welfare of the citizenry, and nurtured the nation's social conscience. All of these were indispensable for American democracy to work. He believed one of government's central obligations was to help Americans who needed help. Roosevelt's "bodyguard of lies," to borrow a phrase from Churchill, did not extend to betraying the very people he pledged to help, especially America's military.

Roosevelt's mentors shared the belief in the importance of doing good for the public, and each of them, like Franklin, had their own "rendezvous with destiny." As Eleanor, dressed in mourning, sat next to Franklin's body on the long train ride from Warm Springs to Washington, D.C., thousands of people lined the train tracks to pay their respects. The journey was reminiscent of the one returning Lincoln's body for burial back home in Illinois. It was the beginning of a new phase in her journey of becoming an American icon in her own right. With the help of Louis Howe, she had transformed the role of the first lady, not only serving as a hostess for social affairs but also by being the most effective first lady in history, championing civil rights for women and African Americans, rescuing Jewish refugees, and advocating for international peace.

From the outset of Truman's presidency, she was a close advisor and made history again when Truman appointed her as the first United States delegate to the United Nations. She served as chair of the Human Rights Commission and worked tirelessly to draft the Universal Declaration of Human Rights, which the General Assembly adopted in 1948. In 1952, she resigned from her post in the United Nations to allow President Eisenhower to appoint his own person. She volunteered to assist the American Association for the United Nations and was an American representative to the World Federation of the U.N. Associations. She later became chair of the associations' Board of Directors, and President John F. Kennedy in 1961 appointed her to the National Advisory Council of the then newly created Peace Corps and chair of the President's Commission on the Status of Women. Besides writing a multivolume autobiography, she wrote numerous articles and more than twenty-five other books. As pain and fatigue plagued her, she moved to Val-Kill, her special home in Hyde Park. On November 7, 1962, she died. President John F. Kennedy, the son of Ambassador Joe Kennedy, issued a statement declaring that her "loss will be deeply felt by all those who admired her tireless idealism or benefitted from her good works or wise counsel."[13] She remains the metric for all first ladies. More biographies have been written about her than most American presidents.

Churchill outlived Franklin, Stalin, and Eleanor. On the morning of March 5, 1953, Stalin's tyranny came to an ignominious end: He was found dead on the floor of his dacha, the cause of death later certified as a cerebral hemorrhage. He died before he could begin a purge of Jews, whom he had accused of planning to assassinate Communist leaders.

When Churchill traveled to Potsdam to meet with Truman and Stalin, votes were still being counted in the British election of 1945, and he brought the leader of the opposition party, Clement Atlee, in case he lost. He did, and Atlee took his place in the remaining negotiations among the Big Three. For the next six years, Churchill led the opposition in Parliament. In 1951, he was reelected prime minister. He enjoyed a good relationship with Truman but not with Eisenhower, whom he did not trust and who returned the favor. Though he was desperate to hold on to his position, he retired in 1955 because of a debilitating stroke. His mental and physical health kept waning, preventing him from further work and travel, even to receive honorary American citizenship. Outliving President Kennedy, who was assassinated in 1963, Churchill had a final stroke on January 12, 1965. He died on the seventieth anniversary of his father's death. His state funeral was the first for a non-royal since William Gladstone's in 1898. Today, near Churchill's memorial at Westminster is a bust honoring FDR.

Churchill's legacy has been mixed. He often was on the wrong side of history, as reflected in his racist attitudes and policies, his tyrannical efforts to keep British territories in line, misleading statements during the war, harsh treatment of Mahatma Gandhi, and propensity to be resolute in war but less charitable in peace. Yet, the unique role he played during World War II, standing alone among nations to face the Nazi threat, has never been forgotten: In 2002, he was rated the greatest Briton ever and a runner-up for *Time* magazine's person of the twentieth century. (Einstein won the honor.) In the same year that Stalin died, Churchill won the Nobel Prize for

Literature for "his mastery of historical and biographical description as well as for brilliant oratory in defending exalted human values."[14]

After twelve years in Roosevelt's cabinet, Frances Perkins was the longest serving labor secretary in American history. Subsequently, she served for eight years as a member of the U.S. Civil Service Commission, stepping down after her husband's death in 1952. In her remaining years, she delivered lectures around the country on employment inequities and the history of labor and taught at the Cornell University School of Industrial and Labor Relations until her death in 1965. Today, the building housing the United States Labor Department is named for Frances Perkins.

Other mentors, who died before Roosevelt, left different legacies. Louis Howe, so important to Roosevelt's rise to the presidency and Eleanor's entry into politics, was fondly remembered by those with whom he worked with and given enormous credit for his educating Franklin and Eleanor on the arts of campaigning and governing. But, given the absence of any written records from him, there has been only one biography, written by a cousin, which detailed his eccentricities and political impact.

Theodore Roosevelt remains the third most popular subject of presidential biographies, besting Franklin, whose biographies rank fourth. (The construction of the Mount Rushmore National Monument, completed in Franklin's third term in 1941, burnished Teddy's legacy.) Yet his legacy has often been reassessed, and his persistently racist views have diminished his luster. His philosophy of governance has further complicated his legacy, since it was a precursor to modern Democratic presidents, beginning with Franklin, rather than to modern Republican presidents.

Woodrow Wilson's progressive legacy has withered, because of his unapologetic racism, including supporting the Jim Crow system demeaning African Americans and defending segregation in the armed forces and public life. Though critics have often assailed Wilson for praising the movie *Birth of a Nation*, which venerated the rise of the Ku Klux Klan, Wilson's biographer, Scott Berg, finds not only the absence of support for such a claim but also a different statement from Wilson at the time stating, "I have always felt that this was a very unfortunate production and I wish most sincerely that its production might be avoided, particularly in communities where there are so many colored people."[15] Nonetheless, the record of Wilson's racism led Princeton University, where he was once president, to drop his name from its School of Public International Affairs.

Andrew Jackson is no longer venerated as he once was, given his persistent racism and slaughter of Native Americans. Yet Abraham Lincoln paid homage to Jackson for his proclamation against state nullification of federal laws, which significantly informed his first inaugural address and rationale for defending the inviolability of the Union. Jackson's official portrait was the only presidential portrait Lincoln hung in his office at the White House. Hoping to associate himself with Jackson's toughness, Donald Trump hung his portrait when he was the forty-fifth president. When Joe Biden followed Trump into the White House, he replaced the Jackson portrait with one of Franklin Roosevelt.

Harry Hopkins, indispensable aide, was in the hospital when Roosevelt died, though he attended the funeral. Less than a year later, he died. Like Howe, he left a legacy of devotion to Roosevelt, and like Roosevelt, he worked himself to death for his country. He was fifty-five.

Henry Morgenthau lived several more decades, during which he extended his exemplary public service. Though he had no background in finance, he served for more than a decade as treasury secretary, until Truman called his bluff when Morgenthau threatened to resign in protest over Truman's failure to take him to the Potsdam Conference. (Truman named his friend Jimmy Byrnes secretary of state, correcting Roosevelt's failure to replace Hull with Byrnes.)

Morgenthau played major roles in finding safe refuge for Jewish refugees during and after the war, developing financial support for the new nation of Israel, and helping to steer the country away from financial ruin in the aftermath of the war. He died in 1967. His son Robert, for whom Justice Sonia Sotomayor once worked, was the longest serving district attorney of New York County.

Henry Stimson, who retired from government service in 1945, served under five presidents—more than any American in his era—

William Howard Taft, Woodrow Wilson, Herbert Hoover, Franklin Roosevelt, and Harry Truman. Though a lifelong Republican, Stimson put country before party more than once. Stimson was a visionary, who anticipated the risks and benefits of the Atomic Age. He predicted that the impact of the atomic bomb extended well beyond military needs, including but not limited to diplomacy, world affairs, business, economics, and science. He believed countries, including the United States and Russia, should work together to deliver their weapons to a neutral sovereign, such as the United Nations. Not many of his contemporaries agreed with him. His memoirs, largely written before he died on October 20, 1950, remain a valuable, insightful resource on executive leadership during the Second World War.

When a friend asked Stimson who was the "best" president he served, Stimson replied that it depended on the meaning of "the best." He said that if the metric was who was the most *efficient* person to be president, his answer was William Howard Taft. As president, Taft had maintained that presidents only had the powers expressly given to them in the Constitution. In office, he acted like a judge, who only pursued a course of action, such as balancing the budget, after he had thoroughly studied and found the appropriate support for taking it. But, if asked to name the greatest president, Stimson answered, "Roosevelt." He never said which one, since he believed both "understood the use of power" and "knew the enjoyment of power."[16]

While Stimson's appraisal of Roosevelt might have been begrudging, given Stimson's longstanding service to the Republican Party and Republican presidents, Stimson was hardly the only Republican to acknowledge Roosevelt's greatness as a leader. Indeed, a final measure of a leader may be how those who opposed him, or had good reason to question him, regarded his political impact. No one criticized Roosevelt more harshly in his lifetime than the Ohio senator known as Mr. Republican, Robert Taft, the eldest son of Chief Justice Taft. On Roosevelt's passing, Taft said that "the President's death removed the greatest figure of our time at the very climax of his career and shocks the world to which his words and actions were more important than any other man. He dies a hero of the war, for he literally worked himself to death in the service of the American people."

Though long a critic of Roosevelt, Republican senator Arthur Vandenberg of Michigan had been persuaded by Roosevelt of America's moral leadership in the world. He said Roosevelt "left an imperishable imprint on the history of America and the world."[17] Such generous comments speak volumes of the era and the man who made himself the modern model of presidential leadership.

Acknowledgments

IF WRITING THE STORY OF Abraham Lincoln's mentors, as I did in 2020, is akin to climbing a mountain, writing the story of Franklin D. Roosevelt's mentors is like climbing a mountain range. Each is daunting, and I could not have done either biography alone.

To begin with, I benefitted enormously, in researching and writing about FDR's mentors, from the help and generosity of several repositories of FDR papers, including the Library of Congress, Harvard University, the Groton School, and the FDR Library. My visits to the Roosevelt estate and the cottage Val-Kill in Hyde Park, New York, were illuminating, as was my visit to FDR's boarding school. Mark Melchior, the Groton School's head librarian, generously gave me the space and access to review Groton's excellent archive of FDR-related materials, including correspondence, memoirs, and other documents regarding Endicott Peabody's decades-long relationship with FDR. On visits to Germany, France, and Italy, I tracked the Allies' movements as they advanced on Germany in the final year of World War II.

The support I received from my home institution, the University of North Carolina at Chapel Hill, was indispensable. I am especially grateful to Kerrie-Ann Yanique Rowe and Nicole Downing for their outstanding research support, for funding from the UNC Law School, and for the indefatigable research assistance of UNC Law

School students Sam Lahne, Allison Kraynek, and Regan Metzger. Thanks as well to Mike Morgan in the History Department for his insights and suggestions on FDR, particularly in the realm of foreign affairs.

Jane Dystel, my agent, and Ned Wahl deserve credit for encouraging me to do this book, and my friend and law school classmate Nick Theodorou provided invaluable feedback on each page of the manuscript. My family—my wife Deborah and sons Ben, Daniel, and Noah—were helpful sounding boards and editors throughout the writing of this manuscript, and thanks to my mother-in-law Sally Schwartz for her enthusiastic proofreading. Jane deserves credit, too, for her support, confidence, and candor.

Bibliography

Ashburn, Frank D. *Peabody of Groton: A Portrait*. New York: Coward McCann, 1944.

Baker, Leonard. *Back to Back: The Duel Between FDR and the Supreme Court*. New York: Macmillan Company, 1967.

Berg, Scott A. *Wilson*. New York: G. P. Putnam's Sons, 2013.

Berle, Adolf, and Gardiner Means. *The Modern Corporation and Private Property*. New York: Harcourt, Brace & World, 1932.

Black, Allida M. "Eleanor Roosevelt (1884–1962): First Lady, Social Welfare Advocate, Human Rights Leader." *Social Welfare History Project*, 2010.

Black, Conrad. *Franklin Delano Roosevelt: Champion of Freedom*. New York: Public Affairs, 2003.

Boffey, Philip M. "Theodore Roosevelt at Harvard." *Harvard Crimson*, December 12, 1957.

Borah, William Edgar, and Grace Hileman. *William Edgar Borah Papers*. Library of Congress, Manuscript Division, Washington, D.C.

Brands, H. W. *Traitor to His Class: The Privileged Life and Radical Presidency of Franklin Delano Roosevelt*. New York: Doubleday, 2008.

Breitman, Richard, and Allan J. Lichtman. *FDR and the Jews*. Boston: Harvard University Press, 2013.

Burner, David. *Herbert Hoover: A Public Life*. New York: Alfred A. Knopf, 1979.

Burns, James MacGregor. *FDR's Last Journey*. Maryland: New Word City, 2017.

Burns, James MacGregor. *Roosevelt: The Lion and the Fox, 1882–1940*. New York: Open Road Media, 2012. First published 1956 by Harcourt, Brace & World (New York).

Chase, Stuart. *A New Deal*. New York: The MacMillan Company, 1932.

Cook, Blanche Wiesen. *Eleanor Roosevelt, Volume 1: The Early Years, 1884–1933*. New York: Viking Penguin (1992).

Cox, James M. *Journey Through My Years*. New York: Simon & Schuster, 1946.

Dallek, Robert. *Franklin D. Roosevelt: A Political Life*. New York: Viking, 2017.

Daniels, Josephus. *The Life of Woodrow Wilson, 1856–1924*. New York: Praeger, 1971. First published 1924 by The John H. Winston Company, Philadelphia.

Daniels, Josephus. *The Wilson Era: Years of Piece, 1910–1917*. North Carolina: The University of North Carolina Press, 1944.

Downey, Kirstin. *The Woman Behind the New Deal: The Life of Frances Perkins, FDR's Secretary of Labor and His Moral Conscience*. New York: Anchor Books, 2009.

Doyle, William. *Inside the Oval Office: The White House Tapes from FDR to Clinton*. New York: Kodansha America, 1999.

Drury, Allen. *A Senate Journal, 1943–1945*. New York: McGraw-Hill, 1963.

Eisenhower, Dwight D. *Crusade in Europe*. New York: Doubleday & Company, 1948.

Elliott Roosevelt Papers, 1929–1952. Franklin D. Roosevelt Presidential Library & Museum, Hyde Park, New York.

Fenster, Julie M. *FDR's Shadow: Louis Howe, the Force That Shaped Franklin and Eleanor Roosevelt*. New York: Palgrave Macmillan, 2009.

Flynn, John T. *The Roosevelt Myth*. New York: The Devin-Adair Company (1948).

Fohlen, Claude. "De Gaulle and Franklin D. Roosevelt." *FDR and His Contemporaries* (C. A. van Minnen and J. F. Sears, eds.) London: Palgrave Macmillan, 1992.

Franklin D. Roosevelt: Day by Day. Pare Lorentz Center at the FDR Presidential Library, Hyde Park, New York.

Freidel, Frank. *Franklin D. Roosevelt: A Rendezvous with Destiny*. New York: Little, Brown, 1990.

Golway, Terry. *Frank and Al: FDR, Al Smith, and the Unlikely Alliance that Created the Modern Democratic Party*. New York: St. Martin's Press, 2018.

Golway, Terry. *Machine Made: Tammany Hall and the Creation of Modern American Politics*. New York: Liveright Publishing Corporation, 2014.

Graham, Hugh Davis. "The Paradox of Eleanor Roosevelt: Alcoholism's Child." *Virginia Quarterly Review* (Spring 1987).

Grew, Joseph C. *Turbulent Era: A Diplomatic Record of Forty Years, 1904–1945*. Boston: Houghton Mifflin, 1952.

Harriman, W. A., Papers, Library of Congress, Washington, D.C.

Harriman, W. Averell, and Elie Abel. *Special Envoy to Churchill and Stalin, 1941–1946*. New York: Random House, 1975.

Harry L. Hopkins Papers, 1928–1946. Franklin D. Roosevelt Presidential Library & Museum, Hyde Park, New York.

Hassett, William. *Off the Record with FDR: 1942–1945*. New Jersey: Rutgers University Press, 1958.

Helicher, Karl. "The Education of Franklin D. Roosevelt." *Presidential Studies Quarterly* 12, no. 1 (1982): 50–53.

Hoover, Herbert. *The Challenge to Liberty*. New York: Scribner, 1935.

Ickes, Harold L. *The Secret Diary of Harold L. Ickes, Vol. 3: The Lowering Clouds, 1939–1941*. New York: Simon & Schuster, 1954.

John F. Kennedy, Presidential Papers, President's Office Files, John F. Kennedy Presidential Library and Museum, Boston, Massachusetts.

Joint Committee on the Investigation of the Pearl Harbor Attack. Report, June 20, 1946. United States Government Printing Office, 1946.

Keynes, John Maynard. "From Keynes to Roosevelt: Our Recovery Plan Assayed; The British Economist Writes an Open Letter to the President Finding Reasons, in Our Policies, for Both Hopes and Fears." *New York Times*, December 31, 1933.

Kimball, Warren F. *The Juggler: Franklin Roosevelt as Wartime Statesman*. New Jersey: Princeton University Press, 1991.

Kintrea, Frank. "'Old Peabo' and the School." *American Heritage*, October/November 1980.

Lash, Joseph P. *Eleanor and Franklin: The Story of Their Relationship Based on Eleanor Roosevelt's Private Papers*. New York: W. W. Norton & Company, 1971.

Lelyveld, Joseph. *His Final Battle: The Last Months of Franklin Roosevelt*. New York: Alfred A. Knopf, 2016.

Leuchtenberg, William. *Franklin D. Roosevelt and the New Deal: 1932–1940*. Philadelphia: Harper Torchbooks, 1963.

Lodge, Henry Cabot. The League of Nations Must Be Revised (1919). *Congressional Record*, 66th Cong., 1st sess., 1919, 3779–3784.

Michaelis, David. *Eleanor*. New York: Simon & Schuster, 2020.

Moley, Richard. *After Seven Years*. New York: Harper and Brothers, 1939.

Nasaw, David. *The Patriarch: The Remarkable Life and Turbulent Times of Joseph P. Kennedy*. New York: The Penguin Press, 2012.

Newman, Roger. *Hugo Black: A Biography*. New York: Fordham University Press, 1997.

Perkins, Frances. *The Roosevelt I Knew*. New York: The Viking Press, 1946.

Perry, Mark. *The Most Dangerous Man in America: The Making of Douglas MacArthur*. New York: Basic Books, 2015.

Rabalais, Steven. *General Fox Connor: Pershing's Chief of Operations and Ei-senhower's Mentor.* Pennsylvania: Casemate Publishers, 2016.

Rauchway, Eric. *Winter War: Hoover, Roosevelt, and the First Clash over the New Deal.* New York: Basic Books, 2018.

Robinson, Corinne Roosevelt. *My Brother Theodore Roosevelt.* New York: Charles Scribner's Sons, 1921.

Roosevelt, Eleanor. "Keepers of Democracy." *Virginia Quarterly Review* 15 (January 1939).

Roosevelt, Eleanor. *The Autobiography of Eleanor Roosevelt.* New York: Harper & Brothers, 1961.

Roosevelt, Eleanor. *This I Remember.* New York: Harper & Brothers, 1949.

Roosevelt, Eleanor, Papers, Digital Edition, George Washington University.

Roosevelt, Franklin D. Executive Order 8802: Prohibition of Discrimination in the Defense Industry, June 25, 1941. Executive Order, 1862-2011, General Records of the United States Government, Record Group 11, National Archives Building, Washington, D.C.

Roosevelt, Franklin Delano. *FDR's Fireside Chats.* Russell D. Buhite & David W. Levy, eds. Norman, Oklahoma: University of Oklahoma Press, 1992.

Roosevelt, Franklin D., Master Speech File, 1898–1945. Franklin D. Roosevelt Presidential Library & Museum, Hyde Park, New York.

Roosevelt, Franklin D., Papers as President: The President's Official File, 1933–1945. Franklin D. Roosevelt Presidential Library & Museum, Hyde Park, New York.

Roosevelt, James, and Bill Libby. *My Parents: A Differing View.* Illinois: Playboy Press, 1976.

Roosevelt, Theodore. *Theodore Roosevelt: An Autobiography.* New York: The Macmillan Company, 1913.

Roosevelt, Theodore. *The Strenuous Life; Essays and Addresses.* Philadelphia: Gebbie and Company, 1903.

Rosenman, Samuel I., and Jerry N. Hess. *Oral History Interview with Judge Samuel I. Rosenman, New York, NY, October 15, 1968 and April 23, 1969.* Harry S. Truman Library & Museum, Independence, Missouri.

Rosenman, Samuel I, ed. *The Public Papers and Addresses of Franklin D. Roosevelt, vol. I–IV.* New York: MacMillan Company, 1941.

Rothman, Lily. "It's Not the Story That Was Buried: What Americans in the 1930s Really Knew About What Was Happening in Germany." *Time,* July 10, 1933.

Schwartz, Thomas Alan. *America's Germany: John J. McCloy and the Federal Republic of Germany.* Boston: Harvard University Press, 1991.

Sherwood, Robert. *Roosevelt and Hopkins: An Intimate History*. New York: Harper & Brothers, 1948.

Simon, James F. *FDR and Chief Justice Hughes: The President, the Supreme Court, and the Epic Battle Over the New Deal*. New York: Simon & Schuster, 2012.

Smith, Jean Edward. *FDR*. New York: Random House, 2007.

Smith, Kathryn. *The Gatekeeper: Missy LeHand, FDR, and the Untold Story of the Partnership that Defined a Presidency*. New York: First Touchstone, 2017.

Stiles, Lela. *The Man Behind Roosevelt: The Story of Louis McHenry Howe*. Ohio: World Publishing Company, 1954.

Stimson, Henry L., Papers. Manuscripts and Archives, Yale University Library, New Haven, Connecticut.

Stokes, Harold Phelps. "Groton Celebrates Its Fiftieth Year; The School's Founder, the Rev. Endicott Peabody, Still Carries on at 77 the Tradition Between Masters and Boys." *New York Times*, June 3, 1934.

Stoler, Mark A., and Daniel D. Holt, eds. *The Papers of George Catlett Marshall*. Baltimore: Johns Hopkins University Press, 1981–2003.

Sun, Cornell. "The Gold Coast." *Harvard Crimson*, October 13, 1928.

Tugwell, Rexford Guy. *The Brains Trust*. New York: Viking Press, 1968.

Tugwell, Rexford Guy. *The Democratic Roosevelt*. New York: Doubleday, 1957.

Wallace, Gregory. *America's Soul in the Balance: The Holocaust, FDR's State Department, and the Moral Disgrace of an American Aristocracy*. Texas: Greenleaf Book Group Press, 2012.

Ward, Geoffrey C. *Closest Companion: The Unknown Story of the Intimate Friendship Between Franklin Roosevelt and Margaret Suckley*. New York: Houghton Mifflin, 1995.

Ward, Geoffrey C. *Before the Trumpet: Young Franklin Roosevelt, 1882–1903*. New York: Vintage Books, 2014. First published 1985 by Harper & Row (New York).

Ward, Geoffrey C. *A First-Class Temperament: The Emergence of Franklin Roosevelt, 1905–1928*. New York: Harper & Row, 1989.

Ward, Geoffrey C. "The Roosevelts at Harvard." *The Gold Coaster: The Alumni Magazine of Adams House, Harvard College*, 2014.

Welles, Sumner. *Statement by the Acting Secretary of State, the Honorable Sumner Welles, July 23 1940 [The Welles Declaration]*. Digital Archive, History and Public Policy Program, Woodrow Wilson International Center for Scholars, Washington, D.C.

White, Walter. *A Man Called White: The Autobiography of Walter White.*
    New York: Viking Press, 1948.
Wills, Matthew B. *Wartime Missions of Harry L. Hopkins.* New York: Ivy
    House Publishing Group, 1996.
Woodin, W. H. "Woodin Defines Reopening Steps." *New York Times*, March
    12, 1933.
Woolner, David B. *The Last 100 Days: FDR at War and at Peace.* New York:
    Basic Books, 2017.
Woolverton, John H. with James Bratt. *A Christian and a Democrat: A Re-
    ligious Biography of Franklin D. Roosevelt.* Michigan: William B.
    Eerdmans Publishing Company, 2019.

Endnotes

AUTHOR'S NOTE: In the Endnotes that follow, I draw heavily on primary materials, including voluminous electronic data bases on the life and education of Franklin D. Roosevelt; memoirs, correspondence, and diaries of key figures and mentors in FDR's life and education (and the same of course for Eleanor); newspaper archives, public speeches, and statements by and about FDR; FDR's Fireside Chats; and newspaper columns and magazines. I rely as well on many excellent secondary resources on the life and political education of Franklin D. Roosevelt.

CHAPTER ONE

1. Franklin Roosevelt, Fireside Chat, April 14, 1938.
2. Frank Freidel, *Franklin D. Roosevelt: A Rendezvous with Destiny*, 4–5 (1990) (quoting Franklin D. Roosevelt).
3. Geoffrey C. Ward, *Before the Trumpet: Young Franklin Roosevelt*, 66 (1985) (quoting Sara); James MacGregor Burns, *Roosevelt: The Lion and the Fox, 1882–1940*, 34 (2017).
4. Geoffrey C. Ward, *Before the Trumpet: Young Franklin Roosevelt*, 112 (1985) (quoting Dora).
5. Theodore Roosevelt, *Autobiography*, 8 (1913).
6. Corinne Roosevelt Robinson, *My Brother Theodore Roosevelt*, 106 (2016).
7. Phillip M. Boffey, "Theodore Roosevelt at Harvard," *Harvard Crimson*, December 12, 1957 (quoting Henry Pringle).
8. Geoffrey C. Ward, "The Roosevelts at Harvard," *Gold Coaster*, 2014 (quoting Theodore Roosevelt).
9. Theodore Roosevelt, quoted on PBS, *The American President*, April 13, 2000.

10. Theodore Roosevelt, diary entry, February 14, 1884.
11. See Paul Grondahl, *I Rose Like a Rocket: The Political Education of Theodore Roosevelt* (Bison Books, 2007).
12. Frank D. Ashburn, *Peabody of Groton: A Portrait*, 49 (1944).
13. Geoffrey C. Ward, *Before the Trumpet: Young Franklin Roosevelt, 1882–1905*, 169 (1985).
14. Harold Phelps Stokes, "Groton Celebrates its Fiftieth Year: The School's Founder, the Rev. Endicott Peabody, Still Carries on at 77 the Tradition Between Masters and Boys," *New York Times*, June 3, 1934; Geoffrey C. Ward, *Before the Trumpet: Young Franklin Roosevelt*, 171 (quoting the brochure).
15 Frank Kintrea, "'Old Peabo' and the School," *American Heritage*, October/November 1980 (quoting Harriman).
16. Edward N. Saveth, "Education of an Elite," *History of Education Quarterly* 28, no. 3 (Autumn 1988), 367-386.
17. Geoffrey C. Ward, *Before the Trumpet: Young Franklin Roosevelt*, 180 (quoting Peabody).
18. Geoffrey C. Ward, *Before the Trumpet: Young Franklin Roosevelt*, 184 (citation omitted in original).
19. Geoffrey C. Ward, *Before the Trumpet: Young Franklin Roosevelt*, 180–181.
20. Geoffrey C. Ward, *Before the Trumpet: Young Franklin Roosevelt*, 182.
21. George C. Ward, *Before the Trumpet: Young Franklin Roosevelt*, 189 (citation omitted in original).
22. American Legends Interviews: Louis Auchincloss (2010). When asked in the interview about his "impression of Endicott Peabody," Auchincloss answered, "He was a man of deep faith. But he was summed up by Stewart Alsop, whose brother John was in my form: 'The Rector was a great man. He was also a bit of a shit.'"
23. Geoffrey C. Ward, *Before the Trumpet: Young Franklin Roosevelt*, 190.
24. Geoffrey C. Ward, *Before the Trumpet: Young Franklin Roosevelt*, 186.
25. Frank D. Ashburn, *Peabody of Groton: A Portrait*, 88 (1944).
26. Cornell Sun, "The Gold Coast," *Harvard Crimson*, October 13, 1928.
27. Jerome Karabel, First Chapter, "The Chosen," *New York Times*, October 30, 2005.
28. Karl Helicher, "The Education of Franklin D. Roosevelt," *Presidential Studies Quarterly* 12, no. 1 (1982): 50-53.
29. James MacGregor Burns, *Roosevelt: The Lion and the Fox, 1882–1940*, 19 (1956).
30. James MacGregor Burns, *Roosevelt: The Lion and the Fox, 1882–1940*, 20 (1956).

31. James MacGregor Burns, *Roosevelt: The Lion and the Fox, 1882–1940*, 20 (1956).

32. James MacGregor Burns, *Roosevelt: The Lion and the Fox, 1882–1940*, 20 (1956).

33. Eleanor Roosevelt, *The Autobiography of Eleanor Roosevelt*, 3 (1961).

34. Eleanor Roosevelt, *The Autobiography of Eleanor Roosevelt*, 4 (1961).

35. Hugh Davis Graham, "The Paradox of Eleanor Roosevelt: Alcoholism's Child," *Virginia Quarterly Review*, Spring 1987.

36. Allida M. Black, "Eleanor Roosevelt (1884–1962): First Lady, Social Welfare Advocate, Human Rights Leader," *Social Welfare History Project* (2010).

37. Eleanor Roosevelt, *The Autobiography of Eleanor Roosevelt*, 15.

38. Eleanor Roosevelt, *The Autobiography of Eleanor Roosevelt*, 6.

39. Gail Collins, A Review of Eleanor by David Michaelis, The Franklin Delano Roosevelt Foundation, Adams House, Harvard College, October 6, 2020.

40. Jonathan Yardley, "The Roosevelt Cousins Growing," *Washington Post*, November 18, 2001.

41. Hazel Rowley, *Franklin and Eleanor: An Extraordinary Marriage* (Macmillan, 2010).

42. Jean Edward Smith, *FDR*, 37 (2008).

43. James MacGregor Burns, *Roosevelt: The Lion and the Fox, 1882–1940*, 26.

44. James MacGregor Burns, *Roosevelt: The Lion and the Fox, 1882–1940*, 26.

45. James MacGregor Burns, *Roosevelt: The Lion and the Fox, 1882–1940*, 26.

46. Eleanor Roosevelt, *The Autobiography of Eleanor Roosevelt*, 74.

47. Geoffrey C. Ward, *A First-Class Temperament: The Emergence of Franklin Roosevelt, 1905–1928*, 64 (1989) (quoting President Butler and then-Governor Roosevelt).

48. Robert B. Charles, "Legal Education in the Late Nineteenth Century: Through the Eyes of Theodore Roosevelt," *American Journal of Legal History* 37, no. 3 (July 1993), 233–272.

CHAPTER 2

1. "Here's the Famous Populist Speech Theodore Roosevelt Gave Right After Being Shot," *Business Insider*, October 14, 2011, https://www.business insider.com/heres-the-famous-populist-speech-teddy-roosevelt-gave -right-after-getting-shot-2011-10.

2. Grenville Clark, "Franklin D. Roosevelt, 1882–1945: Five Harvard Men Pay Tribute to His Memory," *Harvard Alumni Bulletin* 452 (April 28, 1945): 47.

3. Meredith Hindley, "The Roosevelt Bond: Politics and War Brought Teddy Roosevelt and Franklin Ever Closer," *Humanities* 35 (September/October 2014).
4. *Poughkeepsie Eagle*, October 7, 1910.
5. Jean Edward Smith, *FDR*, 65, 68.
6. Jean Edward Smith, *FDR*, 70.
7. Geoffrey Cobb, "Al Smith Was Political Trailblazer," *Irish Echo*, March 1, 2022.
8. Jean Edward Smith, *FDR*, 72.
9. Jean Edward Smith, *FDR*, 79.
10. Harris Chailkin, "Frances Perkins: She Boldly Went Where No Woman Had Gone Before," *American Social Worker* (Winter 2012).
11. Frances Perkins, *The Roosevelt I Knew*, 9, 11 (1946).
12. Theodore Roosevelt, "The Man with the Muck Rake," speech given on April 15, 1906.
13. Interview with the *New York Times*, January 22, 1911.
14. Jean Edward Smith, *FDR*, 73.
15. James F. Simon, *FDR and Chief Justice Hughes: The President, the Supreme Court, and the Epic Battle over the New Deal*, 79 (2012).
16. Josephus Daniels, "Franklin Roosevelt as I Knew Him," *News and Observer*, Raleigh, N.C. (October 23, 1932).
17. Jean Edward Smith, *FDR*, 73–75.
18. H. W. Brands, *Traitor to His Class*, 70.
19. H. W. Brands, *Traitor to His Class*, 69–70.
20. Lela Stiles, *The Man Behind Roosevelt*, 32 (1954).
21. Julie M. Fenster, *FDR's Shadow: Louis Howe, the Force That Shaped Franklin and Eleanor Roosevelt*, 79 (2009).
22. Julie M. Fenster, *FDR's Shadow: Louis Howe, the Force That Shaped Franklin and Eleanor Roosevelt*, 79.
23. Julie M. Fenster, *FDR's Shadow: Louis Howe, the Force That Shaped Franklin and Eleanor Roosevelt*, 97.
24. H. W. Brands, *Traitor to His Class*, 70.
25. Elliott Roosevelt, Franklin D. Roosevelt Library, Hyde Park, N.Y., June 20, 1979.
26. In 1906, Roosevelt won the Nobel Peace Prize for negotiating the end of the Russo-Japanese [as per Britannica, Wikipedia, other online sources] War. His award sparked the first controversy in the history of the prize, because liberals in Sweden considered him a "military mad" imperialist.
27. See Theodore Roosevelt's Corollary to the Monroe Doctrine (1905) and Annual Message to Congress, December 6, 1904.

28. A. Scott Berg, *Wilson*, 216.

29. A. Scott Berg, *Wilson*, 216.

30. H. W. Brands, *Traitor to His Class*, 74.

31. Jill Lepore, "The Tug of War: Woodrow Wilson and the Power of the Presidency," *The New Yorker*, September 2, 2013.

32. Julie M. Fenster, *FDR's Shadow: Louis Howe, the Force That Shaped Franklin and Eleanor Roosevelt*, 98.

33. Jean Edward Smith, *FDR*, 98.

34. James MacGregor Burns, *Roosevelt: The Lion and the Fox 1882–1940*, 50.

35. Jean Edward Smith, *FDR*, 98.

36. James MacGregor Burns, *Roosevelt: The Lion and the Fox 1882–1940*, 53.

37. Julie M. Fenster, *FDR's Shadow: Louis Howe, the Force That Shaped Franklin and Eleanor Roosevelt*, 9.

38. Robert Dallek, *Franklin D. Roosevelt: A Political Life*, 55 (2017).

39. H. W. Brands, *Traitor to His Class*, 88.

40. Jean Edward Smith, *FDR*, 112.

41. Jean Edward Smith, *FDR*, 113.

42. Jean Edward Smith, *FDR*, 112–113.

43. Jean Edward Smith, *FDR*, 113.

44. Josephus Daniels, *The Wilson Era* (1944).

45. Lela Stiles, *The Man Behind Roosevelt*, 57.

46. Josephus Daniels, Orders Governing the Movements of the Rudder, General Order No. 98, May 18, 1914.

47. Josephus Daniels, Orders Governing the Movements of the Rudder, General Order No. 98, May 18, 1914.

48. Thomas Buell, "Of Ships and the Men Who Sail Them," *Washington Post*, August 3, 1986.

49. Josephus Daniels, Orders Governing the Movements of the Rudder, General Order No. 98, May 18, 1914.

50. Robert Dallek, *Franklin D. Roosevelt: A Political Life*, 56.

51. Jean Edward Smith, *FDR*, 113.

52. Robert Dallek, *Franklin D. Roosevelt: A Political Life*, 57.

53. *The Roosevelts: The Fire of Life (1910–1919)*, episode 3, https://video.kqed .org/video/roosevelts-part-3-fire-life-1910-1919/.

54. Meredith Hindley, "The Roosevelt Bond: Politics and War Brought Teddy Roosevelt and Franklin Delano Roosevelt Ever Closer," *Humanities* 35, no. 5 (September/October 2014).

55. Robert Dallek, *Franklin D. Roosevelt: A Political Life*, 58.

56. Robert Dallek, *Franklin D. Roosevelt: A Political Life*, 62.

57. Conrad Black, *Franklin Delano Roosevelt: Champion of Freedom*, 74, 270 (2003).

58. Mary Alexander and Marilyn Childress, "The Zimmerman Telegram," *Social Education* 45, no. 4 (April 1981): 266.

59. Josephus Daniels, *The Life of Woodrow Wilson*, chap. 23 (1971).

60. Transcript, April 2, 1917: Address to Congress Requesting a Declaration of War Against Germany, Miller Center, University of Virginia.

61. H. W. Brands, *Traitor to His Class*, 125.

62. Foundations of the League of Nations, ungeneva.org.

63. Henry Cabot Lodge, August 12, 1919 (Digital Public Library of America).

64. James Cox, *Journey Through My Years*, 232 (1946).

65. Jean Edward Smith, *FDR*, 165–186.

66. Julie Fenster, *FDR's Shadow: Louis Howe, the Force That Shaped Franklin and Eleanor Roosevelt*, 123.

67. Jean Edward Smith, *FDR*, 165–186.

68. Jean Edward Smith, *FDR*, 47, 77, 148.

69. Robert Dallek, *Franklin D. Roosevelt: A Political Life*, 68-70; Frank Freidel, *Franklin D. Roosevelt: A Rendezvous with Destiny*, 33–36.

70. J. Roosevelt with Bill Libby, *My Parents: A Differing View*, 101–102 (1976).

71. Jean Edward Smith, *FDR*, 139–164.

72. Eleanor Roosevelt, *The Autobiography of Eleanor Roosevelt*, 195.

73. David Michaelis, *Eleanor*, 198.

CHAPTER 3

1. Warren Harding, Campaign Speech, "Return to Normalcy," May 14, 1920.

2. Amy Berish, *FDR and Polio*, Franklin D. Roosevelt Museum and Library, https://www.fdrlibrary.org/polio.

3. Frank Freidel, *Franklin D. Roosevelt: A Rendezvous with Destiny*, 41.

4. Jean Edward Smith, *FDR*, 191.

5. Interview with Frances Perkins, May 1953; Eleanor Roosevelt, *This Is My Story*, 331–332 (1937).

6. Frank Freidel, *Franklin D. Roosevelt: A Rendezvous with Destiny*, 42.

7. Theodore Roosevelt, Address to the Assemblage on "The Strenuous Life," April 10, 1899.

8. Jean Edward Smith, *FDR*, 193.

9. Jean Edward Smith, *FDR*, 195.

10. Jean Edward Smith, *FDR*, 195.

11. Jean Edward Smith, *FDR*, 195.

12. Jean Edward Smith, *FDR*, 195.
13. Eleanor Roosevelt, *The Autobiography of Eleanor Roosevelt*, 117–118.
14. Eleanor Roosevelt, "My Day," February 19, 1955.
15. Joseph P. Lash, *Eleanor and Franklin*, 277 (1971).
16. Jean Edward Smith, *FDR*, 213–215.
17. H. W. Brands, *Traitor to His Class*, 184–185.
18. Terry Golway, *Machine Made: Tammany Hall and the Creation of Modern American Politics* (2014).
19. Franklin D. Roosevelt, Nominating Speech for Al Smith for the Democratic Party Nomination for President, June 26, 1924.
20. Richard Voulahan, "Gov. Smith Is Put in Nomination Amid Wild Cheer/Carnival of Enthusiasm Is Let Loose by Tribute to Franklin D. Roosevelt," *New York Times*, June 28, 1928; Frank Freidel, *Franklin D. Roosevelt: A Rendezvous with Destiny*, 195–196.
21. Frank Freidel, *Franklin D. Roosevelt: A Rendezvous with Destiny*, 52.
22. Richard Voulahan, "Gov. Smith Is Put in Nomination Amid Wild Cheer/Carnival of Enthusiasm Is Let Loose by Tribute to Franklin D. Roosevelt," *New York Times*, June 28, 1928.
23. Terry Golway, *Frank and Al: FDR, Al Smith, and the Unlikely Alliance That Created the Modern Democratic Party* (2018).
24. Robert Dallek, *Franklin D. Roosevelt: A Political Life*, 96.
25. Robert Dallek, *Franklin D. Roosevelt: A Political Life*, 93.
26. Blanche Wiesen Cook, *Eleanor Roosevelt, Volume 1: The Early Years, 1884–1933*, 352 (1992).
27. Robert Dallek, *Franklin D. Roosevelt: A Political Life*, 93.
28. Robert Dallek, *Franklin D. Roosevelt: A Political Life*, 97.
29. Jean Edward Smith, *FDR*, 224.
30. Robert Dallek, *Franklin D. Roosevelt: A Political Life*, 98; Frank Freidel, *Franklin D. Roosevelt: A Rendezvous with Destiny*, 53–54; Brands, *Traitor to His Class*, 209-211.
31. Jean Edward Smith, *FDR*, 226–227.
32. H. W. Brands, *Traitor to His Class*, 215.
33. Frank Freidel, *Franklin D. Roosevelt: A Rendezvous with Destiny*, 46.
34. Robert Dallek, *Franklin D. Roosevelt: A Political Life*, 102.
35. Robert Dallek, *Franklin D. Roosevelt: A Political Life*, 102.
36. Robert Dallek, *Franklin D. Roosevelt: A Political Life*, 102.
37. Kirstin Downey, *The Woman Behind the New Deal*, 96–97.
38. Frances Perkins, *The Roosevelt I Knew*, 3–5, 30, 32, 33.
39. H. W. Brands, *Traitor to His Class*, 222.
40. Frank Freidel, *Franklin D. Roosevelt: A Rendezvous with Destiny*, 57.

41. Robert Dallek, *Franklin D. Roosevelt: A Political Life*, 103.
42. James MacGregor Burns, *Roosevelt: The Lion and the Fox, 1882–1940*, 205.
43. Robert Dallek, *Franklin D. Roosevelt: A Political Life*, 102.
44. H. W. Brands, *Traitor to His Class*, 223.
45. Frank Freidel, *Franklin D. Roosevelt: A Rendezvous with Destiny*, 59.
46. Jean Edward Smith, *FDR*, 238.
47. Frank Freidel, *Franklin D. Roosevelt: A Rendezvous with Destiny*, 60.
48. Jean Edward Smith, *FDR*, 241.
49. Kirstin Downey, *The Woman Behind the New Deal*, 111.
50. *New York Times*, April 27, 1930.
51. H. W. Brands, *Traitor to His Class*, 223.
52. Frances Perkins, *The Roosevelt I Knew*, 96.
53. Frank Freidel, *Franklin D. Roosevelt: A Rendezvous with Destiny*, 61.
54. Jean Edward Smith, *FDR*, 243.
55. Jean Edward Smith, *FDR*, 245.
56. Robert Dallek, *Franklin D. Roosevelt: A Political Life*, 106.
57. *New York Times*, November 4, 1930.
58. Robert Dallek, *Franklin D. Roosevelt: A Political Life*, 106.
59. Robert Dallek, *Franklin D. Roosevelt: A Political Life*, 106.

CHAPTER 4

1. Lela Stiles, *The Man Behind Roosevelt*, 166.
2. Alden Whitman, "Farley, 'Jim' to Thousands, Was the Master Political Organizer and Salesman," *New York Times*, June 10, 1976.
3. Jean Edward Smith, *FDR*, 262.
4. Also a graduate of Columbia's law school, Rosenman most desired a seat on the New York Supreme Court, on which he served from 1936 to 1943 while also working for Roosevelt.
5. Raymond Moley, *After Seven Years*, 17 (1939).
6. Adolph Berle and Gardiner Means, *The Modern Corporation and Private Property* (1932).
7. Raymond Moley, *After Seven Years*, 22 (1939).
8. Rex Tugwell, *The Brains Trust*, xi–xii (1968).
9. Raymond Moley, *After Seven Years*, 15 (1939).
10. Raymond Moley, *After Seven Years*, 20 (1939).
11. Bernard Sternsher, "Tugwell's Appraisal of FDR," *Western Political Quarterly* 15, no. 1, 67–93 (1962).

12. Julie M. Fenster, *FDR's Shadow: Louis Howe, the Force That Shaped Franklin and Eleanor Roosevelt*, 216–217.

13. Herbert Hoover, Statement on Unemployment Relief, February 3, 1931.

14. Franklin D. Roosevelt Speeches: The Forgotten Man, April 7, 1932.

15. Franklin D. Roosevelt Speeches: The Oglethorpe Address, May 22, 1932.

16. Jean Edward Smith, *FDR*, 265.

17. Lela Stiles, *The Man Behind Roosevelt*, 171–172.

18. John T. Flynn, *The Roosevelt Myth* (1948).

19. Lionel V. Patenaude, "The Garner Switch to Roosevelt: 1932 Democratic Convention," *Southwestern Historical Quarterly* 79, no. 2, 189–204 (1975).

20. There were many close advisors to credit with Roosevelt's victory, including Howe. In fact, Louis received more letters than he could count that congratulated him on helping to steer Roosevelt to the presidency. Frances Perkins, for example, wrote, "Yours was a great job, and I cannot tell you how appreciative are those of us who have knowledge of what you were doing. Particularly because I disagreed with you about some things, I want you to know how fine I think the total was." Many prominent people wrote congratulatory messages to Franklin, including financier Bernard Baruch, who told Howe, "There are few people who know of your devotion and unswerving loyalty [to FDR] during the past many years.... It is seldom one sees such unselfishness." Julie Fenster, *FDR's Shadow: Louis Howe, the Force That Shaped Franklin and Eleanor Roosevelt*, 221.

21. Franklin D. Roosevelt, Address Accepting the Presidential Nomination at Democratic National Convention in Chicago, July 2, 1932.

22. Ronald G. Shafer, "The Woman Who Helped a President Change America During His First 100 Days," *Washington Post*, March 14, 2021.

23. Stuart Chase, *A New Deal* (1932).

24. Herbert Hoover National Historic Site, "Adversity Leads to Opportunity," https://www.nps.gov/articles/adversity-leads-to-opportunity.htm.

25. David Burner, *Herbert Hoover: A Public Life*, 102 (1979).

26. Matthew Shafeer, *Hoover and 20th Century Presidents: Franklin D. Roosevelt*, April 8, 2020.

27. W. G. Thiemann, "President Hoover's Efforts on Behalf of FDR's 1932 Nomination," *Presidential Studies Quarterly* 24, no. 1, Domestic Goals and Foreign Policy Objectives, 87–91 (1994).

28. Michael Duffy, "Even Headstrong Generals Must Answer to Somebody," *Time*, October 21, 2016.

29. Rexford G. Tugwell, *The Democratic Roosevelt*, 348–350 (1957).

30. Mark Perry, *The Most Dangerous Man in America: The Making of Douglas MacArthur* (2015).

31. Kenneth S. Davis, "FDR as a Biographer's Problem," *American Scholar* 52 (1983).

32. Raymond Moley, *After Seven Years*; Rex Tugwell, *The Brains Trust*.

33. Raymond Moley, *After Seven Years*.

34. Jean Edward Smith, *FDR*, 278.

35. Lela Stiles, *The Man Behind Roosevelt*, 166.

36. Jean Edward Smith, *FDR*, 281.

37. *America at the Crossroads: The Election of 1932*, fdr4freedomgs.org, https://fdr4freedoms.org/wp-content/themes/fdf4fdr/Downloadable PDFs/I_FDRBeforethePresidency/05_AmericaattheCrossroads.pdf.

38. Herbert Hoover, Address at Madison Square Garden, October 31, 1932.

39. Franklin D. Roosevelt, Campaign Speech, November 7, 1932.

40. Franklin D. Roosevelt, Brief Remarks at Biltmore Hotel, November 8, 1932.

41. Lela Stiles, *The Man Behind Roosevelt*, 218.

42. President-Elect Franklin D. Roosevelt, Brief Statement from His Home on 65th Street, November 9, 1932.

43. Eleanor Roosevelt, *The Autobiography of Eleanor Roosevelt*, 196–202.

44. Eric Rauchway, *Winter War: Hoover, Roosevelt, and the First Clash over the New Deal*, 63 (2018).

45. Jean Edward Smith, *FDR*, 293.

46. Jean Edward Smith, *FDR*, 294.

CHAPTER 5

1. Andrew Jackson, Second Inaugural Address, March 4, 1833.

2. John H. Wolverton with James Bratt, *A Christian and a Democrat*, 34 (2019).

3. Edward G. Lengel, "Franklin Delano Roosevelt's Historic First Inauguration" (March 4, 1933), White House Historical Association.

4. Sugit Raman, "Felix Frankfurter and His Proteges: Reexamining the 'Happy Hot Dogs,'" *Journal of Supreme Court History*, May 21, 2014.

5. Ronald Shafer, "The Most Contentious Transition before Trump and Biden: Herbert Hoover and FDR," *Washington Post*, May 24, 2021.

6. Franklin D. Roosevelt, First Inaugural Address, March 4, 1933.

7. John H. Wolverton with James Bratt, *A Christian and a Democrat*, 1.

8. Frances Perkins, *The Roosevelt I Knew*, 141.

9. David W. Houck and Mihaela Nocasian, "FDR's First Inaugural Address: Text, Context, and Reception," *Rhetoric and Public Affairs* 5, no. 4 (Winter 2002): 649–678.

10. Franklin D. Roosevelt, First Inaugural Address, March 4, 1933.

11. Franklin D. Roosevelt, Press Conference from the Oval Study in the White House, April 19, 1933.

12. Raymond Moley, *After Seven Years* (1939).

13. Raymond Moley, *After Seven Years*, 48, 369–370 (1939).

14. Eleanor Roosevelt, *The Autobiography of Eleanor Roosevelt* (1961).

15. Eric Rauchway, *Winter War: Hoover, Roosevelt, and the First Clash over the New Deal* (2018); Ronald G. Shafer, "The Most Contentious Transition before Trump and Biden: Herbert Hoover and FDR," *Washington Post*, November 9, 2020.

16. W. H. Woodin, "Woodin Defines Reopening Steps," *New York Times*, March 12, 1933, 63.

17. "Treasury Secretary Woodin Says National Banking Holiday Not to Be Extended," UPI Archives, March 6, 1933; William Silber, "Why Did FDR's Bank Holiday Succeed?," *Economic Policy Review* 15 (Federal Reserve Bank of New York), 19 (2019).

18. They were not all men: My great aunt Bernice Bernstein headed to Washington after graduating first in her class at the University of Wisconsin Law School. She worked closely with Frances Perkins to launch Social Security.

19. William Leuchtenberg, *Franklin D. Roosevelt and the New Deal, 1932–1940*, 63–64 (1963).

20. William Leuchtenberg, *Franklin D. Roosevelt and the New Deal, 1932–1940*, 64 (1963).

21. William Leuchtenberg, *Franklin D. Roosevelt and the New Deal, 1932–1940*, 79 (1963).

22. William Leuchtenberg, *Franklin D. Roosevelt and the New Deal, 1932–1940*, 80 (1963).

23. Warner Garner, "Pebbles from the Path Behind," *Green Bag* 9, 271, 272.

24. Seth P. Waxman, "The Physics of Persuasion: Arguing the New Deal," *Core*, October 8, 1999.

25. William Leuchtenberg, *Franklin D. Roosevelt and the New Deal, 1932–1940*, 81.

26. Raymond Moley, *After Seven Years* (1938).

27. William Leuchtenberg, *Franklin D. Roosevelt and the New Deal, 1932–1940*, 92.

28. Herbert Hoover, *The Challenge to Liberty* (1953).

29. Franklin D. Roosevelt, Fireside Chat Number 6: On Government and Capitalism, September 30, 1934.

30. Frank Freidel, *Franklin D. Roosevelt: A Rendezvous with Destiny*, 141 (1990).

31. 290 U.S. 398 (1934).

32. 291 U.S. 502 (1934).

33. 293 U.S. 388 (1935).

34. *A.L.A. Schecter Poultry v. United States*, 295 U.S. 495 (1935).

35. David Dalin, "Old Isaiah," *Jewish Review of Books* (Summer 2016). In calling Brandeis "Isaiah," both Roosevelt and his inner circle manifested their still lingering antisemitism.

36. Franklin D. Roosevelt, Press Conference, May 30, 1935.

37. *Morehead v. New York ex rel. Tipaldo*, 298 U.S. 587 (1936).

38. Geoffrey C. Ward, *Closest Companion: The Unknown Story of the Intimate Friendship Between Franklin Roosevelt and Margaret Suckley* (1995).

39. Geoffrey C. Ward, *Closest Companion: The Unknown Story of the Intimate Friendship Between Franklin Roosevelt and Margaret Suckley* (1995).

40. "Rexford Tugwell, 1891–1979," *Washington Post*, July 29, 1979.

41. Frances Perkins, *The Roosevelt I Knew*, 239 (1946).

42. William Leuchtenberg, "When Franklin Roosevelt Clashed with the Supreme Court—and Lost," *Smithsonian*, May 2005, smithsonianmag.com.

43. Sebastian Edwards, *The London Monetary and Economic Conference of 1933*, NBER Working Papers Series, February 2017.

44. Cordell Hull, "Memoirs of Cordell Hull: Friction with Moley Recalled by Secretary," *New York Times*, January 30, 1948.

45. Julie Victa, *FDR and the London Economic Conference: The Impact of Personality on Decision-Making*, February 26, 2016, longdom.org.

46. H. W. Brands, *Traitor to His Class*, 372.

47. The Papers of Franklin D. Roosevelt, Part I, 1933–1945.

48. Jean Edward Smith, *FDR*, 363.

49. Jean Edward Smith, *FDR*, 363.

50. Robert Dallek, *Franklin D. Roosevelt: A Political Life*, 243 (2017).

51. Blanche Wiesen Cook, *Eleanor Roosevelt, Volume 2: The Defining Years, 1933–1938*, 353 (1999).

52. Eleanor Roosevelt, *This I Remember*, 145 (1949).

53. Robert Dallek, *Franklin D. Roosevelt: A Political Life*, 232n (2017).

54. Patrick Cox, *Not Worth a Bucket of Warm Spit*, History News Network, https://historynewsnetwork.org/article/53402.

55. Franklin D. Roosevelt, Speech, January 8, 1936.

56. Franklin D. Roosevelt, Speech, January 8, 1936.

57. Michael Hiltzik, "FDR, Too, Was Denounced as 'Socialist,'" *Los Angeles Times*, https://enewspaper.latimes.com/infinity/article_share.aspx?guid =38b26cf1-c6e4-4a16-ab90-3b541252dd2a.

58. Robert Dallek, *Franklin D. Roosevelt: A Political Life*, 268 (2017).

CHAPTER 6

1. James MacGregor Burns, *Roosevelt: The Lion and the Fox, 1882–1940*, 684 (2017).

2. Robert Dallek, *Franklin D. Roosevelt: A Political Life*, 243 (2017).

3. Franklin D. Roosevelt, Second Inaugural Address, January 20, 1937.

4. Franklin D. Roosevelt, Second Inaugural Address, January 29, 1937.

5. Franklin D. Roosevelt, State of the Union, January 6, 1937.

6. Robert Dallek, *Franklin D. Roosevelt: A Political Life*, 272 (2017).

7. Robert Dallek, *Franklin D. Roosevelt: A Political Life*, 270 (2017).

8. Jean Edward Smith, *FDR*, 392.

9. Robert Dallek, *Franklin D. Roosevelt: A Political Life*, 272 (2017).

10. Franklin D. Roosevelt, Speech on Supreme Court Reform, March 4, 1937.

11. Franklin D. Roosevelt, Fireside Chat, March 9, 1937.

12. Jean Edward Smith, *FDR*, 384.

13. Robert Dallek, *Franklin D. Roosevelt: A Political Life*, 275 (2017).

14. Leonard Baker, *Back to Back: The Duel Between FDR and the Supreme Court*, 149–173 (1967).

15. Leonard Baker, *Back to Back: The Duel Between FDR and the Supreme Court*, 149–173 (1967).

16. Borah Statements: Reorganization of the Federal Judiciary: Hearing on S. 1392 before the S. Comm. on the Judiciary, 75th Congress, 13–21 (1937).

17. Richard Friedman, "Chief Justice's Letter on Court-Packing," *Journal of Supreme Court History* 22, no. 1 (1997): 76–86.

18. Jean Edward Smith, *FDR*, 391.

19. Senate Leaders, Alben Barkley, senate.gov., https://www.senate.gov/ about/origins-foundations/parties-leadership/barkley-alben.htm.

20. Roger Newman, *Hugo Black: A Biography* (1997).

21. Alpheus T. Mason, *Harlan Fiske Stone: Pillar of the Law*, 469 (1956).

22. Roger Newman, *Hugo Black: A Biography* (1997).

23. Hugo Black, Radio Address on KKK Membership, October 1, 1937.

24. William Leuchtenberg, "A Klansman Joins the Court," *University of Chicago Law Review* 41, no. 1 (1973).

25. David Garrow, "The Tragedy of William O. Douglas," *Nation*, March 27, 2003, thenation.com.

26. Jean Edward Smith, *FDR*, 391–392.

27. Jean Edward Smith, *FDR*, 393.

28. Jean Edward Smith, *FDR*, 397.

29. John Maynard Keynes, "From Keynes to Roosevelt: Our Recovery Plan Assayed," *New York Times*, December 31, 1933.

30. James MacGregor Burns, *Roosevelt: The Lion and the Fox, 1882–1940*, 336 (1956).

31. William Leuchtenberg, "Franklin D. Roosevelt: Domestic Affairs," millercenter.org.

32. William Leuchtenberg, *Franklin D. Roosevelt and the New Deal*, 274.

33. Franklin D. Roosevelt, Message to Congress, April 29, 1938.

34. H. W. Brands, *Traitor to His Class*, 501 (2008).

35. Jean Edward Smith, *FDR*, 399.

36. Jean Edward Smith, *FDR*, 401.

37. Jean Edward Smith, *FDR*, 402–403.

38. Eleanor Roosevelt, *This I Remember*, 349 (1949).

39. Eleanor Roosevelt, "Keepers of Democracy," speech given on January 15, 1939.

40. Walter White, *A Man Called White*, 169 (1948).

41. Franklin D. Roosevelt, State of the Union, January 4, 1939.

42. H. W. Brands, *Traitor to His Class*, 504.

43. Franklin D. Roosevelt—Foreign Affairs, presidentprofiles.com.

44. Frank Freidel, *Franklin D. Roosevelt: A Rendezvous with Destiny*, 348, 349 (1990).

45. Harold Ickes, *The Secret Diary of Harold L. Ickes, Volume 3: The Lowering Clouds, 1939–1941*, 216 (1955).

46. H. W. Brands, *Traitor to His Class*, 537.

47. H. W. Brands, *Traitor to His Class*, 569.

48. David Dilks, *Neville Chamberlain*, Volume One, *Pioneering and Reform, 1869–1929* (1984).

49. Herman Eberhardt, "Artifact Highlight: The Sphinx," National Archives, FDR Blogs, May 29, 2020.

50. James MacGregor Burns, *Roosevelt: The Lion and the Fox*, 411.

51. David Nasaw, *The Patriarch: The Remarkable Life and Turbulent Times of Joseph P. Kennedy*, 371–398 (2012).

52. James MacGregor Burns, *Roosevelt: The Lion and the Fox*, 425.

53. Jean Edward Smith, *FDR*, 459.

54. J. Samuel Walker, "The New Deal and the Guru," *American Heritage* 40 (March 1989).

55. Eleanor Roosevelt, *This I Remember*, 216.

56. Eleanor Roosevelt, Speech to the Democratic National Convention, July 18, 1940.

57. James MacGregor Burns, *Roosevelt: The Lion and the Fox*, 423.

58. Oral History Interview by Jerry N. Hess with Judge Samuel I. Rosenman, in New York, NY, October 15, 1968.

59. *Franklin D. Roosevelt Day by Day: November 1940*, FDR Library: Pare Lorentz Film Center (2011).

60. H. W. Brands, *Traitor to His Class*, 574.

61. Franklin Delano Roosevelt, FDR's Campaign Promise in Boston, Massachusetts (October 30, 1940).

62. News Conference with President Franklin D. Roosevelt, December 17, 1940.

63. H. W. Brands, *Traitor to His Class*, 575, 577.

CHAPTER 7

1. Letter to James Madison, April 30, 1789. Washington wrote the letter on his first day as president.

2. Franklin D. Roosevelt, Fourth Annual Message to Congress, January 6, 1941.

3. International Churchill Society (March 1, 2009).

4. Thomas Alan Schwartz, *America's Germany: John J. McCloy and the Federal Republic of Germany* (1991).

5. Franklin D. Roosevelt, Third Inaugural Address, January 20, 1941.

6. Franklin D. Roosevelt, Third Inaugural Address, January 20, 1941.

7. Franklin Delano Roosevelt, Fireside Chat from Washington, D.C.: FDR Warns of Fifth Column, May 27, 1940; Harold Ickes, *The Secret Diary of Harold L. Ickes, Volume 3: The Lowering Clouds, 1939–1941*, 208–212 (1955).

8. Franklin D. Roosevelt, Third Inaugural Address, January 20, 1941.

9. Franklin D. Roosevelt, Navy Day Speech on the Attack on the Destroyer Kearny, October 27, 1941.

10. Franklin D. Roosevelt, Annual Message, January 6, 1941.

11. Robert Sherwood, *Roosevelt and Hopkins: An Intimate History* (1948).

12. Christopher Hohman, *Whither Thou Goest I Shall Go: Harry Hopkins' Adventure in the United Kingdom*, 1941, StMU Research Scholars, stmuscholars.org, December 15, 2021.

13. Jean Edward Smith, *FDR*, 488.

14. Jean Edward Smith, *FDR*, 491.

15. Erik Larson, *The Splendid and the Vile: A Saga of Churchill, Family, and Defiance during the Blitz*, 346 (2020).

16. Christopher Hohman, *Whither Thou Goest I Shall Go: Harry Hopkins' Adventure in the United Kingdom*, 1941, StMU Research Scholars, stmu scholars.org, December 15, 2021.

17. Christopher Hohman, *Whither Thou Goest I Shall Go: Harry Hopkins' Adventure in the United Kingdom*, 1941, StMU Research Scholars, stmu scholars.org, December 15, 2021.

18. Christopher Hohman, *Whither Thou Goest I Shall Go: Harry Hopkins' Adventure in the United Kingdom*, 1941, StMU Research Scholars, stmu scholars.org, December 15, 2021.

19. Frank Freidel, *Franklin D. Roosevelt: A Rendezvous with Destiny*, 364.

20. Lily Rothman, "'It's Not That the Story Was Buried': What Americans in the 1930s Really Knew About What Was Happening in Germany," *Time*, July 10, 2018.

21. Melissa Mart, "Eleanor Roosevelt, Liberalism, and Israel," *Shofar: An Interdisciplinary Journal of Jewish Studies* 24 (2006): 58–89.

22. Richard Breitman and Allan J. Littman, *FDR and the Jews* (2013).

23. Richard Breitman and Allan J. Littman, *FDR and the Jews* (2013).

24. Robert Dallek, *Franklin D. Roosevelt: A Political Life*, 422.

25. Franklin D. Roosevelt, Press Conference, June 24, 1941.

26. Sumner Welles, The Welles Declaration, July 23, 1940.

27. Executive Order 8802: Prohibition of Discrimination in the Defense Industry, June 25, 1941.

28. Report from Harry Hopkins to FDR, August 1, 1941.

29. W. Averell Harriman and Elie Abel, *Special Envoy to Churchill and Stalin, 1941–1945* (1975).

30. FDR Churchill Press Conference, August 14, 1941.

31. Robert Dallek, *Franklin D. Roosevelt: A Political Life*, 429–432.

32. Matthew B. Wills, *Wartime Missions of Harry L. Hopkins*, 26 (1996); Franklin Delano Roosevelt, Navy Day Address: FDR Uses Counterfeit Nazi Invasion Map to Turn America Against Germany, October 27, 1941.

33. Admiral Stark Memorandum to FDR, July 12, 1941.

34. Jean Edward Smith, *FDR*, 516–517.

35. Joseph Grew, *Turbulent Era: A Diplomatic Record of Forty Years, 1904–1945*, ed. W. Johnson (1952).

36. Jean Edward Smith, *FDR*, 521–522.

37. Jean Edward Smith, *FDR*, 519–523.

38. Jean Edward Smith, *FDR*, 523–524.

39. Jean Edward Smith, *FDR*, 520–521.

40. Jean Edward Smith, *FDR*, 525.

41. Jean Edward Smith, *FDR*, 527.

42. Frank Feidel, *Franklin D. Roosevelt: A Rendezvous with Destiny*, 400.

43. Robert Dallek, *Franklin D. Roosevelt: A Political Life*, 439.

44. Frank Freidel, *Franklin D. Roosevelt: A Rendezvous with Destiny*, 404–405.

45. Frank Freidel, *Franklin D. Roosevelt: A Rendezvous with Destiny*, 405.

46. Jean Edward Smith, *FDR*, 537.

47. "The Attack on Pearl Harbor United Americans Like No Other," *Washington Post*, December 7, 2016.

48. Frank Freidel, *Franklin D. Roosevelt: A Rendezvous with Destiny*, 405.

49. Report, Joint Committee on the Investigation of the Pearl Harbor Attack, June 20, 1946.

50. Franklin D. Roosevelt, Day of Infamy Speech, December 7, 1941.

51. Frantz Jantzen, "From the Urban Legend Department: McReynolds, Brandeis, and the Myth of the 1924 Photograph," *Journal of Supreme Court History* 40 (October 18, 2015): 325; Todd C. Peters, "Cancelling Justice? The Case of James Clark McReynolds," *University of Richmond Public Interest Law Review* 24 (2021): 59.

52. Albert Lawrence, *Biased Justice: James C. McReynolds of the United States Supreme Court* (2005).

53. Henry Abraham, *Justices and Presidents* (2007).

CHAPTER 8

1. Peter Grier, "Pearl Harbor Day: How Did Adolph Hitler React?," *Christian Science Monitor*, December 7, 2011.

2. H. W. Brands, *Traitor to His Class*, 636–637.

3. First Washington Conference, National Archives, December 1941.

4. Diaries of Henry Stimson, December 28, 1941.

5. Address to Joint Session of Congress, December 26, 1941.

6. Franklin D. Roosevelt, Annual Message to Congress, January 6, 1942.

7. Frank Freidel, *Franklin D. Roosevelt: A Rendezvous with Destiny*, 492.

8. Frank Freidel, *Franklin D. Roosevelt: A Rendezvous with Destiny*, 411–412.

9. Franklin D. Roosevelt, State of the Union, January 6, 1942.

10. Franklin D. Roosevelt, Fireside Chat, February 23, 1942.

11. Robert Dallek, *Franklin D. Roosevelt: A Political Life*, 455–456.

12. Carl Cannon, "Untruth and Consequences," *Atlantic* (January-February 2007).

13. Winston Churchill, *War Memoirs* (November 30, 1943).

14. Franklin D. Roosevelt, Fireside Chat, February 23, 1942.
15. William Doyle, "Franklin Roosevelt: The Creative Executive," in *Inside the Oval Office: The White House Tapes from FDR to Clinton* (1999).
16. William Doyle, *Inside the Oval Office: The White House Tapes from FDR to Clinton* (1999).
17. Warren F. Kimball, "Franklin Roosevelt: The Creative Executive," in *The Juggler: Franklin Roosevelt as Wartime Statesman*, 7 (1991).
18. William Doyle, "Franklin Roosevelt: The Creative Executive," in *Inside the Oval Office: The White House Tapes from FDR to Clinton* (1999).
19. William Doyle, "Franklin Roosevelt: The Creative Executive," in *Inside the Oval Office: The White House Tapes from FDR to Clinton* (1999).
20. William Doyle, "Franklin Roosevelt: The Creative Executive," in *Inside the Oval Office: The White House Tapes from FDR to Clinton* (1999).
21. William Doyle, "Franklin Roosevelt: The Creative Executive," in *Inside the Oval Office: The White House Tapes from FDR to Clinton* (1999).
22. Report by Jimmie Doolittle, on Halsey-Doolittle Raid, April 1942.
23. Cable, Winston Churchill to Franklin D. Roosevelt, June 13, 1942.
24. Jean Edward Smith, *FDR*, 565.
25. Frank Freidel, *Franklin D. Roosevelt: A Rendezvous with Destiny*, 461–464.
26. Frank Freidel, *Franklin D. Roosevelt: A Rendezvous with Destiny*, 461–464.
27. Jean Edward Smith, *FDR*, 568.
28. H. W. Brands, *Traitor to His Class*, 737.
29. Jean Edward Smith, *FDR*, 588–598.
30. The Papers of George Catlett Marshall, 103 (Larry I. Bland & Sharon Ritenour Stevens eds., 1981–2003).
31. H. W. Brands, *Traitor to His Class*, 745.
32. Steven Rabalais, *General Fox Connor: Pershing's Chief of Operations and Eisenhower's Mentor*, XIV (2016).
33. Dwight Eisenhower, *Crusade in Europe*, 18 (1948).
34. Lt. Col. Diana Bodner, *The Relationship Between Fox Conner and Dwight Eisenhower*, U.S. Army War College, April 9, 2002.
35. Franklin D. Roosevelt, Fireside Chat, June 5, 1944.
36. Franklin D. Roosevelt, Fireside Chat, June 12, 1944.
37. History of American Journalism: World War II on the Air: Edward R. Murrow and the Broadcasts That Riveted a Nation, December 13, 1942, University of Kansas website.
38. Gregory Wallace, *America's Soul in the Balance: The Holocaust, FDR's State Department, and the Moral Disgrace of an American Aristocracy*, 189–190 (2012).
39. Jean Edward Smith, *FDR*, 582–583.

40. David Michaelis, *Eleanor*, 84, 175 (2020).
41. Hugh Rawson, "Why Do We Say That?," *American Heritage*, April/May 2003, americanheritage.com.
42. Eleanor Roosevelt, *This I Remember*, 216.
43. Franklin D. Roosevelt, Speech Before the International Brotherhood of Teamsters Union, Washington, D.C., September 23, 1944.
44. Frank Freidel, *Franklin Delano Roosevelt: A Rendezvous with Destiny*, 563.
45. Frank Freidel, *Franklin Delano Roosevelt: A Rendezvous with Destiny*, 567.

CHAPTER 9

1. Kathryn Smith, *The Gatekeeper: Missy LeHand, FDR, and the Untold Story of the Partnership That Defined a Presidency* (2017).
2. Roosevelt had nominated Wallace in spite of the strong urgings of most of his advisors not to do so. They worried it squandered the goodwill Roosevelt needed with Congress to rebuild the country after the war.
3. John F. Woolverton and James D. Bratt, *A Christian and a Democrat: A Religious Biography of Franklin D. Roosevelt*, 54–55 (2019).
4. William Hassett, *Off the Record with FDR: 1942–1945* 238 (1958).
5. William Hassett, *Off the Record with FDR: 1942–1945*, 239.
6. William Hassett, *Off the Record with FDR: 1942–1945*, 238–239.
7. Eleanor Roosevelt, "My Day," November 22, 1944.
8. John F. Woolverton with James D. Bratt, *A Christian and a Democrat: A Religious Biography of Franklin D. Roosevelt*, 52.
9. John F. Woolverton with James D. Bratt, *A Christian and a Democrat: A Religious Biography of Franklin D. Roosevelt*, 53.
10. Inauguration Day 1945: FDR's Ceremony at the White House, National World War II Museum, January 20, 2021.
11. Eleanor Roosevelt, *Memoirs*; Inauguration Day 1945: FDR's Ceremony at the White House, National World War II Museum, January 20, 2021.
12. Franklin D. Roosevelt, Fourth Inaugural Address, January 20, 1945.
13. Franklin D. Roosevelt, Fourth Inaugural Address, January 20, 1945.
14. David B. Woolner, *The Last 100 Days: FDR at War and at Peace*, 26 (2017).
15. Jean Edward Smith, *FDR*, 629; Frank Freidel, *Franklin D. Roosevelt*, 581.
16. Frank Freidel, *Franklin D. Roosevelt: A Rendezvous with Destiny*, 588.
17. Frank Freidel, *Franklin D. Roosevelt: A Rendezvous with Destiny*, 592.
18. Frank Freidel, *Franklin D. Roosevelt: A Rendezvous with Destiny*, 594–595.
19. Frank Freidel, *Franklin D. Roosevelt: A Rendezvous with Destiny*, 595.

20. Franklin D. Roosevelt, Address to Joint Session of Congress, March 1, 1945.

21. Frances Perkins, *The Roosevelt I Knew*, 395.

22. Franklin D. Roosevelt, Public Papers and Addresses, 586, 578.

23. Jean Edward Smith, *FDR*, 632–633.

24. H. W. Brands, *Traitor to His Class*, 809.

25. Franklin D. Roosevelt, Address to Joint Session of Congress, March 1, 1945.

26. Robert Dallek, *Franklin D. Roosevelt: A Political Life*, 616–618.

27. Franklin D. Roosevelt to the Chairman of the Council of People's Commissars of the Soviet Union (Stalin), telegram.

28. Warren F. Kimball, *The Juggler*, 179.

29. Warren F. Kimball, *The Juggler*, 179.

30. Franklin D. Roosevelt to the Chairman of the Council of People's Commissars of the Soviet Union (Stalin), telegram.

31. Franklin D. Roosevelt, State of the Union Message, January 6, 1945.

32. Allen Drury, *A Senate Journal*, 373 (1963).

33. Frank Freidel, *Franklin D. Roosevelt: A Rendezvous with Destiny*, 598–599.

34. Frank Freidel, *Franklin D. Roosevelt: A Rendezvous with Destiny*, 600.

35. Frank Freidel, *Franklin D. Roosevelt: A Rendezvous with Destiny*, 604.

36. Joseph Lelyveld, *His Final Battle: The Last Months of Franklin Roosevelt*, 313 (2016).

37. H. W. Brands, *Traitor to His Class*, 809.

38. Frank Freidel, *Franklin D. Roosevelt: A Rendezvous with Destiny*, 604.

39. Frank Freidel, *Franklin D. Roosevelt: A Rendezvous with Destiny*, 606.

40. Warren Kimball, *The Juggler*, 180.

41. Jean Edward Smith, *FDR*, 635.

42. Frank Freidel, *Franklin D. Roosevelt: A Rendezvous with Destiny*, 605–606.

EPILOGUE

1. Letter from Dumas Malone to Justice Felix Frankfurter, January 14, 1941.

2. Robert Dallek, *Franklin D. Roosevelt: A Political Life*, 619.

3. W. A. Harriman, Memorandum of Conversation by the Ambassador in the Soviet Union, April 13, 1945.

4. Claude Fohlen, "De Gaulle and Franklin D. Roosevelt," in *FDR and His Contemporaries*, 33–44 (1992).

5. "Eisenhower Regrets Policy of Total Surrender; Asserts Roosevelt Erred in His World War II Goal; Says the Fear of U.S. Terms Sparred Nazis to Fight," *New York Times*, December 21, 1944. It is hard to imagine "reason"

informed Hitler's dreams of world conquest and exterminating Jews and other minorities or that Germans might have had more success assassinating Hitler in the absence of a demand for unconditional surrender.

6. "Japanese Premier Voices 'Sympathy,'" *New York Times*, April 15, 1945.
7. "Nazi Press Calls Death a 'Miracle,'" *New York Times*, April 15, 1945.
8. William Leuchtenberg, "The FDR Years: On Roosevelt and His Legacy," *Washington Post*.
9. James MacGregor Burns, *FDR's Last Journey* (2017).
10. James MacGregor Burns, *The Lion and the Fox*, 458.
11. Michael J. Gerhardt, *Lincoln's Mentors: The Education of a Leader*, 415 (2020).
12. Susan King, "FDR Knew How to Act as President," *Los Angeles Times*, December 10, 2012.
13. President John F. Kennedy, Statement of the President on the Death of Mrs. Eleanor Roosevelt, November 7, 1962.
14. The Nobel Prize in Literature 1953, NobelPrize.org, Nobel Prize Outreach, December 8, 2022.
15. A. Scott Berg, *Wilson*, 349.
16. David H. Schmitz, *Henry L. Stimson: The First Wise Man* (2000).
17. Jean Edward Smith, *FDR*, 636.

Index